Test Bank

Small Business Management
An Entrepreneurial Emphasis

THIRTEENTH EDITION

Justin G. Longenecker
Baylor University

Carlos W. Moore
Baylor University

J. William Petty
Baylor University

Leslie E. Palich
Baylor University

Prepared by

Charlie T. Cook, Jr.
University of West Alabama

THOMSON
SOUTH-WESTERN

Australia · Canada · Mexico · Singapore · Spain · United Kingdom · United States

Test Bank for Small Business Management:, an Entrepreneurial Emphasis, 13th Edition
Justin G. Longenecker, Carlos W. Moore, J. William Petty, Leslie E. Palich

Prepared by
Norm Bryan
Georgia State University

VP/Editorial Director:
Jack W. Calhoun

VP/Editor-in-Chief:
Dave Shaut

Sr. Publisher:
Melissa Acuna

Executive Editor:
John Szilagyi

Developmental Editor:
Ohlinger Publishing Services

Marketing Manager:
Jacquelyn Carillo

Production Editor:
Robert Dreas

Manager of Technology, Editorial:
Vicky True

Technology Project Editor:
Kristen Meere

Web Coordinator:
Karen Schaffer

Manufacturing Coordinator:
Doug Wilke

Printer:
Globus Printing
Minster, Ohio

Art Director:
Anne Marie Rekow

Cover Designer:
Grannan Graphic Design/Brenda Grannan

Cover Image:
Guildhaus Photographics

Printed in the United States of America
2 3 4 5 08 07 06

ISBN: 0-324-22617-9

For more information about our products, contact us at:

Thomson Learning Academic Resource Center

1-800-423-0563

Thomson Higher Education
5191 Natorp Boulevard
Mason, OH 45040
USA

Asia (including India)
Thomson Learning
5 Shenton Way
#01-01 UIC Building
Singapore 068808

Australia/New Zealand
Thomson Learning Australia
102 Dodds Street
Southbank, Victoria 3006
Australia

Canada
Thomson Nelson
1120 Birchmount Road
Toronto, Ontario
M1K 5G4
Canada

Latin America
Thomson Learning
Seneca, 53
Colonia Polanco
11560 Mexico
D.F.Mexico

UK/Europe/Middle East/Africa
Thomson Learning
High Holborn House
50/51 Bedford Row
London WC1R 4LR
United Kingdom

Spain (including Portugal)
Thomson Paraninfo
Calle Magallanes, 25
28015 Madrid, Spain

CONTENTS

Correlation Table for Chapter 1—The Entrepreneurial Life

	Learning Objectives	Question Type	Definition Define new term, recall facts	Concept Understand or relate concepts	Application Apply knowledge, analyze data
1	Discuss the availability of entrepreneurial opportunities and give examples of successful business started by entrepreneurs	T/F		1	2,3,4
		MC		1,2,3	4
		ES			
2	Explain the nature of entrepreneurship and how it is related to small business.	T/F	5,6,7,8,9		
		MC	6,7	5,8	
		ES			
3	Identify some motivators or rewards of entrepreneurial careers.	T/F	14,15	10,11,12,13,16	
		MC	9,10,11,16,17	12	13,14,15,18,19, 20
		ES	2	1	
4	Describe the various types of entrepreneurs and entrepreneurial ventures.	T/F	17,18	20	19
		MC	21,22,23,24,25, 26,27,28	29	30,31
		ES	3,4		
5	Identify five potential advantages of small entrepreneurial firms.	T/F		21,22,23,24,25	
		MC	33	32,34,35,36	
		ES			
6	Discuss factors related to readiness for entrepreneurship and getting started in an entrepreneurial career.	T/F		26,27,28,29,30, 31	32,33
		MC		38,40,41,43,44,	37,39,42,45,46, 47,48
		ES	6	5	
7	Explain the concept of an entrepreneurial legacy and the challenges involved in crafting a worthy legacy.	T/F		50	
		MC			
		ES			
	You Make the Call	ES		7,8,9,10	

Total Number of Test Questions: 93 (33 True/False; 50 Multiple-Choice; 10 Essay)

Chapter 1—The Entrepreneurial Life

TRUE/FALSE

1. An entrepreneurial career can provide an exciting life and substantial personal rewards while also contributing to the welfare of society.

   ANS: T REF: p. 1 OBJ: TYPE: C

2. When the Souto Brothers founded Rowland Coffee Roasters, they decided it was best for their enterprise to compete against rivals based on price.

   ANS: F
   The Souto Brothers differentiate their coffee roasting business by focusing on superior products and building customer loyalty.

   REF: p. 2 OBJ: 1-1 TYPE: A

3. Kenny Kramm's idea for FlavorX has been a success because other pharmacies recognized its value and readily adopted Kramm's unique system.

   ANS: T
   FlavorX is an example of the social value of entrepreneurship

   REF: p. 4 OBJ: 1-1 TYPE: A

4. Annie Beiler founded Aunt Annie's by first developing a better-tasting pretzel and then building a successful, growing, and profitable business on that foundation.

   ANS: T REF: p. 5 OBJ: 1-1 TYPE: A

5. The term *entrepreneur* is understood in this text to refer only to founders of small businesses.

   ANS: F
   According to the text, *entrepreneur* refers to founders, franchisees, second-generation members of family-owned firms, and owner-managers who buy out the founders of existing firms.

   REF: p. 6 OBJ: 1-2 TYPE: D

6. The terms *founder* and *entrepreneur* are mutually exclusive.

   ANS: F
   According to the definition in the text, founders are considered to be entrepreneurs.

   REF: p. 10 OBJ: 1-2 TYPE: D

7. An owner-manager is a person who founds a new business.

   ANS: F

An owner-manager may be an individual who bought out the founder(s) of an existing firm (or later owners) and thus is not necessarily the one who started the firm.

REF: p. 6 OBJ: 1-2 TYPE: D

8. According to the definition of entrepreneur given in Chapter 1, owner-managers who buy out founders of existing firms may be classified as entrepreneurs.

ANS: T REF: p. 6 OBJ: 1-2 TYPE: D

9. The universally accepted definition of the term *small business* is based on the number of people employed by the firm.

ANS: F
There have been a number of attempts to define the term *small business*, using such criteria as the number of employees, sales volume, and value of assets, but there is no universally accepted definition.

REF: p. 7 OBJ: 1-2 TYPE: D

10. Three primary rewards of entrepreneurship are thought to be profit, independence, and personal fulfillment.

ANS: T REF: p. 8-9 OBJ: 1-3 TYPE: C

11. Some estimate that entrepreneurs are four times more likely to be millionaires than are those who work for others.

ANS: T REF: p. 8 OBJ: 1-3 TYPE: C

12. Most startups are initiated by entrepreneurs who have visions of getting rich.

ANS: F
Most startups are initiated by entrepreneurs who are satisfied with that which they consider to be a reasonable profit from their ventures.

REF: p. 8 OBJ: 1-3 TYPE: C

13. A large percentage of small business owners cite their desire to be their own boss as the main reason they left their previous employers.

ANS: T REF: p. 8 OBJ: 1-3 TYPE: C

14. Persons who leave their homeland and go into business for themselves in a new country would be described as entrepreneurial *refugees*.

ANS: T REF: p. 8 OBJ: 1-3 TYPE: D

15. A *refugee* is a person who tried entrepreneurship, failed, and sought refuge in corporate employment.

ANS: F

A refugee is an individual who has left an undesirable environment by going into business for him/herself.

REF: p. 8 OBJ: 1-3 TYPE: D

16. Being an entrepreneur can often bring a sense of dignity or significance that makes life worth living.

ANS: T REF: p. 9 OBJ: 1-3 TYPE: C

17. *"Second-stage" entrepreneurs* are entrepreneurs who take over the operations of a successful ongoing business from its founder.

ANS: T REF: p. 10 OBJ: 1-4 TYPE: D

18. Entrepreneurial teams are formed by bringing together two or more persons who together function as entrepreneurs.

ANS: T REF: p. 11 OBJ: 1-4 TYPE: D

19. A mechanic who starts an independent garage can best be thought of as an *opportunistic entrepreneur*.

ANS: F
This is an *artisan entrepreneur*-i.e., one who operates the business using his or her technical skills as opposed to communication and managerial skills.

REF: p. 12 OBJ: 1-4 TYPE: A

20. Between 1976 and 2000, women's share of total self-employment remained fairly constant.

ANS: F
Between 1976 and 2000, women's share of total self-employment grew from 22 percent to 38 percent.

REF: p. 12 OBJ: 1-4 TYPE: C

21. Small and entrepreneurial firms cannot hold their own or gain an edge over successful, more powerful businesses.

ANS: F
Small firms can indeed compete against their larger rivals by focusing on customers' needs, providing high-quality goods and services, operating with greater integrity, using innovative methods, or findings low-cost solutions.

REF: p. 13-14 OBJ: 1-5 TYPE: C

22. Business opportunities exist for any size firm, as long as they can provide products or services that customer's desire.

ANS: T REF: p. 13 OBJ: 1-5 TYPE: C

23. Small firms are at a great disadvantage when it comes to competing based on customer service.

ANS: F
Due to their flexibility (e.g., fewer levels of bureaucracy and adaptable corporate policies), small firms have an advantage when it comes to offering superior customer service.

REF: p. 13 OBJ: 1-5 TYPE: C

24. In service businesses, quality performance is closely linked to customer service.

ANS: T REF: p. 13 OBJ: 1-5 TYPE: C

25. Many entrepreneurs are innovators, individuals who are often better at identifying improved ways of doing things.

ANS: T REF: p. 14 OBJ: 1-5 TYPE: C

26. Older people are often discouraged from starting businesses because of family responsibilities and interests in retirement programs.

ANS: T REF: p. 16 OBJ: 1-6 TYPE: C

27. The ideal age for starting a business appears to be between 40 and 50.

ANS: F
The ideal age for starting a business appears to be between the mid-20s and mid-30s.

REF: p. 16 OBJ: 1-6 TYPE: C

28. Entrepreneurs are essentially like the general population in their personal characteristics.

ANS: F
Compared to the general population, entrepreneurs are noted for their willingness to take moderate risks, strong self-confidence, and a passion for business.

REF: p. 16 OBJ: 1-6 TYPE: C

29. Most entrepreneurs have an external locus of control.

ANS: F
Most entrepreneurs tend to have an *internal* locus of control.

REF: p. 16 OBJ: 1-6 TYPE: C

30. If they identify closely with their ventures, entrepreneurs may bear psychic risk as they face the possibility of business failure.

ANS: T REF: p. 16 OBJ: 1-6 TYPE: C

31. The four primary routes to entrepreneurship are buying an existing business, starting a new business, opening a franchised business, and entering a family business.

ANS: T REF: p. 0 OBJ: 1-6 TYPE: C

32. The offer by a friend to sponsor you as an Amway distributor might be called a precipitating event.

    ANS: T REF: p. 16 OBJ: 1-6 TYPE: A

33. Unexpectedly stumbling across a business opportunity could be considered a precipitating event.

    ANS: T REF: p. 16 OBJ: 1-6 TYPE: A

MULTIPLE CHOICE

1. Compared to large corporations, small businesses
   a. play just as important a part in the economy.
   b. attract more attention and make more headlines in the media.
   c. are not as important to the well-being of society.
   d. are highly visible.

   ANS: A REF: p. 7 OBJ: TYPE: C

2. Sundra Ryce's SLR Contracting & Service Company is a success for all of the following reasons EXCEPT:
   a. She had experience in construction.
   b. She used her startup resources carefully
   c. She relied on set-aside contracts.
   d. She had access to family financing.

   ANS: C REF: p.4 OBJ: 1-1 TYPE: C

3. The argument developed in Chapter 1 about entrepreneurial opportunities holds that
   a. potentially profitable opportunities exist at all times.
   b. the biggest barrier to seizing opportunities is lack of capital.
   c. minorities are effectively blocked from exploiting opportunities.
   d. approximately 99 percent of all opportunities involve some form of retailing.

   ANS: A REF: p. 5 OBJ: 1-1 TYPE: C

4. Jarred Holmes, a college senior, is evaluating his prospects as an independent business owner. As a practical matter, he should realize that
   a. no major entrepreneurial successes have been realized in the last three decades.
   b. the upper limit for entrepreneurial profits is somewhere between $750,000 and $1 million.
   c. an entrepreneur can never earn as much as a major corporate executive.
   d. any individual is free to enter into business for him/herself.

   ANS: D REF: p. 6 OBJ: 1-1 TYPE: A

5. Which of the following is classified as an entrepreneur?
   a. A manager in a large corporation
   b. A financial manager in a small firm
   c. An owner-manager who bought out the founder of a firm
   d. A salaried technician in a rapidly-growing high-tech firm

   ANS: C REF: p. 6 OBJ: 1-2 TYPE: C

6. Which of the following is excluded from the definition of *entrepreneur* given in the book?

a. Founder
b. Second generation owner-manager
c. Franchisee
d. A salaried manager who has a flair for innovation

ANS: D REF: p. 6 OBJ: 1-2 TYPE: D

7. Using the textbook's criteria for defining a small business, Portland Ceramics isn't a small business if it
   a. is financed by one or only a few individuals.
   b. is considerably smaller than larger firms in the industry.
   c. is engaged in geographically dispersed operations.
   d. has fewer than 100 employees.

ANS: C REF: p. 7 OBJ: 1-2 TYPE: D

8. The size standard for small business used in the textbook would exclude firms that
   a. have more than 10 employees.
   b. have more than 100 employees.
   c. have more than two owners.
   d. sell products of services outside the local community.

ANS: B REF: p. 7 OBJ: 1-2 TYPE: C

9. The three primary rewards or incentives for entrepreneurs are
   a. independence, personal fulfillment, and profit.
   b. love of country, independence, and freedom from long hours.
   c. preserving the capitalistic system, an easy life, and financial rewards.
   d. serving self, love of country, and independence.

ANS: A REF: p. 8-9 OBJ: 1-3 TYPE: D

10. Lydia Kurze works as a senior network administrator and is dissatisfied with stifling bureaucratic environment of her job. She considering venturing out on her own as a consultant. If she carries through with her intentions, she would be considered a ___________.
    a. pariah
    b. dilettante
    c. emigrant
    d. refugee

ANS: D REF: p. 8 OBJ: 1-3 TYPE: D

11. Miriam Motif is an example of Stanley and Danko's *The Millionaire Next Door*. She is ___ more times likely to be a millionaire than those who work for others.
    a. two
    b. four
    c. ten
    d. forty

ANS: B REF: p. 8 OBJ: 1-3 TYPE: D

12. Individuals are typically pulled toward entrepreneurship by the hope of obtaining
    a. an easy life.
    b. financial rewards.
    c. freedom from long hours.
    d. job security.

ANS: B REF: p. 8 OBJ: 1-3 TYPE: C

13. Valerie Weatherspoon has been described as a "free spirit." She has tolerated but seldom appreciated parental, academic, or even job authority. The factor most likely to lure her to entrepreneurship is
   a. profit opportunities.
   b. freedom to operate independently.
   c. enjoyment of doing what she likes to do.
   d. satisfaction in serving the community through the business.

   ANS: B REF: p. 8 OBJ: 1-3 TYPE: A

14. A corporate manager chafes under red tape and bureaucratic regulations until finally deciding to start a separate business. The apparent reward being sought is
   a. community service.
   b. a satisfying way of life.
   c. independence.
   d. the satisfaction of working with people.

   ANS: C REF: p. 8 OBJ: 1-3 TYPE: A

15. The daughter of an entrepreneur disliked her father's criticism and eventually decided to quit the family business and show her father that she could start her own business. The daughter is a
   a. corporate opportunist.
   b. feminist advocate.
   c. potential housewife.
   d. refugee.

   ANS: D REF: p. 8 OBJ: 1-3 TYPE: A

16. Sally Forthright, a single mother, opened a florist shop to support her family after losing her job in a corporate layoff. She is __________.
   a. a woman without a portfolio.
   b. a parental refugee.
   c. a reluctant entrepreneur.
   d. an independent refugee.

   ANS: C REF: p. 8 OBJ: 1-3 TYPE: D

17. A reluctant entrepreneur is a woman who
   a. leaves her children with a babysitter to follow a secretarial career.
   b. divorces her husband because of his intense preoccupation with his business.
   c. starts her own business after her grown children return to live with her.
   d. leaves a family business to show that she can do it on her own.

   ANS: C REF: p. 8 OBJ: 1-3 TYPE: D

18. When a large business like IBM or General Motors downsizes and lays off workers, some of these displaced employees decide to start their own businesses. They are best described as
   a. foreign refugees.
   b. welfare profiteers.
   c. reluctant entrepreneurs.
   d. corporate entrepreneurs.

   ANS: C REF: p. 8 OBJ: 1-3 TYPE: A

19. A camera hobbyist starts a photographic supplies store. The most obvious reward for this entrepreneur is the opportunity to
   a. serve other photography enthusiasts.
   b. experience personal fulfillment.
   c. be independent.
   d. work with people.

   ANS: B REF: p. 9 OBJ: 1-3 TYPE: A

20. A prospective entrepreneur wants to find a career doing what she enjoys most-designing and selling clothing. She might be drawn to try an entrepreneurial venture in order to realize
   a. personal fulfillment.
   b. substantial long-term profits.
   c. freedom from control of a managerial hierarchy.
   d. a sense of self-esteem as a result of building her own business.

   ANS: A REF: p. 9 OBJ: 1-3 TYPE: A

21. A person who starts a business is classified as a
   a. founder.
   b. general manager.
   c. franchisee.
   d. marginal-firm manager.

   ANS: A REF: p. 10 OBJ: 1-4 TYPE: D

22. Gill Balstock started his business after inventing an environmentally-friendly disposal foam container for dairy products. His son Larry now runs the business while Gill pursues other projects. Gill is a(n) ____________ and Larry is a(n) ____________.
   a. founder, follow-on entrepreneur
   b. initiator, instigator
   c. founder, franchisee
   d. founder, second-stage entrepreneur

   ANS: D REF: p. 10 OBJ: 1-4 TYPE: D

23. Amar V. Bhide considers the growth potential of marginal startups to be
   a. poor at best.
   b. moderate with great late-stage potential.
   c. exceptionally fast.
   d. exceptionally fast and large.

   ANS: A REF: p. 10 OBJ: 1-4 TYPE: D

24. Characteristics of artisan entrepreneurs include all of the following EXCEPT:
   a. They are paternalistic.
   b. They are good delegators.
   c. They use few capital resources.
   d. Their time orientation is short.

   ANS: B REF: p. 11 OBJ: 1-4 TYPE: D

25. A small firm that is profitable but provides only a very modest return to the entrepreneur is
   a. an attractive small company.
   b. a high-potential venture.
   c. a franchise.
   d. a microbusiness.

   ANS: D REF: p. 10 OBJ: 1-4 TYPE: D

26. Small businesses that have great prospects for growth are called ______.
    a. gorillas
    b. antelopes
    c. jaguars
    d. gazelles

ANS: D REF: p. 10 OBJ: 1-4 TYPE: D

27. A firm that provides substantial profits to its owner is called a(n) _________.
    a. franchise
    b. high-potential venture
    c. attractive small firm
    d. lifestyle business

ANS: C REF: p. 10 OBJ: 1-4 TYPE: D

28. An entrepreneurial team is a group composed of
    a. individuals who work together in the same firm as entrepreneurs.
    b. the entrepreneur plus the firm's banker, CPA, and attorney.
    c. the firm's managers.
    d. SBA officials who provide counseling to aspiring entrepreneurs.

ANS: A REF: p. 11 OBJ: 1-4 TYPE: D

29. We would expect an opportunistic entrepreneur to be
    a. paternalistic.
    b. reluctant to delegate authority.
    c. unwilling to plan for future growth.
    d. well educated in non-technical matters.

ANS: D REF: p. 29 OBJ: 1-4 TYPE: C

30. A woman wants to start a construction company. She should realize that
    a. women have never successfully started construction businesses having more than two or three employees.
    b. people (for example, some male loan officers) may not take her seriously simply because she is a woman.
    c. it will be impossible for her to break into the "good old boy network".
    d. gender differences are a fact of life (for example, construction is a male industry, beauty shops are usually female owned, and so on), and therefore she should stay with the pattern.

ANS: B REF: p. 12 OBJ: 1-4 TYPE: A

31. Amy Mendez is contemplating opening her own business. She should
    a. stick to traditional fields for women (such as women's clothing stores or beauty shops) since nontraditional fields are virtually closed to women.
    b. realize that many banks will be slow to offer loans because she is a woman.
    c. realize that she is going against the flow, in that the proportion of women-owned firms is decreasing slightly.
    d. know that women-owned firms are basically part-time businesses.

ANS: B REF: p. 12 OBJ: 1-4 TYPE: A

32. Given that they often compete against powerful companies, it is imperative that entrepreneurs
    a. try to make their businesses as large as capital will permit.
    b. achieve a level of complacency that will allow them to maintain their sanity.
    c. exploit the opportunities that are available to them.

d. consider diversifying into multiple markets to protect against bankruptcy.

ANS: C REF: p. 13 OBJ: 1-5 TYPE: C

33. Potential advantages of small entrepreneurial firms include:
a. Customer focus
b. Quality performance
c. Special niche
d. All of these.

ANS: D REF: p. 13,15 OBJ: 1-5 TYPE: D

34. Compared to their larger competitors, small firms may be better positioned to provide good customer service because they
a. do not struggle as much with bureaucracy.
b. tend to have established corporate policies that emphasize a customer focus.
c. have a narrow range of products or services to offer.
d. refuse to be distracted by other developments in the industry.

ANS: A REF: p. 13 OBJ: 1-5 TYPE: C

35. Because many entrepreneurs are innovators, they
a. are unable to build strong organizations.
b. usually keep a close eye on the innovations generated by big companies.
c. tend to see different and often better ways of doing things.
d. are usually engineers by training.

ANS: C REF: p. 14 OBJ: 1-5 TYPE: C

36. Entrepreneurs often produce innovations related to
a. multiple patents.
b. new ways of doing business.
c. competitive intelligence.
d. market identification.

ANS: B REF: p. 14 OBJ: 1-5 TYPE: C

37. A prospective entrepreneur is 36 years old. She realizes that, other things being equal, her age may affect her chances for success. She should
a. go for it-her age is ideal.
b. wait eight to ten years.
c. realize that prospects were much better when she was in her early 20s.
d. try entrepreneurship only if someone else in the family has an independent source of income.

ANS: A REF: p. 16 OBJ: 1-6 TYPE: A

38. The ideal period of life for starting a business is
a. between the mid-20s and mid-30s.
b. during the 20s.
c. between the late 20s and early 40s.
d. between 40 and 55.

ANS: A REF: p. 16 OBJ: 1-6 TYPE: C

39. When a 32-year-old construction worker launches a construction firm after seven years' experience in that industry, he
    a. has experienced a precipitating event.
    b. is facing a forced-choice career.
    c. is launching his venture during the ideal time of life for starting a business.
    d. is part of an entrepreneurial team.

    ANS: C REF: p. 16 OBJ: 1-6 TYPE: A

40. Compared to the general population, entrepreneurs tend to have
    a. a passion for business.
    b. an external locus of control.
    c. an aversion to risk.
    d. a high need for affiliation.

    ANS: A REF: p. 16 OBJ: 1-6 TYPE: C

41. In comparison to the general population, entrepreneurs have a
    a. higher internal locus of control.
    b. lower internal locus of control.
    c. higher external locus of control.
    d. similar locus of control.

    ANS: A REF: p. 16 OBJ: 1-6 TYPE: C

42. A professor of entrepreneurship is trying to identify students who are the best prospects for entrepreneurial careers. Based on prior research and especially the work of J. B. Rotter, she is looking for students having a
    a. high external locus of control.
    b. low external locus of control.
    c. high internal locus of control.
    d. low internal locus of control.

    ANS: C REF: p. 16 OBJ: 1-6 TYPE: A

43. One drawback of entrepreneurship is the
    a. routine and boring work.
    b. requirement that the business pay a minimum wage.
    c. need to participate in civic activities.
    d. risk of business failure.

    ANS: D REF: p. 16 OBJ: 1-6 TYPE: C

44. In terms of willingness to assume risks, entrepreneurs show
    a. low risk-taking propensity.
    b. moderate risk-taking propensity.
    c. high risk-taking propensity.
    d. extremely high risk-taking propensity.

    ANS: B REF: p. 16 OBJ: 1-6 TYPE: C

45. A prospective entrepreneur is evaluating the suitability of his own characteristics for an entrepreneurial career. He realizes that he should be prepared to assume

a. moderate risks.
b. no risks-that is, he should plan to operate conservatively.
c. risks similar to those a gambler assumes in Las Vegas.
d. psychological risks but not financial risks.

ANS: A REF: p. 16 OBJ: 1-6 TYPE: A

46. Being passed over for promotion prompted an employee to quit and start her own business. This perceived injustice served as
a. a forced-choice event.
b. an open-window event.
c. a free-choice event.
d. a precipitating event.

ANS: D REF: p. 16 OBJ: 1-6 TYPE: A

47. Which of the following situations might be a *precipitating event*?
a. Getting laid off by General Motors
b. Making a new firm's first sale
c. Getting a working-capital loan for $25,000 from a local bank
d. Changing the organizational structure of a small department store

ANS: A REF: p. 16 OBJ: 1-6 TYPE: A

48. A 32-year-old manager lost his job because of cutbacks in staff, so he immediately made plans to open his own business. For him, the loss of a job was
a. a window of opportunity.
b. a loss of self-confidence.
c. a precipitating event.
d. evidence of an external locus of control.

ANS: C REF: p. 16 OBJ: 1-6 TYPE: A

49. A small business's advantages of finding a special niche include all of the following EXCEPT:
a. avoiding intense competition
b. serving a particular geographic
c. having room for expansion
d. diminishing overall profitability

ANS: D REF: p. 15 OBJ: 1-6 TYPE: C

50. An entrepreneur's concern that his values continued to be reflected in the ways in which his firm conducts business after he retires is an example of the concept of ________.
a. self-assessment
b. entrepreneurial legacy
c. activity trade-offs
d. psychological aggrandizement

ANS: B REF: p. 17 OBJ: 1-7 TYPE: C

ESSAY

1. Identify and explain three major types of rewards for entrepreneurs.

ANS:
- *Profit.* The desire to make money is a factor in most ventures, but it is thought to be less significant than independence as an overall driving force. However, it can

provide powerful motivation for some individuals.

- *Independence.* This involves a desire to be one's own boss and avoid having others tell one what to do.
- *Personal Satisfaction.* The life-style provided by some independent business ventures is inherently enjoyable. The hobbyist who goes into business illustrates this fact.

REF: p. 8-9 OBJ: 1-3 TYPE: C

2. How is the concept of personal fulfillment related to entrepreneurship?

   ANS:
   Some people are drawn to entrepreneurship by their desire to do good, to make some positive contribution to their communities.

   REF: p. 9-10 OBJ: 1-3 TYPE: D

3. Explain the nature of and the differences among microbusinesses, attractive small firms, and high-potential ventures.

   ANS:
   Microbusinesses provide only a very limited return to their owners. Such firms may be consistently unable to generate much profit; however, they are not necessarily failing. Attractive small firms offer substantial profit (e.g., $100,000 to $300,000 or more annually) but not spectacular rewards. High-potential (or *gazelle*) ventures are those like Dell and Microsoft, which can turn entrepreneurs into multimillionaires. Of course, they also include less spectacular successes that still earn very high profits.

   REF: p. 10 OBJ: 1-4 TYPE: D

4. Distinguish between artisan entrepreneurs and opportunistic entrepreneurs. Describe the distinctive features of each.

   ANS:
   Artisan entrepreneurs tend to "fly by the seat of their pants." They typically have only technical training, lack good communication skills, display a paternalistic outlook, are reluctant to delegate authority, use only one or two capital sources, use personal sales efforts, and think in terms of a short time orientation. Opportunistic entrepreneurs, on the other hand, are more broadly educated, avoid paternalism, delegate authority when desirable, employ various types of marketing strategies and sales efforts, frequently obtain capital from a number of sources, and plan for future growth.

   REF: p. 11-12 OBJ: 1-4 TYPE: D

5. What is the ideal age for starting a business, and what are the principal factors involved? Discuss.

   ANS:
   The ideal time is that period of life between the mid-20s and mid-30s, when entry into business is most easily accomplished. The key factors are education, some experience, acquisition of sufficient capital, and avoidance of getting locked into an attractive corporate career with retirement benefits, family obligations, financial commitments, and so on.

   REF: p. 16 OBJ: 1-6 TYPE: C

6. List and briefly explain the six categories of "desirable and acquirable attitudes and behaviors" found in Timmons and Spinelli's research on entrepreneurial characteristics.

ANS:
1. *Commitment and determination.* Such entrepreneurs are tenacious, decisive, and persistent in problem solving.
2. *Leadership.* Such entrepreneurs are self-starters and team builders and focus on honesty in their business relationships.
3. *Opportunity obsession.* Such entrepreneurs are aware of market and customer needs.
4. *Tolerance of risk, ambiguity, and uncertainty.* Such entrepreneurs are risk takers, risk minimizers, and uncertainty tolerators.
5. *Creativity, self-reliance, and adaptability.* Such entrepreneurs are open-minded, flexible, uncomfortable with the status quo, and quick learners.
6. *Motivation to excel.* Such entrepreneurs are goal oriented and aware of their weaknesses and strengths.

REF: p. 16 OBJ: 1-6 TYPE: D

7. **You Make the Call - Situation 1**
In the following statement, a business owner attempts to explain and justify his preference for slow growth in his business.
I limit my growth pace and make every effort to service my present customers in the manner they deserve. I have some peer pressure to do otherwise by following the advice of experts—that is, to take on partners and debt to facilitate rapid growth in sales and market share. When tempted by such thoughts, I think about what I might gain. Perhaps I could make more money, but I would also expect a lot more problems. Also, I think it might interfere somewhat with my family relationships, which are very important to me.

Question 1 Should this venture be regarded as entrepreneurial? Is the owner a true entrepreneur?
Question 2 Do you agree with the philosophy expressed here? Is the owner really doing what is best for his family?
Question 3 What kinds of problems is this owner trying to avoid?

ANS:
1. Whether this is entrepreneurial depends on one's definition. The owner may or may not be a founder—the key issue in some definitions of a "true" entrepreneur. In this text, we use a looser definition of entrepreneur, which could include this owner-manager regardless of whether he founded the business. The venture is apparently not the high-growth, high-potential type. It may well be what we have called an "attractive small company."
2. This question calls for opinions and permits some discussion of the conflicting values and rewards in business. Some may feel the owner is insufficiently motivated to grow and even to serve his own family properly in that way. Others will see the family values and careful growth as appropriate. The question permits the instructor to discern the general orientation of students in a class. How many, after discussion, will give a vote of commendation to this owner? You might ask students to guess the owner's age.

3. The owner is apparently avoiding or reducing problems related to inadequate customer service and product/service quality—areas of difficulty in a rapidly growing business. Also, the personnel and management functions (e.g., delegation, finding qualified key people) are simplified by slow growth. Slow growth may either postpone a transition to professional management or permit a more orderly transition to it.

REF: p. 21 OBJ: YMTC TYPE: C

8. **You Make the Call - Situation 2**
Nineteen-year-old Kiersten Berger, now in her second year at a local community college, has begun to think about starting her own business. She has taken piano lessons since she was seven years old and is regarded as a very good pianist. The thought has occurred to her that she could establish a piano studio and offer lessons to children, young people, and even adults. The prospect sounds more attractive than looking for a salaried job when she graduates in a few months.

Question 1 If Kiersten Berger opens a piano studio, will she be an entrepreneur?
Question 2 Which type of reward(s) will be greatest in this venture?
Question 3 Even though she is an artisan, she will need to make decisions of a business nature. What decisions or evaluations may be especially difficult for her?

ANS:
1. Yes, even though this piano studio would be a small business (better described as a microbusiness, in this case), it is a new firm that she is starting. Those who launch new businesses are very much entrepreneurs.
2. The payoffs of a satisfying life (for one who loves music) and also independence would seem to be the greatest. The reward that looks least likely is making money. This business is not likely to generate substantial profits. In fact, a key question is whether it will produce sufficient profits to survive. The business might need to begin as a part-time operation.
3. Some of the questions she will face relate to marketing her services. What is the potential market? What kind of competition exists? How can she attract customers? What prices should she establish so that she can generate sufficient revenue and still attract customers? What will a projected income statement show in terms of net profits?

REF: p. 21 OBJ: YMTC TYPE: C

9. **You Make the Call - Situation 3**
Dover Sporting Goods Store occupies an unimpressive retail location in a small city in northern Illinois. Started in 1935, it is now operated by Duane Dover—a third-generation member of the founding family. He works long hours trying to earn a reasonable profit in the old downtown area. Dover's immediate concern is an announcement that Wal-Mart is considering opening a store at the southern edge of town. As Dover reacts to this announcement, he is overwhelmed by a sense of injustice. Why should a family business that has served the community honestly and well for 60 years have to fend off a large corporation that would take big profits out of the community and give very little in return? Surely, he reasoned, the law must offer some kind of protection against big business predators of this kind. Dover also wonders whether small stores such as his have ever been successful in competing against business giants like Wal-Mart.

Question 1 Is Dover's feeling of unfairness justified? Is his business entitled to some type of legal protection against moves of this type?

Question 2 How should Dover plan to compete against Wal-Mart, if and when this becomes necessary?

ANS:

1. Dover's feeling is understandable but difficult to defend rationally. The business has prospered, to some extent at least, by functioning in a free enterprise system. Capitalism does not protect one from competition. The law, of course, offers some protection from unscrupulous competition—for example, practices such as predatory pricing designed to drive competitors out of business.

2. Large retailers and discounters are more successful in some fields than in others. They are very strong, for example, in drugs, lumber, and general merchandise. In sporting goods, small firms continue to compete very well. Wal-Mart's forte will be price competition. Dover must emphasize those factors that give small firms unusual strength: personal attention, excellent product knowledge, product lines that exceed those of a discount chain, advertising programs tailored to the interests of their customers, attractiveness (and possibly renovation) of physical facilities, and activities that will gain attention in the news media and thereby deny Wal-Mart a news monopoly. In brief, the store should do everything it does better than its competitor is able to do. If this family business can be an aggressive, bold competitor, it can continue to survive and do well.

   Meg Whittemore (a writer for *Nation's Business*) describes a small hardware business threatened by the advent of Wal-Mart in Sterling, Colorado. To cope with the new competition, the owners of the hardware store dropped product lines in which Wal-Mart was strongest and concentrated on basic hardware lines—paint, tools, electrical items, plumbing, carpentry supplies, lawn and garden supplies—and offering customers advice and instructions on how to use those items. In these areas, they could do better than Wal-Mart, and their sales tripled after Wal-Mart moved into town.

REF: p. 21 OBJ: YMTC TYPE: C

10. **You Make the Call - Situation 4**

When Amy Clark was growing up, her father owned several service stations, where she pumped gas and developed some knowledge of station operation. When she graduated from high school, Amy entered business college and trained to be a secretary. She married soon after school, and her husband entered the service station business. Recently, Amy decided that she would like to operate a station of her own. A station with three service bays and facilities for minor auto repair is available, but she would have to persuade the oil company—the same one that franchises her husband's station—that she is qualified to have a franchise. Clark has expressed her philosophy as follows: "I'm a person who likes to get things done. I like to keep excelling and to do bigger and better things than I've ever done before. I guess that's why I'd like to have a station of my own."

Question 1 Evaluate Amy Clark's qualifications for the proposed venture. Should the oil company accept her as a dealer?

Question 2 As a female entrepreneur, what problems should she anticipate in relationships with customers, employees, the franchising oil company, and her family?

ANS:

1. Amy Clark's prior work in a service station is excellent because it gave her knowledge of the "nitty-gritty" of the business. We have no information as to the extent of her management experience, but, as wife of the owner, she may have exercised some supervision. Her education as a secretary is not ideally suited for this career. However, her motivations and the need for achievement evident in her comments fit the mold of the classic entrepreneur. Ask: What additional information should you as an oil company manager wish to have? The oil company would be interested in the nature of Clark's service station experience and whether her husband's station had done repair work.

2. As a woman entrepreneur, she will need to be sensitive to various relationships, especially in the beginning stages. Customers—especially males—may be cautious when considering repair work, but few customers would base gasoline purchases on the sex of the business owner. Some employees may be sensitive to female supervision if they have never been supervised by a woman manager previously. This may be particularly true of blue-collar employees who are limited in education and breadth of experience. The oil company no doubt deals principally with male dealers. Depending on their experience and background, divisional managers may or may not be receptive to entrepreneurial roles for women. We are given little information on the quality of family relationships. An element of possible competition will be introduced if both husband and wife operate stations, so effective communication and mutual trust are important. Ask: If you were the oil company's divisional manager making the decision, how would you deal with this issue?

   What Actually Happened Clark was awarded the franchise she sought. She was the first woman in her city to obtain such a franchise. She admitted that she had a hard time convincing corporate officials to allow her to open a station. After operating the station for a while, she commented:

   > *A business like this can be operated just as easily by a woman as a man. The few women who are pioneering in the service station business are laying the groundwork for other women to follow.*

   In the first year of operation, Clark and her husband both won the oil company's award for excellence, an award given to only 100 firms nationally. In a typical week, she works from 50 to 60 hours—in the office, stockroom, or driveway. She hires employees to do repair work and other service station duties. Only one seemed to have an attitude problem, and he is no longer employed. She has, in fact, developed a good relationship with employees. She has also found excellent acceptance by customers, especially women and senior citizens. She requires attendants to assist women and older customers even at self-service pumps, and she writes personal thank-you notes to customers who have their cars repaired at her station. Her marriage is as stable as ever.

REF: p. 0 OBJ: YMTC TYPE: C

Correlation Table for Chapter 2—Entrepreneurial Integrity

	Learning Objectives	Question Type	Definition Define new term, recall facts	Concept Understand or relate concepts	Application Apply knowledge, analyze data
1	Define integrity and understand its importance to small businesses.	T/F	4	1,2,3,5,6,7,8,9, 10,11,12,13,14	
		MC	3,14,22	1,2,6,7,8,9,11,12,1 3	4,5,10
		ES			1
2	Explain how integrity applies to various stakeholder groups, including owners, customers, employees, and the community.	T/F	21,23,24	15,16,17,18,19, 20,22	
		MC	19,28,29,30	15,16,17,18,20, 21,22,23,24,26, 27	25
		ES		4	
3	Identify challenges to integrity that arise in small businesses and explain the benefits of integrity to small firms.	T/F		25,26,27,28,29, 30,31	
		MC		33,34,35,36,37, 38	31,32
		ES		2,3	
4	Explain the impact of the Internet and globalization on the integrity of small businesses.	T/F	35	32,33,34,35,36, 37,38	
		MC	39,46	49,50	40,41,42,43,44,45, 47,48
		ES		5	
5	Describe practical approaches for building a business with integrity.	T/F			
		MC	51		
		ES			
6	Describe the costs and opportunities of environmental-ism to small businesses.	T/F			
		MC			
		ES			
	You Make the Call	ES		6,7,8	

Total Number of Test Questions: 95 (35 True/False; 51 Multiple-Choice; 9 Essay)

Chapter 2—Entrepreneurial Integrity

TRUE/FALSE

1. Many entrepreneurs are people of principle, and integrity regulates their quest for profits.

   ANS: T REF: p. 27 OBJ: 2-1 TYPE: C

2. Small businesses that practice skimming of income are acting unethically and illegally.

   ANS: T REF: p. 34 OBJ: 2-1 TYPE: C

3. Income-tax cheating by small business is sufficiently widespread to be recognized as a general problem.

   ANS: T REF: p. 34 OBJ: 2-1 TYPE: C

4. According to a recent survey, many small business owners experienced ethical problems pertaining to the environment, but very few of them reported ethical problems in relationships with customers.

   ANS: F
   The survey actually showed that *few* small business owners experienced ethical problems pertaining to the environment, but *many* of them reported ethical problems in relationships with customers.

   REF: p. 28 OBJ: 2-1 TYPE: D

5. Sales people must often walk a fine line between persuasion and deception.

   ANS: T REF: p. 30 OBJ: 2-1 TYPE: C

6. Direct selling practices such as pyramid schemes and front-loading are unethical.

   ANS: T REF: p. 30 OBJ: 2-1 TYPE: C

7. Unlike employees in small firms, those who work for large corporations face pressure from various sources to act in ways that conflict with their own sense of what is right and wrong.

   ANS: F
   These pressures are indeed great for employees in large firms, but small firm employees also face these pressures.

   REF: p. 34 OBJ: 2-1 TYPE: C

8. In a survey of employees of small firms, approximately two-thirds of the respondents said they did not feel any pressure to compromise their own ethical standards.

   ANS: T REF: p. 32 OBJ: 2-1 TYPE: C

9. Few of those responding to a recent survey believe it would be seriously unethical for an employer to monitor its employees' e-mail.

ANS: F
A survey conducted by the Society of Financial Services found that 44 percent of workers surveyed consider it seriously unethical for employers to monitor employee e-mail.

REF: p. 36 OBJ: 2-1 TYPE: C

10. Unethical business behaviors take place in every country, but some countries must deal with more serious forms of illegal business activity than others.

ANS: T REF: p. 37 OBJ: 2-1 TYPE: C

11. Temptations and pressures to act unethically are thought to be greater in big business than in small business.

ANS: F
As a result of their size and low public profile, temptations and pressures to act unethically are thought to be greater in *small* business than in *big* business.

REF: p. 35 OBJ: 2-1 TYPE: C

12. The essence of ethical relativism is captured in the following statement: "When in Rome, do as the Romans do."

ANS: T REF: p. 38 OBJ: 2-1 TYPE: C

13. Small firm owners may be tempted to rationalize bribery as a way of offsetting what seems to be a competitive disadvantage.

ANS: T REF: p. 35 OBJ: 2-1 TYPE: C

14. In a recent study cited in the textbook, entrepreneurs were more willing than other businesspeople to condone collusive bidding and the duplicating of copyrighted computer software without payment to the manufacturer.

ANS: T REF: p. 35 OBJ: 2-1 TYPE: C

15. Business practices and other behaviors reflect the underlying values of the leaders and employees of a business.

ANS: T REF: p. 38 OBJ: 2-2 TYPE: C

16. Judeo-Christian values have traditionally been left in the churches and synagogues and have not entered the marketplace.

ANS: F
Judeo-Christian values have traditionally served as the general body of beliefs underlying business behavior.

REF: p. 38 OBJ: 2-2 TYPE: C

17. Religious values and other deeply felt convictions strengthen a manager's resolve to act ethically in the face of temptation.

ANS: T REF: p. 38 OBJ: 2-2 TYPE: C

18. Without a strong commitment to integrity on the part of small business leadership, ethical standards can easily be compromised.

ANS: T REF: p. 39 OBJ: 2-2 TYPE: C

19. Because they are in contact with a much larger body of employees, the ethical influence of a leader in a large business is more pronounced than is that of a leader in a small firm.

ANS: F
The personal ethical influence of the leader *decreases* as a firm grows larger because his or her influence is diffused over a larger organization.

REF: p. 40 OBJ: 2-2 TYPE: C

20. Small business owners cannot formulate codes of ethics; they must be issued by law or by professional associations.

ANS: F
At some point, the owner-manager of a firm should formulate a code of ethics similar to that of most large corporations.

REF: p. 40 OBJ: 2-2 TYPE: C

21. Codes of ethics should not only express the principles that members of the firm should follow but also give examples of situations likely to be faced.

ANS: T REF: p. 40 OBJ: 2-2 TYPE: D

22. The purpose of a Better Business Bureau is to promote ethical conduct by businesses in a community.

ANS: T REF: p. 42 OBJ: 2-2 TYPE: C

23. Better Business Bureaus serve primarily as assistants to district attorneys, helping expose corrupt business practices.

ANS: F
The function of Better Business Bureaus is twofold: (1) to provide information about companies to consumers and (2) to resolve disputes concerning purchases.

REF: p. 42 OBJ: 2-2 TYPE: D

24. Bait advertising is considered unethical because the business lures customers with an attractive price only to try to convince them to purchase more expensive products or services.

ANS: T REF: p. 41 OBJ: 2-2 TYPE: D

25. One study cited in the textbook found entrepreneurs tend to be more narrowly focused on profits and thus less socially responsible than CEOs of large businesses.

ANS: T REF: p. 33 OBJ: 2-3 TYPE: C

26. Acting in a socially responsible manner can be costly to small businesses because acting in the public interest always requires spending money, which reduces profits.

ANS: F REF: p. 34 OBJ: 2-3 TYPE: C

27. The Baucus and Baucus study of 255 corporations found that returns on assets and sales of law-abiding firms only marginally higher than those convicted of corporate wrongdoing, indicating that socially responsible practices have, at best, a minimal long-term impact on profits.

ANS: F REF: p. 34 OBJ: 2-3 TYPE: C

28. Only large corporations can afford to be socially responsible.

ANS: F
While it is true that entrepreneurs tend to be less socially sensitive than CEOs of large corporations, most entrepreneurs still accept some degree of social responsibility.

REF: p. 34 OBJ: 2-3 TYPE: C

29. Socially responsible activities may be consistent with a firm's long-term profit objective.

ANS: T REF: p. 34 OBJ: 2-3 TYPE: C

30. The goodwill gained from benefiting the community may be worth more than it costs.

ANS: T REF: p. 34 OBJ: 2-3 TYPE: C

31. Research has always shown that socially responsible practices have a negative impact on profits.

ANS: F
A study by Baucus and Baucus has shown that socially responsible practices can have a *positive* impact on profits.

REF: p. 34 OBJ: 2-3 TYPE: C

32. Employer monitoring of employees' Internet activities has become so commonplace that it is no longer a subject for debate.

ANS: F REF: p. 36 OBJ: 2-4 TYPE: C

33. The Internet is a prime venue for fraudulent activities.

ANS: T REF: p. 37 OBJ: 2-4 TYPE: C

34. Businesses that operate on the Internet can safely ignore the ethical standards that exist in other countries.

ANS: F REF: p. 37 OBJ: 2-4 TYPE: C

35. An Internet innovation known as *donuts* were developed so that Web sites could recognize return visitors and thus generate a customized and personalized response.

ANS: F
This is an innovation known as *cookies*, not *donuts*.

REF: p. 36 OBJ: 2-4 TYPE: D

36. In most cases, the pressures of environmentalism have contributed to the profitability of small firms.

ANS: F
Though some small businesses have been in a position to benefit from the general emphasis on the environment, a good numbers are adversely affected by environmental protections.

REF: p. 42 OBJ: 2-4 TYPE: C

37. The interests of small business owners and environmentalists are not always in conflict.

ANS: T REF: p. 42 OBJ: 2-4 TYPE: C

38. Most small firms pass on the costs of environmental regulation to customers.

ANS: F
A small firm can pass on these costs only in a favorable market situation.

REF: p. 42 OBJ: 2-4 TYPE: C

MULTIPLE CHOICE

1. While unethical practices do exist, it is good that many small firms strive to achieve the highest standards of ________ in their business relationships.
   a. truthfulness
   b. relativism
   c. synchronous behavior
   d. congruity

   ANS: A REF: p. 27 OBJ: 2-1 TYPE: C

2. One glaring example of poor ethics practiced by small businesses in general is
   a. lack of pollution controls.
   b. untruthful labeling of products.
   c. lack of loyalty to employees.
   d. fraudulent reporting of income and expenses for income tax purposes.

   ANS: D REF: p. 34 OBJ: 2-1 TYPE: C

3. Skimming is an unethical business practice involving

a. failure to report all income on tax returns.
b. employees taking cash from the cash register.
c. sales associates offering gifts and inducements to purchasers.
d. managers of competing firms agreeing to charge high prices.

ANS: A REF: p. 34 OBJ: 2-1 TYPE: D

4. A prospective small business owner wonders what types of ethical problems may prove most difficult. If the business is typical, the owner should realize that problems are most likely to relate to
a. environmental issues.
b. relationships with customers and competitors.
c. human resource decisions.
d. banking relationships.

ANS: B REF: p. 27 OBJ: 2-1 TYPE: A

5. A small business owner finds that his salesperson has lied to a customer about test results on a new product. The owner recognizes that this breach of good ethics falls into the category of
a. management processes and relationships.
b. governmental obligations and relationships.
c. human resources decisions.
d. relationships with customers and competitors.

ANS: D REF: p. 28 OBJ: 2-1 TYPE: A

6. After issues related to customers and competitors, the second most common category of ethical issues that challenge small businesses is concerned with
a. the treatment of employees.
b. international relations.
c. public relations.
d. harmful production processes.

ANS: A REF: p. 27 OBJ: 2-1 TYPE: C

7. A nationwide survey showed that no pressure to act unethically was felt by what proportion of individuals holding managerial and professional positions in small business?
a. 0 (zero-None report pressure.)
b. 30.1%
c. 62.4%
d. 72.3%

ANS: B REF: p. 32 OBJ: 2-1 TYPE: C

8. Temptations and pressures to act unethically are such that small firms are
a. less vulnerable than large firms.
b. more vulnerable than large firms.
c. as vulnerable as large firms.
d. not subject to the temptations and pressures facing large firms.

ANS: B REF: p. 34 OBJ: 2-1 TYPE: C

9. Small firms are likely to be tempted to act unethically because
a. founders or owners of small businesses are usually crooked.
b. breaking the rules often seems to be the only way to make a profit and survive.
c. small businesses are exempt from federal regulations.

d. Better Business Bureaus don't deal with small businesses.

ANS: B REF: p. 35 OBJ: 2-1 TYPE: C

10. A local building inspector suggested to a small business owner that a generous "tip" would help speed up the process of gaining approval for some new construction. The power of a small business firm to resist such pressure is
    a. greater than that of a big business.
    b. less than that of a big business.
    c. equal to that of a big business.
    d. dependent on the type of construction.

ANS: B REF: p. 35 OBJ: 2-1 TYPE: A

11. In a recent study of small business ethics, entrepreneurs were more likely than other business managers and professionals to be unethical with respect to issues that
    a. were not visible to the community.
    b. directly affected the environment.
    c. directly affected profits.
    d. were perceived as important to production operations.

ANS: C REF: p. 33 OBJ: 2-1 TYPE: C

12. The hallmarks of business integrity include all of the following EXCEPT:
    a. duplicity.
    b. reliability.
    c. honesty.
    d. fairness.

ANS: A REF: p. 25 OBJ: 2-1 TYPE: C

13. Integrity is as much about *what to do* as it is
    a. *when to do it.*
    b. *where it fits in.*
    c. *who it affects.*
    d. *who to be.*

ANS: D REF: p. 25 OBJ: 2-1 TYPE: C

14. Ethical issues
    a. seldom involve legal issues.
    b. are questions of right and wrong.
    c. are always clearly defined.
    d. often resolve themselves.

ANS: B REF: p. 27 OBJ: 2-1 TYPE: D

15. Entrepreneurs who are deeply committed to ethical values operate their businesses in ways that reflect
    a. the standard practices of the industry.
    b. their personal interpretations of those values.
    c. profit motivations above all others.
    d. their personal religious values.

ANS: B REF: p. 25 OBJ: 2-2 TYPE: C

16. Unethical business practices often decline when firms
    a. collude with one another.
    b. face challenging business situations.
    c. set a flexible code of ethics.
    d. cooperate to organize a Better Business Bureau.

ANS: D REF: p. 42 OBJ: 2-2 TYPE: C

17. Milton Friedman argues that businesses
    a. should avoid social responsibility whenever it is possible to do so.
    b. should be required to use their resources meet their social responsibilities.
    c. can only earn profits if they do so in a socially responsible manner.
    d. are justified in being socially responsible only if doing so increases the firm's value.

ANS: D REF: p. 29 OBJ: 2-2 TYPE: C

18. Marc Katz is an example of
    a. how an employee's integrity can contribute to a business's success.
    b. how an entrepreneur's integrity contributes to a business's success.
    c. how a customers' lack of integrity can affect the operations of a firm.
    d. how an entrepreneur's lack of integrity can cause a business failure.

ANS: B REF: p. 30 OBJ: 2-2 TYPE: C

19. When Jean Romano lost her job at Deepcanyon.com, she
    a. felt the firm lacked integrity how it managed its employees.
    b. sued the firm for being summarily dismissed without explanation for cause.
    c. started her own successful employment agency based on her experience there.
    d. believed that the firm dealt fairly with her regarding the closure of the business.

ANS: D REF: p. 32 OBJ: 2-2 TYPE: D

20. The John E. Long family was charged by the IRS with income tax fraud for failing to record the cash they collected for admission to their country folk art shows. This illegal practice is known as _______.
    a. cash diversion
    b. gunkholing
    c. skimming
    d. mattress-stuffing

ANS: C REF: p. 34 OBJ: 2-2 TYPE:C

21. The ethical influence of a leader of a small business is
    a. relatively minor.
    b. overpowered by profit concerns of stockholders.
    c. less important than the views of others within the firm.
    d. more pronounced than that of a leader of a large corporation.

ANS: D REF: p. 39 OBJ: 2-2 TYPE: C

22. In a small business, the most important key to ethical performance is
    a. a code of ethics.
    b. the personal integrity of the founder or owner.
    c. a training program based on the code of ethics.
    d. the amount of legislation affecting the organization.

ANS: B REF: p. 40 OBJ: 2-2 TYPE: C

23. The most important influence on ethics in a small business is
    a. the accountant or bookkeeper who keeps honest financial records.
    b. the salesperson who quotes a fair price to customers.
    c. the founder or owner whose values are put into practice.

d. the existence of a written code of ethics.

ANS: C REF: p. 40 OBJ: 2-2 TYPE: C

24. A code of ethics becomes increasingly appropriate and necessary as a small business
    a. expands its credit sales and acquires more customers who buy on credit.
    b. begins to market products in other countries.
    c. grows larger, with a consequent lessening of the owner's personal influence.
    d. increases borrowing to the extent that one-third of its assets are financed by borrowing.

ANS: C REF: p. 40 OBJ: 2-2 TYPE: C

25. In drawing up a code of ethics, a small business owner should adopt a code
    a. provided by the Ethics Resource Center of Washington, D.C.
    b. that outlines ethical principles and gives examples.
    c. that outlines ethical principles but avoids examples.
    d. suggested by the Better Business Bureau.

ANS: B REF: p. 40 OBJ: 2-2 TYPE: A

26. A Better Business Bureau should
    a. help enforce laws regulating conduct of local businesses.
    b. promote ethical conduct on the part of business firms in the community.
    c. provide free consumer education classes.
    d. lobby for improved legislation to protect consumers.

ANS: B REF: p. 42 OBJ: 2-2 TYPE: C

27. One function of a Better Business Bureau is to
    a. survey businesses in a community to determine which are ethical.
    b. take legal action against businesses for unethical conduct.
    c. provide customers with free buying guidelines and information about local companies.
    d. advertise against unethical business practices.

ANS: C REF: p. 42 OBJ: 2-2 TYPE: C

28. Better Business Bureaus are
    a. federal government agencies established by Congress.
    b. part of the Chamber of Commerce.
    c. organizations composed of business firms.
    d. associations of religious groups interested in the improvement of business ethics.

ANS: C REF: p. 42 OBJ: 2-2 TYPE: D

29. Bait advertising consists of an
    a. alluring but insincere offer to sell a product.
    b. attempt to sell a product that adversely affects the environment.
    c. attempt to sell a defective and possibly unsafe product.
    d. advertisement of expensive products.

ANS: A REF: p. 41 OBJ: 2-2 TYPE: D

30. Bait advertising attempts to
    a. conceal product defects.

b. lure customers with the intention of selling them a different product.
c. use customer service as an incentive to buy a product.
d. persuade users to purchase products that may be injurious to their health or welfare.

ANS: B REF: p. 41 OBJ: 2-2 TYPE: D

31. A small computer retailer makes every effort to satisfy customer needs—both before and after the sale. However, this retailer regards social problems such as hunger and juvenile crime as being beyond the scope of his business. We can correctly describe this firm's management as having recognized
a. some degree of social responsibility in its commitment to customers.
b. the existence of social responsibilities but having failed to do anything about them.
c. ethical obligations to customers but no social responsibilities.
d. social responsibility as the domain of big business.

ANS: C REF: p. 33 OBJ: 2-3 TYPE: A

32. An example of a firm that would least likely be recognized as socially responsible is
a. a farm that specializes in organically grown produce.
b. a builder that constructs energy-efficient homes.
c. a manufacturer of pollution-control equipment.
d. a high fee, low return investment company.

ANS: D REF: p. 33 OBJ: 2-3 TYPE: A

33. Social responsibilities go far beyond a firm's relationships with customers, and typically include diverse areas such as
a. protection of the environment.
b. educational activism.
c. consumer protection for all business dealings within the community.
d. protection of religious liberties.

ANS: A REF: p. 42 OBJ: 2-3 TYPE: C

34. The viewpoint expressed in the textbook is that social responsibility should be recognized by
a. manufacturing firms in particular, since they tend to pollute more.
b. businesses that operate in communities with greater social needs.
c. small businesses.
d. any firm that wants to make profits quickly.

ANS: C REF: p. 33 OBJ: 2-3 TYPE: C

35. There is a limit to the possible social responsiveness of small businesses because they must
a. make a profit to survive.
b. be responsive to their customers.
c. first of all be fair to their employees.
d. not harm the environment.

ANS: A REF: p. 33 OBJ: 2-3 TYPE: C

36. Though it is sometimes expensive to make socially responsible choices,
a. small businesses should be exempt from environmental regulations.
b. manufacturing concerns always have lower profits.
c. long-term and short-term profits are invariably reduced.

d. businesses must recognize that profits are not the only important factor.

ANS: D REF: p. 34 OBJ: 2-3 TYPE: C

37. Which of the following sayings would best summarize the relationship between social responsibility and small firm performance?
   a. Crime pays.
   b. Nice guys can finish first.
   c. A bird in the hand is worth two in the bush.
   d. Better to be the head of a chicken than the tail of a cow.

ANS: B REF: p. 34 OBJ: 2-3 TYPE: C

38. The ethical standards of entrepreneurs
   a. are unaffected by profit motives.
   b. are affected by profit motives.
   c. are seldom challenged by real-world events.
   d. are higher overall than those of corporate managers.

ANS: B REF: p. 34 OBJ: 2-3 TYPE: C

39. A data file that is electronically sent to the customer's computer when other requested materials are downloaded from a Web site is known as
   a. a cookie.
   b. a saucer.
   c. an inverted collector.
   d. a contact signature.

ANS: A REF: p. 36 OBJ: 2-4 TYPE: D

40. Environmentalism poses the greatest threat to small
   a. iron foundries.
   b. drugstores.
   c. movie theaters.
   d. auto repair shops.

ANS: A REF: p. 42 OBJ: 2-4 TYPE: A

41. An example of an industry especially vulnerable to efforts to protect the environment is the _____ industry.
   a. glass manufacturing
   b. military construction
   c. restaurants
   d. pet-food processing

ANS: D REF: p. 42 OBJ: 2-4 TYPE: A

42. A pet-food manufacturer has returned from a seminar on environmentalism and wishes to act responsibly in this area. Which of the following actions will accomplish this purpose?
   a. Increase the firm's gross margins
   b. Reduce product prices
   c. Eliminate undesirable processing odors
   d. Increase service to customers

ANS: C REF: p. 42 OBJ: 2-4 TYPE: A

43. A small manufacturer is concerned about a possible cost disadvantage caused by expensive environmental requirements. She should realize that her own firm's competitive position is best served by restrictions imposed by
   a. city ordinances.
   b. county requirements.
   c. state laws.
   d. federal legislation.

ANS: D REF: p. 42 OBJ: 2-4 TYPE: A

44. Bob's Bistro and Come-by & Take-out are two restaurants located within one mile of each other, but they operate within two separate city jurisdictions. Which of the following best describes the legal and competitive situation for these two businesses?
   a. Local environmental laws may prove discriminatory by forcing higher costs on one competitor than the other.
   b. Federal law may create a competitive advantage for one of these two restaurants.
   c. The legal situation will not impact the competitive situation of these two businesses.
   d. These two firms have equal chances of competing because they both tap the same market.

ANS: A REF: p. 42 OBJ: 2-4 TYPE: A

45. Raymond Cassion, a café owner, is also a member of the city council. Cassion believes that a proposed ordinance requiring restaurants in the city to be smoke-free would be good for consumers. Cassion's vote for the proposed ordinance would
   a. create an unfair advantage for his restaurant.
   b. increase operating costs for his restaurant.
   c. aid most consumers without handicapping any particular restaurant in the city.
   d. run contrary to the whole idea of social responsibility.

ANS: C REF: p. 30 OBJ: 2-4 TYPE: A

46. Websense Inc. found that ___ percent of employees in small businesses it surveyed visited Web sites unrelated to their work.
   a. 49
   b. 18
   c. 26
   d. 64

ANS: A REF: p. 37 OBJ: 2-4 TYPE: D

47. A U.S. manager is upset with his overseas representative in Fannelstan for paying a small "access fee" to a local customs official to ensure the expedited release of a customer order. The manager's belief such payments are wrong reflects his sense of _________.
   a. cultural insensitivity
   b. ethical elitism
   c. ethical imperialism
   d. cultural integrity

ANS: C REF: p. 37 OBJ: 2-4 TYPE: A

48. The saying "When in Rome, do as the Romans do" reflects a philosophy of _________.
   a. ethical insensitivity
   b. ethical elitism
   c. ethical imperialism
   d. ethical relativism

ANS: D REF: p. 38 OBJ: 2-4 TYPE: A

49. If a student copies his favorite record album and gives it away to a friend to use, the student is engaged in the theft of _________ property.
a. collective
b. intangible
c. intellectual
d. real

ANS: C REF: p. 37 OBJ: 2-4 TYPE: C

50. As the Internet continues to grow, it is safe to assume that property rights will
a. become less difficult to protect.
b. become more difficult to protect.
c. become an irrelevancy of the past.
d. become universally assumable.

ANS: B REF: p. 37 OBJ: 2-4 TYPE: C

51. A web site lists a digital camera at sale price that is twenty percent less than the online prices of its competitors. When a customer attempts to purchase the camera online, the customer is redirected to web page that offers a different camera at a higher price, with the disclaimer that the originally-offered camera is out-of-stock for an "indefinite period." The web site is engaging in __________.
a. in-cart conversion
b. customer deflection
c. aggressive merchandising
d. bait advertising

ANS: D REF: p. 41 OBJ: 2-5 TYPE: A

ESSAY

1. Give an example of an unethical practice that might tempt a small business in each of the following areas: marketing, management, and finance or accounting.

ANS:
Unethical marketing practices include bait advertising, price fixing among competitors, deceptive selling practices, and improper inducements to buy. Unethical management practices include discrimination in hiring and promotions; unfair work assignments, dismissals, and layoffs; and dishonesty in communications with employees. Unethical financial or accounting practices include not only understating profits to reduce taxes, but withholding or disguising unpleasant financial conditions to mislead bankers, stockholders, or others with a need to know.

REF: p. 28 OBJ: 2-1 TYPE: A

2. What are some important social responsibilities of small businesses?

ANS:
Small firms, as well as large ones, have responsibilities to their communities, their customers, and their employees. Protecting the environment from pollution and conserving resources such as soil, water, endangered species, and old-growth forests benefit not only personal interests but those of future generations as well. Small businesses have an opportunity to sponsor worthwhile charitable causes within the community, simultaneously making a positive impact and obtaining goodwill. Treating people fairly rather than manipulating them for gain is a social responsibility both large and small businesses should assume, through responsiveness to consumers and through fair labor practices. Other issues might also be mentioned.

REF: p. 33, 42 OBJ: 2-3 TYPE: C

3. Discuss the relationship between profits and social responsibility in the small firm.

ANS:
Some of the points that should be made are the following:

- Some socially responsible actions are consistent with the profit goal-particularly long-run profits.
- Profits are a limiting factor. A business cannot survive if it gives away all of its profits.
- Some actions for community betterment are very costly—e.g., eliminating pollution from an iron foundry.
- There are motivations for social responsibility that go beyond profits.
- A firm that consistently ignores social responsibility may contribute to the passing of restrictive legislation and possibly alienate customers.

REF: p. 33-34 OBJ: 2-3 TYPE: C

4. How are Better Business Bureaus formed, and how do they contribute to ethical business behavior?

ANS:
Better Business Bureaus are formed by privately owned business firms as an effort to self-police. They work with consumers who need guidance in purchasing or who believe they have been subjected to unethical treatment. They attempt to resolve disputes between customers and businesses. They also draw up codes of ethics, such as the code of values shown in the textbook.

REF: p. 41 OBJ: 2-2 TYPE: C

5. What are some of the ways in which small businesses may gain from consumerism, and what are some dangers?

ANS:
Consumerism deals with the rights of consumers to purchase high-quality goods and services at a fair price. Since small firms have traditionally been strong in attending to customer needs, they have a competitive advantage in the marketplace. Small firms are more able to be flexible in meeting customers' desires and in providing excellent service. The threat of consumerism is the result of ever-increasing consumer expectations and the increased likelihood that customers will sue.

REF: p. 30-31 OBJ: 2-4 TYPE: C

6. **You Make the Call - Situation 1**
Sally started her consulting business a year ago and has been doing very well. About a month ago, she decided she needed to hire someone to help her since she was getting busier and busier. After interviewing several candidates, she decided to hire the best one of the group, Mary. She called Mary on Monday to tell her she had gotten the job. They both agreed that she would start the following Monday and that Mary could come in and fill out all the hiring paperwork at that time.

On Tuesday of the same week, a friend of Sally's called her to say that she had found the perfect person for Sally. Sally explained that she had already hired someone, but the friend insisted. "Just meet this girl. Who knows, maybe you might want to hire her in the future!"

Rather reluctantly, Sally consented. "Alright, if she can come in tomorrow, I'll meet with her, but that's all."

"Oh, I'm so glad. I just know you're going to like her!" Sally's friend exclaimed.

And Sally did like her. She liked her a lot. Sally had met with Julie on Wednesday morning. She was everything that Sally had been looking for and more. In terms of experience, Julie far surpassed any of the candidates Sally had previously interviewed, including Mary. On top of that, she was willing to bring in clients of her own which would only increase business. All in all, Sally knew this was a win-win situation. But what about Mary? She had already given her word to Mary that she could start work on Monday.
Source: SBA Management Institute, "Business Ethics: The Foundation of Effective Leadership," http://www.onlinewbc.org, September 27, 2000.

Question 1 What decision on Sally's part would contribute most to the success of her business?
Question 2 What ethical reasoning would support hiring Mary?
Question 3 What ethical reasoning would support hiring Julie?

ANS:

1. Hiring Julie seems to be the best choice. The fact that she is superior to the other candidates, based on experience and ability, suggests that she should be able to contribute most to the business. (Of course, one might also argue that hiring Julie is more ethical and that ethical decisions pay off in the long run.)
2. Sally has given her word to applicant Mary. She has told Mary that she has the job. The starting time has been specified. Since the instructions were verbal, it is probably not legally enforceable. However, does the principle of keeping ones promise allow for backing down at this stage? Mary may already have made commitments in view of the new job, and that fact that Mary needs the job to support her family makes this especially difficult.
3. Can the instructions to Mary be construed as merely tentative? If the agreement with Mary is not yet finalized, the job is still open until Monday. It might be argued that Sally can hire Julie and still be ethical. The welfare of Sally's own family would pull in this direction, even though it would be a big disappointment to Mary. Which of these positions or arguments is more persuasive?

REF: p. 32 OBJ: YMTC TYPE: C

7. **You Make the Call - Situation 2**
Software piracy is rampant in China. As a result, a bootleg copy of the latest release of Microsoft's Windows, which normally sells for more than $100 when purchased through a legitimate vendor, can be found on the streets of Shanghai for as little as $1. An assistant manager working for the Chinese subsidiary of an American educational services firm ponders the question of whether or not to buy 325 copies of pirated software through a local source for $1 each. Purchasing through an authorized vendor would cost about 100 times more. He recognizes that he is up against extremely strong competitors that usually purchase pirated software to control costs, so paying the price for legitimate copies could make it difficult for the subsidiary to stay in business. Furthermore, social standards in China do not emphasize proprietary property rights.

Question 1 Is the assistant manager acting with integrity if he purchases unauthorized copies of the software on the street?
Question 2 What might be the long-term effects of deciding to buy the pirated software? Of insisting on buying only legitimate copies of the software?
Question 3 What course of action do you recommend? Why?

ANS:

1. Based on the position taken in the chapter, the assistant manager would not be acting with integrity if he purchased unauthorized copies of the software, though it may be expensive to make the right choice in this situation. The logic behind intellectual property rights is that these offer protections that encourage the development of more innovations that can benefit all of society, so there is a greater purpose behind making the "right" decision.

2. As mentioned above, buying pirated goods discourages new innovation, which leads to less economic development and lower quality of life for society over the long run. It also encourages others to do the same thing, which could spill over to one's own customers. In other words, if it is widely known that you engage in this activity, then your customers may follow your example and buy counterfeit versions of the products you sell (assuming these exist). In any case, your customers, lenders, and other important stakeholders could legitimately conclude that the standards of integrity of the company are low and thus come to distrust the firm, which could have serious effects on the company. On the other hand, refusing to buy illegitimate goods would avoid these potential problems, despite short-term costs. It is also important to mention that the purchase of counterfeit goods is against the law (even in China), though enforcement of the law is usually very weak.

3. Hopefully, students will choose, on principle, to avoid the purchase of unauthorized goods. However, it will seem proper to some students to decide to purchase the pirated software with the thought that doing so will boost the competitive position of the firm and thus protect the financial interests of the owners of the company. Other justifications for both courses of action are likely to vary considerably.

REF: p. 35 OBJ: YMTC TYPE: C

8. **You Make the Call - Situation 3**
A self-employed commercial artist reports taxable income of $7,000. Actually, her income is considerably higher, but much of it takes the form of cash for small projects and thus is easy to conceal. She considers herself part of the "underground economy" and defends her behavior as a tactic that allows her small business to survive. If the business were to fail, she argues, the government would receive even less tax revenue.

Question 1 Is the need to survive a reasonable defense for the practice described here?
Question 2 If the practice of concealing income is widespread, as implied by the phrase "underground economy," is it really wrong?

ANS:
1. The explanation offered by the commercial artist sounds more like a rationalization than a defense. Even if the firm is fighting for its very survival, the practice described is clearly illegal. It is difficult to justify a clearly illegal practice as being ethical.
2. In other words, is it wrong if everybody is doing it? The answer is yes—the practice is wrong. She is violating the law and would be subject to fines and/or imprisonment. It appears that this person is concealing substantial amounts, although this is not spelled out. The illegal conduct of others does not excuse flagrant violation of the law.

REF: p. 35 OBJ: YMTC TYPE: C

Correlation Table for Chapter 3—Getting Started

	Learning Objectives	Question Type	Definition Define new term, recall facts	Concept Understand or relate concepts	Application Apply knowledge, analyze data
1	Identify several factors that determine whether an idea for a new venture is a good investment opportunity.	T/F	5,6	1,2,3,4,7,8,9,10, 11,12	
		MC		1,2,3,4,5,	
		ES		1,2,3	
2	Give several reasons for starting a new business from scratch rather than buying a franchise or an existing business.	T/F		13,14,	
		MC		8	
		ES			
3	Distinguish among the different types and sources of startup ideas.	T/F			
		MC	14,15,16	6,7,17,19,20,23	12,13,18,21,22
		ES			
4	Describe external and internal analyses that might shape new venture opportunities.	T/F	15,16,23,25,27, 28,29,30,	17,18,19,20,21, 22,24,26,31	
		MC	30,31,36,37,38	9,10,11,24,26,27, 28,29,32,33,34, 35,39	25
		ES		4	
5	Explain broad-based strategy options and focus strategies.	T/F	32,36,39,40	33,34,35,37,38, 41	
		MC	42,44,48,50,51	41,52,53	40,43,45,46,47, 49
		ES	7	5,6	
	You Make the Call	ES		8,9,10,11,12	

Total Number of Test Questions: (41 True/False; 52 Multiple-Choice; 12 Essay)

Chapter 3—Getting Started

TRUE/FALSE

1. "Me, too" strategies are used by very few new ventures.

   ANS: F
   In reality, most new ventures (especially in service industries) are founded on "me, too" strategies.

   REF: p. 52 OBJ: 3-1 TYPE: C

2. Many new businesses are formed as a result of the entrepreneur's previous work experience, through which he or she sees ways to improve or modify a product.

   ANS: T REF: p. 53 OBJ: 3-1 TYPE: C

3. Some possibilities for new startup ideas based on knowledge gleaned from a present or recent job are modifying an existing product, improving a service, or duplicating a business concept in a different location.

   ANS: T REF: p. 53-54 OBJ: 3-1 TYPE: C

4. Hobbies of retiring business executives can spawn startup ideas.

   ANS: T REF: p. 54 OBJ: 3-1 TYPE: C

5. *Serendipity* is a term describing a new product idea resulting from deliberate search activities.

   ANS: F
   Serendipity refers to making desirable *accidental* discoveries, not engaging in deliberate search efforts.

   REF: p. 54 OBJ: 3-1 TYPE: D

6. Serendipity is the faculty for making desirable discoveries by accident.

   ANS: T REF: p. 54 OBJ: 3-1 TYPE: D

7. Magazines and other periodicals are excellent sources of startup ideas.

   ANS: T REF: p. 55 OBJ: 3-1 TYPE: C

8. Startups are more likely to be successful when the entrepreneur first evaluates his or her own capabilities and then looks for a new product or service idea, as opposed to beginning with a need in the marketplace and then relating those to personal capabilities.

   ANS: F
   Startups that are launched by first identifying when a marketplace needs are more likely to be successful, especially when the business is related to consumer goods and services.

REF: p. 56 OBJ: 3-1 TYPE: C

9. The invention of the pocket protector by electrical engineer Gerson Strassberg in 1952 was the result of his deliberate search for a solution to problem of leaking ballpoint pens.

ANS: F
The invention of the pocket protector by electrical engineer Gerson Strassberg in 1952 happened by accident.

REF: p. 54 OBJ: 3-1 TYPE: C

10. Business guru Peter Drucker believes entrepreneurs should consider no more than two or three sources of opportunity to avoid being sidetracked as they prepare to launch or grow their enterprises.

ANS: F
Business guru Peter Drucker believes entrepreneurs should consider seven sources of opportunity as they prepare to launch or grow their enterprises.

REF: p. 54 OBJ: 3-1 TYPE: C

11. Given their limited market scope and size, only three of Porter's five forces are relevant to small businesses.

ANS: F REF: p. 57 OBJ: 3-1 TYPE: C

12. The *industry environment* is made up of very broad factors that influence all—or at least most—businesses in a society.

ANS: F REF: p. 56 OBJ: 3-1 TYPE: C

13. An entrepreneur who starts his or her own business, rather than buying an existing business, avoids the undesirable precedents, policies, procedures, and legal commitments of the existing firm.

ANS: T REF: p. 50 OBJ: 3-2 TYPE: C

14. Either a new product or a superior location can serve as a foundation for a successful new venture.

ANS: T REF: p. 50 OBJ: 3-2 TYPE: C

15. The *general environment* is very narrow and includes the forces that directly impact a firm and its competitors.

ANS: F
It is the *industry environment* that impacts only a firm and its competitors. The *general environment* is broad in its impact, since it influences all or most businesses in a society.

REF: p. 56 OBJ: 3-4 TYPE: D

16. The *industry environment* can best be defined as the combined forces that directly impact a given firms and its competitors.

ANS: T REF: p. 56 OBJ: 3-4 TYPE: D

17. The general environment is more narrowly defined than the industry environment because it focuses on specific segments, such as those relating to the economy, sociocultural trends, and geopolitical developments.

ANS: F
The general environment (comprised of economic, sociocultural, political/legal, technological, ecological, and global segments) is more broadly defined than the industry environment in that the former affects all (or at least most) businesses in a society, whereas the industry environment affects only a given firm and its relevant competitors.

REF: p. 56 OBJ: 3-4 TYPE: C

18. The general environment is positive in its impact on the small firm and its performance.

ANS: F
The general environment is a two-edged sword in that it can open up new opportunities to the small firm or threaten its existence.

REF: p. 56 OBJ: 3-4 TYPE: C

19. Developments in the technological segment of the general environment have created significant opportunities for many new and creative small businesses.

ANS: T REF: p. 57 OBJ: 3-4 TYPE: C

20. Buyers, suppliers, substitute products, competitive rivalry, and new entrants all represent forces within an industry.

ANS: T REF: p. 57 OBJ: 3-4 TYPE: C

21. The industry forces identified by Michael Porter have very little impact on a small firm's success.

ANS: F
The collective impact of Porter's five forces on the firm's industry is widely recognized and will thus have an indirect impact on the firm's success.

REF: p. 57 OBJ: 3-4 TYPE: C

22. Strong industry forces tend to lead to low profits, whereas weak forces yield high profits.

ANS: T REF: p. 57 OBJ: 3-4 TYPE: C

23. The bargaining power of suppliers is encouraging for small businesses attempting to enter an industry.

ANS: F REF: p. 57 OBJ: 3-4 TYPE: D

24. Change may be the most important source of opportunities for entrepreneurial firms.

ANS: T REF: p. 54 OBJ: 3-4 TYPE: C

25. The entrepreneurs are usually drawn to opportunities that others reject because they misread their potential.

ANS: F
Entrepreneurs who understand industry influences can better assess market opportunities and guard against threats to their ventures.

REF: p. 57 OBJ: 3-4 TYPE: D

26. Research has shown that most entrepreneurs generate their business ideas by searching external sources of ideas.

ANS: F
Research has shown that these are more often generated from personal expertise, not from external sources.

REF: p. 60 OBJ: 3-4 TYPE: C

27. Resources can be either tangible or intangible in nature.

ANS: T REF: p. 59 OBJ: 3-4 TYPE: D

28. Capabilities are best viewed as a loose collection of several resources.

ANS: F
Organizational resources do not comprise organizational capabilities until they are *integrated* in some meaningful way.

REF: p. 59 OBJ: 3-4 TYPE: D

29. Core competencies are those resources and capabilities that provide a firm with a competitive advantage over its rivals.

ANS: T REF: p. 59 OBJ: 3-4 TYPE: D

30. SWOT analysis provides a concise overview of a firm's strategic situation.

ANS: T REF: p. 60 OBJ: 3-4 TYPE: D

31. In practice, a SWOT analysis is usually based on a dynamic view of the firm and its situation.

ANS: F
SWOT analysis is often based as a static view of the firm and its situation, which is unfortunate since the firm's strategy will always be dynamic (changing).

REF: p. 60 OBJ: 3-4 TYPE: C

32. Following a cost-based strategy can give a small firm a competitive advantage.

ANS: T REF: p. 62 OBJ: 3-5 TYPE: D

33. A cost-based strategy requires a firm to create and sustain differentiation in the marketplace.

ANS: F
It is a differentiation-based strategy that requires a firm to create and sustain differentiation in the marketplace.

REF: p. 63 OBJ: 3-5 TYPE: C

34. A differentiation-based strategy usually does not lead to a competitive advantage in business.

ANS: F
A differentiation-based strategy is one of two general options that can lead to a competitive advantage.

REF: p. 63 OBJ: 3-5 TYPE: C

35. A firm that is able to create and sustain product and/or service differentiation will most likely be a successful performer in the marketplace.

ANS: T REF: p. 63 OBJ: 3-5 TYPE: C

36. Small firms are pursuing a focus strategy if they adapt their efforts to concentrating on a specific niche within the market.

ANS: T REF: p. 63 OBJ: 3-5 TYPE: D

37. In marketing terms, a focus strategy depends upon market segmentation.

ANS: T REF: p. 63-64 OBJ: 3-5 TYPE: C

38. Focus strategies are very popular because they allow small firms to operate in the gap that exists between larger competitors.

ANS: T REF: p. 64 OBJ: 3-5 TYPE: C

39. Mitch Frankenberg and Jennifer Fredreck's Paw House Inn is an example of the application of a cost-based strategy to solve a specific problem

ANS: F
It is an example of a focus strategy restricted to a single subset of customers—dog owners.

REF: p. 65 OBJ: 3-5 TYPE: D

40. Zane's Cycles in Branford, Connecticut lost its competitive advantage when it changed its broad-based market strategy to one that focused on a market segment that turned out to be too small to sustain the firm.

ANS: F
Zane's Cycles is successful because it has focused on providing superior customer service to build customer loyalty.

REF: p. 65 OBJ: 3-5 TYPE: D

41. The experience of Minnetonka, a small firm widely recognized as the first to introduce liquid hand soap, is an example of how a focus strategy can be difficult to imitate.

ANS: F REF: p. 66 OBJ: 3-5 TYPE: C

MULTIPLE CHOICE

1. When people become infatuated with a business idea, they tend to ____________ the difficulty of developing market receptivity to that idea.
   a. ignore
   b. underestimate
   c. overestimate
   d. quickly calculate

   ANS: B REF: p. 50 OBJ: 3-1 TYPE: C

2. Which of the following is a criteria used to judge whether a new business idea is a good investment opportunity?
   a. The market need is defined so clearly that timing of introduction is unimportant.
   b. The proposed business can achieve a durable or sustainable competitive advantage.
   c. The return on investment must be just high enough to allow for errors and mistakes.
   d. The opportunity must be financially rewarding, regardless of the entrepreneur's abilities.

   ANS: B REF: p. 50 OBJ: 3-1 TYPE: C

3. Different types of small business ownership opportunities include all of the following *except*
   a. startups.
   b. bailouts.
   c. family businesses.
   d. franchises.

   ANS: B REF: p.50 OBJ: 3-1 TYPE: C

4. According to Amar Bhide, a professor at Columbia University, "______________ with products that do not serve clear and important needs cannot expect to be 'discovered' by enough customers to make a difference."
   a. startups.
   b. buyouts.
   c. family business.
   d. franchises.

   ANS: A REF: p. 49 OBJ: 3-1 TYPE: D

5. Fundamental requirements of a good investment opportunity include all but which of the following?
   a. The timing must be right.
   b. The business must be able to achieve a sustainable competitive advantage.
   c. There must be a good fit between the entrepreneur and the opportunity.
   d. There can be no more than one fatal flaw.

   ANS: D REF: p.50 OBJ: 3-1 TYPE: C

6. Reasons for developing a startup, rather than pursuing other alternatives, include all of the following *except*
   a. invention of a new product or service.
   b. the existence of established customers or clientele.
   c. freedom to select location, equipment, products/services, employees, suppliers, and bankers.
   d. avoidance of undesirable precedents, policies, procedures, and legal commitments of existing firms.

   ANS: B REF: p.50 OBJ: 3-3 TYPE: C

7. Questions that a would-be entrepreneur should consider before deciding to implement a startup include all but which of the following?
   a. Will I acquire the benefit of the experience of the prior owner?
   b. How do I identify a genuine opportunity?
   c. What are some of sources for new ideas?
   d. What are the different types of startup ideas I should consider?

   ANS: A REF: p. 50 OBJ: 3-3 TYPE: C

8. Attractiveness of a target market _________ as the time required to breakeven in the market _________.
   a. increases, decreases.
   b. increases, increases.
   c. decreases, decreases.
   d. is unchanged, decreases.

   ANS: A REF: p. 51 OBJ: 3-2 TYPE: C

9. An example of a Type A startup idea is
   a. a new microsponge technology allowing oils to be contained inside billions of microscopic sponges.
   b. a baby stroller that pushes more easily and is more difficult to overturn than previous designs.
   c. opening a new hamburger stand on the corner with no unique product differentiation.
   d. using satellite dish technology to form a mobile satellite transmitter and receiver business.

   ANS: C REF: p. 52 OBJ: 3-3 TYPE: A

10. An example of a Type B startup idea is
   a. a new microsponge technology allowing oils to be contained inside billions of microscopic sponges.
   b. a baby stroller that pushes more easily and is more difficult to overturn than previous designs.
   c. opening a new hamburger stand on the corner with no unique product differentiation.
   d. a new mail-order business selling a foreign-produced item never sold domestically before.

   ANS: A REF: p. 52 OBJ: 3-3 TYPE: A

11. As described in the textbook, a Type A idea involves
   a. a technically new process.
   b. performing an old function in a new and improved way.
   c. using prior work experience as a basis for starting a new business.

d. providing customers with a product or service absent in their market but available elsewhere.

ANS: D REF: p. 52 OBJ: 3-3 TYPE: D

12. As described in the textbook, a Type B idea involves
    a. a technically new process.
    b. performing an old function in a new and improved way.
    c. using prior work experience as a basis for starting a new business.
    d. providing customers with a product or service absent in their market but available elsewhere.

ANS: A REF: p. 52 OBJ: 3-3 TYPE: D

13. As described in the textbook, a Type C idea involves
    a. a technically new process.
    b. performing an old function in a new and improved way.
    c. using prior work experience as a basis for starting a new business.
    d. providing customers with a product or service absent in their market but available elsewhere.

ANS: B REF: p. 52 OBJ: 3-3 TYPE: D

14. What type of idea accounts for the largest number of startups?
    a. A technically new process
    b. Performing an old function in a new and improved way
    c. Using prior work experience as a basis for starting a new business
    d. Providing customers with a product or service absent in their market but available elsewhere

ANS: B REF: p. 52 OBJ: 3-3 TYPE: C

15. An example of a Type C startup idea is
    a. a new microsponge technology allowing oils to be contained inside billions of microscopic sponges.
    b. a baby stroller that pushes more easily and is more difficult to overturn than previous designs.
    c. opening a new hamburger stand on the corner with no unique product differentiation.
    d. using satellite dish technology to form a mobile satellite transmitter and receiver business.

ANS: B REF: p. 52 OBJ: 3-3 TYPE: A

16. According to a study by the National Federation of Independent Business Foundation, new product ideas for small business startups originate from all of the following *except*
    a. prior work experience.
    b. personal interests and hobbies.
    c. a chance happening.
    d. existing records of a business.

ANS: D REF: p. 53 OBJ: 3-3 TYPE: C

17. According to a study by the National Federation of Independent Business Foundation, the most common source of new product ideas for small business startups is

a. prior work experience.
b. personal interests and hobbies.
c. a chance happening.
d. existing records of a business.

ANS: A REF: p. 53 OBJ: 3-3 TYPE: C

18. An example of an idea for a new startup from a hobby is
a. a coin collector, who bought and sold coins for years to build a personal collection, deciding to become a coin dealer.
b. a furniture salesperson seeing the possibility of opening a new furniture store in a different area of the city.
c. a sharpshooter, who shot holes in a pair of her boyfriend's jeans during an argument, hearing him get complimented on the way they look.
d. a purposeful exploration to find a new idea.

ANS: A REF: p. 54 OBJ: 3-3 TYPE: A

19. An example of an idea for a new startup from an accidental discovery is
a. a coin collector, who bought and sold coins for years to build a personal collection, deciding to become a coin dealer.
b. a furniture salesperson seeing the possibility of opening a new furniture store in a different area of the city.
c. a sharpshooter, who shot holes in a pair of her boyfriend's jeans during an argument, hearing him get complimented on the way they look.
d. a purposeful exploration to find a new idea.

ANS: C REF: p. 54 OBJ: 3-3 TYPE: A

20. The most productive deliberate search approach for new businesses starts by looking at
a. prior work experience.
b. personal interests and hobbies.
c. a chance happening.
d. marketplace needs.

ANS: D REF: p. 56 OBJ: 3-3 TYPE: C

21. Which of the following is a recognized segment of the general environment?
a. The industry segment
b. The global segment
c. The information segment
d. The human factors segment

ANS: B REF: p. 57 OBJ: 3-4 TYPE: C

22. Trade between the United States and Mexico has increased since the enactment of the North American Free Trade Agreement. This factor is related to the _________ element of the general environment.
a. technological
b. global
c. ecological
d. sociocultural

ANS: B REF: p. 57 OBJ: 3-4 TYPE: A

23. All of the following are specified by Michael Porter as factors that determine the nature and degree of competition in an industry *except*
    a. threat of new competitors.
    b. rivalry among existing competitors.
    c. industry cost/price structure.
    d. bargaining power of buyers and/or suppliers.

    ANS: C REF: p. 57 OBJ: 3-4 TYPE: C

24. Which of the following is one of the factors that determines the nature and degree of competition in an industry, as identified by Michael Porter in his book *Competitive Advantage*?
    a. The interest of small businesses
    b. Bargaining power of competitors
    c. Threat of substitute products or services
    d. The macroeconomy

    ANS: C REF: p. 57 OBJ: 3-4 TYPE: C

25. Competitive advantage in an industry is protected by
    a. barriers to entry.
    b. potential substitute products.
    c. intra-industry competition
    d. deregulation .

    ANS: A REF: p. 51 OBJ: 3-4 TYPE: C

26. An increase in the bargaining power of suppliers
    a. increases both the attractiveness and the profitability of the target market.
    b. decreases both the attractiveness and the profitability of the target market.
    c. decreases the attractiveness and increases the profitability of the target market.
    d. increases the attractiveness and decreases the profitability of the target market.

    ANS: B REF: p. 58 OBJ: 3-4 TYPE: C

27. Proprietary information and regulatory protection represent
    a. entry barriers.
    b. exit barriers.
    c. competitive barriers.
    d. mobility barriers.

    ANS: A REF: p. 51 OBJ: 3-4 TYPE: D

28. Substitute products
    a. often place a ceiling on prices charged within an industry.
    b. represent those items manufactured by direct rivals within an industry.
    c. are usually cheaper than the products they can replace.
    d. are always a serious threat to rivals in an industry.

    ANS: A REF: p. 57 OBJ: 3-4 TYPE: D

29. Based on William A. Sahlman's suggestions, which of the following is a question about competitors that should be answered by the business plan?

a. Are there ways to co-opt potential or actual competitors by forming alliances?
b. How easily can new competitors enter the industry?
c. Do small businesses have special advantages when competing in the industry?
d. What is the average size of competitors?

ANS: A REF: p. 59 OBJ: 3-4 TYPE: C

30. According to Peter Drucker, the means by which the entrepreneur either creates new wealth-producing resources or endows existing resources with enhanced potential for creating wealth is
a. creativity.
b. innovation.
c. capital spending.
d. collaborating with competitors.

ANS: B REF: p. 54 OBJ: 3-4 TYPE: C

31. Which of the following is one of the seven sources of opportunities in the environment recognized by Peter Drucker?
a. The unbelievable
b. The undeniable
c. The incongruous
d. The new

ANS: C REF: p. 55 OBJ: 3-4 TYPE: C

32. An increase in the rivalry among existing competitors in a target market
a. increases both the attractiveness and the profitability of the target market.
b. decreases both the attractiveness and the profitability of the target market.
c. decreases the attractiveness and increases the profitability of the target market.
d. increases the attractiveness and decreases the profitability of the target market.

ANS: B REF: p. 58 OBJ: 3-4 TYPE: C

33. A(n) _____ exists when multiple resources are integrated and then deployed to the firm's advantage.
a. networked resource
b. common intangible
c. capability
d. industry edge

ANS: C REF: p. 59 OBJ: 3-4 TYPE: D

34. Resources are best described as
a. those basic inputs that a firm uses to conduct its business.
b. only those features that are visible and easy to quantify.
c. the firm's lending capacity.
d. capabilities that can be exploited.

ANS: A REF: p. 59 OBJ: 3-4 TYPE: D

35. A SWOT analysis can be described best as
a. a means of assessing the firm's industry situation.
b. an assessment of the internal strengths and weakness of the firm.
c. a dynamic analysis of the firm's current situation.

d. a concise overview of the firm's strategic situation.

ANS: D REF: p. 60 OBJ: 3-4 TYPE: D

36. Observations about the external environment and organizational potentials can be brought together by means of
a. an alignment strategy.
b. the in-and-out assessment.
c. a SWOT analysis.
d. common sense critique.

ANS: C REF: p. 60 OBJ: 3-4 TYPE: C

37. Generally speaking, a strategy is
a. an action plan that guides resource investments.
b. a formal statement of what the firm intends to do.
c. an expanded description of the firm's mission statement.
d. most effective when it is designed to reflect the tactics that are common within an industry.

ANS: A REF: p. 61 OBJ: 3-5 TYPE: D

38. The two broad strategies for building a competitive advantage are the _______________ strategies.
a. cost-based and differentiation-based
b. price-advantage and cost-advantage
c. marketing-advantage and price-advantage
d. focus-advantage and marketing-advantage

ANS: A REF: p. 62-63 OBJ: 3-5 TYPE: C

39. Which type of strategy requires a firm to be the lowest-cost producer within the market?
a. Price-based
b. Marketing-based
c. Efficiency-based
d. Cost-based

ANS: D REF: p. 62 OBJ: 3-5 TYPE: D

40. Marketplace Farms is a regional cooperative of apple and orange growers. In order to compete against larger regional growers, Marketplace Farms relies on low-cost migrant workers instead of machines and inexpensive packaging processes. (That is, it uses individual hand-packaging instead of assembly lines.) Marketplace Farms is relying on a
a. price-based strategy.
b. marketing-based strategy.
c. efficiency-based strategy.
d. cost-based strategy.

ANS: D REF: p. 62 OBJ: 3-5 TYPE: A

41. A differentiation-based strategy requires that a firm
a. be the lowest-cost provider in an industry.
b. emphasize the uniqueness of its product or services.
c. achieve the highest resource efficiency in an industry.

d. be the lowest-priced competitor in an industry.

ANS: B REF: p. 63 OBJ: 3-5 TYPE: D

42. Containers Etc. manufactures household containers. In contrast to traditional market designs, all of Containers Etc.'s products are microwaveable and child-proof and come in an assortment of 35 colors. Accordingly, Containers Etc. is pursuing a _______________ strategy.
    a. product-based
    b. differentiation-based
    c. concept-based
    d. efficiency-based

ANS: B REF: p. 63 OBJ: 3-5 TYPE: A

43. Mark Michaels is the owner of Delectable Delights, a specialty store offering chocolates, candies, and fruit baskets. After a recent analysis of the competitive environment, Michaels concluded that three distinct consumer segments exist for his products-A, B, and C consumers. In an effort to maximize the effectiveness of its strategy, Michaels has decided to focus on fulfilling the needs of A consumers. He is employing a ____________ strategy.
    a. multisegmentation
    b. selective
    c. focus
    d. concentration

ANS: C REF: p. 63 OBJ: 3-5 TYPE: A

44. Elegant Writings, a small creator of high-quality fountain pens, segmented its market into five distinct groups of consumers. The firm then decided to target only the segment labeled "affluent business executives." By doing so, the management hopes to establish a small, viable market for its products while simultaneously avoiding direct competition with larger competitors. Elegant Writings is following a ____________ strategy.
    a. selective
    b. market focus
    c. focus
    d. cost-based

ANS: C REF: p. 63 OBJ: 3-5 TYPE: A

45. A focus strategy is best described as
    a. an attempt to compete directly with industry giants.
    b. a domestic marketing strategy.
    c. a strategy that isolates the firm from market forces.
    d. targeting the high end of a market.

ANS: C REF: p. 63 OBJ: 3-5 TYPE: D

46. Carol Weinstock, who runs Technographics, a company that designs greeting cards for computer users, is employing
    a. a focus strategy.
    b. an unsegmented strategy.
    c. a multisegmentation strategy.
    d. a marketing mix strategy.

ANS: A REF: p. 63 OBJ: 3-5 TYPE: A

47. Which of the following does *not* indicate a focus strategy?
   a. Strict concentration on a single subset of customers
   b. Concentration on a single product
   c. Concentration on multiple products for the total market
   d. Restriction to a single geographical region

ANS: C REF: p. 64 OBJ: 3-5 TYPE: D

48. Entrepreneurs' choices that affect the nature of a small firm and its basic direction are known as
   a. market-based decisions.
   b. tactical decisions.
   c. strategic decisions.
   d. focus-based decisions.

ANS: C REF: p. 65 OBJ: 3-5 TYPE: D

49. According to Michael Porter, a focus strategy can erode when
   a. the strategy is protected.
   b. the target segment's differences from other segments narrow.
   c. new firms reconstruct the industry.
   d. demand for the product grows and thus attracts new competitors.

ANS: B REF: p. 66 OBJ: 3-5 TYPE: C

50. Which of the following is a cause for erosion of a small firm's focus strategy?
   a. Consumer demand grows.
   b. New firms reconstruct the industry.
   c. Differences between segments grow larger.
   d. The focus strategy is imitated.

ANS: D REF: p. 66 OBJ: 3-5 TYPE: C

ESSAY

1. Which of the three different categories of new venture ideas accounts for the most startup ventures?

   ANS:
   Type C startup ideas probably account for the largest number of all new venture startups. These ideas result in modifications to existing products and services. Therefore, they have less risk and already have a market that provides a customer base. Of course, they will fail if the market does not perceive that an old function is being performed in a new and improved manner.

   REF: p. 52 OBJ: 3-1 TYPE: C

2. Compare prior work experience with accidental discovery and deliberate search as a source of startup ideas.

   ANS:

Prior work experience is probably the most prolific source of startup ideas. It produces ideas that are related to the individual's skills and knowledge. Accidental discovery (serendipity), on the other hand, is like lightning—it may strike at any time and be totally unrelated to the individual's background. Deliberate search has the potential for producing ideas of many kinds and escapes the limitations inherent in relying on prior work experiences for inspiration.

REF: p. 54 OBJ: 3-1 TYPE: C

3. Compare the different approaches to deliberate search for new venture ideas.

ANS:
Entrepreneurs can begin by either evaluating their own abilities and ideas or assessing market needs or opportunities. Either approach can produce viable new venture ideas, but students should note that the latter approach has produced more successful startups, especially those offering consumer goods and services.

REF: p. 54 OBJ: 3-1 TYPE: C

4. List the five factors that determine the nature and degree of competition in an industry, as presented by Michael Porter in his book *Competitive Advantage*.

ANS:
- New competitors
- Substitute products/services
- Rivalry
- Suppliers
- Buyers

REF: p. 57 OBJ: 3-4 TYPE: C

5. Name and describe the two broad-based strategy options that a firm can select when pursuing a competitive advantage in the marketplace.

ANS:
The myriad strategies firms employ can ultimately be condensed into two-cost-based strategy and differentiation-based strategy. The cost-based strategy requires a firm to be the lowest-cost producer in its market, employing practices ranging from using low-cost labor to installing highly efficient manufacturing equipment. Using creative approaches, small firms can be very competitive using this type of strategy.
Differentiation-based strategies are based on product or service differentiation. That is, firms using this strategy must offer a product or service that is perceived to be unique in some way (e.g., convenient to operate, recognized as user-friendly) that the consumer desires.

REF: p. 62-63 OBJ: 3-5 TYPE: C

6. What marketing activities suggest that a small firm is following a focus strategy?

ANS:
- Strict concentration on a single market segment
- Concentration on a single product
- Restriction to a single geographical region

- Emphasis on substantive superiority of the product or service

REF: p. 63 OBJ: 3-5 TYPE: C

7. What are the four conditions under which a segmented market can erode?

ANS:

- The focus strategy is imitated.
- The target segment becomes structurally unattractive because the structure erodes or because demand simply disappears.
- The target segment's differences from other segments narrow.
- New firms subsegment the industry.

REF: p. 64 OBJ: 3-5 TYPE: D

8. **You Make the Call—Situation 1**

Marty Lane worked for a card company specializing in invitations and announcements. Every day for 25 years, he went to an office, sat at a desk, and took orders over the phone. He hated it. He was bored out of his mind. He didn't know what to do.

So he began skimming the business opportunities section of the Sunday *New York Times.* He wasn't sure what he was looking for. At almost 50 years of age, he had few business skills. Accounting was a foreign language to him. He figured that if he ever bought a business, it would have to be one that didn't require much specialized knowledge—something that would be relatively easy to manage. He considered a franchise, but he found that the good ones were very expensive. Then he came across an Italian-bread route for sale. He thought "How difficult could it be to run a delivery route?" He called the phone number in the ad and spoke with the business broker who was handling the sale.

It turned out that the route was in Queens, New York, not far from where Lane and his wife, Annabelle, lived. It was a one-person operation. The individual owned the company for 20 years and took home about $65,000 a year. He wanted $200,000 for the business, but he was willing to help finance the deal. If Lane would put $60,000 down, he could pay the balance over five years at 10 percent interest, or about $35,000 a year. That would leave Lane with an annual income of $30,000 until the debt was paid. Combined with Annabelle's salary, it would be enough to make ends meet. If he worked hard, moreover, he could expect his sales, and his income, to grow by 10 to 15 percent a year.

It seemed perfect. Lane went to meet with the owner and returned sounding even more enthusiastic. "This is a can't-miss deal," he told his wife. "The guy has signed contracts with all the places he delivers to, and none of them is more than 25 miles from here. I could do the entire route in seven hours."

However, Annabelle wasn't buying. "You're not quitting your job until you talk to an expert," she said. Lane agreed to meet with a broker.

On the date of the meeting, Lane brought all his paperwork along. He laid out the terms of the deal in great detail. "What do you think?" he asked.

The broker said, "Tell me something, Marty. Do you like this business?"

He shrugged. "I can't really say. I haven't tried it yet."

"What's involved in it besides picking up the bread and delivering it to the stores?"

"I'm not sure," he said. "Whatever it is, it can't be that complicated."

"What happens if the truck breaks down?" "I don't know," he said. "I guess I'll just work it out."

After asking Lane a series of questions along those lines, the broker finally said, "Listen, Marty. You want to know if this deal makes sense from a financial standpoint. That's easy to check. The guy has an income tax return, and his sales are verifiable. This isn't a cash business, after all. He sells to delis and supermarkets. They pay by check. We can go over his expense figures and make sure they're realistic, but my guess is that the deal is OK. If you're asking me whether I could negotiate him down a little, the answer is probably yes."

Lane turned to his wife: "See, I told you he'd approve."

The broker said, "I didn't approve anything. Only you can do that, and you're not ready to."

"What do you mean?" he asked.

"You haven't done your homework," the broker said. "You don't know what you're actually going to do in this business, and you don't know if you'll be happy doing it."

"How am I going to find that out?" Lane asked.

Question 1 How would you suggest that Lane find out if he would be happy in this business?
Question 2 Would you recommend that Lane buy the business, given the asking price and terms of the deal?
Question 3 Is Lane relying too much on nonquantitative factors?

ANS:

1. Several points are relevant to this question. First of all, there are no guarantees of happiness for the buyer of a new business, so Lane will never know for sure whether he would be happy with the business before actually getting involved. However, this does not mean that Lane should not think about whether the business offers a good fit for him. He could get a better idea of this through conversations with owners of similar businesses. Further, he could assess his potential for happiness in the business if he worked as an employee for a similar firm. At the very least, he should ask to spend a few days working the route with the current owner to get a feel for the ins-and-outs of the operation. This would also provide a more realistic estimate of how much work/time would be involved in managing the business. Finally, Lane needs to invest more effort in evaluating the profit potential of the route since he will surely be unhappy operating a venture that turns out to be unsuccessful.

2. The broker seems to suggest that the numbers work out for the deal (assuming the information provided is accurate), and he seems confident that the seller may drop his price a bit in negotiations. However, there are a number of "softer" issues that Lane needs to think through, including the fact that he seems less than excited about the business he is thinking of entering and has not considered a number of circumstances that are sure to emerge (e.g., equipment breakdowns). So, the biggest questions are non-financial in nature.

3. Nonquantitative factors are usually considered in the purchase of a business, including existing and anticipated competition, market potential, future community development, legal commitments of the business, union contracts that must be honored, the quality and adequacy of existing buildings and other assets, and product pricing. Lane has emphasized additional nonquantitative matters such as the location of the business and other convenience factors, but his primary interest seems to be in the potential of the business to provide happiness. From a rational/financial perspective, he is placing too much emphasis on the nonquantitative, but this is common among small business owners and is not necessarily bad since he intends to be very involved in the operation of the route.

REF: p. 68-69 OBJ: YMTC TYPE: C

9. **You Make the Call—Situation 2**

Amy Wright is the owner of Fit Wright Shoes, a manufacturer of footwear located in Alice, Texas. Her company has pledged that all customers will have a lifetime replacement guarantee on all footwear bought from the company. This guarantee applies to the entire shoe, even though another company makes parts of the product.

Question 1 Do you think a lifetime guarantee is too generous for this kind of product? Why or why not?
Question 2 What impact will this policy have on quality standards in the company? Be specific.

Question 3 What alternative customer service policies would you suggest?

ANS:

1. A lifetime guarantee is much too generous, because the average life of shoes is no more than a few years.
2. A lifetime guarantee would require excellent total quality management in all phases of the business. All supplies would need to pass stern quality tests, and the shoes produced would have to pass high-quality examinations.
3. A two-year guarantee might represent quality to the consumer and would be far less expensive to support.

REF: p. 69 OBJ: YMTC TYPE: C

10. **You Make the Call—Situation 3**
Jay Sorenson of Portland, Oregon, created a product called the Java Jacket, which is a patented honeycombed insulating sleeve that slides over a paper cup containing a hot beverage to make it comfortable to hold. Having introduced the new product to the market, Sorenson has already cut deals with coffeehouses, specialty stores, and convenience stores nationwide. He started the business with $15,000 in 1993, but his 2003 sales were projected to be between $12 and 15 million. Sorenson is now in a position where he would like to continue expanding his business, but he is concerned that large and established competitors could introduce their own variations of the same product.
Source: Don Debelak, "Send in the Clones," *Entrepreneur,* September 2003, pp. 128–132.

Question 1 Will the market for Sorenson's product continue to grow in the years ahead?
Question 2 If he is successful, what sources of competition should he expect?
Question 3 What steps would you recommend that he take to protect his company from the onslaught of competition that is likely to come?

ANS:

1. With the escalating consumption of coffee in the United States and abroad, it would seem that the potential for market growth for Sorensen's product is likely to grow. However, the greater concern is with the probability of larger competitors coming into the market and taking business away from Sorenson, which is the focus of question 2 below.
2. There are two general sources of competition on which Sorenson should keep an eye. The first of these is large competitors that have the resources to develop a similar product and use their market power to pry sales away from Sorenson. Their advantages from scale economies could be substantial and make it hard for Sorenson to maintain his position. Since the product is likely to become commodity-like in the future, he may also see competition from overseas manufacturers that can easily tap into low-cost labor and drive prices down to the point that Sorenson will find it difficult to make a profit.
3. There are several steps that Sorenson can take to maintain/grow his position in the market. For example, he could find an advantage that customers will notice and value (e.g., superior design or function), come up with a clever name that people find easy to remember, and/or promote brand identity vigorously. He could also be constantly on the lookout for ways to drive down his costs (e.g., expand sales to increase economies of scale, keep overhead low) and search relentlessly for ways to reach new customers.

REF: p. 69 OBJ: YMTC TYPE: C

11. **You Make the Call—Situation 4**
Stuart Mize had worked with his father in a successful building materials business. The family had sold the company, and Mize had received a portion of the sales price. After several months, he began thinking about starting or buying a company. One of his hobbies was backpacking; he had hiked the highest peaks in 30 of the 50 states. In his search for a new business, Mize heard of a company that made small trailers for motorcycles. These trailers were fairly popular with retirees who were cyclists and with individuals who liked to travel on motorcycles in order to go where a car could not go.

After several meetings, Mize and the current owner of the firm negotiated a selling price and the deal was consummated. Immediately after the purchase, Mize moved the business from its present location to his hometown, several hundred miles away.

Question 1 Why should Mize buy the company instead of starting his own firm?
Question 2 What are the pros and cons for Mize of buying this particular business?
Question 3 Do you think Mize made a mistake in moving the business to his hometown?

ANS:

1. There may be three main reasons:
   - If the existing business has been successful in the past, it already has an ability to attract customers, control costs, and make a profit. The success in the past will show what it should likely be in the future under similar market conditions.
   - Mize can save time and effort in acquiring personnel, inventories, and facilities and developing relationships with suppliers and banks.
   - Mize may get a good price in buying the business if (1) the seller is old and wants to quit or (2) the location is deteriorating.
2. Pros:
   - Reducing the amount of planning for a new business
   - Getting a benefit from the existing customers and suppliers
   - Starting his business without losing much time in selecting and ordering products
   - Getting a benefit from the historical records of the business

   Cons:
   - The difficulty of changing precedents such as employees' salaries, procedures, and legal commitments
   - The risk of creating a burden on future cash flow caused by the purchase price
3. If the historical data of the business indicate that the existing location can provide good sales and profit, Mize's decision may have been a mistake. In relocating, he has to face uncertainty as to whether the new location can provide enough cyclists or motorcyclists as customers to make a high level of profit.

REF: p. 0 OBJ: YMTC TYPE: C

12. **You Make the Call—Situation 5**
Salvatore Indigo recently retired from a successful corporate career in information technology. He is presently casting about for a business opportunity that will allow him time to pursue his life-long gardening hobby. He has been in contact with a business broker who has located what appears to be an ideal business opportunity. The owners of a successful online home-based business selling premium-quality gardening implements and supplies are interested in cashing out their investment. The broker has indicated that the current owners are "motivated" to sell immediately.

Question 1 Why should Salvatore buy the company instead of starting his own firm?
Question 2 What are the pros and cons for Salvatore of buying this particular business?

ANS:
1. There may be four main reasons:

• If the business has been successful in the past, it already has an ability to attract customers, control costs, and make a profit. The success in the past will show what it should likely be in the future under similar market conditions.
• Salvatore can save time and effort in acquiring customers, inventories, and facilities and developing relationships with suppliers.
• Salvatore may be able to purchase the business at a good price if the sellers are truly "motivated" to sell. He should be cautious and attempt to determine what factors are actually motivating the present owners to sell the business.

• Salvatore's background in information technology, knowledge of gardening, and prior business experience will be useful when he takes possession of the business.

2. Pros:
• Reducing the amount of planning for a new business.
• Getting a benefit from the existing customers and suppliers.
• Starting his business without losing much time in selecting and ordering products.
• Getting a benefit from the historical records of the business.
• The business and its requirements are a good fit with Salvatore's employment background and his personal interests.

Cons:
• The difficulty of changing precedents such as employees' salaries, procedures, and legal commitments.
• The risk of creating a burden on future cash flows caused by the purchase price.

• The risk of that the business may consume more of Salvatore's time than he is willing to sacrifice—after all, he is "retired."

REF: p. 0 OBJ: YMTC TYPE: C

Correlation Table for Chapter 4—Franchises and Buyouts

	Learning Objectives	Question Type	Definition Define new term, recall facts	Concept Understand or relate concepts	Application Apply knowledge, analyze data
1	Identify the major pros and cons of franchising.	T/F		1,2,3,4,5,6,7.8,9 10	
		MC		1,4,5,7	2,3,6
		ES		1	
2	Explain franchising options and the structure of the industry.	T/F	11, 15	12,16	13,14
		MC	8,9,10,11,12,13, 14,16,17,18		15
		ES		2,3	
3	Describe the process for evaluating a franchise opportunity.	T/F	31	17,18,19,20,21, 22,23,24,25,26, 27,28,29,30,32, 33	
		MC	24,33,39,	19,20,21,22,25, 26,27,28,29,30, 32,34,35,36,37, 38,40,41,44	23,31,42,43
		ES		4	
4	List four reasons for buying an existing business and describe the process of evaluating a business.	T/F	35	34,36,37,38,39, 40,41,42	
		MC	45,47,50	46,48,49	
		ES		5	
	You Make the Call	ES		6,7,8,9,10	

Total Number of Test Questions: 101 (41 True/False; 50 Multiple-Choice; 10 Essay)

Chapter 4—Franchises and Buyouts

TRUE/FALSE

1. Because of unique characteristics of franchising, the success rate for franchises is higher than the success rate for nonfranchised businesses.

   ANS: T REF: p. 73 OBJ: 4-1 TYPE: C

2. A franchise is typically attractive because it offers training, financial assistance, and operating benefits.

   ANS: T REF: p. 73 OBJ: 4-1 TYPE: C

3. The failure rate for independent small businesses is comparable to that for franchised businesses.

   ANS: F
   Results show that franchisees are much more often successful than nonfranchised businesses.

   REF: p. 73 OBJ: 4-1 TYPE: C

4. Franchising organizations frequently extend financial assistance to franchise applicants that seem to be suitable prospects with a high probability of success.

   ANS: T REF: p. 75 OBJ: 4-1 TYPE: C

5. The franchisee is seldom required to pay the complete cost of establishing the business.

   ANS: T REF: p. 75 OBJ: 4-1 TYPE: C

6. Association with a well-respected franchisor is often helpful to a franchisee, but it is unlikely to improve the new business's prospects for obtaining bank loans.

   ANS: F
   Association with a well-respected franchisor may improve a franchisee's credit standing with banks, either by establishing a proven program of financial controls, by providing a financially sound cosigner to a loan (i.e., the franchisor), or both.

   REF: p. 75 OBJ: 4-1 TYPE: C

7. One of the benefits of becoming a franchisee is sharing profits with the franchisor.

   ANS: F
   A franchisee enjoys benefits such as rights to use the franchisor's nationally advertised trademark or brand name and its tested methods of marketing and management, but sharing profits with the franchisor is one of the drawbacks of a franchise for the franchisee.

   REF: p. 77 OBJ: 4-1 TYPE: C

8. The entrepreneur who enters into a franchising agreement does not acquire the right to use the franchisor's trademark or brand name.

ANS: F
In reality, one of the greatest benefits an entrepreneur gains by entering a franchise agreement is the right to use the franchisor's trademark and brand name.

REF: p. 76 OBJ: 4-1 TYPE: C

9. Three shortcomings of franchising include cost, restrictions on operations, and loss of independence.

ANS: T REF: p. 76 OBJ: 4-1 TYPE: C

10. In many cases, a franchisor will receive payments in the form of royalties that are based on a percentage of the franchisee's gross income.

ANS: T REF: p. 77 OBJ: 4-1 TYPE: C

11. Franchising is typically defined as a marketing system revolving around a two-party legal agreement whereby a franchisor is granted the privilege to conduct business as an individual owner according to the methods and terms specified by the franchisee.

ANS: F
It is the franchisor who specifies the methods and terms of conduct and grants business privileges to the franchisee, not the other way around.

REF: p. 77 OBJ: 4-2 TYPE: D

12. The potential value of any franchise arrangement is defined by the rights outlined in the franchise contract.

ANS: T REF: p. 78 OBJ: 4-2 TYPE: C

13. Burger King is an example of a company that uses business format franchising.

ANS: T REF: p. 79 OBJ: 4-2 TYPE: A

14. The Coca-Cola Company is an example of a product and trade name franchisor.

ANS: T REF: p. 79 OBJ: 4-2 TYPE: A

15. A franchising strategy whereby a single franchisee owns more than one unit in a given area is typically referred to as a multiple-unit ownership strategy.

ANS: F
This type of entrepreneur is called an "area developer".

REF: p. 79 OBJ: 4-2 TYPE: D

16. Most franchisors are involved only with the outlets they have franchised.

ANS: F
Most franchisors own one or more outlets that are not franchised (sometimes called *company-owned stores*).

REF: p. 79 OBJ: 4-2 TYPE: C

17. Business publications such as *The Wall Street Journal* and *Entrepreneur* are excellent sources of advertising from franchisors.

ANS: T REF: p. 81 OBJ: 4-3 TYPE: C

18. The franchisor being evaluated should be a primary source of information about a franchise.

ANS: T REF: p. 84 OBJ: 4-3 TYPE: C

19. It is important for potential franchisees to remember that many financial figures provided by franchisors are only estimates.

ANS: T REF: p. 84 OBJ: 4-3 TYPE: C

20. Existing franchisees are a valuable source of information about franchises.

ANS: T REF: p. 84 OBJ: 4-3 TYPE: C

21. Small business firms have little opportunity to franchise in other countries.

ANS: F
The opportunity to franchise in other countries (especially Canada) is great, and this opportunity continues to grow as geopolitical developments open up more markets abroad.

REF: p. 84 OBJ: 4-3 TYPE: C

22. The appeal of foreign markets is substantial, but the task of franchising abroad is not easy.

ANS: T REF: p. 84 OBJ: 4-3 TYPE: C

23. If the franchisor insists, it is best to sign a franchise contract quickly before other entrepreneurs take advantage of the opportunity.

ANS: F
You should be skeptical of a franchisor who pressures you to sign a contract without time for proper investigation.

REF: p. 81 OBJ: 4-3 TYPE: C

24. One of the drawbacks of becoming a franchisor is the reduction in control.

ANS: T REF: p. 78 OBJ: 4-3 TYPE: C

25. To reduce costs, a franchise consultant can substitute for a licensed attorney experienced in the evaluation of legal documents related to franchising agreements.

ANS: F
Franchise consultants are not necessarily attorneys, an experienced franchise attorney should evaluate all legal documents.

REF: p. 0 OBJ: 4-3 TYPE: C

26. One drawback of becoming a franchisor relates to the increase in required operating support.

ANS: T REF: p. 78 OBJ: 4-3 TYPE: C

27. Though less recognized franchises exist, these rarely have the success rate of high profile, large franchisors, such as McDonald's.

ANS: F
Many of these less recognized franchises are quite successful, including Snap-on-tools and CleanNet USA.

REF: p. 76 OBJ: 4-3 TYPE: C

28. Because the offering and sale of a franchise are more intensely regulated by state and federal laws than is the establishment of a new business, individuals and/or firms involved in negotiating a franchise arrangement have limited need for legal counsel.

ANS: F
Because franchise contracts are complex documents that serve as the legal basis for the franchised business, it is important to consult legal counsel before signing such an agreement.

REF: p. 85 OBJ: 4-3 TYPE: C

29. Aside from consulting an attorney, a potential franchisee should avoid using other sources of assistance.

ANS: F
A prospective franchisee should use as many sources of help as is practical.

REF: p. 85 OBJ: 4-3 TYPE: C

30. The franchise disclosure requirements of the Federal Trade Commission specify that franchisors must provide potential franchisees with written disclosures providing important information about the franchisor, the franchised business, and the franchise relationship, and allow them at least ten business days to review it.

ANS: T REF: p. 85 OBJ: 4-3 TYPE: C

31. The UFOC is the Uniform Franchise Offering Circular.

ANS: T REF: p. 85 OBJ: 4-3 TYPE: D

32. Third-party coverage is of little use in evaluating the credibility of information provided directly by the franchisor.

ANS: F
Third-party coverage helps in evaluating the credibility of information provided directly by the franchisor.

REF: p. 81 OBJ: 4-3 TYPE: C

33. A disclosure document is a detailed statement of such information as the franchisee's finances, experience, and involvement in litigation.

ANS: F
A disclosure document is a detailed statement of such information as the **franchisor's** finances, experience, size, and involvement in litigation.

REF: p. 84 OBJ: 4-3 TYPE: C

34. The buyer of an existing business typically acquires its personnel, inventories, physical facilities, established banking connections, and ongoing relationships with trade suppliers.

ANS: T REF: p. 86 OBJ: 4-4 TYPE: C

35. Specialized brokers who handle all the arrangements associated with closing a buyout are called matchmakers.

ANS: T REF: p. 87 OBJ: 4-4 TYPE: D

36. The advice of lawyers and accountants, if employed, should be strictly followed.

ANS: F
Since the consequences of a business purchase, good or bad, are borne by the buyer, the prospective new business owner should never let the experts make the decision for him/her.

REF: p. 87 OBJ: 4-4 TYPE: C

37. Financial statements can mislead a potential purchaser trying to develop an accurate business valuation.

ANS: T REF: p. 88 OBJ: 4-4 TYPE: C

38. A firm's financial statements should not be adjusted because they conform with generally accepted accounting principles.

ANS: F
Financial statements should be adjusted by a potential buyer so that they reflect realistic values-e.g., property that has recently appreciated in value and receivables that are actually worth less than their stated value.

REF: p. 88 OBJ: 4-4 TYPE: C

39. As part of the valuation process, a buyer should scrutinize the seller's balance sheet to see whether asset book values are realistic.

ANS: T REF: p. 88 OBJ: 4-4 TYPE: C

40. Valuing a company is an easy task that results in a precise figure.

ANS: F
Valuing a business is neither easy nor exact, even under the best of circumstances.

REF: p. 88 OBJ: 4-4 TYPE: C

41. The purpose of determining the value of a business is to provide a benchmark for use in negotiating the purchase price of the business.

ANS: T REF: p. 88 OBJ: 4-4 TYPE: C

42. Legal commitments of an existing business are not a factor that needs to be evaluated by a prospective buyer.

ANS: F
Although only indirectly related to a firm's future cash flows and financial position, legal considerations can be an important nonquantitative factor in valuing a business.

REF: p. 88 OBJ: 4-4 TYPE: C

MULTIPLE CHOICE

1. All of the following are considered attractive characteristics of franchising *except*
   a. higher success rates than for alternative methods.
   b. entrepreneurial independence.
   c. financial and training assistance.
   d. operating benefits.

   ANS: B REF: p. 73 OBJ: 4-1 TYPE: C

2. Which of the following franchisors has a well-implemented franchisee training program?
   a. Snap-on-Tools
   b. WFC
   c. CleanNet USA
   d. McDonalds

   ANS: D REF: p. 73 OBJ: 4-1 TYPE: A

3. An entrepreneur would choose a franchise over an independent startup most likely because of the
   a. decision freedom it provides.
   b. guidance it provides for organizational structure.
   c. high probability of success.
   d. opportunities to meet and share ideas with other executives.

   ANS: C REF: p. 73 OBJ: 4-1 TYPE: A

4. The cost of a franchise may include
   a. royalty payments.
   b. high executive salaries.
   c. a one-time federal franchise tax.
   d. higher-than-usual labor costs.

ANS: A REF: p. 77 OBJ: 4-1 TYPE: C

5. Investment costs related to franchising include all of the following *except*
   a. insurance premiums and legal fees.
   b. inventory and supply costs.
   c. building and equipment costs.
   d. royalty payments.

ANS: D REF: p. 77 OBJ: 4-1 TYPE: C

6. Tom Jones is a college student with no business experience. Jones is most likely to worry about his decision to become a franchisee primarily because of the
   a. restrictions on business operations.
   b. restrictions on company growth.
   c. requirement to work at least 40 hours per week.
   d. increase in entrepreneurial independence.

ANS: A REF: p. 78 OBJ: 4-1 TYPE: A

7. Consider this quote: "If you can't follow somebody else, don't buy a franchise." Which characteristic of a franchise does this describe?
   a. High success rate
   b. Restrictions on growth
   c. Loss of entrepreneurial independence
   d. Location problems

ANS: C REF: p. 78 OBJ: 4-1 TYPE: C

8. The term *franchising* was derived from
   a. a Gallic word meaning "to sell or bargain for another."
   b. the archaic Norman form of "franshen" meaning "to trade with strangers."
   c. a French word meaning "freedom" or "exemption from duties."
   d. the Dutch trading term meaning "to drive a fair bargain."

ANS: C REF: p. 78 OBJ: 4-2 TYPE: D

9. An entity or individual granted the right to conduct business according to specified methods and terms of another party is known as a
   a. franchisor.
   b. franchisee.
   c. franchise.
   d. licensee.

ANS: B REF: p. 73 OBJ: 4-2 TYPE: D

10. A legal agreement between two parties in a franchise arrangement is referred to as a
    a. master license.
    b. franchise contract.
    c. requirements contract.
    d. franchise consent draft.

ANS: B REF: p. 78 OBJ: 4-2 TYPE: D

11. An entity or individual that grants another party the right to conduct business according to specified methods and terms is known as a
    a. franchisor.
    b. franchisee.
    c. franchise.
    d. licenser.

    ANS: A REF: p. 73 OBJ: 4-2 TYPE: D

12. The franchising strategy whereby an individual or firm is granted the legal right to own more than one unit of a franchised business is known as
    a. development franchising.
    b. multiple-unit ownership.
    c. piggyback franchising.
    d. aggregate ownership.

    ANS: B REF: p. 79 OBJ: 4-2 TYPE: D

13. Individuals or firms that possess the legal right to open multiple outlets in a given area are referred to as
    a. development franchisees.
    b. area developers.
    c. piggyback franchisees.
    d. multiple-unit owners.

    ANS: B REF: p. 79 OBJ: 4-2 TYPE: D

14. The rights conveyed by a franchising agreement are referred to as
    a. franchising rights.
    b. franchise claims.
    c. franchise interests.
    d. the franchise.

    ANS: D REF: p. 78 OBJ: 4-2 TYPE: D

15. Products and trade name franchising is best illustrated by the system offered by
    a. Dr. Pepper.
    b. Mail Boxed Etc.
    c. Burger King.
    d. Holiday Inn.

    ANS: A REF: p. 78 OBJ: 4-2 TYPE: A

16. Business format franchising is best illustrated by the system offered by
    a. Goodyear Tires.
    b. Coca-Cola.
    c. Burger King.
    d. Dr. Pepper.

    ANS: C REF: p. 79 OBJ: 4-2 TYPE: D

17. A _______ is an independent firm or individual acting as a sales agent with the responsibility for finding new franchisees within a specified territory.
    a. multiple-unit franchisor
    c. franchisor representative

b. area developer
d. master licensee

ANS: D REF: p. 79 OBJ: 4-2 TYPE: D

18. A Krispy Kreme franchise located inside of the local Wal-Mart store is a type of franchise operation referred to as
    a. folded.
    b. internalized.
    c. cooperative.
    d. piggyback.

ANS: D REF: p. 79 OBJ: 4-2 TYPE: D

19. Which source of information is *not* recommended to help a potential franchisee investigate a franchising opportunity?
    a. The franchisors themselves
    b. The franchisor's suppliers
    c. Existing and previous franchisees
    d. Independent, third-party sources

ANS: B REF: p. 81 OBJ: 4-3 TYPE: C

20. Government publications offering information about franchises include
    a. *Franchise Opportunities Handbook.*
    b. *Successful Franchising.*
    c. *Franchising Today.*
    d. *The Wall Street Journal.*

ANS: A REF: p. 81 OBJ: 4-3 TYPE: C

21. One primary source of information for a potential franchisee should be
    a. the franchisor being evaluated.
    b. the franchisor's suppliers.
    c. other parties considering the same franchisor.
    d. other franchisors.

ANS: A REF: p. 84 OBJ: 4-3 TYPE: C

22. Which of the following is an excellent source of information about franchisors?
    a. Any state funded university
    b. Friends and neighbors.
    c. Advertisements in the *Wall Street Journal*
    d. FranchiseAmerica.com

ANS: C REF: p. 81 OBJ: 4-3 TYPE: C

23. Johnny Berrins is considering an investment in a nationally known franchise. With which source of information should he be most concerned?
    a. The franchisor itself
    b. The franchisor's suppliers
    c. Other independent business people he knows
    d. "Infomercials" on the subject

ANS: A REF: p. 84 OBJ: 4-3 TYPE: A

24. Which of the following typically is *not* found in a *disclosure document*?

a. The franchisor's involvement in litigation
b. Key features of the franchisor's experience
c. Details of the franchisor's proprietary technology
d. The franchisor's size

ANS: C REF: p. 84 OBJ: 4-3 TYPE: D

25. Traditionally, U.S. franchisers have done most of their international franchising in
a. Canada.
b. Japan.
c. Mexico.
d. China.

ANS: A REF: p. 84 OBJ: 4-3 TYPE: C

26. Which event has contributed the *least* to the opening of foreign markets to U.S. franchisors?
a. The formation of the European Economic Community
b. The collapse of the Soviet Union
c. The introduction of the Euro as the unit of currency throughout much of Europe
d. The passage of the North American Free Trade Agreement

ANS: C REF: p. 84 OBJ: 4-3 TYPE: C

27. Why would a businessperson wish to become a franchisor?
a. Reduction of capital requirements
b. Reduction in control
c. Sharing of profits
d. Increase in operating support

ANS: A REF: p. 75 OBJ: 4-3 TYPE: C

28. All of the following are benefits of becoming a franchisee *except*
a. increase in management motivation.
b. speed of expansion.
c. reduction of capital requirements.
d. reduction in control.

ANS: D REF: p. 78 OBJ: 4-3 TYPE: C

29. In what way is a franchisee's control over the business greatly reduced?
a. Most franchisors are located near the franchisee.
b. The franchisees are technically employees of the franchisor.
c. The franchisee is bound by the terms the franchise contract.
d. The franchisee is completely dependent on the franchisor for funding.

ANS: C
The franchisee surrenders a considerable amount of independence in signing a franchise contract.

REF: p. 85 OBJ: 4-3 TYPE: C

30. Which of the following is least likely to have an unbiased interest in having a prospective franchisee sign a franchise contract?
a. Investment banker

b. Franchise consultant
c. Franchisor
d. Legal counsel

ANS: C REF: p. 85 OBJ: 4-3 TYPE: C

31. The disclosure statement provided to a prospective franchisee must contain all of the following information Except:
a. franchisor's finances.
b. experience in the market.
c. involvement in litigation.
d. strategic plans for future expansion.

ANS: D REF: p. 84 OBJ: 4-3 TYPE: A

32. Why is the sharing of profits a drawback to becoming a franchisor?
a. The franchisee will not share profits.
b. Only part of the profits from the franchise operation belongs to the franchisor.
c. There are usually no profits to share.
d. The sharing of profits reduces the franchisor's control.

ANS: B REF: p. 77 OBJ: 4-3 TYPE: C

33. The drawbacks of becoming a franchisor include
a. speed of expansion.
b. reduction in control.
c. reduced capital requirements.
d. increased management motivation.

ANS: B REF: p. 78 OBJ: 4-3 TYPE: D

34. The UFOC disclosure must include information on
a. litigation and bankruptcy history
b. investment requirements
c. conditions that would affect renewal, termination, or sale of the franchise.
d. all of these.

ANS: D REF: p. 85 OBJ: 4-3 TYPE: D

35. What accounts for the increase in operating support when an independent business expands by becoming a franchisor?
a. Accounting and legal services
b. Information technology demands
c. The need for decentralization
d. Coordination requirements

ANS: A REF: p. 85 OBJ: 4-3 TYPE: C

36. In addition to consulting an attorney, a potential franchisee should consider using the services of
a. a trusted friend.
b. a financial advisor.
c. as many sources of help as would be practical.
d. an experienced administrator.

ANS: C REF: p. 85 OBJ: 4-3 TYPE: C

37. One of the most important features of the franchise contract is the provision related to
    a. the sale or transfer of the franchise to a government entity.
    b. changes in management.
    c. termination and transfer of the franchise.
    d. termination of contracts with suppliers.

ANS: C REF: p. 85 OBJ: 4-3 TYPE: C

38. The offer and sale of a franchise are regulated by
    a. state laws exclusively.
    b. federal laws exclusively.
    c. both state and federal laws.
    d. Federal Trade Commission laws exclusively.

ANS: C REF: p. 85 OBJ: 4-3 TYPE: C

39. A document called the ______ has, in recent years, been the accepted format for satisfying franchise disclosure requirements.
    a. Uniform Franchise Offering Circular
    b. Franchise Offering Circular
    c. Franchise Circular Agreement
    d. Uniform Franchise Circular Agreement

ANS: A REF: p. 85 OBJ: 4-3 TYPE: D

40. Items covered in the new UFOC include all of the following *except*
    a. litigation.
    b. bankruptcy.
    c. investment requirements.
    d. marketing goals.

ANS: D REF: p. 40 OBJ: 4-3 TYPE: C

41. Most franchise experts recommend that the UFOC be examined carefully by
    a. regulators that specialize in such documents.
    b. a franchise attorney and an accountant.
    c. everyone associated with the potential startup.
    d. suppliers that may be used if the startup is successful.

ANS: B REF: p. 85 OBJ: 4-3 TYPE: C

42. You are considering becoming a franchisee with the Pots-R-Us franchise. You will only be able to determine whether this is a legitimate franchise opportunity or a fraudulent operator by
    a. carefully investigating the company and its product(s).
    b. finding out whether the company has an operational Web site.
    c. researching the industry in which the franchisor is involved.
    d. following your instincts–there is no substitute for intuition.

ANS: A REF: p. 80-81 OBJ: 4-3 TYPE: A

43. Entrepreneur Carrie McAbee's purchase of a Hair Diamond kiosk franchise is an example of

a. how an entrepreneur's lack of due diligence can lead to business failure.
b. the opportunities that piggyback franchises offer to entrepreneurs.
c. how important franchisor support can be to a franchisee's success.
d. why marginal businesses do not make good franchise opportunities.

ANS: C REF: p. 81 OBJ: 4-3 TYPE: A

44. Development of international franchise operations usually involves
a. fewer resources than anticipated.
b. more personnel than resources.
c. little patience and much perseverance.
d. diversion of surplus domestic resources.

ANS: D REF: p. 84 OBJ: 4-3 TYPE: C

45. Certified Business Brokers (http://www.certifiedbb.com) in Houston, Texas, deal with mergers and acquisitions of small and mid-sized companies in the United States. This business is defined in the text as a(n) __________ firm for entrepreneurs seeking to purchase a business
a. matchmaker
b. acquisition agent
c. coordinating specialist
d. prospector

ANS: A REF: p. 87 OBJ: 4-4 TYPE: D

46. Altering the financial records of a firm such that the records do not reflect the true conditional of the firm is
a. "gilding the lilies."
b. "plugging the numbers."
c. "cooking the books."
d. "creative accounting."

ANS: C REF: p. 87 OBJ: 4-4 TYPE: C

47. The exercise of reasonable care in the evaluation of a business opportunity is
a. customary caution.
b. due diligence.
c. scrupulous surveying.
d. duty of care.

ANS: B REF: p. 87 OBJ: 4-4 TYPE: D

48. The purchase price of a business is determined by negotiation between
a. lender and seller.
b. seller and broker.
c. buyer and seller.
d. lender and buyer.

ANS: C REF: p. 89 OBJ: 4-4 TYPE: C

49. When negotiation the purchasing of an existing business, the terms of the sale may become more attractive to the buyer if the expected down payment is
a. reduced.
b. placed in escrow.
c. increased.
d. aged as a receivable.

ANS: A REF: p. 89 OBJ: 4-4 TYPE: C

50. Union contracts are among the many __________ factors in valuing a business.
a. nominative
b. nonessential
c. nonquantitative
d. nonqualitative

ANS: C REF: p. 89 OBJ: 4-4 TYPE: D

ESSAY

1. List the advantages and disadvantages of franchising to a potential franchisee.

   ANS:
   The advantages are training, financial assistance, and operating benefits. The disadvantages are the costs associated with the franchise, operating restrictions, and the loss of entrepreneurial independence.

   REF: p. 74 OBJ: 4-1 TYPE: C

2. Define the terms *franchising*, *franchisor*, and *franchisee*.

   ANS:
   - Franchising--a marketing system revolving around a two-party legal agreement defining the privileges and responsibilities of the involved parties.
   - Franchisor--the party that offers a franchise for sale to potential operators (e.g., McDonalds).
   - Franchisee--the party granted the privilege to sell a product or service and conduct business as an individual owner, with responsibilities to operate in accord with the terms specified by the franchisor.

   REF: p. 73 OBJ: 4-2 TYPE: C

3. Discuss the function of a master licensee.

   ANS:
   A master licensee is a firm or individual that acts as a sales agent (or *middleman*), taking on the contractual responsibility of finding new franchisees within a specified territory. Sometimes a master licensee will provide support services, such as training and warehousing, which are more traditionally provided by the franchisor.

   REF: p. 79 OBJ: 4-2 TYPE: C

4. What options are available to the aspiring franchisee to assist in the evaluation of a franchising opportunity?

   ANS:
   Basically, three sources of information should be tapped: (1) independent, third-party sources, (2) the franchisor itself, and (3) existing and previous franchisees.

   REF: p. 81, 84 OBJ: 4-3 TYPE: C

5. List four reasons for buying an existing business.

   ANS:
   1. To reduce some of the uncertainties and unknowns that must be faced in starting a business from the ground up
   2. To acquire a business with ongoing operations and established relationships with customers and supplier

3. To obtain an established business at a price below what it would cost to start a new business or to buy a franchise
4. To begin a business more quickly than by starting from scratch.

REF: p. 85-86 OBJ: 4-4 TYPE: C

6. **You Make the Call—Situation 1**

Ethan Moore is a college student in Phoenix, Arizona, currently enrolled as an entrepreneurship major at a local university. Moore's home is in Chandler, Arizona, a nearby city, where he is considering purchasing a franchise. The franchise, which caught his interest while he was on a shopping trip to the Tucson Mall, is operated by an Idaho-based gumball company named Gumball Gourmet.

Moore talked to the owner of the franchise at the Tucson Mall while he was stocking the kiosk, which is set up in three tiers with 47 gumball machines and a money changer. The owner mentioned in their brief conversation that this particular kiosk had sold 12,000 gumballs in the last 30-day period.

From information he found at the Gumball Gourmet Web site, Moore determined that franchises are available with as little as a $25,000 investment.

Source: http://www.gumballgourmet.com, September 2003.

Question 1 What other Internet sites might provide helpful information to Moore as he tries to learn more about this franchise?
Question 2 What other questions should Moore have asked the Tucson franchisee?
Question 3 What information might a Uniform Franchise Offering Circular from Gumball Gourmet provide?

ANS:

1. Numerous Web sites could provide helpful information to Moore. Some of these are:
   http://www.ftc.gov
   http://www.franchise.org
   http://www.franchiseconnections.com
   http://www.thefranchisecompany.com
   Moore could also access articles about the franchise by accessing the Web sites of entrepreneurial magazines such as Inc. and Entrepreneur. Most of these type publications archive their articles and provide free access. A word search with an Internet search engine such as Google would definitely locate articles and other web sites related to the franchise.
2. Hopefully, the franchisee Moore spoke with was credible. If so, the sales information regarding the last thirty days should be useful. However, many other questions could have been asked to this person. Some example questions are:
   Did you receive training from the franchisor?
   What support do they provide you now?
   Is your territory restricted?
   How long did it take for you to be profitable?
   What kinds of ongoing fees, if any, do you pay?
   Are there restrictions on your operating methods?
   Can you do your own promotion? Etc, etc.
   If Moore could locate any ex-owners of this franchise they could provide valuable information about the dark side of the franchise, if there is one.
3. The UFOC would provide important information on a variety of items, including litigation and bankruptcy history, investment requirements, and conditions that would affect renewal, termination, or sale of the franchise.

REF: p. 91 OBJ: YMTC TYPE: C

7. **You Make the Call—Situation 2**
Scott Prewitt, 23, his brother Steven Prewitt, 29, and his brother-in-law Tony Mansoor, 21, have no experience in the restaurant business. But one of their goals is to start their own business and move their families from Jackson, Mississippi, to the mountains of western North Carolina. They are considering buying a Back Yard Burgers franchise.

As of March 4, 2003, the Back Yard Burgers, Inc., restaurant system comprised 122 units, including 80 franchised stores. The franchise, with headquarters in Memphis, Tennessee, specializes in charbroiled, freshly prepared food. The company began franchising in 1988 and currently has only U.S. franchises. The company uses a double drive-through concept for most of its restaurants, including the franchise that Prewitt and his family are considering. The Prewitt family is concerned about their inexperience and the harsh weather in the snowy mountains of North Carolina.

Sources: http://www.backyardburger.com; and Tracy Stapp, "Never Say Die," *Entrepreneur,* December 2002, p. 130.

Question 1 How concerned do you think this family should be about their inexperience? Why?
Question 2 Will the proposed location in the mountains be a potential problem for this type of restaurant? Why or why not?

ANS:
1. Lack of experience should not be a major problem. Most franchise purchasers are first-time entrepreneurs. If the franchisor is strong and has a good training program any inexperience will not be a handicap. This particular franchise offers six weeks of training at its headquarters and two additional weeks at the franchisee's location! This franchisor began franchising in 1988, therefore, it is experienced in selecting a franchisee from applicants.
2. Weather is frequently a major consideration in a business's success or failure. Back Yard Burgers had traditionally required a two-drive-thru design for its buildings. However, the Prewitt's were so eager to operate this business they convinced the franchisor to grant an exception and allow them to convert one drive-thru into an inside dining area. Their idea has helped them overcome the weather challenge and become one of the more successful franchises! In fact, nearly all Back Yard Burgers now have some indoor dining area.

REF: p. 91 OBJ: YMTC TYPE: C

8. **You Make the Call—Situation 3**
Judy Patterson, Connie Post, and Kriste Burnside were all friends, working together in the accounting department of a local manufacturing business in Waco, Texas. They enjoyed working out at a local exercise facility during their lunch hour.

One day, they learned that the owner of the gym was planning to move to Arizona and needed to sell the business. "We kind of hoped the owners of the company we worked for would buy it so we'd have free memberships," said Patterson. But that didn't happen, so the three friends formed a corporation to consider the purchase of the franchise.

Source: Mike Copeland, "Trio on Learning Curve," *Waco Tribune-Herald,* April 30, 2000, p. 4B.

Question 1 What sources of information about this franchise would you recommend that the friends consider?
Question 2 Is their work-out experience sufficient to prepare them for ownership of this franchise?
Question 3 Would the three friends be making a wise decision if they decided to buy this franchise? Why or why not?

ANS:

1. The sources of information described in this chapter should, once again, provide the information needed by these three ladies. In this case they should also look carefully at local conditions to make an assessment of the potential for the gym.

2. Probably not! They may have knowledge of accounting issues because of their work experience, but beyond that the odds are they will need help. However, their experience as customers of the gym will be valuable to decisions regarding certain aspects of operations, facilities, and maybe even promotion.

3. Giving an answer to this question will be possible only after the three ladies have carefully evaluated the franchise, the local market potential for the gym, financing arrangements, and their personal relationship to see if a business relationship might work as well as their work-out relationship at the gym has succeeded.

REF: p. 91 OBJ: YMTC TYPE: C

9. **You Make the Call—Situation 4**

Growth prospects have never been brighter for this 22-year-old manufacturer of custom-designed skylights, which has grown to more than $2 million in annual sales by letting light into homes, museums, symphony halls, upscale commercial buildings, and more. The California company ended last year with its strongest sales quarter since its current owners bought the business in 1995. Some 60 percent of its revenues come from jobs within California, where construction has remained steady throughout the economic downturn. Furthermore, the energy crisis has driven up demand for skylights, which pay for themselves in energy savings.

The manufacturer's state-of-the-art products also protect furniture and carpeting against fading from sunlight. The owners of the business are selling because they intend to move overseas. Their 22 staffers, including two installation crews and four sales and marketing professionals, appear willing to stay and help a new owner "illuminate" a variety of new growth opportunities.

The asking price is $675,000, with 60 percent down. The owners will consider financing a portion of the deal.

Source: Based on Jill Andresky Frazer, "A Blue-Sky Deal," *Inc.*, Vol. 24, No. 7(July 2002), p. 40.

Question 1 Should a prospective buyer of this firm investigate other possible reasons why the owners might want to sell? Why or why not?

Question 2 What sales and revenue numbers are needed to evaluate the asking price?

Question 3 What nonquantitative factors might have an impact on the fairness of the asking price?

ANS:

1. Yes. The move overseas can likely be checked out without too much trouble. One might wonder why the business couldn't still be owned as an absentee owner. Nevertheless, any prospective buyer should look for other more negative reasons for the proposed sale.

2. A prospective buyer needs as much financial data as is available. (See Appendix B "Valuing a Business" for more information about this process) Typically, past income and balance sheets for five or more years would be required.

3. There may be community issues related to the manufacturing plant which could impact a "fair" price. Also, the firm may have some legal issues outstanding. The business is very old and all buildings and equipment should be examined closely. And there is the chance that energy conservation may fizzle as suddenly as it sizzled, and the volatility of the construction industry will always be with you. If a prospective buyer can't cope with the uncertainties or with all those bids, he or she should try something simpler.

REF: p. 92 OBJ: YMTC TYPE: C

10. **You Make the Call—Situation 5**
One night, Charles Dunn saw an infomercial on television, that advertised a franchise for a gourmet-coffee store. One month later, he signed a franchise agreement and paid the initial $20,000 fee. He quit his job and took a second mortgage on his home to raise the $100,000 of capital required by the franchisor. Dunn did no market research; he didn't look at other franchises. His store was the first of its kind in the area, and it had no name recognition. Shortly after Dunn opened his doors, another store from the same franchisor opened a few miles away. After another year, Dunn shut down his business.

Question 1 What types of research should Dunn have conducted prior to buying the franchise?
Question 2 What kinds of training should this franchisor have provided to Dunn?
Question 3 What types of contractual issues should Dunn have considered in order to get a better deal?

ANS:

1. Dunn would have substantially increased his probability of success if he had spent more time assessing the franchise and its market potential before buying into it. Specifically, he would have benefited greatly by consulting three basic sources of information (at a minimum). First, he should have looked to independent, third party sources of information. For example, he could have discovered more about the franchise via federal and state government sources (e.g., the FTC's Franchise Opportunity Handbook), trade association publications, and the popular business press. Second, he might have learned a great deal by probing the franchise itself for information about specifics (though such information is best viewed in light of its purpose—to promote the franchise). Finally, Dunn would have learned much by talking with existing and previous franchisees. Taken together, these three sources of information would have revealed important features of the franchise that were unfavorable (e.g., weak territorial exclusions) and may have saved Dunn from a significant loss of investment.

2. One of the features of a franchise that persuades individuals to invest in its services (rather than going it alone) is the training provided. Initial training offered by franchisors often cover operating procedures to be used by the franchisee, but would also address broader topics such as record keeping, inventory control, insurance, and human relations. Of course, the amount and type of training required will depend upon the nature of the product and the type of business. Dunn should not have expected training support as thorough as that offered by McDonald's famed "Hamburger U," but initial and subsequent training would no doubt have been useful to a novice operator like Dunn.

3. Though several contract features are relevant to setting up a franchise agreement, it is clear that the most important issue in Dunn's case relates to the restriction of sales territories. His gourmet coffee store already suffered from limitations such as a lack of name recognition, but it was the opening of a competing store nearby from the same franchise that resulted in the closure of his operation. A careful review of the franchise contract by an experienced operator would have revealed this risk. Advanced warning of this unfavorable feature of the contract could have led to a renegotiation of the terms of the deal (e.g., reduction of franchise fees or insertion of territorial protections in the agreement), or it might have dissuaded Dunn from investing in the franchise in the first place.

REF: p. 0 OBJ: YMTC TYPE: C

Correlation Table for Chapter 5—The Family Business

	Learning Objectives	Question Type	Definition Define new term, recall facts	Concept Understand or relate concepts	Application Apply knowledge, analyze data
1	Discuss the factors that make a family business unique.	T/F	1	3,4,5,6,7,8	2
		MC	5,41	2,4,7,8,42,43	1,3,6,9
		ES		1	
2	Explain the cultural context of a family business.	T/F		9,10,11,12	11,
		MC	11	10,13,44,45	12,47
		ES			
3	Outline the complex roles and relationships involved in a family business.	T/F	22,	13,14,15,16,17, 18,19,20,21	
		MC		15,16,18,19,20, 21,22,23,24,25	14,17,46
		ES		2	
4	Identify management practices that enable a family business to function effectively.	T/F		23,24,25	
		MC		26,27,28,30,32, 48,49	29,31
		ES		3	
5	Describe the process of managerial succession in a family business.	T/F	31,32,33	26,27,28,29,30, 34,35	
		MC	34,36	33,37,39,50	35,38,40
		ES	4	5	
	You Make the Call	ES		6,7,8,9	

Total Number of Test Questions: 94 (35 True/False; 50 Multiple-Choice; 9 Essay)

Chapter 5—The Family Business

TRUE/FALSE

1. When a parent retires completely and turns the firm over to a son or daughter, the firm ceases to be a family business.

   ANS: F
   A firm remains a family business when it passes from one generation to another.

   REF: p. 96 OBJ: 5-1 TYPE: D

2. Even though Ford Motor Company is a big business, family considerations are nonetheless important to the firm.

   ANS: T REF: p. 96 OBJ: 5-1 TYPE: A

3. In a family business, the family's *primary* function it to ensure the profitability and survival of the business.

   ANS: F
   The family's primary goals are the development of members as well as equality of reward opportunities for each member.

   REF: p. 96 OBJ: 5-1 TYPE: C

4. In a family business, there is a possibility for either conflict or harmony between business goals and family goals.

   ANS: T REF: p. 96 OBJ: 5-1 TYPE: C

5. If a business is to survive, its interests cannot be unduly compromised to satisfy family wishes.

   ANS: T REF: p. 97 OBJ: 5-1 TYPE: C

6. Even if a family member contributes to the success of a family business, this does not mean that he or she has the ability to serve the firm in a key position.

   ANS: T REF: p. 98 OBJ: 5-1 TYPE: C

7. One weakness of a family business is the tendency of family members to leave quickly when the business "falls on hard times."

   ANS: F
   Members of the family are drawn to the business because of family ties, and they tend to stick with the business "through thick and thin."

   REF: p. 99 OBJ: 5-1 TYPE: C

8. A major weakness of a family business is that it has greater difficulty than a nonfamily business in focusing on long-run decision making.

ANS: F
A family can take the long-run view more easily than corporate managers who are being evaluated on year-to-year business results.

REF: p. 99 OBJ: 5-1 TYPE: C

9. Though the distinctive values that motivate and guide an entrepreneur in the founding of a firm are important, these cannot serve as a foundation for competitive advantage in the firm.

ANS: F
The distinctive values that motivate and guide an entrepreneur in the founding of a firm *can* serve as a foundation for competitive advantage in the firm. For example, emphasizing intensive customer service may attract business that would normally go to competing firms.

REF: p. 100 OBJ: 5-2 TYPE: C

10. The family firm's total culture consists of three cultural patterns: the family pattern, the financial pattern, and the employee pattern.

ANS: F
These three cultural patterns include the business pattern, the family pattern, and the governance pattern.

REF: p. 101 OBJ: 5-2 TYPE: C

11. A small equipment rental business strives to answer every phone call before the phone rings three times. This practice is part of the firm's organizational culture.

ANS: T REF: p. 99 OBJ: 5-2 TYPE: A

12. A change in leadership may play a role in bringing about a break with traditional methods of operation.

ANS: T REF: p. 101 OBJ: 5-2 TYPE: C

13. In the entrepreneurial family, the natural tendency is to think in terms of a family business career and to push a child in that direction.

ANS: T REF: p. 102 OBJ: 5-3 TYPE: C

14. The family business culture complicates the process of leadership succession.

ANS: T REF: p. 101 OBJ: 5-3 TYPE: C

15. Entrepreneurial couples find that working together in the business strengthens their marriage and that family problems are minimal or nonexistent.

ANS: F

For some couples, the problems that emerge from participation in the business far outweigh the benefits of shared involvement in the enterprise.

REF: p. 102 OBJ: 5-3 TYPE: C

16. Mom or Dad, the founder, may logically assume that a son or daughter will be interested in taking over the family business.

ANS: F
A son or daughter may lack the leadership skills necessary to take over control of the business, or they may have other career aspirations.

REF: p. 103 OBJ: 5-3 TYPE: C

17. Two major factors involved in grooming a son or daughter to enter the family business are the child's aptitude and the child's right to choose a career.

ANS: T REF: p. 103 OBJ: 5-3 TYPE: C

18. Some family businesses benefit from effective collaboration among brothers and sisters.

ANS: T REF: p. 104 OBJ: 5-3 TYPE: C

19. A family business involving two or more children may experience either sibling cooperation or sibling rivalry.

ANS: T REF: p. 104 OBJ: 5-3 TYPE: C

20. To operate effectively, the leader of a family firm must concentrate on dealing with both family members and in-laws within the business.

ANS: T REF: p. 104 OBJ: 5-3 TYPE: C

21. The leader of a family firm may safely ignore in-laws outside the business, though he or she must carefully consider the views of in-laws who are members of the family firm.

ANS: F
In-laws who are "on the sidelines" are also participants in the business and have an important stake in its outcomes; thus, they should not be ignored.

REF: p. 104 OBJ: 5-3 TYPE: C

22. The role of the entrepreneur's spouse in family conflicts can sometimes be described as that of a mediator in business relationships between the entrepreneur and the children.

ANS: T REF: p. 105 OBJ: 5-3 TYPE: D

23. In the family business, family considerations affect only members of the family.

ANS: F

Those employees who are not family members are still affected by family considerations--e.g., being passed over for a deserved promotion that was set aside for a family member.

REF: p. 105 OBJ: 5-4 TYPE: C

24. Nonfamily employees in a family business may be caught in the crossfire between feuding family members.

ANS: T REF: p. 106 OBJ: 5-4 TYPE: C

25. Family retreats are best handled by an outside facilitator, who can help develop an agenda and establish ground rules for discussion.

ANS: T REF: p. 106 OBJ: 5-4 TYPE: C

26. Even if family members lack the capability to run the business, an entrepreneur should always select a successor from this pool of talent.

ANS: F
When capable family members are not available, the entrepreneur may have to bring in outside leadership to avoid a decline in firm performance.

REF: p. 108 OBJ: 5-5 TYPE: C

27. The process of preparing a family member to take over a family business typically takes about one year.

ANS: F
This process usually takes a number of years, and in some cases decades.

REF: p. 109 OBJ: 5-5 TYPE: C

28. The process of preparing a successor for leadership in a family business can take more than a decade.

ANS: T REF: p. 109 OBJ: 5-5 TYPE: C

29. Founders typically try to push their somewhat reluctant children into positions of responsibility more quickly than the children wish.

ANS: F
In some cases, potential successors may be held back by the reluctance of the parent- owner to release control and delegate responsibility.

REF: p. 111 OBJ: 5-5 TYPE: C

30. The most appropriate way for a family firm to deal with younger family members whose abilities are untested is to adopt a policy of "no jobs in the business until you own at least 10 percent."

ANS: F
A period of testing may occur either in the family business or in an outside business.

REF: p. 109 OBJ: 5-5 TYPE: C

31. In Stage I of leadership succession, the pre-business stage, the child begins part-time work in the business.

ANS: F
The child does not begin part-time work in the firm until Stage III, the introductory functional stage.

REF: p. 109 OBJ: 5-5 TYPE: D

32. In Stage II of leadership succession, the introductory stage, the successor becomes acquainted with the family business by playing on the business's premises or around its equipment.

ANS: F
Stage II involves introducing the child to certain people associated with the firm and to other aspects of the business. It is during *Stage I* that a potential successor becomes acquainted with the business as a part of growing up (e.g., by playing on the premises and around the equipment).

REF: p. 109 OBJ: 5-5 TYPE: D

33. In Stage IV of leadership succession, the functional stage, the successor enters full-time employment.

ANS: T REF: p. 109 OBJ: 5-5 TYPE: D

34. Bequeathing equal shares of ownership to children in a family business will probably create havoc in the future functioning of the business.

ANS: T REF: p. 111 OBJ: 5-5 TYPE: C

35. Bequeathing equal amounts of ownership to all heirs, including those outside the business, is obviously the fairest and probably the most efficient way to perpetuate a family firm.

ANS: F
On the surface, bequeathing equal amounts of ownership to all heirs may seem to be the fairest approach, but such an arrangement may play havoc with the future functioning of the firm and hinder its performance.

REF: p. 111 OBJ: 5-5 TYPE: C

MULTIPLE CHOICE

1. In which of the following cases is the business best described as a family business?
   a. The total investment comes from one owner.
   b. The son works in the business part-time during the school year and full-time during the summer.
   c. The firm is extremely small, with less than $100,000 annual sales revenue.
   d. The owner treats the business as a "cash cow," using its income to pay college tuition for her children.

   ANS: B REF: p. 95 OBJ: 5-1 TYPE: A

2. When is a company a family business?

a. When decisions at work have an impact on ones family
b. When a number of family members are employed by the same company
c. When a parent is in a good position to give career advice to a son or daughter
d. When two or more members of a family are involved in a firm's ownership and functioning

ANS: D REF: p. 95 OBJ: 5-1 TYPE: C

3. Which of the following is incorrectly classified as a family business?
a. Levi Strauss and Company
b. Wal-Mart
c. Apple Computer
d. Ford Motor Company

ANS: C REF: p. 96 OBJ: 5-1 TYPE: A

4. In a family business, the interests of the family and the interests of the business are best described as
a. overlapping.
b. conflicting.
c. coinciding.
d. having no relationship with each other.

ANS: A REF: p. 96 OBJ: 5-1 TYPE: C

5. In a family business, business decisions
a. often affect both the business and the family.
b. are never family decisions.
c. are seldom rational decisions.
d. are made by negotiation between family and nonfamily members.

ANS: A REF: p. 96 OBJ: 5-1 TYPE: D

6. The parent-founder of a family business is contemplating the potential conflict between family concerns and business interests. He concludes that a primary family concern is
a. nurture.
b. profitability.
c. survival.
d. avoidance of excessive business debt.

ANS: A REF: p. 96 OBJ: 5-1 TYPE: A

7. The close relationship of business factors and family concerns in a family business has been described as
a. separation of domains.
b. a generational gap.
c. an example of blood being thicker than water.
d. overlapping.

ANS: D REF: p. 96 OBJ: 5-1 TYPE: C

8. A primary benefit deriving from the strength of family relationships is the willingness of family members to
a. adopt new operating methods when needed.
b. act generously in compensating nonfamily employees.

c. sacrifice salaries and dividends when necessary.
d. emphasize short-run profits.

ANS: C REF: p. 99 OBJ: 5-1 TYPE: C

9. Steve, Harry, and Chris, who own and operate a family auto parts store, are experiencing tough times during a downturn in the local economy. To help the store weather these adverse conditions, the brothers agree to each take a 25 percent reduction in salary for a one-year period. This decision
a. demonstrates a weakness of financial management.
b. illustrates an important advantage of a family business.
c. reveals a lack of customer orientation in a family business.
d. reflects a lessening of entrepreneurial ambition in second-generation businesses.

ANS: B REF: p. 99 OBJ: 5-1 TYPE: A

10. A founder's values become part of the family business culture because
a. the founder insists that the values are sound.
b. others in the firm learn what's important and absorb traditions established by the founder.
c. the values coincide with modern management theory.
d. family members follow family traditions without excessive analysis.

ANS: B REF: p. 100 OBJ: 5-2 TYPE: C

11. The set of cultural patterns in a family business includes
a. the business pattern, the governance pattern, and the employee pattern.
b. the business pattern, the governance pattern, and the family pattern.
c. the business pattern, the managerial pattern, and the family pattern.
d. the business pattern, the managerial pattern, and the informal pattern.

ANS: B REF: p. 101 OBJ: 5-2 TYPE: D

12. An example of a business pattern is
a. an emphasis on a patriarchal family tradition.
b. the creation of a governance system in the company.
c. a firm's system of beliefs and behaviors concerning quality.
d. the accepted practices of communication between family members.

ANS: C REF: p. 101 OBJ: 5-2 TYPE: A

13. In passing leadership of a family firm to a new generation, a problem may be encountered because of the existing
a. paternalistic culture.
b. collaborative family culture.
c. participative business culture.
d. advisory board governance pattern.

ANS: A REF: p. 101 OBJ: 5-2 TYPE: C

14. Which of the following is *least* likely to be a problem for the founder of a small manufacturing firm, in passing the business on to his or her son or daughter?
a. Avoiding favoritism among children
b. Preventing the business relationship from damaging the parent-child relationship
c. Motivating the son or daughter to take an interest in the business

d. Introducing the son or daughter to key people, especially outsiders such as bankers

ANS: D REF: p. 102 OBJ: 5-3 TYPE: A

15. One of the most common problems for a founder in passing the business on to a son or daughter is
    a. introducing the child to outsiders such as bankers.
    b. finding a suitable position for the son or daughter within the business.
    c. arranging the transition from part-time to full-time employment.
    d. deciding whether the child has the necessary temperament and ability.

ANS: D REF: p. 102 OBJ: 5-3 TYPE: C

16. An inherent problem for couples involved in a family business is that
    a. conflicts in the business tend to carry over into family life.
    b. hours of work become longer for the wife than for the husband.
    c. wives get the menial tasks to perform.
    d. husbands find their masculinity threatened.

ANS: A REF: p. 102 OBJ: 5-3 TYPE: C

17. While running a family business, a couple is experiencing a strain on family relationships. Which of the following might be the most likely cause of the tension?
    a. The wife holds the top position in the firm.
    b. The husband started the business.
    c. The roles of both parties are carefully defined.
    d. They have a difference of opinion about a business matter.

ANS: D REF: p. 102 OBJ: 5-3 TYPE: A

18. In considering the role of younger family members, the best philosophy is to recognize that
    a. a child should have a right to a job in the business if he or she desires.
    b. no family member should be hired at any level.
    c. children should have a right to prove themselves.
    d. second-generation managers are doomed to failure.

ANS: C REF: p. 103 OBJ: 5-3 TYPE: C

19. From the children's standpoint, one common reason that they may be reluctant to join the family firm is
    a. teenage rebellion.
    b. a desire to prove their abilities in another company.
    c. a desire to make a higher rate of pay.
    d. a desire to help the parent avoid favoritism.

ANS: B REF: p. 103 OBJ: 5-3 TYPE: C

20. Sibling rivalry in a family business
    a. rarely affects nonfamily members in the firm.
    b. may create disagreements about business policy or about siblings' roles within the business.
    c. is unusual since only one child will normally be employed in a family business.
    d. is often good because it spurs healthy business competition.

ANS: B REF: p. 104 OBJ: 5-3 TYPE: C

21. The spouse of the head of a family business may serve the family firm by
    a. making impartial decisions on controversial business matters.
    b. filling the role of a company director.
    c. mediating family disputes.
    d. staying out of the business.

ANS: C REF: p. 105 OBJ: 5-3 TYPE: C

22. In resolving differences among family members in a family business, the entrepreneur's spouse most typically functions as
    a. arbitrator.
    b. mediator.
    c. director.
    d. coach.

ANS: B REF: p. 105 OBJ: 5-3 TYPE: C

23. In-laws create complications in a family business
    a. rarely, since they only married into the family.
    b. only if they are employed in the firm.
    c. only if they are directly competing against another family member for a promotion.
    d. because the more family members become involved in the firm (even indirectly), the more difficult the fairness issue becomes.

ANS: D REF: p. 104 OBJ: 5-3 TYPE: C

24. The entrepreneur's spouse tends to function as worrier for the family business, especially if
    a. in-laws are employed in the firm.
    b. a child is being groomed for future leadership.
    c. the entrepreneur does not communicate sufficiently.
    d. several children are interested in the business.

ANS: C REF: p. 105 OBJ: 5-3 TYPE: C

25. Which of the following is the most appropriate and useful role for the entrepreneur's spouse in maintaining good family relationships in a business?
    a. Worrier
    b. Listener
    c. Evaluator
    d. Appeals judge

ANS: B REF: p. 105 OBJ: 5-3 TYPE: C

26. Concerning the need for good management in the family business, which of the following is one of the "best practices" identified by John L. Ward?
    a. Resist preparing successors for leadership to avoid demoralizing those who are not selected.
    b. Maintain rigid guidelines based on family traditions to guide the company into the future.
    c. Emphasize the attraction and retention of family members.
    d. Stimulate new thinking and fresh strategic insights.

ANS: D REF: p. 105 OBJ: 5-4 TYPE: C

27. To avoid a stifling atmosphere for nonfamily employees in a family business, the owner should
    a. promote only nonfamily members.
    b. avoid all special consideration for family members.
    c. make clear the extent of opportunity for nonfamily members.
    d. minimize discussion about future management changes.

ANS: C REF: p. 106 OBJ: 5-4 TYPE: C

28. To protect the interests of both the family and the business in a family business, the owner should
    a. recognize a basic obligation to supply the family with jobs of some type.
    b. refuse to hire family members but, instead, reward them with dividends.
    c. keep management simple by personally making all personnel decisions affecting family members.
    d. identify the positions, if any, that are reserved for members of the family.

ANS: D REF: p. 106 OBJ: 5-4 TYPE: C

29. A nonfamily employee of a family business complains that the recent promotion of a family member was unfair. The owner should
    a. enter into a discussion of the roles and opportunities for both family members and outsiders.
    b. point out the fact that family members always have the inside track, even though this is disappointing to the bypassed employee.
    c. get the employee to think more positively by describing other attractive features of the employee's job.
    d. shrug his shoulders and acknowledge that a tension always exists and that it can never be satisfactorily dealt with.

ANS: A REF: p. 106 OBJ: 5-4 TYPE: A

30. A family retreat is designed to
    a. bring family members together to openly discuss business matters.
    b. focus on business matters while avoiding extensive communication.
    c. control the lines of communication.
    d. announce the latest policy decisions.

ANS: A REF: p. 106 OBJ: 5-4 TYPE: C

31. A nonfamily employee of a family business is concerned about competing with family members for future career opportunities. To protect her personal interests, the nonfamily employee should
    a. align herself with the CEO.
    b. ask that the manager clarify the extent of opportunities.
    c. seek assurances that she will receive first consideration for promotion, ahead of family members.
    d. leave the firm and seek employment in a nonfamily business.

ANS: B REF: p. 106 OBJ: 5-4 TYPE: A

32. Family retreats, which open lines of communication,
    a. use the father as a communication facilitator.
    b. avoid discussing sensitive issues.
    c. involve family members but not in-laws.
    d. may result in formation of a family council to continue discussion.

ANS: D REF: p. 107 OBJ: 5-4 TYPE: C

33. The process of preparing a family successor for leadership in the family business often takes
    a. weeks.
    b. months.
    c. about one year.
    d. a decade or longer.

ANS: D REF: p. 109 OBJ: 5-5 TYPE: C

34. The son or daughter begins to function as a part-time employee in a family business during the
    a. pre-business stage.
    b. introductory stage.
    c. introductory functional stage.
    d. early succession stage.

ANS: C REF: p. 109 OBJ: 5-5 TYPE: D

35. A business owner tells her banker, "I'd like you to meet my little boy, Johnny, who is going to help me take inventory." This stage of succession is known as the
    a. pre-business stage.
    b. introductory stage.
    c. advanced functional stage.
    d. early succession stage.

ANS: B REF: p. 109 OBJ: 5-5 TYPE: A

36. A successor assumes a supervisory position in a family firm in the
    a. introductory functional stage.
    b. functional stage.
    c. advanced functional stage.
    d. early succession stage.

ANS: C REF: p. 110 OBJ: 5-5 TYPE: D

37. When fathers train their children in the family business, the typical problem is
    a. ambitious fathers.
    b. disloyal children.
    c. reluctant fathers.
    d. capable children.

ANS: C REF: p. 111 OBJ: 5-5 TYPE: C

38. Research has shown that a daughter's role in a family-owned business can often be described as
    a. clearly defined.
    b. a respected cheerleader for the enterprise.
    c. playing the part of "daddy's little girl".
    d. well developed, since their participation in the firm is usually anticipated years in advance.

ANS: C REF: p. 111 OBJ: 5-5 TYPE: A

39. In passing on ownership of a family business, the owner's primary concern should be
    a. tax considerations.

b. allowing each child to have an equal voice in the business.
c. the functioning of the business in the future.
d. nonfamily members of the firm.

ANS: C REF: p. 111 OBJ: 5-5 TYPE: C

40. A founder of a family business is contemplating turning the business over to his five children. One possibility, the founder believes, is to divide ownership equally among the children. This would
a. be impossible.
b. be inherently unfair to the children.
c. potentially hinder the future functioning of the business.
d. require an S corporation.

ANS: C REF: p. 111 OBJ: 5-5 TYPE: A

41. Recent estimates suggest that family firms generate more than ____ of the business revenue in the United States and employ more than ____ of its workforce.

a. one quarter, half
b. half, one quarter
c. one quarter, three-quarters
d. half, half

ANS: A REF: p. 95 OBJ: 5-1 TYPE: D

42. Which of the following family members are less frequently involved in family businesses in the United States?

a. in-laws
b. parents
c. spouses
d. siblings

ANS: A REF: p. 96 OBJ: 5-1 TYPE: C

43. In the operation of their Woodplay franchise, Nicole and Jason Gullege's attitude toward business can be described as
a. take care of the franchise and it will take care of the family.
b. putting the family first and the business second.
c. satisfying their customers is the most important priority.
d. doing business is fun but only if you make it so.

ANS: B REF: p. 98 OBJ: 5-1 TYPE: C

44. The influence of ____________ is shown when an entrepreneur sends personal messages of condolence to customers because her mother who founded the firm always sent them when she was operating the firm.
a. organizational complexities
b. cultural configuration
c. immutable principles
d. core values

ANS: D REF: p. 100 OBJ: 5-2 TYPE: C

45. In the early stages of a family business, according to Dyer, a common cultural configuration consists of a _________ business pattern.
a. paternalistic
b. patriarchal
c. pluralistic
d. platonic

ANS: A REF: p. 101 OBJ: 5-2 TYPE: C

46. Fran and Bob Smithers (wife and husband) own and manage a cleaning service. A potential advantage of this arrangement is that
    a. differences of opinion about the business won't carry over into family lives.
    b. it affords the opportunity to share more of their lives.
    c. the business isn't likely to dissipate their energies.
    d. they can count on working fewer hours in the business.

    ANS: B REF: p. 102 OBJ: 5-3 TYPE: A

47. Billy Newton works part time in his mother's garden supply wholesaling business. According to the results of Sue Briley's survey of the children of owner-managers of family businesses, how likely is Billy to work somewhere else before entering his mother's business?
    a. 25 percent
    b. 40 percent
    c. 55 percent
    d. 70 percent

    ANS: D REF: p. 103 OBJ: 5-2 TYPE: A

48. Making decisions about family business matters quietly and secretly
    a. avoids the embarrassment of airing "dirty linen" in public.
    b. spares the feelings of less involved family members.
    c. will help preserve harmony within family.
    d. can conceal serious differences that become increasingly troublesome.

    ANS: D REF: p. 105 OBJ: 5-4 TYPE: C

49. The Gaylors' succession plan for Al's Formal Wear
    a. was clearly developed and successful.
    b. created frustrations for their four children.
    c. was developed too late to save the firm from failure.
    d. caused the firm to dissolve into two separate business entities.

    ANS: A REF: p. 108 OBJ: 5-4 TYPE: C

50. A parent might attempt to resolve a transfer of ownership by giving active children in the firm's management _________ stock and giving nonactive children ______ stock.
    a. distributed, undistributed
    b. growth, speculative
    c. common, preferred
    d. dowry, canonical

    ANS: C REF: p. 111 OBJ: 5-5 TYPE: C

ESSAY

1. Explain the concept of family and business overlap in a family business.

    ANS:

The family and the business are separate entities, brought together in the complex institution of a family business. It is important to recognize the differences in the two entities' goals. Families are concerned with individual nurture, welfare, and opportunity. Businesses are concerned with production and distribution of goods or services. Employees are concerned with matters of compensation and fair treatment. A good answer will recognize that either harmony or conflict may result. Reconciling the needs of the family and the business calls for skill in management. The students may offer specific suggestions for improving the blend of family and business interests.

REF: p. 96 OBJ: 5-1 TYPE: C

2. Explain the role of the entrepreneur's spouse as it affects a family business and show how it can be made most effective.

ANS:
The spouse's role is often described as mediator. The spouse occupies a unique position, with a strong concern for each member of the family. At the same time, the spouse sees the business with some detachment because he or she is not involved in its everyday operations. The task of creating harmony and minimizing misunderstanding is a major one. The role can be made most effective if the spouse is informed about what is going on in the business. Students should recognize, of course, that individual differences in personality affect the manner in which spouses carry out this role.

REF: p. 104-105 OBJ: 5-3 TYPE: C

3. Outline and explain the relevance of John L Ward's "best practices" for the management of a family firm.

ANS:
Ward identified the following list of "best practices":
a. Stimulate new thinking and fresh strategic insights.
b. Attract and retain excellent nonfamily members.
c. Create a flexible, innovative organization.
d. Create and conserve capital.
e. Prepare successors for leadership.
f. Exploit the unique advantages of family ownership.

Points b and e highlight the need for founders to develop a clear succession plan, which should clarify the future direction of the firm and alleviate uncertainty and suspicion among family members and others. Points a, c, and d are important for all firms as they face business environments that are characterized by increasing change. Finally, point f applies a principle from modern management practices, recognizing that family firm ownership presents unique features, and these should be employed to the advantage of the firm whenever possible.

REF: p. 105 OBJ: 5-4 TYPE: C

4. Describe the model of succession in a family business, giving particular attention to its stages.

ANS:
Leadership succession in a family business is viewed in this model as being a long-term process, extending over the child's lifetime. The stages, which should be explained by the students in some detail, are the following:

Stage I: Pre-business
Stage II: Introductory
Stage III: Introductory functional

Stage IV: Functional
Stage V: Advanced functional
Stage VI: Early succession
Stage VII: Mature succession

REF: p. 109-110 OBJ: 5-5 TYPE: D

5. Discuss the problem of reluctant parents and ambitious children in a family business. Propose solutions.

ANS:
The problem arises because of differences in status and orientation. Parents tend to be conservative, committed emotionally and financially to present directions, and inclined to accept the status quo. Children tend to be oriented to the future, more willing to take risks, and ready for change. The potential for differences is clear and may be explicated in many ways. Students' solutions may include various practices or concepts of good management. Open communication between parents and children—a process that usually increases mutual trust—should be emphasized.

REF: p. 111 OBJ: 5-5 TYPE: C

6. **You Make the Call—Situation 1**
The three Dorsett brothers are barely speaking to each other. "Phone for you" is about all they have to say. It hasn't always been like this. For more than 30 years, Tom, Harry, and Bob Dorsett have run the successful manufacturing business founded by their father. For most of that time, they have gotten along rather well. They've had their differences and arguments, but important decisions were thrashed out until a consensus was reached.

Each brother has two children in the business. Tom's oldest son manages the plant, Harry's oldest daughter keeps the books, and Bob's oldest son is an outside salesman. The younger children are learning the ropes in lower level positions. The problem? Compensation. Each brother feels that his own children are underpaid and that some of his nieces and nephews are overpaid. After violent arguments, the Dorsett brothers just quit talking while each continues to smolder.

The six younger-generation cousins are still on speaking terms, however. Despite the differences that exist among them, they manage to get along with one another. They range in age from 41 down to 25.

The business is in a slump but not yet in danger. Because the brothers aren't talking, important business decisions are being postponed. The family is stuck. What can be done?
Source: "Anger over Money Silences Brothers," *Nation's Business,* Vol. 78, No. 10 (October 1990), p. 62.

Question 1 Why do you think the cousins get along better than their fathers do?
Question 2 How might this conflict over compensation be resolved?

ANS:
1. The present compensation arrangement may indeed be equitable, and the cousins may recognize its fairness. Since the cousins get along well, it seems possible that the compensation argument reflects some other personal differences among the three brothers. On the surface, it seems probable that we are seeing some sibling rivalry at play here, with the children's salaries being used as the way of keeping score.

2. If the firm has a board of directors or an advisory board, this board might be able to make recommendations. Since board members have an interest in the overall success of the firm, they should be able to avoid the personal bias that is apparently at work among the brothers. Also, regardless of who makes the compensation decision, an effort to make it as objectively as possible should be helpful. This would involve an analysis of the cousins' respective duties and possibly some comparison with pay levels for similar positions in other firms. An independent consultant might be helpful if the company has no working board. An imaginative solution is suggested in the following comments by Gerald LeVan:

   In this case, we have a solution that was tried and worked. I suggested the Dorsett brothers come up with a dollar figure that represents total compensation for the six cousins during the coming year. Then the six cousins were asked to divide that total compensation among them as they saw fit, leaving their fathers completely out of the process.

   The cousins jumped at the chance to solve the dilemma that so dumbfounded their fathers. The six met as a group first with their family-business consultant, then by themselves. For 90 minutes they debated the contributions each made to the business and arrived at a solution. They concluded that during the current year, each was being paid his or her appropriate portion of the total compensation available to them. They agreed to share the base pay for the following year in the same proportions. However, they came up with a different approach toward bonuses. "We are all blood," they said. "For that reason, we will share any bonuses equally among us, recognizing that all of us must pull together for the success of the company."

   They found a unique way to present their solution to Tom, Harry, and Bob. Each of the brothers had a favorite niece or nephew, and the cousins knew it. Therefore, the three favorites were tapped to present the new plan to their uncles. It was accepted and the brothers are talking again.

   It is clear that Tom, Harry, and Bob were still engaged in sibling rivalry. They competed through their children, keeping score by their children's compensation. Moving the compensation issue to the younger generation caused some of the brothers' rivalry to subside. In the process, the brothers avoided the issue that had divided them, while passing along the most delicate part of the compensation issue to the next generation. The cousins grew in the process through healthy discussions of each other's contributions to the business. Yet they acknowledged the equal value of kinship when it came to dividing bonuses.

REF: p. 113 OBJ: YMTC TYPE: C

7. **You Make the Call—Situation 2**

Harrison Stevens, second-generation president of a family owned heating and air conditioning business, was concerned about his 19-year-old son, Barry, who worked as a full-time employee in the firm. Although Barry had made it through high school, he had not distinguished himself as a student or shown interest in further education. He was somewhat indifferent in his attitude toward his work, although he did reasonably—or at least minimally—satisfactory work. His father saw Barry as immature and more interested in riding motorcycles than in building a business.

Stevens wanted to provide his son with an opportunity for personal development. As he saw it, the process should begin with learning to work hard. If Barry liked the work and showed promise, he might eventually be groomed to take over the business. His father also held a faint hope that hard work might eventually inspire him to get a college education.

In trying to achieve these goals, Stevens sensed two problems. The first problem was that Barry obviously lacked proper motivation. The second problem related to his supervision. Supervisors seemed reluctant to be exacting in their demands on Barry. Possibly because they feared antagonizing the boss by being too hard on his son, they allowed Barry to get by with marginal performance.

Question 1 In view of Barry's shortcomings, should Harrison Stevens seriously consider him as a potential successor?

Question 2 How could Barry be motivated? Can Stevens do anything more to improve the situation, or does the responsibility lie with Barry?

Question 3 How could the quality of Barry's supervision be improved to make his work experience more productive?

ANS:

1. Barry is not a viable candidate at present, but it is too early to reach a conclusion on this question. To this point, Barry's attitude does not show promise. The father's main hope is that Barry may "grow up" and realize the opportunity that he has.
2. The primary responsibility lies with Barry. He is ultimately responsible for his own destiny. His father can and should do his best to maintain or establish open communication with his son—often a difficult challenge. Also, he should attempt to structure work assignments so that they provide Barry with a challenge.
3. His supervisors must be made to understand that the father wants them to be exacting in their demands on Barry. This will require that Barry's father offer his supervisors consistent support and reassurance. Even with the father's support, a supervisor may tend to think ahead to some future day when Barry will be running the show. Formal performance review procedures might be instituted to make the issue less nebulous and more practical.

REF: p. 113 OBJ: YMTC TYPE: C

8. **You Make the Call—Situation 3**

Siblings Rob, 37, and Julie, 36, work in their family's $15 million medical products firm. Both are capable leaders and have experienced success in their respective areas of responsibility. Compared to Julie, Rob is more introverted, more thorough in his planning, and much better on detail and follow through. In contrast, Julie is more creative, more extroverted, and stronger in interpersonal skills. Since childhood, they have been rather competitive in their relationships. Their 62-year-old father is contemplating retirement and considering the possibility of co-leadership, with each child eventually holding a 50-percent ownership interest.

Question 1 If you were to choose one leader for the firm, based on the brief description above, which sibling would you recommend? Why?

Question 2 What are the strengths and/or weaknesses of the co-leadership idea? Would you favor it or reject it?

Question 3 How could the father secure practical advice to help with this decision?

ANS:

1. Obviously, it would be dangerous to choose a leader for the firm based on the limited information provided for this situation. There isn't enough information to make a *rational* decision. However, if one is forced to choose, it is important that he or she do so using some logic to support the position taken. For example, choosing Julie might be justified since interpersonal skills seem to be more important than is attention to detail when it comes to leading an organization. However, one could choose Rob based on his age, which has no doubt been a factor in their relationship.

2. The strengths would be that this arrangement would allow both siblings to contribute to the leadership and vision of the business and to foster an attitude of cooperation. The weaknesses would be that it is almost impossible to make such an arrangement work. The siblings would have to be exceptional human beings to work together in this way. Very few organizations have been able to succeed with such divided leadership.

3. It would be helpful to consult with someone with relevant experience or knowledge of the situation. Someone with experience in the industry or a business leader who is acquainted with the firm might be able to provide good advice (for example, a banker, attorney, or some other outsider who works with the business). The case presents a good argument for having an active board of directors. Ideally, the board should have the experience that would prepare them to provide some direction on this matter and to act in just such a situation as this.

REF: p. 114 OBJ: YMTC TYPE: C

9. **You Make the Call—Situation 4**

Bill and Simone Taylor have been married for almost thirty years. Their three grown children are independent and successful in their chosen careers. Three years ago, Bill had the opportunity to retire early from his job managing an automotive parts distribution warehouse. He used his retirement bonus to purchase his family's cabinet-making business. Simone was concerned that Bill, who had never worked in the family business, lacked the proper experience to manage the business and that he was making a mistake.

The Taylors mortgaged their home and signed a personal loan from Bill's parents to finance the purchase of the business from Bill's parents, both of whom died shortly thereafter. The personal loan is part of his parents' estate and is to be repaid to the heirs (Bill and his two siblings) within five years. The business began to lose money almost immediately after Bill took over from his father. Worst yet, the Taylors are having difficulty making their mortgage payments and have no present hope of repaying the note left in the estate.

As time has gone by, Bill has come to focus entirely on the business and largely ignores Simone's questions when she expresses her concerns about their increasingly dire financial condition. Bill feels that Simone should be second-guessing him about how to operate the business.

Question 1 What are the major causes of strain in the marriage?
Question 2 Is Simone entitled to a voice in decision making in the business? Explain.
Question 3 What steps would you recommend to improve the marriage and give the business a better chance to succeed?

ANS:

1. Bill and Simone appear to have different perceptions of seriousness of their financial condition and the prospects for future success of their business. Bill simply may not be qualified to manage such a business or Simone may be overly concerned about their present problems. Bill is likely embarrassed of the failure to repay the personal loan or feeling pressured by his siblings to do so. In any case, communication between Bill and Simone is not conducive to their marital relationship. Despite Simone's attempts to communicate, it seems that the couple has failed to express their differences in a mutually constructive manner.

2. It is important that Simone have the opportunity to ask questions and to offer input when business decisions are made. The couple needs to discuss business matters freely—after all, decisions and outcomes will affect them both. And it is insulting to Simone for Bill to ignore her attempts to communicate.

3. It would be good if Bill and Simone would communicate more with an aim toward developing mutual understanding and "getting everyone on the same team." Their expressed attitudes make this seem highly unlikely. A facilitator might be helpful in this case, but it is difficult to see how this could be arranged, given the limited information available in this situation. Nonetheless, it would be a good start if Bill could at least come to see the need for improving communications with Simone.

REF: p. 0 OBJ: YMTC TYPE: C

Correlation Table for Chapter 6—The Business Plan: Visualizing the Dream

	Learning Objectives	Question Type	**Definition** Define new term, recall facts	**Concept** Understand or relate concepts	**Application** Apply knowledge, analyze data
1	Explain what a business plan is, when it is needed, and what form it might take.	T/F	1,2,3,6	4,5,7	
		MC	2,9	1,3,4,5,6,7,8	
		ES		1	
2	Explain how to tell a new venture's story to outsiders, especially investors.	T/F	12	8,9,10,11,13,14, 15,16,17,18,19, 20,21,	22
		MC	15	10,11,12,13,14, 16,17,18,19,20, 21,23,24,25,26, 28,29	22
		ES		2,3	
3	List practical suggestions to follow in writing a business plan and outline the key sections of a business plan.	T/F	26,28,30,31	23,23,25,27,29	
		MC	33,43	27,30,31,32,34, 35,36,37,38,39, 40,41,42,44,45	
		ES		4,5	
4	Identify available sources of assistance in preparing a business plan.	T/F		32,33,34,35	
		MC		47,48,49	46
		ES			
5	Maintain the proper perspective when writing a business plan.	T/F			
		MC		50	
		ES			
	You Make the Call	ES		6,7,8,9	

Total Number of Test Questions: 94 (35 True/False; 50 Multiple-Choice; 9 Essay)

Chapter 6—The Business Plan: Visualizing the Dream

TRUE/FALSE

1. A business plan is a written document that sets out the basic idea underlying a business and its related startup considerations.

   ANS: T REF: p. 117 OBJ: 6-1 TYPE: D

2. As the game plan for a new venture, the business plan focuses on the entrepreneur's bank account and other cash sources.

   ANS: F
   The business plan crystallizes the hope and dreams that motivated the entrepreneur to propose the start of a new business.

   REF: p. 117 OBJ: 6-1 TYPE: D

3. A business plan should describe where you are, where you want to go, and how you plan to get there.

   ANS: T REF: p. 117 OBJ: 6-1 TYPE: D

4. A business plan helps the entrepreneur anticipate the different situations that may occur.

   ANS: T REF: p. 118 OBJ: 6-1 TYPE: C

5. Preparation of a business plan helps to refine a new-venture idea and to make it more practical.

   ANS: T REF: p. 119 OBJ: 6-1 TYPE: C

6. A business plan should project marketing, operational, and financial aspects of a business for the first five to seven years.

   ANS: F
   A business plan should project these aspects of a business for the first 3-7 years.

   REF: p. 124 OBJ: 6-1 TYPE: D

7. A business plan may be prepared for a major expansion of an existing business, as well as for a proposed new business.

   ANS: T REF: p. 119 OBJ: 6-1 TYPE: C

8. One of the primary functions of a business plan is to serve as a selling document-selling your ideas and even yourself to others.

   ANS: T REF: p. 118 OBJ: 6-2 TYPE: C

9. The sole purpose of a business plan is to persuade potential investors to supply funding for the business.

   ANS: F
   This is only one of the primary functions of the business plan. The other is to provide a clearly articulated statement of goals and strategies for internal use.

   REF: p. 117 OBJ: 6-2 TYPE: C

10. A business plan is prepared for external use only–for example, to interest potential investors.

    ANS: F
    A business plan has both internal and external uses.

    REF: p. 117 OBJ: 6-2 TYPE: C

11. One advantage of preparing a formal written plan for a business is the discipline provided for the prospective entrepreneur.

    ANS: T REF: p. 118 OBJ: 6-2 TYPE: C

12. A business plan is a legal document.

    ANS: F
    A business plan is not a legal document. For example, a business plan would not be sufficient to solicit investment, which would require a prospectus or offering memorandum.

    REF: p. 121 OBJ: 6-2 TYPE: D

13. Entrepreneurs typically focus on the positive potential of the startup—what will happen if everything goes right.

    ANS: T REF: p. 122 OBJ: 6-2 TYPE: C

14. The prospective investor usually plays the role of the encourager, often seeing market potential in a business plan that others overlook.

    ANS: F
    The prospective investor tends to play the role of the skeptic, thinking more about what could go wrong than about what could go right.

    REF: p. 122 OBJ: 6-2 TYPE: C

15. Because they have personal resources at risk, prospective investors tend to look carefully at the business plans they receive.

    ANS: F
    Because prospective investors receive so many business plans, they cannot take time to review each in any detailed fashion.

    REF: p. 123 OBJ: 6-2 TYPE: C

16. Investors prefer lengthy business plans because they need details before making an investment decision.

    ANS: F
    The business plan should seldom exceed 40 pages because prospective investors tend to avoid those that would take too long to review.

    REF: p. 123 OBJ: 6-2 TYPE: C

17. Business plans should be prepared so that they are attractive in appearance and well organized.

    ANS: T REF: p. 123 OBJ: 6-2 TYPE: C

18. Business plans should seldom exceed 40 pages in length.

    ANS: T REF: p. 123 OBJ: 6-2 TYPE: C

19. Investors are more product-oriented than market-oriented.

    ANS: F
    Venture capitalists are more *market-oriented* than product-oriented.

    REF: p. 123 OBJ: 6-2 TYPE: C

20. The level of complexity of a business affects how much planning is appropriate.

    ANS: T REF: p. 118 OBJ: 6-2 TYPE: C

21. Time and money are factors that affect the extent of business plan preparation.

    ANS: T REF: p. 118 OBJ: 6-2 TYPE: C

22. When prospective entrepreneurs prepare to write a business plan, they should first consider the amount of time and money they have to spend.

    ANS: T REF: p. 121 OBJ: 6-2 TYPE: A

23. Clear writing gives credibility to the ideas presented in the business plan.

    ANS: T REF: p. 124 OBJ: 6-3 TYPE: C

24. A good business concept may be destroyed by writing that fails to communicate.

    ANS: T REF: p. 124 OBJ: 6-3 TYPE: C

25. Even if the business plan reveals sensitive information (e.g., details of an advanced technology or the specifics of a marketing plan), prospective investors can be trusted with that knowledge.

    ANS: F
    Highly sensitive information should not be included in the business plan; the entrepreneur should submit only a summary of the plan to avoid exposing important details.

REF: p. 124-125 OBJ: 6-3 TYPE: C

26. The executive summary of a business plan presents a firm's history and its form of organization.

ANS: F
It is the *company overview* (not the executive summary) that contains this information.

REF: p. 128 OBJ: 6-3 TYPE: D

27. The business plan should never include photographs because these tend to make the plan look unprofessional.

ANS: F
If a new or unique physical product is to be offered and a working prototype is available, a photograph of it should be included in the *Product and/or Services Plan* section of the business plan.

REF: p. 130 OBJ: 6-3 TYPE: C

28. The marketing plan should identify user benefits and show evidence of consumer interest.

ANS: T REF: p. 130 OBJ: 6-3 TYPE: D

29. Though all financial statements are important, the cash flow statement deserves special attention.

ANS: T REF: p. 131 OBJ: 6-3 TYPE: C

30. Pro forma financial statements reflect the past financial performance of a firm.

ANS: F
Pro forma financial statements are projections of a firm's *future* financial situation.

REF: p. 130 OBJ: 6-3 TYPE: D

31. The *Financial Plan* section of a business plan should include balance sheets and income statements on an annual basis and cash flow statements on a monthly basis, all projected out 2-3 years.

ANS: F
The *Financial Plan* section should include balance sheets, income statements, and cash flow statements on an annual basis for five years, as well as cash budgets on a monthly basis for the first year and on a quarterly basis for the second and third years.

REF: p. 130 OBJ: 6-3 TYPE: D

32. A computer may properly be used in a new business operation but not in preparation of the business plan.

ANS: F
Computers can facilitate the preparation of a business plan.

REF: p. 132 OBJ: 6-4 TYPE: C

33. With the right assistance from professional sources (e.g., attorneys, accounting firms, incubator services), the entrepreneur can avoid direct involvement in developing the business plan.

ANS: F
The entrepreneur must be the primary planner because his or her ideas are essential to producing a business plan that is realistic and believable.

REF: p. 132 OBJ: 6-4 TYPE: C

34. Incubator organizations can provide advice on structuring a new business.

ANS: T REF: p. 132 OBJ: 6-4 TYPE: C

35. Most major accounting firms can guide the development of the written business plan.

ANS: T REF: p. 132 OBJ: 6-4 TYPE: C

MULTIPLE CHOICE

1. Which of the following is *not* one of the basic objectives of the business plan?
   a. It identifies the nature and context of the business opportunity.
   b. It outlines the approaches other entrepreneurs have taken in the same industry.
   c. It serves as a tool for raising financial capital.
   d. It highlights factors that will determine whether the venture will be successful.

   ANS: B REF: p. 117 OBJ: 6-1 TYPE: C

2. A business plan is best described as a
   a. crystal ball picture.
   b. money plan.
   c. contingency plan.
   d. game plan.

   ANS: D REF: p. 117 OBJ: 6-1 TYPE: D

3. A business plan should generally project financial and operational aspects of the proposed business for the first
   a. six months.
   b. one year.
   c. three to five years.
   d. seven years.

   ANS: C REF: p. 124 OBJ: 6-1 TYPE: C

4. Writing a business plan should be thought of as
   a. the means to an end product.
   b. an ongoing process.
   c. an absolute essential to the startup of businesses.
   d. a mental exercise.

   ANS: B REF: p. 133 OBJ: 6-1 TYPE: C

5. One aid to assure the understanding of a new business opportunity is a
   a. charter.
   b. written business plan.
   c. computer.
   d. partner.

   ANS: B REF: p. 119 OBJ: 6-1 TYPE: C

6. When an entrepreneur establishes a blueprint for creating a new venture, he or she prepares
   a. an organization chart.
   b. a budget.
   c. a sales analysis.
   d. a business plan.

   ANS: D REF: p. 117 OBJ: 6-1 TYPE: C

7. The answer to the question of whether you need a business plan is
   a. "It just depends."
   b. "It's imperative."
   c. "It's requisite for success."
   d. "It's a no-brainer."

   ANS: A REF: p.118 OBJ: 6-1 TYPE: C

8. Capital-constrained entrepreneurs cannot afford to do much prior analysis and research because
   a. the affordability of properly conducted research is beyond the means at their disposal.
   b. the costs of any mistakes are lower than the risks of missing out on opportunistic actions.
   c. the limited profit potential and high uncertainty of the opportunity they pursue also make the benefits low compared to the costs.
   d. potential competitors could quickly discern the entrepreneurs' intentions and motives from their research.

   ANS: C REF: p. 118 OBJ: 6-1 TYPE: C

9. When Dan Feshbach went looking for equity capital for his company (Mortgage Information Corporation) he usually
   a. made the case for customer revenue.
   b. undersold what he thought the company could do.
   c. avoided talking about his competitors.
   d. emphasized how short product cycles benefited his company.

   ANS: B REF: p. 119 OBJ: 6-1 TYPE: D

10. In the context of business planning, a *prospectus* is viewed as a
    a. financial system.
    b. way to guarantee that every employee in the startup knows his or her role in the company.
    c. marketing document used to solicit investors' monies.
    d. methodology that defines the way every aspect of the business is to be run.

    ANS: C REF: p. 121 OBJ: 6-2 TYPE: C

11. Which of the following in *not* one of the benefits of developing a business plan?
    a. This forces the entrepreneur to consider systematically all of the factors in starting a business.
    b. It ensures that the startup's cash flows are manageable, especially in the first 5-7 years.

c. This imposes needed discipline on the entrepreneur and the management team.
d. This can be helpful in selling the new venture to those within the company.

ANS: B REF: p. 124 OBJ: 6-2 TYPE: C

12. The primary outside users of business plans are
a. suppliers.
b. investors and lenders.
c. customers.
d. government agencies.

ANS: B REF: p. 118 OBJ: 6-2 TYPE: C

13. Which of the following groups would be most interested in a business plan for a new venture?
a. Customers
b. Bankers
c. Supervisors
d. The Internal Revenue Service.

ANS: B REF: p. 120 OBJ: 6-2 TYPE: C

14. Both investors and lenders use the business plan to better understand the
a. type of product or service offered by the new venture.
b. probability that interest rates will rise or fall in the future.
c. potential of other competitors in the same line of business.
d. range of business opportunities available at a given point in time.

ANS: A REF: p. 118 OBJ: 6-2 TYPE: C

15. A business plan is
a. a legal document for raising capital.
b. a prospectus.
c. a selling document.
d. an offering memorandum.

ANS: C REF: p. 118 OBJ: 6-2 TYPE: D

16. A potential investor's single goal is to
a. make as much money as possible.
b. minimize taxes.
c. avoid risk.
d. maximize potential return on investment through cash flows received while minimizing personal risk exposure.

ANS: D REF: p. 122 OBJ: 6-2 TYPE: C

17. In writing the business plan, an entrepreneur should remember that
a. interested investors will commit the time necessary to fully understand the proposed venture.
b. certain features will be appealing to investors, while others are distinctly unappealing.
c. investors are too busy to read through the business plans that come across their desk.
d. the quality of this plan has little bearing on the potential for success in the startup.

ANS: B REF: p. 123 OBJ: 6-2 TYPE: C

18. Investors who read business plans can be described as
    a. one-minute investors.
    b. two-hour investors.
    c. half-day investors.
    d. weekend investors.

    ANS: A REF: p. 123 OBJ: 6-2 TYPE: C

19. An effective business plan should seldom exceed _____ pages in length.
    a. 10
    b. 25
    c. 40
    d. 75

    ANS: C REF: p. 123 OBJ: 6-2 TYPE: C

20. Investors who review business plans typically
    a. look only at brief reports.
    b. read about one-half of a plan.
    c. read plans thoroughly.
    d. read only the marketing and finance sections.

    ANS: A REF: p. 123 OBJ: 6-2 TYPE: C

21. Plans that appeal effectively to investors are
    a. long and thorough.
    b. market-oriented.
    c. product-oriented.
    d. ten or fewer pages.

    ANS: B REF: p. 123 OBJ: 6-2 TYPE: C

22. John Keeler is a prospective entrepreneur who has just presented his business plan to a venture capitalist, enthusiastically pointing out the unique features of a new invention he is promoting. The most likely question in the venture capitalist's mind is:
    a. How strong is the patent protection?
    b. How costly will it be to produce the product?
    c. What is the demand for the product?
    d. What management skills does this venture have?

    ANS: C REF: p. 123 OBJ: 6-2 TYPE: A

23. Prospective investors are most attracted by business plans showing
    a. evidence of customer acceptance of the venture's product or service.
    b. expense projections that are far lower than normal industry ranges.
    c. growth projections that are unbelievably strong.
    d. detailed drawings and engineering details of the proposed product.

    ANS: A REF: p. 123 OBJ: 6-2 TYPE: C

24. Experience has shown that an effective plan should
    a. be very long.

b. be encyclopedic in detail.
c. be brief.
d. emphasize budgets above all else.

ANS: C REF: p. 123 OBJ: 6-2 TYPE: C

25. Prospective investors are likely to consider a new business proposal to be *un*favorable if it
a. focuses on the product or service and provides minimal analysis of marketplace needs.
b. is brief, even if it touches on all of the critical details of the startup.
c. presents financial projections that show the startup will not exceed industry norms.
d. fails to call for custom or applications engineering.

ANS: A REF: p. 123 OBJ: 6-2 TYPE: C

26. When making a decision regarding the extent of planning, an entrepreneur should consider the
a. preferences of employees.
b. complexity of the environment.
c. level of uncertainty of the venture.
d. competitiveness of the product.

ANS: C REF: p. 120 OBJ: 6-2 TYPE: C

27. A poorly conceived business concept
a. is likely to be accepted if the business plan is well written.
b. will not be recognized if the business plan is well written.
c. cannot be rescued by a well written business plan.
d. can still be justified, as long as the entrepreneur can prove that strong market demand exists.

ANS: C REF: p. 124 OBJ: 6-3 TYPE: C

28. A prospectus is
a. a legal document for soliciting investment.
b. the legal document that replaces a draft business plan.
c. a marketing document intended to sell a concept.
d. a document containing confidential business information.

ANS: A REF: p. 121 OBJ: 6-2 TYPE: C

29. The basis of the perceptions of entrepreneurs and investors about a new venture
a. are very different.
b. are somewhat different.
c. are somewhat the same.
d. are identical.

ANS: A REF: p. 122 OBJ: 6-2 TYPE: C

30. ____________ is a section of the business plan that describes the user benefits of the product or service and the type of market that exists.
a. Product and/or services plan
b. Marketing plan
c. Management plan
d. Operating plan

ANS: B REF: p. 130 OBJ: 6-3 TYPE: C

31. The executive summary in a business plan should come
    a. at the beginning.
    b. at the end.
    c. following the finance section.
    d. following the marketing section.

ANS: A REF: p. 128 OBJ: 6-3 TYPE: C

32. Highlights from various sections of a business plan appear in the
    a. financial plan.
    b. general company description.
    c. executive summary.
    d. operating plan.

ANS: C REF: p. 127 OBJ: 6-3 TYPE: C

33. The mission statement is best described as the
    a. path that will lead to successful initiation of a startup.
    b. potential of the business, as conceived.
    c. entrepreneur's personal hopes for the future.
    d. intended strategy and business philosophy for making the entrepreneur's vision a reality.

ANS: D REF: p. 128 OBJ: 6-3 TYPE: D

34. The executive summary part of a business plan should be written
    a. first.
    b. last.
    c. before the finance plan.
    d. before the legal plan.

ANS: B REF: p. 128 OBJ: 6-3 TYPE: C

35. It is most important that the marketing plan
    a. identify user benefits.
    b. show the degree of patent or copyright protection.
    c. summarize the location of potential customers.
    d. identify distribution channels.

ANS: A REF: p. 130 OBJ: 6-3 TYPE: C

36. The marketing plan should follow the establishment of user benefits and document the existence of
    a. sources of financing.
    b. managerial experience.
    c. customer interest.
    d. patent protection.

ANS: C REF: p. 130 OBJ: 6-3 TYPE: C

37. In a business plan, the competition would be discussed in the
    a. financial plan.
    b. general company description.
    c. executive summary.
    d. marketing plan.

ANS: D REF: p. 130 OBJ: 6-3 TYPE: C

38. Ideally, investors like a business plan that shows evidence of
   a. a management staff that will minimize overhead.
   b. a well-balanced managerial team.
   c. an entrepreneur who has studied management.
   d. an entrepreneur who will spend more time managing than selling.

ANS: B REF: p. 130 OBJ: 6-3 TYPE: C

39. In a business plan, discussion of the management plan should detail
   a. the proposed venture's organizational structure.
   b. profiles of employee needs during the first three years of operation.
   c. the projected growth of the proposed venture.
   d. the intended distribution of ownership in the firm.

ANS: A REF: p. 130 OBJ: 6-3 TYPE: C

40. In a business plan, the facilities and location of the proposed venture are described in the
   a. executive summary.
   b. management plan.
   c. operating plan.
   d. product and service plan.

ANS: C REF: p. 130 OBJ: 6-3 TYPE: C

41. In a business plan, the key statement in the financial plan is the
   a. break-even analysis.
   b. estimate of returns and allowances.
   c. salary expense statement.
   d. cash flow statement.

ANS: D REF: p. 131 OBJ: 6-3 TYPE: C

42. In considering the content of a business plan, an entrepreneur should think first and foremost about
   a. how to present factors related to the opportunity.
   b. formulating effective strategies and financial projections.
   c. who will be reviewing the plan.
   d. how to protect the confidentially of the plan.

ANS: A REF: p. 125 OBJ: 6-3 TYPE: C

43. *The big picture* includes all of the following EXCEPT:
   a. the management team.
   b. the regulatory environment.
   c. interest rates.
   d. inflation.

ANS: A REF: p. 126 OBJ: 6-3 TYPE: D

44. The narrative form of an executive summary
   a. is more straightforward than the synopsis form.
   b. allows the author to include hyperbole that builds enthusiasm.
   c. is a better format for ventures that have one dominant advantage.
   d. gives each topic relatively equal treatment.

ANS: C REF: p. 128 OBJ: 6-3 TYPE: C

45. Sources of cash identified by a statement of cash flows include
    a. cash generated from operations.
    b. cash raised from investors.
    c. cash devoted to investments.
    d. all of these.

ANS: D REF: p. 131 OBJ: 6-3 TYPE: C

46. The owner of Alison Sportswear, a small manufacturer of women's tennis apparel, uses a computer in preparing a business plan. She finds that a major advantage of using a computer is that
    a. the planner can easily generate reams of material.
    b. spreadsheets enable the planner to prepare and make changes to the financial reports.
    c. the programs are easy to load and use.
    d. it eliminates the need for proofreading the final product.

ANS: B REF: p. 132 OBJ: 6-4 TYPE: A

47. To facilitate preparation of the financial portion of a business plan and the making of changes in the plan, the writer should use
    a. a sample plan.
    b. a plan preparation manual.
    c. an annuity table.
    d. a computer.

ANS: D REF: p. 132 OBJ: 6-4 TYPE: C

48. Business plan software packages
    a. focus mostly on preparing slides to present the business concept to prospective investors.
    b. spawn creativity and flexibility on the part of the entrepreneur.
    c. help an entrepreneur think through the important issues in starting a new company.
    d. offer a simple formula that leads startups to success.

ANS: C REF: p. 132 OBJ: 6-4 TYPE: C

49. Which of the following is *least* likely to provide assistance in preparing a business plan?
    a. An accounting firm
    b. An incubator organization
    c. An industrial park
    d. A marketing specialist

ANS: C REF: p. 132 OBJ: 6-4 TYPE: C

50. Business planning
    a. is an ongoing process.
    b. is an exacting science.
    c. equals business success.
    d. is none of these.

ANS: A REF: p. 133 OBJ: 6-5 TYPE: C

ESSAY

1. Identify the four basic objectives of preparing a written plan prior to starting a new venture.

ANS:

The four basic objectives are the following:

- It identifies the nature and context of the business opportunity—why does such an opportunity exist?.
- It presents the approach the entrepreneur plans to take to exploit the opportunity.
- It identifies the factors that will most likely determine whether the venture will be successful.
- It serves as a tool for raising financial capital.

REF: p. 117 OBJ: 6-1 TYPE: C

2. Identify the various users of business plans and show how a plan is useful to each.

ANS:
The answer should distinguish between inside and outside users. First, there should be clear recognition that a properly drafted plan can serve as a basis for operation and be used by the firm's management staff. Initial goals, for example, are presented in the plan. Various outside groups are also potential users. Among these are the following:

- Investors and bankers. These are typically the major outside users of a business plan. They use it to determine creditworthiness or investment prospects.
- Suppliers. Suppliers can use the business plan to determine the potential value of a new firm as a customer and the wisdom of extending credit.
- Customers. Occasionally, a business plan is useful in persuading a prospective customer that the business is more than a fly-by-night venture that will disappear quickly.

REF: p. 117 OBJ: 6-2 TYPE: C

3. Discuss the features of business plans that make them attractive or unattractive to prospective investors.

ANS:
Many possibilities could be mentioned. The following are some of the key points cited by Rich and Gumpert as making plans attractive:

- Evidence of marketability of the products or services
- Appreciation of investors' needs
- Explanation of user benefits
- Evidence of an experienced managerial team

Some features that turn off investors are the following:

- Infatuation with the product or service
- Financial projections at odds with industry norms
- Unrealistic growth projections
- Need for custom or applications engineering

REF: p. 123 OBJ: 6-2 TYPE: C

4. Explain the nature and purpose of the executive summary part of a business plan.

ANS:

It is important to emphasize the short amount of attention given to any business plan by a prospective investor. When a plan is being submitted to such sources, therefore, it should show the nature of the venture in a succinct manner. Thus, the executive summary should come at the beginning of the overall plan. It should highlight the significant points from other sections. Ideally, it should also create enough excitement to motivate the reader to read on. It needs to be written very carefully in view of the fact it is the one point of contact with most readers.

REF: p. 127-128 OBJ: 6-3 TYPE: C

5. List the key elements that make up the financial plan component of the business plan and identify important considerations in the construction of the financial plan.

ANS:
The key elements are pro forma statements (projected out five years, or longer), which include

- Financial statements
- Balance sheets
- Income statements
- Statements of cash flows
- Cash budgets (on a monthly basis for the first year and on a quarterly basis for years two and three)

Important considerations include

- Supporting financial projections should be backed up with well-substantiated assumptions and an explanation of computations.
- Statements of cash flows are especially important because a business can be profitable while failing to produce positive cash flows.
- Cash flow statements should identify sources of cash, intended investments, and the purpose of investments.
- Investors will want to know when they can expect to cash out of the investment, so the financial plan should outline mechanisms for exit.

REF: p. 130-131 OBJ: 6-3 TYPE: C

6. **You Make the Call—Situation 1**
When they created Round Table Group (RTG) Inc., Russ Rosenstein and Robert Hull envisioned a company offering one-stop shopping for intellectual expertise. They wanted to help businesspeople, management consultants, and litigation attorneys get answers to important questions from topnotch thinkers anywhere in the world through the Internet.

RTG's plan was to have a kind of SWAT team of professors who would answer questions based on their expertise. A team might consist of one or two professors, who would communicate with the client via e-mail, phone, or videoconferencing on projects that might involve a few hours or a few weeks of input. In the traditional management-consulting model, work on a project often lasts as long as a couple of years, and the team consists of a group of junior analysts, managers, and partners.

RTG assembled a database made up mainly of 3,000 university professors available to consult on an as-needed basis. The firm's fixed costs would be low because the professors would be paid only when they did billable work. But an unexpected wrinkle soon emerged. RTG's customers wanted RTG to start acting more like a traditional consulting firm. Business executives wanted face-to-face contact with the professors giving the information. They also wanted number crunching and follow-up analysis. And they wanted current, customized research.

That has left RTG at a crossroads. Should it try to become a more traditional management-consulting firm or continue to pursue its original mission of providing advice through Internet content and virtual links?

Taking the first path would mean providing support to clients, adding infrastructure and formalizing its operation by dividing it into distinct specialties. That would have the downside of making RTG's competitive point of differentiation murky. But the second path would risk putting off clients who say they want more.
Source: Elena De Lisser, "A Plan May Look Good, but Watch Out for the Real World," Startup Journal, *The Wall Street Journal Online,* http://www.startupjournal.com/howto/management/199908240948-lisser.html, January 15, 2004.

Question 1 What is the basic problem that Rosenstein and Hull need to resolve?
Question 2 What are the advantages and disadvantages of the proposed online consulting and the traditional approach to consulting?
Question 3 What do you think Rosenstein and Hull should do?

ANS:
In this "you make the call," we provide the following comments of three advisors who responded to RTG's dilemma, followed by Rosenzweig's response.

Evan I. Schwartz, author of two books about electronic commerce: "Digital Darwinism" and "Webonomics"

"The concept is a good idea but the original business model was fundamentally flawed, partly because of the way the Internet works and partly because of the way consulting works.

"Working by e-mail, it's difficult to have a good back and forth. With e-mail you talk at each other instead of to each other.

"And you know the way professors are. These guys are juggling so many things, they're doing research, they may have a consulting business on the side, all the political stuff that happens at a university -- and they have students.

"To really put their creative energy into it is a really tough thing to do when they don't have their ego tied into it.

"If you're doing a face-to-face with the professor and he's enhancing his own consulting business, he is going to give it his all. If it's just e-mail, I can't see him giving it top priority.

"The Web has existed in this parallel universe for the past few years, and what companies really need to do is create a hybrid of what traditional business does best and what the Web does best. I think this company at the crossroads should also develop a hybrid biz model. Do traditional consulting tied in with this 'just in time' advice through the Internet.

"RTG could have a staff of face-to-face [full-time] consultants and also have a Web site where you could ask a natural-language query and they send the questions out to the database of professors. Part of this service would be a follow-up service for 90 days.

"But if you want to be a middle-man, you've got to add value to the customer experience and to the professor experience. Maybe you tell the professors that if you work on this client for a certain amount of time, afterward you can be free to pursue the client on your own. Maybe that could be part of their matchmaking. All the great middlemen on the Web are adding value to both the buyer and seller experience.

"The Web is not good for people who putter along. It's probably good [for RTG] to get on to whatever is next as quickly as possible."

Mike Santer of Platinum Venture Partners, a Redwood City, Calif., venture-capital firm that focuses on financing Internet and information-technology companies

"I think there's very limited viability to RTG as it is currently built. It doesn't offer what people need, and before they can be credible to offer what people need, they're going to need to have some kind of aura around the company to make people believe this is a 'go to' source.

"Advice from experts is just one quarter of the whole equation when businesses need help. A business looking for help wants somebody to assess where they are, advise them on how they're doing and where they might go, and help them select a new plan or new products that will help them get to where they want to go. They also want somebody to help them implement those things.

"Maybe Round Table Group doesn't have to be a full-fledged consulting company, but it has to offer components of those four things or links to the ones that it doesn't offer. The Internet is a terrific way to provide those links.

"If it's not going to add bodies to come out and do the actual work, it could have links to people who are local or industry appropriate to the company. If RTG wants to make money, it strikes some kind of arrangement for any referrals.

"Also, college professors are way down on the list of advisers for most businesspeople. The truth is, in the business community, business experience is much more valuable than theoretical kind of stuff.

"Create a star-quality team where you can then build a brand around those people. I would do a dream team of professors but not have 3,000 of them. Then I would have a dream team of business-consulting and business-research firms. Then you'd have a real think tank. That's the kind of excitement the firm should create around its service, because otherwise, who cares?"

Wendy Handler, an entrepreneurship professor at Babson College in Babson Park, Mass.

"There are so many great ideas on the Internet right now. People call into radio talk shows for advice. Why not the Internet? But there's a downside to only consulting through the Internet. Clients need more and want more often. A quick fix isn't always enough even when you have the leading experts in the world. If you're a consultant and you're providing ideas that result in major change, it's very, very important to know those people and have a sense of those people and not just be corresponding via a machine. Meaningful change usually involves more than just an information dump.

"In theory [RTG] is a great idea, but in practice it needs to offer two levels of service: Offer a higher level of service face-to-face if the situation warrants it and if the client and the professor are going to be a good fit. If the client wants more, the professor will enter into a contract to do some more traditional consulting. In moving to this more traditional approach, it doesn't mean that you have to take every client. Some of the professors may only want to be part of the Internet part of the service.

"When clients are asking for something, you should listen. If you listen, you're following a marketing orientation and not just providing a product."

Mr. Rosenzweig's Response

Mr. Rosenzweig bridles at Mr. Santer's suggestion that RTG needs to be more credible and that professors are "way down on the list" of desirable experts for business executives. "Renowned business-school professors actually have lots of real-world business experience.... Many of RTG's consulting professors serve as directors on boards of Fortune 500 companies and have enjoyed stellar former careers in business. [They are] particularly appealing and insightful to clients."

In response to Mr. Schwartz's comment that RTG needs to provide value to both the buying and selling experience, Mr. Rosenzweig says that "for the faculty, RTG provides marketing, administrative services [invoicing, for example] and access to our staff of research analysts [including Ph.D. candidates and M.B.A.s]. For our clients, RTG creates nothing but world-class work products."

Still, there are big changes in the works at RTG. The company needs to move quickly, Mr. Rosenzweig acknowledges, if it hopes to be viable. So it will move away from primarily providing professor referrals.

Mr. Rosenzweig says he is abandoning the "ask questions, we'll get you answers" model he and his partner initially had in mind. He agrees with Prof. Handler that companies must listen to what their customers are saying, and notes that he is already responding.

RTG, which is based in Chicago, is changing gears through a two-pronged approach. It is now offering corporate learning programs, where professors develop customized executive education programs for companies. "Our corporate clients were in need of something that traditional executive programs were not providing: namely, highly customized learning experiences, using the most qualified teachers in the country."

RTG is also emphasizing litigation consulting work, using professors as expert witnesses. Included in that: a video library of 10-minute minilectures from the professors, letting lawyers assess the personalities and presentation skills of prospective testifying experts without traveling, Mr. Rosenzweig says.

Interestingly, in 2004, RTG was on the list of Inc. 5oo companies. Adapting the firm's strategy to customer demands has clearly paid off.

REF: p. 135 OBJ: YMTC TYPE: C

7. **You Make the Call—Situation 2**
A young journalist is contemplating launching a new magazine that will feature wildlife, plant life, and nature around the world. The prospective entrepreneur intends for each issue to contain several feature articles—about the dangers and benefits of forest fires, the features of Rocky Mountain National Park, wildflowers found at high altitudes, and the danger of acid rain, for example. The magazine will make extensive use of color photographs, and its articles will be technically accurate and interestingly written. Unlike *National Geographic,* the proposed publication will avoid articles dealing with the general culture and confine itself to topics closely related to the natural world. Suppose you are a prospective investor examining a business plan prepared by this journalist.

Question 1 What are the most urgent questions you would want the marketing plan to answer?
Question 2 What details would you look for in the management plan?
Question 3 Do you think this entrepreneur would need to raise closer to $1 million or $10 million in startup capital? Why?
Question 4 At first glance, would you consider the opportunity potentially attractive? Why or why not?

ANS:
1. The primary question is whether there are enough potential subscribers to make this a viable venture. The market analysis would be extremely important. Also, the plan for selling the magazine—for attracting subscribers—would be of major interest.
2. The qualifications of the journalist, including both education and experience, would be of crucial importance. Also, this venture would call for more than a "one-man band." What type of management team and what type of technical expertise have been assembled? Organizational arrangements would also be of interest.
3. This publication would need lots of money. If it were to be even remotely like *National Geographic*, financial requirements would be immense. The $10 million estimate is closer to the need.
4. The question asks for an opinion. No doubt most will be inclined to reject the plan unless it presents an extremely impressive case, including a penetrating market analysis.

REF: p. 135 OBJ: YMTC TYPE: C

8. **You Make the Call—Situation 3**
John Martin and John Rose decided to start a new business to manufacture noncarbonated soft drinks. They believed that their location in East Texas, close to high quality water, would give them a competitive edge. Although Martin and Rose had never worked together, Martin had 17 years of experience in the soft drink industry. Rose had recently sold his firm and had funds to help finance the venture; however, the partners needed to raise additional money from outside investors. Both men were excited about the opportunity and spent almost 18 months developing their business plan. The first paragraph of their executive summary reflected their excitement:

The "New Age" beverage market is the result of a spectacular boom in demand for drinks with nutritional value from environmentally safe ingredients and waters that come from deep, clear springs free of chemicals and pollutants. Argon Beverage Corporation will produce and market a full line of sparkling fruit drinks, flavored waters, and sports drinks that are of the highest quality and purity. These drinks have the same delicious taste appeal as soft drinks while using the most healthful fruit juices, natural sugars, and the purest spring water, the hallmark of the "New Age" drink market.

With the help of a well-developed plan, the two men were successful in raising the necessary capital to begin their business. They leased facilities and started production. However, after almost two years, the plan's goals were not being met. There were cost overruns, and profits were not nearly up to expectations.

Question 1 What problems might have contributed to the firm's poor performance?
Question 2 Although several problems were encountered in implementing the business plan, the primary reason for the low profits turned out to be embezzlement. Martin was diverting company resources for personal use, even using some of the construction materials purchased by the company to build his own house. What could Rose have done to avoid this situation? What are his options after the fact?

ANS:
1. The company failed to use the business plan to manage the business. A business plan is more than a device for raising funds—it is the basis for operating a business. If they do not follow their own business plan, entrepreneurs cannot uncover weaknesses or be alerted to sources of danger before crises arise.
2. He could have improved the systems for control of the company's resources. He could also have established segregation of duties and authorization, which would have increased the accountability of each employee. The damage or loss of an asset could have been charged to the employee who had responsibility for that asset.

   One option would be for Jones to pay for the business resources that he used for personal purposes or return them to the company. Firing him from the company will affect the company because Jones is experienced in this business; the current company situation requires a good management team to manage the business.

REF: p. 135-136 OBJ: YMTC TYPE: C

9. **You Make the Call—Situation 4**

Michael Richcreek is the owner of Rolling Wheels Mobile Home Repair, in Swayzee, Indiana, a mobile-home maintenance and repair business he operates on a part-time basis. Richcreek is now trying to acquire financing to buy a mobile-home park with an asking price of $1.2 million; he has approximately $40,000 in cash to invest. He realizes that he would need to prepare a business plan to sell the concept to a prospective investor. But he also recognizes that he does not have the knowledge or expertise to write a business plan, financial plan, or any of the other plans required to secure the funds needed for this venture.

Source: Adapted from Jill Andresky Fraser, "Who Can Help Out with a Business Plan", *Inc.*, Vol. 21, No. 8 (June 1999), pp. 115-117.

Question 1 Given Richcreek's seeming inability to write a business plan, do you think that a computer software package could help him? Why or why not?

Question 2 What are some questions that Richcreek should try to answer before writing a business plan?

Question 3 Given the situation, where should Richcreek go to get help in preparing a business plan? Where should he *not* go for assistance?

ANS:

1. Computer software can be very helpful in preparing a business plan, as long as an entrepreneur does not rely on a one-size-fits-all approach. The software can provide a framework, but the plan must be comprehensive, well researched, and, above all, credible. This can only happen when the entrepreneur gives his/her best thought to the business and its future. The software, if used appropriately, can help the entrepreneur ask the right questions, but it is up to the entrepreneur to make an effective presentation—both in content and format. The software is only a tool in this endeavor.

   Before beginning, you must decide what you want--and need--to get out of a business plan. For Richcreek, the goal is to raise funds. But given his lack of familiarity with the business-planning process, he could benefit in other ways as well by actively involving himself in a rigorous examination of his proposed business venture.

2. To be effective in writing a business plan, you need to be able to answer a lot of difficult questions that relate to the opportunity, the management, the marketing plan, the management team, and the financial plan. Many of these questions are provided in this chapter and ones that follow. But some examples of questions that Richcreek must answer include:

   How does he know that the mobile-home park is worth its asking price of approximately $1.2 million?

   How can he show that the new venture will be a sound and profitable business?

   What does the buyer plan to do to either extend the park's existing record of success or turn it around into a successful venture?

   How will the owner create profits for himself/herself and the investors?

   What is the strategy for paying off any debt that is incurred?

3. If Richcreek is unable to answer such questions, he should seek advice from someone accustomed to working with small companies, start-ups, and owners who lack financial-management expertise. Given his lack of experience, Richcreek might consider seeking advice from the Small Business Administration or the Service Corps of Retired Executives, or SCORE, which introduces business owners to volunteer experts who will advise them on matters such as financial planning. Of course, Richcreek could also go to an investment banker or financial intermediary for more sophisticated advice, but he would need to determine that the higher costs of these groups justify what they can do for him.

REF: p. 0 OBJ: YMTC TYPE: C

Correlation Table for Chapter 7—The Marketing Plan

	Learning Objectives	Question Type	Definition Define new term, recall facts	Concept Understand or relate concepts	Application Apply knowledge, analyze data
1	Describe small business marketing.	T/F	1,4,5	2,3,6,7,8	
		MC	2	1,3,4,5,6,7,10	7,9,11,12,13
		ES		1	
2	Identify the components of a formal marketing plan.	T/F	13	9,10,11,12,14, 15	
		MC	17,18,25	14,16,19,20,21	22,23,24
		ES			
3	Discuss the nature of the marketing research process.	T/F	18	16,17,19,20,21, 22,23,24,25	
		MC		26,28,29,30,31, 32,34,35,36,37	27,33
		ES		2,3	
4	Define market segmentation and its related strategies.	T/F	26,27,28		
		MC	38,39	40	
		ES	4		
5	Explain the different methods of fore-casting sales.	T/F		30,31,32,33,34, 35	
		MC	41,46,47	42,43,44,45,49, 50	48
		ES		5	
	You Make the Call	ES		6,7,8,9	

Total Number of Test Questions: 00 (35 True/False; 50 Multiple-Choice; 9 Essay)

Chapter 7—The Marketing Plan

TRUE/FALSE

1. Small business marketing is best defined as the performance of distribution activities that affect the flow of goods and services from producer to consumer or user.

   ANS: F
   Small business marketing involves numerous activities, many of which occur even before a product is created or made ready for distribution or sale.

   REF: p. 141 OBJ: 7-1 TYPE: D

2. In order to achieve market success, a firm merely needs to concentrate on either providing an excellent product/service or devising an insightful marketing strategy.

   ANS: F
   As suggested by the consumer-oriented philosophy, a firm must also pursue customer satisfaction if it is to be successful.

   REF: p. 142 OBJ: 7-1 TYPE: C

3. Regardless of the type of business, the consumer-oriented marketing philosophy is the best choice among the competing alternatives.

   ANS: T REF: p. 142 OBJ: 7-1 TYPE: C

4. A marketing philosophy that says everything originating with consumer needs is *market-oriented.*

   ANS: F
   It is a *consumer-oriented* marketing philosophy that begins with customer needs.

   REF: p. 142 OBJ: 7-1 TYPE: D

5. Distribution and selling are the essence of marketing.

   ANS: F
   Marketing is far more than just selling, since it involves numerous activities such as identifying the market, assessing the market's potential, and distributing the product or service.

   REF: p. 142 OBJ: 7-1 TYPE: D

6. In a small business, the entrepreneur's marketing philosophy typically shapes the firm's marketing activities.

   ANS: T REF: p. 142 OBJ: 7-1 TYPE: C

7. Customer satisfaction is not the means to achieving a certain goal—it *is* the goal.

ANS: T REF: p. 142 OBJ: 7-1 TYPE: C

8. Because many small business owners have strong production skills, they often attend mostly to the marketing side of the business to compensate.

ANS: F
Many small business owners have strong production skills and are weak in marketing ability, and therefore they attend primarily to production considerations.

REF: p. 142 OBJ: 7-1 TYPE: C

9. A detailed analysis of competitors is an important part of a firm's formal marketing plan.

ANS: T REF: p. 144 OBJ: 7-2 TYPE: C

10. Because of the costs involved, it is typical for a business to formulate only a single sales forecast.

ANS: F
Typically, the sales forecast is a composite of several sales forecasts that are merged together.

REF: p. 144 OBJ: 7-2 TYPE: C

11. Following the completion of the market and competitor analysis, the entrepreneur is ready to write the formal marketing plan.

ANS: T REF: p. 144 OBJ: 7-2 TYPE: C

12. If an entrepreneur anticipates several target markets, each individual segment must have its own corresponding customer profile.

ANS: T REF: p. 144 OBJ: 7-2 TYPE: C

13. Target market analysis refers to identifying and describing the types of customers to whom you will sell, and this is an important part of a new venture marketing plan.

ANS: T REF: p. 144 OBJ: 7-2 TYPE: D

14. Most entrepreneurs have an excellent understanding of the field of rivals against which their new venture will compete.

ANS: F
Entrepreneurs frequently ignore the reality of competition for their new ventures, believing that the marketplace offers no close substitutes or that their success will not attract other entrepreneurs. This is simply not realistic.

REF: p. 144 OBJ: 7-2 TYPE: C

15. The marketing strategy section provides the most detailed information in a formal marketing plan.

ANS: T REF: p. 144 OBJ: 7-2 TYPE: C

16. Marketing research is an effective supplement, but not a replacement, for the intuitive judgment of entrepreneurs.

ANS: T REF: p. 146 OBJ: 7-3 TYPE: C

17. Because of the large amounts of time, effort, and money required, only the largest of firms should consider conducting marketing research.

ANS: F
If it uses practical techniques (such as those outlined in the chapter), small businesses can also conduct marketing research. However, because of the expense involved and their lack of understanding, small businesses do conduct *less* marketing research than do large firms.

REF: p. 147 OBJ: 7-3 TYPE: C

18. Marketing research is defined as the gathering, processing, reporting, and interpreting of marketing information.

ANS: T REF: p. 147 OBJ: 7-3 TYPE: D

19. Small businesses typically conduct less marketing research than big businesses, partly because they lack an understanding of the basic marketing research process.

ANS: T REF: p. 147 OBJ: 7-3 TYPE: C

20. When conducting marketing research, it is important that small business owners be concerned with determining if the research is necessary, if the data obtained will justify the expense, and if the owner is capable of conducting the research.

ANS: T REF: p. 147 OBJ: 7-3 TYPE: C

21. Marketing research is an expensive and complicated process and, therefore, is usually not feasible for small businesses.

ANS: F
Using practical techniques, even a small business can conduct marketing research.

REF: p. 147+ OBJ: 7-3 TYPE: C

22. Researchers typically achieve higher response rates from mail and telephone surveys than from personal interviews.

ANS: F
Personal interviews and telephone surveys typically achieve higher response rates than mail surveys.

REF: p. 149 OBJ: 7-3 TYPE: C

23. Because of the considerable cost, time, and effort associated with pre-testing, it is generally considered necessary only in the case of extensive, complex questionnaires.

ANS: F
A questionnaire should be pre-tested by administering it to a small, but representative, sample of respondents.

REF: p. 149 OBJ: 7-3 TYPE: C

24. Personal interview surveys are attractive as a marketing research method because these are inexpensive to conduct.

ANS: F
Personal interview surveys are expensive, especially compared to alternatives such as mail and telephone surveys.

REF: p. 149 OBJ: 7-3 TYPE: C

25. Small business owners can now buy inexpensive personal computer software that can perform statistical calculations and generate report-quality graphics..

ANS: T REF: p. 149 OBJ: 7-3 TYPE: C

26. A market is best defined as a geographical area that is of commercial interest to the entrepreneur.

ANS: F
A market is a group of customers or potential customers who have purchasing power and unsatisfied needs.

REF: p. 151 OBJ: 7-4 TYPE: D

27. Determining market potential is the process of locating and investigating buying units that have purchasing power and needs that can be satisfied with the product or service being offered.

ANS: T REF: p. 151 OBJ: 7-4 TYPE: D

28. When a strategist divides the total market for a product or service into groups with similar needs, so that each group is likely to respond to the same marketing strategy, he or she is engaging in a practice called *market segmentation.*

ANS: T REF: p. 151 OBJ: 7-4 TYPE: D

29. A small business can determine whether a market is adequate for its plans by checking the *sales forecast.*

ANS: T REF: p. 154 OBJ: 7-5 TYPE: C

30. Sales forecasts are typically expressed in dollars or units.

ANS: T REF: p. 154 OBJ: 7-5 TYPE: C

31. Because sales forecasts revolve around specific target markets, the market should be defined as precisely as possible.

ANS: T REF: p. 154 OBJ: 7-5 TYPE: C

32. Because of the relatively inconsequential amount of sales conducted by a typical small business, the majority of entrepreneurs need not be concerned with formulating accurate sales forecasts.

    ANS: F
    A sales forecast is a critical component of the business plan: therefore, entrepreneurs should engage in forecasting and do so with great care.

    REF: p. 155 OBJ: 7-5 TYPE: C

33. The forecasting process can be characterized by the point at which the process is started and the nature of the predicting variable.

    ANS: T REF: p. 155 OBJ: 7-5 TYPE: C

34. A chain-ratio method of sales forecasting, or a buildup process, is frequently used for consumer products forecasting.

    ANS: F
    Another term for the *chain-ratio* method of sales forecasting is the *breakdown* process, not the *buildup* process.

    REF: p. 156 OBJ: 7-5 TYPE: C

35. A buildup process requires a small business to identify all potential buyers in a target market's submarkets and then combine these estimates to determine the calculated demand.

    ANS: T REF: p. 156 OBJ: 7-5 TYPE: C

MULTIPLE CHOICE

1. Small business marketing involves a number of activities, including
   a. preparing, communicating, and delivering a bundle of satisfaction to a target market.
   b. planning for optimal production efficiency.
   c. identifying alternative technologies.
   d. establishing a sales-oriented marketing philosophy.

   ANS: A REF: p. 141 OBJ: 7-1 TYPE: C

2. A firm's marketing mix consists of _____ activities.
   a. pricing, promotion, and distribution
   b. product, pricing, and promotion
   c. product, promotion, and distribution
   d. product, pricing, promotion, and distribution

   ANS: D REF: p. 142 OBJ: 7-1 TYPE: D

3. Traditionally, marketing philosophies have been categorized as
   a. consumer-oriented and market-oriented.
   b. consumer-oriented, product-oriented, market-oriented, and volume-oriented.
   c. consumer-oriented, market-oriented, sales-oriented, and process-oriented.

d. consumer-oriented, production-oriented, and sales-oriented.

ANS: D REF: p. 142 OBJ: 7-1 TYPE: C

4. U.S. businesses have recently shifted their focus toward a _____ orientation.
   a. market
   b. consumer
   c. production
   d. sales

ANS: B REF: p. 142 OBJ: 7-1 TYPE: C

5. A firm's marketing philosophy determines how strategic marketing activities are used to achieve
   a. efficiency.
   b. customer response.
   c. desirable thought patterns.
   d. business goals.

ANS: D REF: p. 142 OBJ: 7-1 TYPE: C

6. In recent years, the emphasis in U.S. businesses has been on
   a. consumers.
   b. production.
   c. sales.
   d. time-honored values.

ANS: A REF: p. 142 OBJ: 7-1 TYPE: C

7. The _____ marketing philosophy is the preferred approach for all businesses.
   a. product-oriented
   b. market-oriented
   c. sales-oriented
   d. consumer-oriented

ANS: D REF: p. 142 OBJ: 7-1 TYPE: C

8. Every day, associates of Sewell Motors, a Dallas-based auto retailer, strive to exceed the company's expectations of treating the customer as its number one priority. Every action, policy, and ultimate sale is conducted professionally, with consumers' needs in mind. Sewell Motors subscribes to the _____ marketing philosophy.
   a. consumer-oriented
   b. market-oriented
   c. sales-oriented
   d. product-oriented

ANS: A REF: p. 142 OBJ: 7-1 TYPE: A

9. Creators Plus, a modest-size manufacturer of quality crafts, expends considerable resources to ensure that its products are created in the most efficient manner. According to the owner, distribution and promotion are secondary considerations to managing an expedient production process. Creators Plus subscribes to the _______ marketing philosophy.
   a. process-oriented
   b. market-oriented

c. sales-oriented
d. production-oriented

ANS: D REF: p. 142 OBJ: 7-1 TYPE: A

10. The consumer-oriented approach to marketing
a. is just one more business philosophy.
b. focuses solely on customer satisfaction.
c. recognizes first and foremost the need for attaining production efficiency goals.
d. the generally preferred philosophy for all types of businesses.

ANS: D REF: p. 142 OBJ: 7-1 TYPE: C

11. Its decision to produce flavored spring water ice cubes in response to requests from its customers reflects Norway Ice Company's _______ marketing philosophy.
a. production-oriented
b. sales-oriented
c. consumer-oriented
d. response-oriented

ANS: C REF: p. 142 OBJ: 7-1 TYPE: A

12. Koldpak has focused principally on the development of revolutionary new ways of containerizing fresh produce for grocery stores. The firm's marketing philosophy is
a. consumer-oriented.
b. market-oriented.
c. production-oriented.
d. sales-oriented.

ANS: C REF: p. 142 OBJ: 7-1 TYPE: A

13. Adopting a consumer-oriented marketing philosophy is most consistent with
a. quickly gaining highly profitable market returns.
b. eventually achieving long-term market success.
c. the revenue stabilizing effect of large market shares.
d. focusing on the single most profitable consumer segment.

ANS: B REF: p. 142 OBJ: 7-1 TYPE: A

14. The types of sales forecasts that should ideally be prepared include the _________ scenario.
a. rapidly shifting
b. pessimistic
c. predominant
d. contingency

ANS: B REF: p. 144 OBJ: 7-2 TYPE: C

15. Irene Anderson, an experienced entrepreneur, is evaluating her customer profile. She should check
a. her financial ratios to make sure they were calculated correctly.
b. the stability of her funding.
c. her customer benefits to make sure they are consistent with the "Products and Services" section of her business plan.
d. her customer benefits to make sure her competitors offer the same benefits.

ANS: C REF: p. 145 OBJ: 7-2 TYPE: A

16. In the analysis of a market, the customer profile should include a
a. description of consumer weaknesses.

b. summary of production plans.
c. a detailed discussion of major customer benefits provided by the product and/or service.
d. a profile of major markets not targeted.

ANS: C REF: p. 143 OBJ: 7-2 TYPE: C

17. The market analysis section of the marketing plan should include
a. sales options.
b. a customer profile.
c. a statement of marketing tendencies.
d. a summary of market philosophies.

ANS: B REF: p. 142 OBJ: 7-2 TYPE: D

18. The marketing plan should include
a. a competitor analysis.
b. a summary of market assumptions.
c. an analysis of alternative markets.
d. a sales forecast broken down by government industrial classifications.

ANS: A REF: p. 144 OBJ: 7-2 TYPE: D

19. One section of the competitor analysis of a formal marketing plan should include all of the following, *except*
a. competitor's strengths and weaknesses.
b. a list of related products currently being marketed or tested by competitors.
c. the likelihood that competitors will enter the firm's target market.
d. the competitiveness of plans such as warranty and repair policies.

ANS: D REF: p. 144 OBJ: 7-2 TYPE: C

20. The most detailed and scrutinized section of a formal marketing plan is the
a. competitor analysis.
b. marketing strategy.
c. market analysis.
d. consumer analysis.

ANS: B REF: p. 144 OBJ: 7-2 TYPE: C

21. The areas of marketing strategy that should be addressed within the marketing plan are
a. promotional, pricing, distribution, and product/service plans.
b. promotional and pricing plans.
c. promotional and distribution plans.
d. promotional, pricing, and distribution plans.

ANS: A REF: p. 145 OBJ: 7-2 TYPE: C

22. John Smith, a car repair shop owner, is developing the warranty and repair policies for his business. What area of the marketing strategy is he addressing?
a. Promotional plan
b. Total product or service
c. Distribution plan
d. Pricing plan

ANS: B REF: p. 145 OBJ: 7-2 TYPE: A

23. The description of potential customers in a target market is commonly called a
    a. customer profile.
    b. demographic detailing.
    c. Simpkins matrix.
    d. target picture.

ANS: A REF: p. 143 OBJ: 7-2 TYPE: A

24. In the text, which particular demographic did Adorable Pet Photography choose as its target market?
    a. families with young children
    b. first-time pet owners
    c. older married couples
    d. affluent "yuppies"

ANS: C REF: p. 143 OBJ: 7-2 TYPE: A

25. Richard Hagelberg changed the name of his company because
    a. he failed to protect its name by trademarking it.
    b. the name of the company didn't make a positive contribution to sales.
    c. he had chosen a name that was already trademarked.
    d. he wanted to capitalize on the name recognition associated with his Olympic gold medals.

ANS: C REF: p. 145 OBJ: 7-2 TYPE: D

26. The initial step in the marketing research process is to
    a. select a data collection method.
    b. identify consumer/business segments of interest.
    c. identify informational needs.
    d. conduct a preliminary information search.

ANS: C REF: p. 147 OBJ: 7-3 TYPE: C

27. In an effort to ascertain the average dollar amount of credit card purchases at their store, managers of Component City, a stereo and appliance dealer, reviewed in-store copies of credit card sales receipts from the previous three months to evaluate the store's credit card acceptance policies. Component City's managers are conducting marketing research by collecting and analyzing
    a. primary data.
    b. observational data.
    c. questioning data.
    d. secondary data.

ANS: D REF: p. 148 OBJ: 7-3 TYPE: A

28. Primary data collection methods are often classified as
    a. expensive or inexpensive.
    b. observational or questioning.
    c. broad or comprehensive.
    d. issue-related or concept-related.

ANS: B REF: p. 148-149 OBJ: 7-3 TYPE: C

29. Only large firms have the resources to do marketing research. This statement is
    a. more true than false.
    b. a myth.

c. well founded.
d. based on recent research findings.

ANS: B REF: p. 147 OBJ: 7-3 TYPE: C

30. Which of the following is *not* a good source of secondary data for small businesses?
a. software programs that offer useful information.
b. the Small Business Administration.
c. company records.
d. relevant Web sites.

ANS: C REF: p. 148 OBJ: 7-3 TYPE: C

31. Problems typically associated with the use of secondary data include all of the following *except*
a. outdated material.
b. inconsistent units of measure.
c. lack of credibility.
d. limited number of data sources.

ANS: D REF: p. 148 OBJ: 7-3 TYPE: C

32. Techniques used to collect primary data are often classified as _____ and _____ methods.
a. internal/external
b. observational/questioning
c. exploratory/descriptive
d. focus/comprehensive

ANS: B REF: p. 148-149 OBJ: 7-3 TYPE: C

33. Mary Delany, owner of Delany Salsas, is curious to know whether the new packaging for her line of salsas is being noticed by supermarket consumers. Accordingly, she ventures out to the local supermarket and passively watches the reactions of shoppers as they pass by one of the many Delany Salsas displays. Mary Delany is collecting _____ data through _____ methods.
a. secondary/observational
b. primary/questioning
c. primary/observational
d. secondary/questioning

ANS: C REF: p. 148 OBJ: 7-3 TYPE: A

34. Which of the following statements about observational methods is *not* true?
a. They can be very economical.
b. They avoid potential biases.
c. They can be conducted by a human or by mechanical devices.
d. They are a form of secondary data collection.

ANS: D REF: p. 148 OBJ: 7-3 TYPE: C

35. The basic instrument used to guide the researcher and the respondent when surveys are taken is known as a
a. questionnaire.
b. questioning form.
c. interview outline.

d. guide form.

ANS: A REF: p. 149 OBJ: 7-3 TYPE: D

36. Stephanie Kellar used a(n) ________ to gather information that helped her successfully launch her innovative eyelash curler.
a. door-to-door survey
b. in-store coupon
c. student marketing research team
d. Usenet newsgroup

ANS: D REF: p. 149 OBJ: 7-3 TYPE: D

37. Public and university libraries contain a wealth of information in the form of _______ data.
a. anecdotal
b. primary
c. secondary
d. tertiary

ANS: C REF: p. 148 OBJ: 7-3 TYPE: D

38. A _____ is defined as a group of customers or potential customers who have purchasing power and unsatisfied needs.
a. consumer segment
b. target market
c. market
d. consumer market

ANS: C REF: p. 151 OBJ: 7-4 TYPE: D

39. In order to be appropriately considered a market, a group of customers or potential customers must have
a. purchasing power.
b. market power.
c. satisfied needs.
d. correlated needs.

ANS: A REF: p. 151 OBJ: 7-4 TYPE: D

40. Marlene Carlson selected a ________ strategy when she chose to market her Puzzle Toes product to parents with young children.
a. demographic
b. multi-segment
c. single-segment
d. unsegmented

ANS: C REF: p. 154 OBJ: 7-4 TYPE: C

41. A _____ estimates how much of a product or service will be purchased within a market over a defined period of time.
a. market forecast
b. market analysis
c. sales forecast
d. sales analysis

ANS: C REF: p. 154 OBJ: 7-5 TYPE: D

42. Which of the following statements about a sales forecast is true?
a. It is an essential part of the business plan.
b. It can apply to any period of time.
c. It must be stated in terms of dollars or another widely accepted currency (e.g., Euros).

d. It is of limited use to startups.

ANS: A REF: p. 155 OBJ: 7-5 TYPE: C

43. Entrepreneurs should base their market assessments, production schedules, inventory policies, and personnel decisions on
a. techniques of observation.
b. qualitative analysis.
c. intuition alone.
d. the sales forecast.

ANS: D REF: p. 155 OBJ: 7-5 TYPE: C

44. Forecasting sales for a new venture
a. is simplified because the firm's product or service offerings are focused on one or a few areas.
b. should always be done with the assistance of outside consultants.
c. is extremely difficult.
d. is not all that important to the future operation of the firm.

ANS: C REF: p. 155 OBJ: 7-5 TYPE: C

45. Which of the following is *not* one of the limitations encountered by small businesses when they forecast sales?
a. Entrepreneurial inexperience
b. Limited familiarity with the forecasting process
c. Deficient quantitative analysis skills
d. Lack of sources of current information about business trends

ANS: D REF: p. 156 OBJ: 7-5 TYPE: C

46. The sales forecasting procedure in which the forecaster begins with a variable that has a very large scope and then systematically works down to the sales forecast is known as the
a. breakdown process.
b. buildup process.
c. chain-linkage method.
d. bottom-up method.

ANS: A REF: p. 156 OBJ: 7-5 TYPE: D

47. Identifying all buyers in a market's submarkets and then adding up the estimated demand is known as the _____ sales forecasting approach.
a. breakdown process
b. buildup process
c. chain-ratio method
d. bottom-up

ANS: B REF: p. 156 OBJ: 7-5 TYPE: D

48. Ideas Unlimited is a recently established consulting firm that specializes in providing retailers with information about regional sales trends. Typically, retail establishments are classified into three categories (specialty, niche, and general retailers). The current CEO of Ideas Unlimited wants to know the estimated demand in the market for its services. Accordingly, she instructs the firm's marketing department to identify all buyers in each category of retailers and derive a full demand assessment. The CEO is requesting a market demand estimate based on the
    a. breakdown forecasting process.
    b. aggregate forecasting process.
    c. buildup forecasting process.
    d. indirect forecasting process.

    ANS: C REF: p. 156 OBJ: 7-5 TYPE: A

49. With regard to market demand estimation, _____ determines whether the sales forecasting process is direct or indirect.
    a. the industry orientation of the firm
    b. the nature of the predicting variable
    c. the ultimate goal of the entrepreneur
    d. the marketing philosophy of the startup

    ANS: B REF: p. 157 OBJ: 7-5 TYPE: C

50. Using the number of births in a historical record to predict the number of driver licenses issued in subsequent years is an example of the use of a(n) _______ variable in forecasting.
    a. approximating
    b. indirect
    c. surrogate
    d. terminating

    ANS: C REF: p. 157 OBJ: 7-5 TYPE: C

ESSAY

1. List the three major factors that influence the adoption of a particular marketing philosophy.

    ANS:
    - The state of the competition (from weak to strong)
    - The range of interests and abilities of the small business manager (e.g., a leaning toward production over marketing)
    - The manager's vision (a shortsighted manager may emphasize sales over customers' needs)

    REF: p. 142 OBJ: 7-1 TYPE: C

2. Several problems accompany the use of secondary data. What are they?

    ANS:
    - Secondary data can quickly become dated and thereby less useful.
    - The units of measure used in the research that formed the secondary data may not fit the current problem. (For example, sales reported in dollars may need to be stated in units.)
    - Credibility is always a concern in using secondary data. Some sources of secondary data are less trustworthy than others.

REF: p. 148 OBJ: 7-3 TYPE: C

3. What are some of the guidelines that should be followed in developing a questionnaire?

ANS:

- Ask questions that relate to the issue under consideration.
- Select the form of question that is appropriate for the subject and the conditions of the survey; open-ended and multiple-choice forms are two popular options.
- Consider the order of the questions carefully to reduce biases.
- Ask the more sensitive questions near the end of the questionnaire.
- Select the words of each question carefully. They should be as simple, clear, and objective as possible.
- Pre-test the questionnaire, using a small representative sample of respondents.

REF: p. 149 OBJ: 7-3 TYPE: C

4. Define the term market and explain the key ingredients of that definition.

ANS:
The word *market* means different things to different people. However, the textbook defines this term as "a group of customers or potential customers who have purchasing power and unsatisfied needs." The specifics of this definition include three key ingredients:

- The market must have buying units or *customers*; thus it is more than a geographic area.
- Customers in a market must have *purchasing power*, since no transaction can occur without it.
- *Unsatisfied needs* provide the buyer with the motivation to complete a purchase.

REF: p. 151 OBJ: 7-4 TYPE: D

5. What are the major elements of the formal marketing plan and what is the purpose of each of these elements?

ANS:
The formal marketing plan should include three sections: market analysis, assessment of the competition, and marketing strategy. Market analysis describes customers in the target market (based on data from both primary and secondary sources) which then leads to profiles of customers and sales forecasts for each targeted segment of the market. To assess the competition, it is important to determine the strengths and weaknesses of rival firms, products that are being tested or marketed by competitors, and the potential for the entry of new competitors into the target market. The marketing strategy of the firm should be described with considerable detail, focusing primarily on marketing decisions related to (1) the total product and/or service (e.g., name selection), (2) promotion of the product or service, (3) distribution concerns, and (4) pricing of the product or service.

REF: p. 143-144 OBJ: 7-5 TYPE: C

6. **You Make the Call—Situation 1**

In 1991, brothers Josh and Seth Frey were driving an ice cream truck. After buying a former postal vehicle and converting it into a dessert-mobile, they operated it between semesters at the University of Wisconsin at Madison. Seth, a senior, planned to join the corporate world after graduating, but Josh was enjoying being his own boss. Josh felt he had finally figured out his future, but he didn't want to be the neighborhood ice cream guy for the rest of his life.

What else could he sell? Care packages. Josh was impressed that a few dorms at his university offered care packages for parents to send to their kids. How could Josh improve on the product? The care packages should be offered campus-wide, he thought.

Source: Geoff Williams, "Staying Power," *Entrepreneur*, Vol. 26, No. 6 (June 1998), p. 154.

Question 1 What type of research could Josh use to estimate demand for the care packages?
Question 2 How could he develop a sales forecast for his product?
Question 3 Would the Internet be helpful to his marketing plan?

ANS:

1. To answer this question, Josh needs to determine his informational needs. For example, will he need primary data to move forward, or will secondary data suffice? Secondary (previously compiled) data are cheaper to gather than are primary (new) data. There are numerous sources of the former, but these are often dated, incompatible, or less than credible. Both primary and secondary data may be of use in this case, but primary data are likely to be necessary if Josh is to answer the questions that are relevant to his specific enterprise. If Josh decides that primary data are required, he will need to determine whether observational (learning by observing) or questioning (surveys and experimentation) methods are best.

2. There are two general "starting points" for developing a sales forecast—breakdown and buildup. The breakdown process begins with a variable that is very large in scope and then systematically works down to the sales forecast. Applied to Josh's venture, the breakdown process would begin by determining the size of the entire potential market (e.g., all parents of students at universities in Wisconsin) and then forecast sales by estimating the percentage of that market that are likely to buy. The buildup approach would start by identifying all potential buyers in relevant submarkets and then add up the estimated demand. To do this, Josh may want to calculate the number of parents of students at the University of Wisconsin at Madison and then compute potential demand by estimating the percentage of these who are likely to be interested in purchasing care packages. By applying this percentage (or a figure adjusted to specific conditions) to other campuses, Josh would be able to forecast total sales. (Table 7-3 may be helpful in walking the students through the specifics of the breakdown process when applied to the care package venture.)

3. Josh may find the Internet beneficial to his efforts, especially when it comes to challenges such as finding and gathering secondary data and promoting his product to prospective customers. Given that he is tapping a market segment that is likely to be educated and thus Internet connected and comfortable with high-tech applications, the Internet may be more helpful than it would be for most startups. For example, he could include the venture's Web address with all advertising to create a tech-savvy image (which should appeal to his target market) and facilitate use of his service by making prices and distribution information readily available.

REF: p. 159 OBJ: YMTC TYPE: C

7. **You Make the Call—Situation 2**
Alibek Iskakov has opened a small café named Oasis in Kokshetau, a city in Kazakhstan. In order to get primary data on the market for his café, he conducted a survey of 100 people—45 men and 55 women. Forty-eight respondents were between 18 and 24 years old, 38 were between 25 and 50 years old, and 14 were over 50 years old. The survey asked the following questions:

1. How often do you visit restaurants?
2. What is your favorite restaurant in Kokshetau? Why?
3. What is the most important factor for you in choosing a restaurant?
4. Would a small, neat café with traditional food appeal to you?
   a. (If no) Why not?
   b. (If yes) When would you patronize it?
5. How much are you willing to pay for dinner?

Question 1 What are the strengths and weaknesses of the sample used in this survey?
Question 2 Evaluate the questions used in the survey.

ANS:
1. The main strength of the survey is based on the profile of the sample, namely, it includes men and women and they range in age from young to old. This strength assumes that the target audience for the restaurant is both men and women of all ages. Another strength of the survey is that it was conducted by a native of the local culture, which adds an important element of reliability to the survey. Answers to an outsider's questions might not be as truthful. On the other hand, the size of the sample size is one of its weaknesses. A bigger sample would reduce the risk of sampling error in the responses. Other issues regarding the sample must be addressed in order to determine another weakness. For example, how was the sample collected? Were the respondents selected based on convenience or based on a quota system to fit the customer profile? Answers to these questions would allow one to assess the weaknesses of the sample. In other words, who are the 100 respondents in the sample? How were they selected?
2. Some of the wording of individual questions could be changed to enhance their precision. For example, question one asked, "How often do you visit restaurants?" Does the word "visit" mean to actually eat at the restaurant? Also, question 3 asks for the most important factor for "...you in choosing a restaurant?" Does Iskakow know that the person being interviewed makes this decision, or is it the spouse or someone else in the family group? Also, all questions use an open-ended format. This may be okay in Kokshetau, but in some cultures it would be necessary to provide choices for some of the questions.

REF: p. 159 OBJ: YMTC TYPE: C

8. **You Make the Call—Situation 3**
Mary Wilson is a 31-year-old wife and mother who wants to start her own company. She has no previous business experience but has an idea for marketing an animal grooming service, with an approach similar to that used for pizza delivery. When a customer calls, she will arrive in a van in less than 30 minutes and will provide the grooming service. Many of her friends think the idea has promise but dismiss her efforts to seriously discuss the venture. However, Wilson is not discouraged; she plans to purchase the van and the necessary grooming equipment.

Question 1 What target market or markets can you identify for Wilson? How could she forecast sales for her service in each market?
Question 2 What advantage does her business have over existing grooming businesses?
Question 3 What business name and promotional strategy would you suggest that Wilson use?

ANS:

1. There appear to be at least two markets for this service. One is the elderly and handicapped who are not able to take their pets to grooming salons. The other market is those customers who do not like leaving their pets in a shop all day because the animals get nervous. Wilson may also be able to serve some of the overload that periodically builds up in grooming shops.

   Forecasting sales will be difficult prior to beginning operations. However, Wilson may be able to obtain secondary data on pet ownership from the local library. With an estimate of what market share she might expect, a sales forecast could be generated.

2. Probably the biggest advantage to Wilson's service is the time factor. A client can have the service performed very soon after identifying the need. The owner can also be available at the grooming van to offer grooming instructions. The customer does not incur transportation costs or the inconvenience of transporting the pet.

3. The actual company is named All Breed Mobile Grooming, which is not necessarily an outstanding choice. A shorter, more descriptive name that connotes the convenience of the service might be better.

   Presently, word-of-mouth has been the primary form of promotion. The outside of the mobile van could be used for promotion; the painting would need to be done professionally. An advertisement in the Yellow Pages would be advisable. An occasional television commercial might work well also.

REF: p. 159+ OBJ: YMTC TYPE: C

9. **You Make the Call—Situation 4**
Carson Smith is an employee of a small family-owned manufacturing plant located in his hometown of Malone, Mississippi. One day, while waiting to see someone at a competitor's business, he noticed a memo tacked to a bulletin board and read it. The memo described a forthcoming promotional campaign and details of a new pricing strategy. Upon leaving the plant, Smith returned to his office and informed management of the details of the memo.

Question 1 Is this a legitimate form of marketing research? Why or why not?
Question 2 Do you consider Smith's behavior to constitute spying?
Question 3 What would you have done in his situation?

ANS:

1. This is observational research, and it raises an important ethical question. Is information obtained by observational research in the public domain, or should the researcher obtain permission to use such information? There is no clear answer.

2. If the bulletin board was positioned in the area where Carson was asked to wait, then it would be difficult to categorize this as spying. If he wandered into a restricted area, then his actions could justifiably be called spying.

3. Answers will, of course, vary. Some students may suggest that they would have simply asked someone in the office if it was okay to look at the bulletin board. Others may argue that any helpful information that the management of Carson's company would not otherwise have had should not be obtained in this manner.

REF: p. 0 OBJ: YMTC TYPE: C

Correlation Table for Chapter 8—The Human Resource Plan: Managers, Owners, Allies, and Directors

	Learning Objectives	Question Type	Definition Define new term, recall facts	Concept Understand or relate concepts	Application Apply knowledge, analyze data
1	Describe the characteristics and value of a strong management team.	T/F		1,2,3,4,5	
		MC		1,2,4	3
		ES		1,2	
2	Explain the common legal forms of organization used by small businesses.	T/F	7,9,12,15	6,8,10,11,13,14, 16,17,18,19,20, 21	
		MC	10,11,12,19	5,6,7,8,9,13,14, 14,16,17,18,20, 21,22,23,25,26, 29	24,27,28
		ES		3,4,5,6	
3	Identify factors to consider in choosing among the primary legal forms of organization, including tax consequences.	T/F		22,23,24,25,26, 27,28,29,30,32, 33	31
		MC	36	30,31,32,33,34, 35,37,38	39,40,
		ES			
4	Describe the unique features and restrictions of three specialized organizational forms: limited partnerships, S corporations, and limited liability companies.	T/F	35,36,37,38	34,39	
		MC	41	42,45	43,44
		ES	7		
5	Explain the nature of strategic alliances and their uses in small businesses.	T/F	40	41	
		MC	50	46,47,48,49	
		ES			
6	Describe the effective use of boards of directors and advisory councils.	T/F		42,43,44	
		MC			
		ES			
	You Make the Call	ES		8,9,10,11	

Total Number of Test Questions: 105 (44 True/False; 50 Multiple-Choice; 11 Essay)

Chapter 8—The Human Resource Plan

TRUE/FALSE

1. In reviewing business plans, investors show great concern for the quality of venture leadership.

   ANS: T REF: p. 163 OBJ: TYPE: C

2. A management team is often stronger than an individual entrepreneur because it provides a diversity of skills and assurance of continuity.

   ANS: T REF: p. 164 OBJ: 8-1 TYPE: C

3. Effective collaboration by members of a management team requires personal compatibility and cooperation of team members.

   ANS: T REF: p. 165 OBJ: 8-1 TYPE: C

4. The concept of balance on the management team means that the entrepreneur should not be wrapped up too much in one area, such as sales or production, but be well rounded.

   ANS: F
   Balance on the management team suggests that *members of the team* have different and complementary competencies, not that the *entrepreneur* has balanced interests.

   REF: p. 165 OBJ: 8-1 TYPE: C

5. Any weakness in the management of a new business will mean its certain failure, since no one outside the business will be able to provide management assistance.

   ANS: F
   If the management talent of a new business has weaknesses, these can be augmented with assistance from external professional organizations (e.g., a commercial bank, a law firm, a certified public accounting firm).

   REF: p. 165 OBJ: 8-1 TYPE: C

6. The sole proprietorship is usually the most appropriate form of business organization for a new small business.

   ANS: T REF: p. 165 OBJ: 8-2 TYPE: C

7. A sole proprietorship is a business owned by one person.

   ANS: T REF: p. 165 OBJ: 8-2 TYPE: D

8. There are no limits on the owner's personal liability in a sole proprietorship.

ANS: T REF: p. 165 OBJ: 8-2 TYPE: C

9. The sole proprietorship is a business owned by two or more people but operated by only one person.

ANS: F
A sole proprietorship is a business that is owned by one person.

REF: p. 165 OBJ: 8-2 TYPE: D

10. Sole proprietors often benefit from fringe benefits such as tax-free insurance plans.

ANS: F
Sole proprietors are owners (not employees) and thus cannot enjoy the advantage of tax-free fringe benefits.

REF: p. 165 OBJ: 8-2 TYPE: C

11. Creating a partnership allows a business to pool the managerial talents and capital of those individuals joining together as partners.

ANS: T REF: p. 166 OBJ: 8-2 TYPE: C

12. A partnership is a legal form of organization in which two or more individuals are forced to carry on, as co-owners, a business for profit.

ANS: F
Partnerships are formed when two or more individuals *choose* to operate a business for profit.

REF: p. 166 OBJ: 8-2 TYPE: D

13. Partners must contribute capital or assets to form a partnership.

ANS: F
Individuals may become partners without contributing capital or having a claim to assets at the time of dissolution.

REF: p. 166-167 OBJ: 8-2 TYPE: C

14. Partners always share profits and losses equally.

ANS: F
Partners share profit/losses equally, except where they have agreed to a different ratio.

REF: p. 169 OBJ: 8-2 TYPE: C

15. Agency power is the ability of any partner to legally bind in good faith other partners in a contract or agreement.

ANS: T REF: p. 169 OBJ: 8-2 TYPE: D

16. Good faith, together with reasonable care in the exercise of managerial duties, is required of all partners in a business.

ANS: T REF: p. 167 OBJ: 8-2 TYPE: C

17. Ownership in a corporation is evidenced by stock certificates.

ANS: T REF: p. 170 OBJ: 8-2 TYPE: C

18. A corporation's charter should be brief, in accord with state law, and broad in the statement of the firm's powers.

ANS: T REF: p. 170 OBJ: 8-2 TYPE: C

19. An ownership interest does not automatically confer a right to act for or to share in the management of a corporation.

ANS: T REF: p. 170 OBJ: 8-2 TYPE: C

20. As in a partnership, ownership in a corporation is readily transferable.

ANS: F
Ownership in a corporation is readily transferable, but this is not the case with partnerships.

REF: p. 171 OBJ: 8-2 TYPE: C

21. To transfer ownership in a corporation, it is only necessary to transfer shares of stock.

ANS: T REF: p. 170 OBJ: 8-2 TYPE: C

22. The death of a majority stockholder of a corporation results in the dissolution of the corporation.

ANS: F
A corporation offers continuity, regardless of the status of individual investors; therefore, the death of a stockholder (even one with a majority position in the company) does not affect the corporation's existence.

REF: p. 171 OBJ: 8-3 TYPE: C

23. The desire for continuity of a business might be one reason to organize as a corporation rather than as a partnership.

ANS: T REF: p. 171 OBJ: 8-3 TYPE: C

24. The liability of owners is not affected by the form of business organization selected.

ANS: F
Sole proprietorships and general partnerships involve unlimited liability, whereas forming a corporation limits the liability of owners to the extent of their investment in the business.

REF: p. 171 OBJ: 8-3 TYPE: C

25. The death of the sole proprietor terminates the business entity.

ANS: T REF: p. 171 OBJ: 8-3 TYPE: C

26. A corporation's life span is equal to that of its owners.

ANS: F
A corporation offers continuity, so it's life span is not affected by that of its owners.

REF: p. 171 OBJ: 8-3 TYPE: C

27. One of the disadvantages of the corporate form of organization is the limited liability of its owners.

ANS: F
The limited liability to owners is one of the *advantages* of the corporate form.

REF: p. 171 OBJ: 8-3 TYPE: C

28. One of the advantages of a sole proprietorship is its continuity.

ANS: F
Continuity is an advantage of a corporation, but this is one of the *drawbacks* of the sole proprietorship.

REF: p. 171 OBJ: 8-3 TYPE: C

29. The form of ownership of a business has no effect on income taxes.

ANS: F
Under the law, different forms of organizations receive different tax treatment.

REF: p. 173 OBJ: 8-3 TYPE: C

30. A sole proprietorship must be registered with the state to obtain its legal charter.

ANS: F
Sole proprietorships usually do not require legal registration or even the payment of a filing fee.

REF: p. 173 OBJ: 8-3 TYPE: C

31. Jesse Roth plans to open a new business that will deal in buying, selling, and trading baseball cards, so he will be required to obtain legal registration.

ANS: F
Roth's enterprise will most likely be operated as a sole proprietorship, and this organizational form requires no legal registration.

REF: p. 165 OBJ: 8-3 TYPE: A

32. A partnership reports the income it earns to the Internal Revenue Service, but the partnership itself does not pay any taxes.

ANS: T REF: p. 174 OBJ: 8-3 TYPE: C

33. Holding stock issued pursuant to Section 1244 of the Internal Revenue Code (i.e., Section 1244 stock) offers no financial protection against corporate failure.

ANS: F
If Section 1244 stock becomes worthless, the loss (up to $100,000 on a joint tax return) may be treated as an ordinary tax-deductible loss.

REF: p. 174 OBJ: 8-3 TYPE: C

34. Limited partners have limited personal liability.

ANS: T REF: p. 174 OBJ: 8-4 TYPE: C

35. A limited partnership must have at least two general partners and one or more limited partners.

ANS: F
Limited partnerships involve at least *one* general partner and one or more limited partners.

REF: p. 174 OBJ: 8-4 TYPE: D

36. An S corporation may have no more than 35 stockholders.

ANS: F
S corporations are permitted to have as many as 75 stockholders (husbands and wives counting as a single stockholder).

REF: p. 175 OBJ: 8-4 TYPE: D

37. The name *S corporation* comes from the Internal Revenue Code, which permits corporations to retain the limited-liability feature of regular corporations while being taxed as partnerships.

ANS: T REF: p. 175 OBJ: 8-4 TYPE: D

38. S corporations can have nonresident alien stockholders.

ANS: F
S corporations are not permitted to have nonresident alien stockholders.

REF: p. 175 OBJ: 8-4 TYPE: D

39. The limited liability company differs from the C corporation in that the former avoids financial complications from double taxation.

ANS: T REF: p. 175 OBJ: 8-4 TYPE: C

40. A strategic alliance is an organizational relationship that links two or more independent business entities in some common endeavor.

ANS: T REF: p. 176 OBJ: 8-5 TYPE: D

41. Large manufacturing firms sometimes match their financial resources with the creativity of small manufacturing firms by means of strategic alliances.

ANS: T REF: p. 176 OBJ: 8-5 TYPE: C

42. The board of directors is elected by the stockholders of a corporation.

ANS: T REF: p. 178 OBJ: 8-6 TYPE: C

43. Some entrepreneurs have found an active board of directors to be both practical and beneficial.

ANS: T REF: p. 178 OBJ: 8-6 TYPE: C

44. Objectivity is a particularly valuable contribution of outside directors to the small firm.

ANS: T REF: p. 179 OBJ: 8-6 TYPE: C

MULTIPLE CHOICE

1. The importance of a strong management group in a new venture is evidenced by the
   a. attitudes of investors.
   b. eagerness of new entrepreneurs to sign up for management seminars.
   c. comparative profit data compiled by the Internal Revenue Service.
   d. reading interests of new management teams, who seek management books and periodicals.

   ANS: A REF: p. 164 OBJ: 8-1 TYPE: C

2. The key to strong management in a new firm is
   a. balance, with each member having competence in at least one area.
   b. financial competence of the chief executive.
   c. a strong marketing manager.
   d. close friendship among all members of the team.

   ANS: A REF: p. 165 OBJ: 8-1 TYPE: C

3. The owner of a new venture wants to supplement the managerial talent of its management team by drawing on outside assistance. Which of the following would be the *least* likely source of help?
   a. A commercial bank
   b. A certified public accounting firm
   c. An attorney
   d. The Small Business Administration

   ANS: D REF: p. 165 OBJ: 8-1 TYPE: A

4. Most of the reasons for failure in many high growth ventures may be traced to
   a. a weak business concept.
   b. a lack of adequate resources.
   c. poor market timing.
   d. specific flaws in the venture team.

   ANS: D REF: p. 164 OBJ: 8-1 TYPE: C

5. A sole proprietor
   a. assumes all losses of the business.
   b. assumes no profits.
   c. receives tax-free fringe benefits.
   d. assumes no losses.

   ANS: A REF: p. 165 OBJ: 8-2 TYPE: C

6. The owner of a sole proprietorship
   a. owns the business.
   b. bears no risks.
   c. is an employee of the business.
   d. shares profits.

   ANS: A REF: p. 165 OBJ: 8-2 TYPE: C

7. The most rudimentary form of business organization among small businesses is the
   a. corporation.
   b. general partnership.
   c. sole proprietorship.
   d. limited partnership.

   ANS: C REF: p. 165 OBJ: 8-2 TYPE: C

8. A disadvantage of a sole proprietorship is
   a. the complexity of the organization.
   b. the cost of starting the business.
   c. the lack of limits on personal liability.
   d. the difficulty of distribution.

   ANS: C REF: p. 165 OBJ: 8-2 TYPE: C

9. A key characteristic of a partnership is that each partner
   a. must contribute capital to the business.
   b. shares in company assets upon the dissolution of the partnership.
   c. is capable of legally contracting.
   d. must manage the business.

   ANS: C REF: p. 166 OBJ: 8-2 TYPE: C

10. Which of the following legal forms of an organization allows owners to contribute no capital but still play a part in managing the business and share in its profits?
    a. S corporation
    b. C Corporation
    c. Partnership
    d. Sole proprietorship

    ANS: C REF: p. 166 OBJ: 8-2 TYPE: D

11. Which of the following best defines a partnership?
    a. A business owned and operated by one person
    b. A voluntary association of two or more persons to carry on, as co-owners, a business for profit

c. The governing body for corporate activity
d. An organization in which each owner has limited personal liability

ANS: B REF: p. 166 OBJ: 8-2 TYPE: D

12. In a partnership, each partner has agency power, which means that
a. upon the death of one partner, the remaining partners can operate the business.
b. a partner can legally bind all members of the firm.
c. an executor can act as a partner.
d. a partner can compete in business and remain a partner.

ANS: B REF: p. 169 OBJ: 8-2 TYPE: D

13. A corporation
a. is chartered under state laws.
b. is chartered under federal laws.
c. remains in existence only as long as its owners are alive.
d. shifts liability of its debts to its owners.

ANS: A REF: p. 170 OBJ: 8-2 TYPE: C

14. Which of the following entities is liable for a corporation's debts?
a. Stockholders
b. Board of directors
c. The corporation itself
d. The corporation's president

ANS: C REF: p. 170 OBJ: 8-2 TYPE: C

15. For a corporate charter to be obtained,
a. one or more persons must apply to the secretary of state for permission to incorporate.
b. the owner(s) must agree to be interviewed by a state department official.
c. the owner(s) must negotiate an incorporation fee.
d. the partners involved must outline a division of assets.

ANS: A REF: p. 170 OBJ: 8-2 TYPE: C

16. A corporate charter should be
a. very detailed.
b. prepared by an attorney.
c. brief in the statement of the firm's power.
d. lengthy and precise.

ANS: B REF: p. 170 OBJ: 8-2 TYPE: C

17. Permission to incorporate a business comes from the
a. board of directors.
b. stockholders.
c. government, usually through a secretary of state.
d. corporate officers.

ANS: C REF: p. 170 OBJ: 8-2 TYPE: C

18. A typical common stockholder of a corporation

a. has the right to act for the firm.
b. has the right to receive declared dividends.
c. can always buy new stock in proportion to stock already owned.
d. can fire employees of the corporation.

ANS: B REF: p. 170 OBJ: 8-2 TYPE: C

19. The right to buy new shares of stock in proportion to stock already owned is called a
a. stock right.
b. stock option.
c. Section 1244 right.
d. pre-emptive right.

ANS: D REF: p. 170 OBJ: 8-2 TYPE: D

20. A basic legal principle involving stockholders is that
a. an ownership interest in a corporation does not confer a legal right to manage the firm.
b. the board of directors cannot elect the principal owner as president.
c. all dividends are nontaxable.
d. stockholders cannot buy new stock until it is offered for public sale.

ANS: A REF: p. 170 OBJ: 8-2 TYPE: C

21. A corporate charter should
a. be detailed.
b. be in accord with state law.
c. include bylaws.
d. indicate profit potential.

ANS: B REF: p. 170 OBJ: 8-2 TYPE: C

22. Stockholders have limited liability unless they
a. are active in the management of the corporation.
b. personally endorse company notes.
c. own preferred stock.
d. convert their shares to partnership status.

ANS: B REF: p. 170 OBJ: 8-2 TYPE: C

23. Upon the death of the majority stockholder in a corporation, direct control may pass to
a. an heir's dependents.
b. an executor.
c. the founder of the firm.
d. employees as directed by an employee stock ownership plan.

ANS: B REF: p. 171 OBJ: 8-2 TYPE: C

24. The residual assets of a sole proprietorship belong to the __________ after the owner's death.
a. owner's heirs
b. primary investors
c. general partners
d. creditors

ANS: A REF: p. 171 OBJ: 8-2 TYPE: A

25. A strong partnership requires that partners who

a. are honest, healthy, capable, and contribute assets to the partnership.
b. honest, healthy, capable, and compatible with the other partners.
c. honest, healthy, capable, and legally unencumbered.
d. honest, healthy, capable, and willing to participate actively in the partnership.

ANS: B REF: p. 167 OBJ: 8-2 TYPE: C

26. Any person capable of ________ may legally become a business partner.
a. assenting to liability
b. contracting
c. contributing capital
d. having a claim on assets

ANS: B REF: p. 166 OBJ: 8-2 TYPE: C

27. A partner can purchase a new copier for the partnership without consulting the other partners because each partner has _____ power.
a. agency
b. purchasing
c. separability
d. fiduciary

ANS: A REF: p. 169 OBJ: 8-2 TYPE: A

28. A partner in ABC construction business who invests in XYZ construction business that is a direct competitor has violated his _________ duty to the ABC partnership.
a. agency
b. concomitant
c. fiduciary
d. intermediary

ANS: A REF: p. 169 OBJ: 8-2 TYPE: A

29. Characteristics of a corporation which of the following:
a. artificial being
b. visible
c. tangible
d. immutable

ANS: A REF: p. 170 OBJ: 8-2 TYPE: C

30. Ownership in a corporation
a. is difficult to transfer.
b. is more easily transferable than ownership in other forms of organization.
c. is transferred in much the same way as stock in a partnership.
d. noticeably affects the operation of the business.

ANS: B REF: p. 171 OBJ: 8-3 TYPE: C

31. Unlimited liability for business debts is imposed on
a. shareholders in a C corporation.
b. shareholders in an S corporation.
c. sole proprietors.
d. limited partners.

ANS: C REF: p. 165 OBJ: 8-3 TYPE: C

32. In selecting the type of legal organization to use for a new small business, which of the following is a major consideration?
a. Profitability
b. Management control
c. Available benefits

d. Procedures for termination or liquidation

ANS: B REF: p. 165 OBJ: 8-3 TYPE: C

33. In a limited partnership, which of the following remains bound by all debts of the business?
    a. Limited partner
    b. Special partner
    c. Partner with the greatest capital investment
    d. General partner

ANS: D REF: p. 175 OBJ: 8-3 TYPE: C

34. Which of the following reflects how a partnership pays taxes?
    a. It doesn't pay any taxes.
    b. It pays taxes as a partnership.
    c. The partners each pay taxes on the total income.
    d. The partners do not pay taxes if they own Section 1244 stock.

ANS: A REF: p. 174 OBJ: 8-3 TYPE: C

35. In the event of corporate failure, which of the following types of stock can be treated as an ordinary tax-deductible loss?
    a. Section 1744 stock
    b. Common stock
    c. Preferred stock
    d. Section 1244 stock

ANS: D REF: p. 174 OBJ: 8-3 TYPE: C

36. A recent IRS report shows that ____ percent of businesses are established as corporations.
    a. 8
    b. 13
    c. 21
    d. 33

ANS: C REF: p. 171 OBJ: 8-3 TYPE: D

37. Max Baer chose to operate his production studio as a sole proprietorship even though his attorney cautioned that he was
    a. reducing its overall profit potential.
    b. increasing his taxable income.
    c. exposing himself to unlimited personal liability.
    d. violating an existing partnership agreement.

ANS: C REF: p. 171 OBJ: 8-3 TYPE: C

38. Formal control and function control in small corporations usually rests in ______ individuals.
    a. a few
    b. many
    c. the same
    d. a limited number of

ANS: C REF: p. 172 OBJ: 8-3 TYPE: C

39. Section 1244 stock somewhat protects the stockholder in a corporate failure
    a. by guaranteeing its par value against corporate assets.
    b. by converting to a redeemable bearer bond
    c. because the loss may be treated as an ordinary tax-deductible loss.
    d. because its value must be backed by

if the corporation fails. Treasury securities.

ANS: C REF: p. 174 OBJ: 8-3 TYPE: A

40. The income from a limited partnership is taxed at the same rate as
a. ordinary income
b. municipal dividends
c. C corporation dividends
d. extraordinary income

ANS: A REF: p. 174 OBJ: 8-3 TYPE: A

41. To be eligible to be an S corporation, a firm must
a. have more than 75 stockholders.
b. have no nonresident alien stockholders.
c. have two or more classes of stock outstanding.
d. be international in scope.

ANS: B REF: p. 175 OBJ: 8-4 TYPE: D

42. S corporations are taxed as
a. proprietorships.
b. partnerships.
c. C corporations.
d. domestic corporations.

ANS: B REF: p. 175 OBJ: 8-4 TYPE: C

43. Lauren Hassell, a partner in Jales & Jales Bonding Company, manages its day-to-day operations. She is considered to be a ________ partner.
a. directing
b. general
c. limited
d. operating

ANS: B REF: p. 174 OBJ: 8-4 TYPE: A

44. A(n) ___________ would be the choice for a form of organization if you intend to provide extensive fringe benefits for owners or employees that would not be treated as taxable income to employees.
a. sole proprietorship
b. partnership
c. C corporation
d. Limited liability company

ANS: C REF: p. 174 OBJ: 8-4 TYPE: A

45. The limited liability company form of organization
a. avoids the double taxation of C corporations.
b. affords less protection from liability than partnerships.
c. is a poor choice for new businesses.
d. can offer stock incentives to employees.

ANS: A REF: p. 175 OBJ: 8-4 TYPE: C

46. A strategic alliance is
a. an organizational relationship that links two separate businesses.
b. an unimportant organizational form in today's business environment.
c. an attempt to duplicate efforts between two firms.
d. a strategy that, as a result of its unwieldy nature, is falling from practice.

ANS: A REF: p. 176 OBJ: 8-5 TYPE: C

47. Large manufacturers have been known to form strategic alliances with small manufacturers in order to benefit from the smaller firms'
    a. financial resources.
    b. operational expertise.
    c. research and development.
    d. creativity.

    ANS: D REF: p. 176 OBJ: 8-5 TYPE: C

48. Looking to the future, strategic alliances represent ____________ for small entrepreneurial firms.
    a. a serious threat
    b. a monopolistic combination
    c. promising opportunities
    d. a prohibitively expensive strategy

    ANS: C REF: p. 176 OBJ: 8-5 TYPE: C

49. A stockholder in a Subchapter S corporation
    a. is not allowed to vote in elections to choose members of the S corporation's board of directors.
    b. cannot vote by proxy at stockholders' meetings.
    c. cannot become a member of the board of directors.
    d. cannot be a nonresident alien.

    ANS: D REF: p. 175 OBJ: 8-6 TYPE: C

50. A corporation's board of directors
    a. is the governing body for corporate activity.
    b. directly manages the corporation.
    c. determines the taxability of dividends.
    d. usually designs the organizational structure of the firm.

    ANS: A REF: p. 178 OBJ: 8-6 TYPE: D

ESSAY

1. Explain the importance of a strong management team for a new venture.

   ANS:
   The answer should recognize that the management team may consist of one person or a group of individuals and that it may include professionals who are not supervisors. The importance of strong management is evidenced by the success and failure record of business firms, with weak management being a primary cause of failure. Venture capitalists also attest to the importance of management in their review of business plans.

   REF: p. 164 OBJ: 8-1 TYPE: C

2. Discuss the concept of a balanced management team.

   ANS:

A balanced management team assumes a venture large enough to have more than one individual. Balance refers to having the necessary diverse skills somewhere in the team. Not everyone, for example, needs to know financial management, but someone needs to be the financial manager.

REF: p. 164 OBJ: 8-1 TYPE: C

3. Identify the six forms of legal organization discussed in the text.

ANS:
The three general forms are the sole proprietorship, the partnership, and the corporation. There are three specialized organizational forms. A limited partnership is an alternative form of partnership. The S corporation is an alternative form of corporation. Finally, limited liability companies represent an organizational form with unique features.

REF: p. 165-170, 174-175 OBJ: 8-2 TYPE: C

4. Identify some of the advantages and disadvantages of a sole proprietorship.

ANS:
The advantages of a sole proprietorship are that it is simple to organize, its owner benefits totally from profits, and it is the cheapest way to start a business. The disadvantages of a sole proprietorship are that there are no limits on personal liability for the owner and the death of the proprietor terminates the business entity.

REF: p. 165 OBJ: 8-2 TYPE: C

5. What are the qualifications of partners?

ANS:
Any person capable of contracting may legally become a business partner. No capital investment or sharing in assets is required to become a partner. A successful partnership requires individuals who are honest, healthy, capable, and compatible.

REF: p. 166-167 OBJ: 8-2 TYPE: C

6. What are the rights of stockholders in a corporation?

ANS:
Stockholders cast one vote per share at stockholders' meetings. Stockholders can vote for directors; the board of directors thus elected is the governing body for corporate activity. Stockholders receive dividends in proportion to stock holdings. Each stockholder can typically buy new shares, in proportion to stock already owned, before these are offered for public sale.

REF: p. 170 OBJ: 8-2 TYPE: C

7. What is the principal advantage of an S corporation, and why is it given this name?

ANS:

A principal disadvantage of a *regular* corporation is that it is subject to the corporate income tax, which results in double taxation when retained earnings are distributed to shareholders, who are thus taxed a second time. A solution to this problem is the S corporation, which allows stockholders to be taxed as partners. This means that the corporation's taxable income is distributed to owners to be taxed as part of their personal income. This type of corporation gets its name from the Subchapter S section of the Internal Revenue Code, which allows for this form of business organization.

REF: p. 175 OBJ: 8-4 TYPE: D

8. **You Make the Call—Situation 1**
Ted Green and Mark Stroder became close friends as 16- year-olds when both worked part-time for Green's dad in his automotive parts store. After high school, Green went to college, while Stroder joined the National Guard Reserve and devoted his weekends to auto racing. Green continued his association with the automotive parts store by buying and managing two of his father's stores.

In 1995, Green conceived the idea of starting a new business that would rebuild automobile starters, and he asked Stroder to be his partner in the venture. Originally, Stroder was somewhat concerned about working with Green because their personalities are so different. Green has been described as outgoing and enthusiastic, while Stroder is reserved and skeptical. However, Stroder is now out of work, and so he has agreed to the offer. They will set up a small shop behind one of Green's automotive parts stores. Stroder will do all the work; Green will supply the cash.

The "partners" have agreed to name the business STARTOVER, and now they need to decide on a legal form of organization.

Question 1 How relevant are the individual personalities to the success of this entrepreneurial team? Do you think Green and Stroder have a chance to survive their "partnership"? Why or why not?

Question 2 Do you consider it an advantage or a disadvantage that the members of this team are the same age?

Question 3 Which legal form of organization would you propose for STARTOVER? Why?

Question 4 If Stroder and Green decided to incorporate, would STARTOVER qualify as an S corporation? If so, would you recommend this option? Why or why not?

ANS:

1. Personalities of partners are extremely relevant to the success of a business. The fact that Green and Stroder were close friends as teenagers suggests that they will be able to get along with each other. Since they have agreed to have Stroder do all the work, there should not be many opportunities for a "personality clash." This should be a fair arrangement. If not, problems may arise regardless of the personalities involved.

2. In most cases it is probably an advantage. World views often vary from age to age, and they can influence individual priorities regarding money, family, and life in general. However, the amount of experience, which usually comes with age, is about the same for each of these young entrepreneurs, and this may prove to be a major limitation of the team.

3. A limited partnership may be a good selection. Green is only supplying cash, and he would be the limited partner. It appears that he has greater personal assets than Stroder, and this arrangement would limit Green's exposure to liability claims that might arise through activities of the business.

4. The STARTOVER business should qualify for S corporation status. It is a domestic business; there are fewer than 35 stockholders, and all are individuals; and the business does not own stock in another corporation. This probably is not a favorable option, however. None of the tax advantages of an S corporation would appear to be attractive at this time. If, at a later date, there is a strong need for growth capital, the entrepreneurs may want to consider incorporation and declare S status.

REF: p. 182 OBJ: YMTC TYPE: C

9. **You Make the Call—Situation 2**
Matthew Freeman started a business in 1993 to provide corporate training in project management. He initially organized his business as a sole proprietorship. Until 1999, he did most of his work on a contract basis for Corporation Education Services (CES). Under the terms of his contract, Freeman was responsible for teaching 3- to 5-day courses to corporate clients—primarily *Fortune 1000* companies. He was compensated according to a negotiated daily rate, and expenses incurred during a course (hotels, meals, transportation, etc.) were reimbursed by CES. Although some expenses were not reimbursed by CES (such as those for computers and office supplies), Freeman's expenses usually amounted to less than 1 percent of his revenues.

In 1999, Freeman increasingly found himself working directly with corporate clients rather than contracting with CES. Over the years, he had considered incorporating but had assumed the costs and inconveniences of this option would outweigh the benefits. However, some of his new clients said that they would prefer to contract with a corporation rather than with an individual. And Freeman sometimes wondered about potential liability problems. On the one hand, he didn't have the same liability issues as some other businesses—he worked out of his home, clients never visited his home office, all courses were conducted in hotels or corporate facilities, and his business involved only services. But he wasn't sure what would happen if a client were dissatisfied with the content and outcomes of his instruction. Finally, he wondered whether there would be tax advantages to incorporating.

Question 1 What are the advantages and disadvantages of running the business as a sole proprietorship? As a C corporation?

Question 2 If Freeman decided to incorporate his business, which types of corporations could he form? Which type would you recommend? Why?

ANS:

1. Matthew Freeman must decide whether to remain organized as a sole proprietorship or incorporate his business. Because he is already operating as a sole proprietorship, this would place the least administrative burden on him. He would have fewer reporting requirements. Taxes on his business income would be reported on Schedule C of his personal income taxes. He would also be required to file quarterly estimated tax payments. As a sole proprietorship, however, he has unlimited personal liability for any debts incurred by the business and any lawsuits brought against the business. Thus, his personal property (e.g., house, cars) is at risk. In his particular situation, he will also lose some business if he remains a sole proprietorship because some large companies will not deal with a sole proprietor. Furthermore, Freeman is not considered an employee and cannot enjoy tax-free fringe benefits such as insurance and hospitalization. And when organized as a sole proprietorship no other person can conduct business for the company. These disadvantages of a sole proprietorship can be overcome by incorporating.

   If incorporated, Freeman will enjoy limited liability and his personal assets will not be at risk. As an employee of the corporation, he will be entitled to certain fringe benefits. As a corporation, his business may also have greater legitimacy in the eyes of other organizations, including large corporations and lending institutions. Incorporation will, however, involve costs and administrative burdens to establish the corporation. He must draw up legal documents (e.g., articles of incorporation) and issue stock to begin the corporation. This process is usually done in consultation with a lawyer and/or a Certified Public Accountant. The on-going reporting requirements for a corporation are more burdensome than for a sole proprietorship. Corporate records must be maintained and accounts must be kept separate from all personal accounts. Depending on the type of corporation chosen (see notes for next question), Freeman may be subject to double taxation.

2. Freeman may choose either a "C corporation" or an "S corporation". Each of these offers the advantage of limited liability and the legitimacy needed for constituents that would prefer not to deal with a sole proprietorship. In choosing between the options, then, other issues should be considered. The primary consideration seems to be the tax implications.

   A " C corporation" must pay corporate income taxes on any income. If dividends are declared, the corporation first pays corporate income tax on these and then individual shareholders pay personal income tax on the dividends. An "S corporation" allows a business to have the benefit of limited liability while being taxed as a partnership. Taxable income and losses are passed to the stockholders rather than the corporation paying corporate income taxes. Thus, dividends are not subject to double taxation. An "S corporation" is limited in many other respects (e.g., no more than 75 shareholders, only one class of stock, corporation must be domestic), but none of these are relevant for Freeman's decision. Thus, it appears that the "S corporation" provides the necessary benefits with the least tax burden.

REF: p. 183 OBJ: YMTC TYPE: C

10. **You Make the Call—Situation 3**
For years, a small distributor of welding materials had followed the practice of most small firms, treating the board of directors as merely a legal necessity. Composed of two co-owners and a retired steel company executive, the board was not a working board. But the company, run informally with traditional management methods, was profitable.

After attending a seminar, the majority owner decided that a board might be useful for more than legal or cosmetic purposes. Thus, he invited two outsiders—both division heads of larger corporations—to join the board. This brought the membership of the board to five. The majority owner believed the new members would be helpful in opening up the business to new ideas.

Question 1 Can two outside members on a board of five make any real difference in the way the board operates?
Question 2 Evaluate the owner's choices for board members.
Question 3 What will determine the usefulness or effectiveness of this board? Do you predict that it will be useful? Why or why not?

ANS:
1. Two new members can definitely make a difference if the chairman of the board wishes to use them. Voting control is necessary only to force changes. In this case, the majority owner wanted the contributions of the two new members.

2. The new board members should be familiar with modern management approaches and able to critique this distributor's use of traditional management methods. Greater diversity of background might possibly be better—for example, having a financial manager or an owner of another small firm as one of the members.

3. The usefulness of this board will depend on the chairman's ability to draw on the thinking of the outsiders and to tolerate their questions. The chances for success are better if the owner is thoroughly convinced of the importance of this step and not merely excited over a new, hot idea.

   What Actually Happened. With the new directors' help, the chairman installed an operating budget and began drafting a long-term plan. These initial steps represented a move toward modernization of this firm's management.

REF: p. 183 OBJ: YMTC TYPE: C

11. **You Make the Call—Situation 4**
Jeremy Jenkins, who operates a 30-truck freight hauling business in Florida, tries to show what he calls "fairness, firmness, and friendliness" in dealing with employees. The firm's personnel include drivers, mechanics, and clerical and secretarial employees. Jenkins's approach has contributed to an atmosphere of reasonably good employee relationships. However, Jenkins is finding that the paperwork associated with payroll preparation, government regulation, tax reporting, and other personnel matters is becoming burdensome. It is also placing heavy demands on his office staff.

An outside leasing company has offered to take over much of the firm's human resource management work by transferring personnel to its own payroll. The cost would be 3 percent of payroll. Additional benefits and services, including training classes on subjects such as workplace violence and sexual harassment, are available at additional cost. Jenkins is pondering the feasibility of contracting with the leasing company.

Question 1 How can Jenkins be sure that the leasing company is reputable and that he will receive real value for the money?

Question 2 How would transferring employees to the leasing company be likely to affect employee relationships within Jenkins's firm? Will employee loyalty be transferred to the new "employer"?

Question 3 What steps should Jenkins take before entering into an agreement?

ANS:

1. Jenkins should engage in some basic research, such as calling other users of the service and asking about their experiences with the company. He might also gain useful assessments from trade associations and other business groups.
2. Transferring employees to a leasing company is unlikely to have much affect on employee relationships. It shifts the burden of paperwork to the leasing company, but Jenkins' company would still make all decisions regarding hiring, compensation, work assignments, promotions, etc. Employee loyalty will remain with Jenkins' firm since that is where they will continue to work—the transfer will go largely unnoticed by the employees.
3. Jenkins should take the following steps: (1) check out the leasing company, (2) evaluate the benefits to ensure the service is financially beneficial, (3) explain the possibility of the transfer with key employees—emphasizing that it will only affect paperwork, and (4) ask an informed (outside) advisor to look over the agreement. These precautions should help Jenkins avoid a serious misstep when making a final decision regarding employee leasing.

REF: p. 0 OBJ: YMTC TYPE: C

Correlation Table for Chapter 9—The Location Plan

	Learning Objectives	Question Type	Definition Define new term, recall facts	Concept Understand or relate concepts	Application Apply knowledge, analyze data
1	Describe the five key factors in locating the brick-and-mortar startup.	T/F	11	1,3,4,6,7,8,9,10, 12,13,14,16,17, 18,19	2,5,15
		MC	7,15	1,2,3,4,8,9,11,12, 13,14,16,17,18	5,6,10
		ES		1,2	
2	Discuss the challenges of designing and equipping a physical facility.	T/F		20,21,22,25	23,24,26
		MC		19,20,24,25	21,22,23,26
		ES		3,4	
3	Understand both the attraction and the challenges of creating a home-based startup.	T/F		27,28,29,30,31, 32	
		MC	27	28,29,30	31
		ES		5	
4	Understand the potential benefits of locating a startup on the Internet.	T/F	33,50	34,35,36,37,38, 39,40,41,42,43, 44,45,46,47,48, 49	
		MC	32,34,40,44,48, 54,	33,35,36,37,38, 39,41,46,47,49, 50,51,53	42,43,45,52,55
		ES			
	You Make the Call	ES		6,7,8,9	

Total Number of Test Questions: 114 (50 True/False; 55 Multiple-Choice; 9 Essay)

Chapter 9—The Location Plan

TRUE/FALSE

1. For many entrepreneurs, choosing a location for a small business is a one-time decision—made only when the business is first established or purchased.

   ANS: T REF: p. 187 OBJ: 9-1 TYPE: C

2. The site location is more important for a painting contractor than for a dress shop.

   ANS: F
   Given that convenience for customers is more important to retail operations, location will be more important for the dress shop than for the painting contractor.

   REF: p. 187 OBJ: 9-1 TYPE: A

3. Startups in any location will still get off the ground, but long-term performance of the business may be weakened if the location is a poor one.

   ANS: F
   If the choice of a site is particularly poor, the business may never be able to get off the ground, even with adequate financing and superior managerial ability.

   REF: p. 187 OBJ: 9-1 TYPE: C

4. When criteria are evaluated in selecting the location for a new business, one factor may be more important in a given situation, but each factor always has an influence.

   ANS: T REF: p. 188 OBJ: 9-1 TYPE: C

5. Customer accessibility is important in locating an electrical contracting firm.

   ANS: F
   Retails outlets and service firms typically must be located so as to make access convenient for target customers, but this would not be true for an electrical contracting firm.

   REF: p. 188 OBJ: 9-1 TYPE: A

6. All other factors being equal, retail and services businesses will find little advantage in selecting a location near the center of the market.

   ANS: F
   For retail and services firms, one of the foremost considerations in selecting a location should be access to customers, so a central location would be advantageous in most cases.

   REF: p. 188 OBJ: 9-1 TYPE: C

7. In selecting a location, retailers are not all that concerned about customer accessibility.

ANS: F
The primary concern of retailers should be locating so as to make access convenient to customers, since their success depends on a consistent flow of customer traffic.

REF: p. 188 OBJ: 9-1 TYPE: C

8. Customer accessibility is vital in industries in which the cost of shipping the final product is high relative to the product's value.

ANS: T REF: p. 189 OBJ: 9-1 TYPE: C

9. Other factors being equal, new retail and services businesses prefer to locate in areas of declining population.

ANS: F
Because access to potential customers is an important consideration in selecting a location, new retail and services businesses often will not locate in an area of declining population.

REF: p. 189 OBJ: 9-1 TYPE: C

10. Locating close to niche market customers often requires placement at a site that otherwise would be less than desirable.

ANS: T REF: p. 189 OBJ: 9-1 TYPE: C

11. States establish *enterprise zones* in order to locate businesses where they can take advantage of the services of other businesses located in the same general area.

ANS: F
States establish *enterprise zones* in order to bring jobs to economically deprived areas.

REF: p. 189 OBJ: 9-1 TYPE: D

12. Manufacturers are one type of business that must be located conveniently for customers.

ANS: F
It is important for manufacturers to be located near the inputs they use because of the weight of raw materials and the cost of their shipment.

REF: p. 189-190 OBJ: 9-1 TYPE: C

13. The critical factor in locating factories is customer accessibility and convenience.

ANS: F
Manufacturers are mostly concerned with locating near raw materials and suitable labor, not with customer accessibility.

REF: p. 190 OBJ: 9-1 TYPE: C

14. If the cost of shipping the finished product is high, the factory should probably be located near a source of raw materials.

ANS: F
Locating near a source of raw materials is important when these inputs are heavy and costly to ship, but this may not apply to the shipping of the finished products of that firm.

REF: p. 190 OBJ: 9-1 TYPE: C

15. The primary factor in determining the location for a sawmill would probably be proximity to the market.

ANS: F
To be economical, a business like a sawmill should locate near the source of raw materials.

REF: p. 190 OBJ: 9-1 TYPE: A

16. From a practical business standpoint, choosing to locate a business in one's home community offers no advantages.

ANS: F
Locating a business in one's home community can offer several advantages—e.g., understanding the community, establishing credit, friends as customers.

REF: p. 190 OBJ: 9-1 TYPE: C

17. Unfortunately, choosing a hometown location for personal reasons is illogical.

ANS: F
Locating a business in one's home community is not necessarily illogical; in fact, doing so offers certain advantages.

REF: p. 190 OBJ: 9-1 TYPE: C

18. Many entrepreneurs recognize the value of talking to local realtors to determine site availability and appropriateness.

ANS: T REF: p. 191 OBJ: 9-1 TYPE: C

19. Sometimes an attorney can insert special clauses into a lease agreement that will allow the lessee to exit the agreement under certain circumstances.

ANS: T REF: p. 191 OBJ: 9-1 TYPE: C

20. Recent observations have shown that most businesses are started in a new building.

ANS: F
In reality, new businesses are typically started in an existing building with major or minor remodeling.

REF: p. 191 OBJ: 9-2 TYPE: C

21. A building's functional attributes determine its suitability for the operation of a business.

ANS: T REF: p. 192 OBJ: 9-2 TYPE: C

22. Manufacturing equipment can be categorized as general-purpose and special-purpose.

ANS: T REF: p. 193 OBJ: 9-2 TYPE: C

23. Bottling machines and auto assembly line machinery are examples of general-purpose equipment.

ANS: F
Bottling machines and auto assembly line machinery represent two kinds of special-purpose equipment.

REF: p. 193 OBJ: 9-2 TYPE: A

24. A milking machine in a dairy is a type of general-purpose equipment.

ANS: F
A milking machine would be more accurately categorized as a type of special-purpose equipment.

REF: p. 193 OBJ: 9-2 TYPE: A

25. Small retailers need merchandise display racks and other equipment, but these are usually less expensive than that which is required for a factory operation.

ANS: T REF: p. 193 OBJ: 9-2 TYPE: C

26. To maximize sales and profits, a discount shoe store should create an atmosphere similar to that of better department stores, with thick carpets, indirect lighting, and big easy chairs.

ANS: F
Stores that cater to low-income customers should concentrate on simplicity, and the installation of luxury fixtures creates an environment that is inconsistent with low price.

REF: p. 193 OBJ: 9-2 TYPE: A

27. To function successfully, owners of home-based businesses need to establish both spatial and nonspatial boundaries between the business and the home.

ANS: T REF: p. 195 OBJ: 9-3 TYPE: C

28. Juggling the needs of business clients and family members can be so stressful that the home business must be relocated.

ANS: T REF: p. 195 OBJ: 9-3 TYPE: C

29. If they are based in the owner's home, a business must conform to local zoning ordinances.

ANS: T REF: p. 195 OBJ: 9-3 TYPE: C

30. Recent business-application technologies that enable home-based businesses to compete are also contributing to an increase in the number of these firms.

ANS: T REF: p. 196 OBJ: 9-3 TYPE: C

31. Because of its complexity, modern technology has had no noticeable effect in expanding the number of home-based businesses.

ANS: F
Advances in business-application technology have been a major catalyst in the rapid growth of home-based businesses.

REF: p. 196 OBJ: 9-3 TYPE: C

32. Technology now allows long-distance phone calls to be placed over the Internet.

ANS: T REF: p. 196 OBJ: 9-3 TYPE: C

33. A brick-and-mortar store is actually a general term that refers to any retail outlet dealing in building supplies.

ANS: F
A brick-and-mortar store is the traditional physical store from which often operate.

REF: p. 187 OBJ: 9-4 TYPE: D

34. The technical nature of the Internet makes e-commerce too expensive for small firms.

ANS: F
This is obviously not true since many e-commerce sites have been successfully launched with relatively small budgets.

REF: p. 196 OBJ: 9-4 TYPE: C

35. E-commerce is really nothing more than a new way of taking orders, supplementing the capabilities of the phone or fax machine.

ANS: F
A Web site can facilitate the taking of orders, but e-commerce offers much more to both customers and firms.

REF: p. 196 OBJ: 9-4 TYPE: C

36. To be an online success, a firm must be the first to enter a market through the Internet.

ANS: F
The first firm to get involved in a market via the Internet may have an edge in defining and developing that market, but this firm will not necessarily have a monopoly on success.

REF: p. 196 OBJ: 9-4 TYPE: C

37. E-commerce can provide a benefit to small firms by compressing the sales cycle and easing cash flow difficulties.

ANS: T REF: p. 196 OBJ: 9-4 TYPE: C

38. One of the ways that the Internet has impacted small firms is by bringing new life and technology to the management of customer service.

ANS: T REF: p. 196 OBJ: 9-4 TYPE: C

39. The world of e-commerce tends to conform around a few basic business models.

ANS: F
The real world of e-commerce contains endless combinations of business models.

REF: p. 197 OBJ: 9-4 TYPE: C

40. B2B success stories generally receive more publicity than B2C ventures.

ANS: F
Actually, B2B success stories generally receive *less* publicity than B2C ventures, so the potential of the former is often overlooked.

REF: p. 197 OBJ: 9-4 TYPE: C

41. All B2B firms are fairly much alike.

ANS: F
B2B firms can be very different from one another, emphasizing features as varied as sales transactions, building products to customer specifications, auctioning goods and services, etc.

REF: p. 197 OBJ: 9-4 TYPE: C

42. New versions of B2B e-commerce models continue to develop and evolve.

ANS: T REF: p. 0198 OBJ: 9-4 TYPE: C

43. Most of the time, customers go to a brick-and-mortar store with the intent of shopping or purchasing.

ANS: T REF: p. 198 OBJ: 9-4 TYPE: C

44. B2C startups offer only one main advantage over brick-and-mortar retailing—transaction speed.

ANS: F
The B2C model offers three main advantages over brick-and-mortar retailing: speed of access, speed of transaction, and round-the-clock access to products and services.

REF: p. 198 OBJ: 9-4 TYPE: C

45. One of the things that many B2C firms offer is an electronic environment where customers can experience a sense of community.

ANS: T REF: p. 198 OBJ: 9-4 TYPE: C

46. One of the advantages B2C businesses have over traditional retailers is that they can quickly change product mixes and prices, as well as the appearance of the store (that is, the Web site).

ANS: T REF: p. 198 OBJ: 9-4 TYPE: C

47. It is possible for an entrepreneur to do business over the Internet without either a Web site or storefront.

ANS: T REF: p. 198 OBJ: 9-4 TYPE: C

48. In the beginning, the only sources of revenue for online sites were from charges for access and user subscription fees.

ANS: T REF: p. 199 OBJ: 9-4 TYPE: C

49. The role of a Web site can range from merely offering content and information to enabling complex business transactions.

ANS: T REF: p. 198 OBJ: 9-4 TYPE: C

50. One of the extensions of the brick-and-mortar store is the contact-and-mortar strategy.

ANS: F
The click-and-mortar strategy is an extension of the brick-and-mortar store.

REF: p. 199 OBJ: 9-4 TYPE: D

MULTIPLE CHOICE

1. Which of the following is a true statement about location decisions?
   a. Franchisers never assist entrepreneurs with location decisions.
   b. Location decisions have an enduring effect on business operations.
   c. Location decisions should be made independently of consumer needs.
   d. The location decision is equally critical to all types of businesses.

   ANS: B REF: p. 187 OBJ: 9-1 TYPE: C

2. A good reason for relocating a typical manufacturing business is to
   a. stabilize income taxes.
   b. increase customer traffic.
   c. get closer to raw materials.
   d. provide free-flow space.

   ANS: C REF: p. 190 OBJ: 9-1 TYPE: C

3. Site-related factors that should be taken into consideration when one is selecting a retail location include
   a. future advertising costs.
   b. the labor supply.
   c. raw material availability.
   d. customer accessibility.

   ANS: D REF: p. 188 OBJ: 9-1 TYPE: C

4. For small service or retail businesses, the top priority in location decisions is
   a. personal preference.
   b. resource availability.
   c. customer accessibility.
   d. environmental conditions.

   ANS: C REF: p. 189 OBJ: 9-1 TYPE: C

5. Customer accessibility is the most critical factor in evaluating a specific site for a
   a. clothing manufacturer.
   b. drugstore.
   c. plumber.
   d. software development company.

   ANS: B REF: p. 189 OBJ: 9-1 TYPE: A

6. Roger Hemingway is analyzing regional differences in seeking a location for a new firm. He just read a *Wall Street Journal* article that ranked states according to the favorability of tax laws. Based on this information, he has decided to give further attention to one of the best states, which is
   a. Wyoming.
   b. Massachusetts.
   c. Ohio.
   d. New York.

   ANS: A REF: p. 189 OBJ: 9-1 TYPE: A

7. Which of the following is an initiative of the U.S. government to assist small firms?
   a. Inspire America!
   b. The Small Business Administration's Expanding Enterprise program
   c. Empowerment Zones/Enterprise Communities
   d. Coalition for Commerce

   ANS: C REF: p. 189 OBJ: 9-1 TYPE: D

8. Which of the following is *not* an environmental condition affecting selection of a business location?
   a. Competition
   b. Weather and climate
   c. Laws and regulations
   d. Raw material availability

   ANS: D REF: p. 189 OBJ: 9-1 TYPE: C

9. Basic considerations that enter into the selection of a location for a manufacturing business normally include
   a. availability of raw materials.
   b. customer accessibility.
   c. neighborhood conditions.
   d. federal income taxes.

   ANS: A REF: p. 189 OBJ: 9-1 TYPE: C

10. In a location decision, the raw materials availability factor is particularly important for a

a. CPA.
b. manufacturer.
c. management consultant.
d. venture capitalist.

ANS: B REF: p. 189 OBJ: 9-1 TYPE: A

11. For manufacturers, which of the following is a top priority in location decisions?
a. Personal preference
b. Environmental conditions
c. Closeness to raw materials
d. Customer accessibility

ANS: C REF: p. 189 OBJ: 9-1 TYPE: C

12. Personal reasons for choosing one's hometown as a location for a new business venture include the fact that
a. the entrepreneur knows the landmarks around his or her home community.
b. credit can be established more easily.
c. friends and relatives line up new customers.
d. this reduces the risk of operations.

ANS: B REF: p. 191 OBJ: 9-1 TYPE: C

13. Which of the following is *not* a potential advantage of establishing a small business in one's home community?
a. Appreciation of the atmosphere of the community
b. More extensive knowledge of consumer tastes
c. Greater ability to establish favorable credit arrangements
d. Increased stability of operations

ANS: D REF: p. 191 OBJ: 9-1 TYPE: C

14. A new business might best begin
a. in a foreign country.
b. in a business incubator.
c. in the classroom setting.
d. at the start of a tax year.

ANS: B REF: p. 191 OBJ: 9-1 TYPE: C

15. Facilities that rent space only to new businesses and that provide services for them are called
a. industrial parks.
b. community development centers.
c. shopping centers.
d. business incubators.

ANS: D REF: p. 191 OBJ: 9-1 TYPE: D

16. One of the greatest contributions that incubator facilities provide to small businesses include
a. shared manufacturing space.
b. postal services.
c. management assistance.

d. university sponsorship.

ANS: C REF: p. 191 OBJ: 9-1 TYPE: C

17. The primary advantage an entrepreneur gains by leasing rather than buying facilities is
    a. receipt of an investment tax credit.
    b. a decrease in investment risk.
    c. a decrease in the amount of promotion required.
    d. a customized layout.

ANS: B REF: p. 191 OBJ: 9-1 TYPE: C

18. For many new firms, the most important reason to lease rather than buy a facility is
    a. avoidance of a large cash outlay.
    b. freedom in modifying the building.
    c. avoidance of interest payments.
    d. avoidance of liability lawsuits.

ANS: A REF: p. 191 OBJ: 9-1 TYPE: C

19. The functional requirements of a business should determine the
    a. geographic location of the business.
    b. suitability of a building.
    c. labor requirements.
    d. spatial requirements.

ANS: B REF: p. 192 OBJ: 9-2 TYPE: C

20. Which of the following layouts arranges special-purpose equipment along a production line in the sequence in which it is used?
    a. Product layout
    b. Process layout
    c. Free-flow layout
    d. Self-service layout

ANS: A REF: p. 193 OBJ: 9-2 TYPE: C

21. Drill presses or lathes would be grouped together in a
    a. process layout.
    b. product layout.
    c. grid layout.
    d. continuous-flow layout.

ANS: A REF: p. 193 OBJ: 9-2 TYPE: A

22. An example of special-purpose equipment is a
    a. lathe.
    b. bottling machine.
    c. drill press.
    d. ripsaw.

ANS: B REF: p. 193 OBJ: 9-2 TYPE: A

23. Harry Hardwick is starting a job-order machine shop and is buying such used equipment as lathes, planing mills, and drill presses. The equipment he plans to use is
    a. special-purpose equipment.
    b. automated equipment.
    c. general-purpose equipment.
    d. product-layout equipment.

    ANS: C REF: p. 193 OBJ: 9-2 TYPE: A

24. Special-purpose equipment is generally difficult for small manufacturers to use unless
    a. the plant has mostly short production runs.
    b. the plant produces a standardized product in a large enough volume.
    c. the plant is set up in a process layout.
    d. the plant can be used for multiple purposes.

    ANS: B REF: p. 193 OBJ: 9-2 TYPE: C

25. Using special-purpose equipment in the manufacturing process typically results in
    a. increased operator errors.
    b. higher costs of processing.
    c. a rise in accident rates.
    d. greater output per machine-hour of operation.

    ANS: D REF: p. 193 OBJ: 9-2 TYPE: C

26. Helen Artz is planning to open a high-fashion clothing store for young professional women. She knows that the fixtures she acquires for the store should be
    a. economical.
    b. elegant.
    c. practical.
    d. feminine.

    ANS: B REF: p.193 OBJ: 9-2 TYPE: A

27. A home-based business is one located in
    a. a local area of family-occupied houses.
    b. the city of the business owner.
    c. the city recognized as the industry home, where similar businesses are located.
    d. the owner's personal residence.

    ANS: D REF: p. 193 OBJ: 9-3 TYPE: D

28. Businesses that operate in the home
    a. can increase profits by decreasing costs.
    b. require customer traffic.
    c. are called family businesses.
    d. are less common today than they were 10 years ago.

    ANS: A REF: p. 194 OBJ: 9-3 TYPE: C

29. Operating a home-based business successfully requires that the owner
    a. change locations when the business is over one year old.
    b. make a cost analysis that clearly divides costs between the business and the home.

c. establish spatial and nonspatial boundaries between the business and the home.
d. keep the baby at home while working.

ANS: C REF: p. 195 OBJ: 9-3 TYPE: C

30. The owner of a home-based business can establish boundaries between the business and the home by
a. setting aside specific space for the business.
b. using an outside bookkeeping service.
c. selling to wholesalers rather than to ultimate consumers.
d. limiting his or her participation in community activities.

ANS: A REF: p. 195 OBJ: 9-3 TYPE: C

31. A woman is planning to establish a business in her residence. In order to maintain a proper balance between family and business matters, she should
a. establish spatial and nonspatial boundaries.
b. design a business-style letterhead that gives no hint of a home location.
c. buy an answering machine.
d. install a computer with a modem.

ANS: A REF: p. 195 OBJ: 9-3 TYPE: A

32. E-commerce refers to
a. B2B models of doing business.
b. the facilitation of business by making initial contact by electronic means.
c. the paperless exchange of business information via the Internet.
d. a form of business that involves online trades and auctions.

ANS: C REF: p. 196 OBJ: 9-4 TYPE: D

33. The Internet provides an alternative to
a. bricks-and-mortar stores.
b. clicks-and-mortar strategies.
c. B2B businesses.
d. B2C businesses.

ANS: A REF: p. 196 OBJ: 9-4 TYPE: C

34. The traditional physical store is sometimes referred to as the ________________ store.
a. classic commerce
b. real experience
c. tangible alternative
d. bricks-and-mortar

ANS: D REF: p. 187 OBJ: 9-4 TYPE: D

35. E-commerce innovators
a. have an extra edge in defining and developing a market.
b. automatically have a monopoly on success.
c. are few and far between.
d. are almost all out of business today.

ANS: A REF: p. 196 OBJ: 9-4 TYPE: C

36. Why does electronic commerce benefit small firms?
    a. Small firms are often "tech savvy", which allows them to embrace innovations more quickly.
    b. Large firms have complex business plans that fail to direct investment toward the Internet.
    c. Without e-commerce, small firms often lack the resources to expand beyond local markets.
    d. The government has committed significant resources to encourage small firms to go online.

    ANS: C REF: p. 196 OBJ: 9-4 TYPE: C

37. For small businesses, the Internet tends to blur ____________ boundaries.
    a. industry
    b. geographic
    c. skill-dependent
    d. technological

    ANS: B REF: p. 196 OBJ: 9-4 TYPE: C

38. The Internet has brought new life and technology to the old-fashioned notion of
    a. customer service.
    b. the "push sell".
    c. the firm's production orientation.
    d. strategic management.

    ANS: A REF: p. 197 OBJ: 9-4 TYPE: C

39. The heart of Electronic Customer Relationship Marketing is a
    a. focus on customization.
    b. conscientious work force.
    c. flexible distribution system.
    d. consumer-centric data warehouse.

    ANS: D REF: p. 197 OBJ: 9-4 TYPE: C

40. A group of shared characteristics, behaviors, and goals that a firm follows in a particular business situation is known as a
    a. business model.
    b. strategic plan.
    c. firm strategy.
    d. business profile.

    ANS: A REF: p. 197 OBJ: 9-4 TYPE: D

41. Which of the following is *not* one of the major categories of e-commerce businesses?
    a. Consumer-to-business
    b. Business-to-consumer
    c. Business-to-business
    d. Auction sites

    ANS: A REF: p. 197-198 OBJ: 9-4 TYPE: C

42. Dell Computer Corporation deals directly with corporate customers online and builds computers to specifications *after* an order is placed, which reduces the firm's storage and carrying costs. This illustrates that B2B firms can create
    a. greater efficiency in their selling.
    b. greater efficiency it their buying.
    c. synergies between buying and selling.
    d. market reach through e-commerce.

    ANS: A REF: p. 198 OBJ: 9-4 TYPE: A

43. John Pearson created Acme Online to allow paper suppliers to compete for manufacturers' orders over the Internet in live auctions. This model would best be described as
    a. consumer-to-business.
    b. business-to-consumer.
    c. business-to-business.
    d. consumer-to-consumer.

    ANS: C REF: p. 197 OBJ: 9-4 TYPE: A

44. In the B2B model, the customers can best be described as
    a. businesses.
    b. consumers.
    c. franchisees.
    d. auction participants.

    ANS: A REF: p. 197 OBJ: 9-4 TYPE: D

45. Amazon.com represents the classic ______ firm.
    a. B2B
    b. B2C
    c. C2C
    d. online auction

    ANS: B REF: p. 198 OBJ: 9-4 TYPE: A

46. Which of the following is *not* one of the advantages B2C models have over bricks-and-mortar retailing?
    a. Speed of access
    b. Speed of transaction
    c. 24/7 service
    d. Superior customer service

    ANS: D REF: p. 198 OBJ: 9-4 TYPE: C

47. Customers who avoid doing business online are often reluctant to do this because
    a. they have had a bad online purchase experience in the past.
    b. it is difficult to predict how much time it will take to ship the product.
    c. Web sites are difficult to navigate.
    d. they are reluctant to purchase a product without first seeing it.

    ANS: D REF: p. 198 OBJ: 9-4 TYPE: C

48. Web-based businesses that provide customers with the ability to list products for potential buyers are called

a. Internet auction sites.
b. B2B sites.
c. B2C sites.
d. C2B sites.

ANS: A REF: p. 198 OBJ: 9-4 TYPE: D

49. Revenues from auction sites are derived for the most part from
a. banner ads.
b. listing fees and commissions on sales.
c. corporate sponsors.
d. investors.

ANS: B REF: p. 198 OBJ: 9-4 TYPE: C

50. One costly process that can often be performed more cheaply online is
a. management distribution.
b. providing information to customers in a timely fashion.
c. locating new employees.
d. identifying emerging technologies.

ANS: B REF: p. 198-199 OBJ: 9-4 TYPE: C

51. B2B firms, in particular, use e-commerce to reduce costs associated with
a. sales force management.
b. inventory processing.
c. product distribution.
d. customer contact.

ANS: A REF: p. 197 OBJ: 9-4 TYPE: C

52. Amazon.com and other firms like it appear to be establishing customer relationships on the Web
a. because these provide a positive cash flow to the company.
b. to measure the potential of market interest.
c. with the hope of cashing in on these at a later date.
d. with increasing ease.

ANS: C REF: p. 198 OBJ: 9-4 TYPE: A

53. During the early days of e-commerce, the model of choice was based on
a. sales.
b. content.
c. advertising information.
d. market identification.

ANS: B REF: p. 198 OBJ: 9-4 TYPE: C

54. A variation of the content model is sometimes called the __________ model.
a. information
b. sales
c. advertising detail
d. market identification

ANS: A REF: p. 198 OBJ: 9-4 TYPE: D

55. Steve Evans started a Web-based business offering a mechanism for buying and selling antiques. Evans has set up his company using the ____________ model.
    a. transaction-based
    b. content-based
    c. information-based
    d. premium-based

    ANS: A REF: p. 199 OBJ: 9-4 TYPE: A

ESSAY

1. In deciding on the location for a business, the entrepreneur must consider five major factors. Identify these factors and briefly summarize the impact each factor has on the entrepreneur's decision.

   ANS:
   - *Entrepreneur's Personal preference*. Advantages of locating in the home community include appreciation of the atmosphere, ability to establish credit, and familiarity with bankers and potential customers.
   - *Environmental business conditions*. Competition, laws, and tax structures may affect location decisions.
   - *Resource availability*. Land, water supply, labor supply, transportation facilities, raw materials, and waste disposal bear on location costs. Resource availability is especially important for manufacturers.
   - *Customer accessibility*. This factor is especially important to retailers and service firms.
   - *Availability and costs of sites*. Cost-saving alternatives include the use of shared facilities (e.g., business incubators, executive suites) and facility leasing (which also reduce cash outlay and investment risk).

   REF: p. 187 OBJ: 9-1 TYPE: C

2. List and describe the critical resource considerations that should guide the location decision?

   ANS:
   Factors that might be cited include the following:
   - *Closeness to Raw Materials*. If required raw materials are not abundantly available in all areas, the areas in which they are abundant may offer special locational advantages, especially if the firm's operations transform heavy or bulky raw materials into product that are easy to transport.
   - *Suitability of the labor supply*. Depending upon the nature of its production process, a firm's labor may need to examine labor factors such as availability, wage rates, productivity, and labor relations.
   - *Availability of transportation*. Retailers must consider the ability of customers to travel to its outlets and manufacturers should assess its ability to ship goods from a given location.

   REF: p. 190 OBJ: 9-1 TYPE: C

3. List an discuss the challenges that entrepreneurs face in designing the physical facilities for their businesses.

ANS:
When specifying building requirements, the entrepreneur must avoid committing to a space that is too large or too luxurious. At the same time, the space should not be too small or too austere for efficient operation. Buildings do not produce profits directly; they merely house the operations and personnel that do so. Therefore, the ideal building is practical, not pretentious.

The general suitability of a building for a given type of business operation depends on the functional requirements of the business. For example, a restaurant should ideally be on one level. Other important factors are the age and condition of the building, fire hazards, heating and air conditioning, lighting and restroom facilities, and entrances and exits. Obviously, these factors are weighted differently for a factory operation than for a wholesale or retail operation. But in any case, the comfort, convenience, and safety of the business's employees and customers must not be overlooked.

REF: p. 192 OBJ: 9-2 TYPE: C

4. Distinguish between general-purpose and special-purpose equipment in a factory setting, and cite the advantages of each.

ANS:
General-purpose equipment consists of machines that can be used in a variety of ways. Examples are lathes, drill presses, saws, and hand tools. Their advantage is flexibility. A job-order shop, for example, needs this type of equipment.

Special-purpose equipment, on the other hand, performs a specific function, such as filling bottles. It lacks flexibility and is appropriate for processes involving large production runs. Most small businesses are unable to use this equipment because they are not engaged in mass production.

REF: p. 193 OBJ: 9-2 TYPE: C

5. List and explain the attractions and challenges of operating a home-based business.

ANS:
Attractions include financial considerations (increasing profits by reducing costs) and family lifestyle considerations (to spend more time around family members). Challenges include managing family/business conflicts (business and family activities that interfere with one another), preserving the firm's business image (maintaining an image of professionalism at the home when clients visit), and dealing with legal issues (avoiding zoning ordinance violations, complying with tax regulations, obtaining appropriate insurance coverage).

REF: p. 194-195 OBJ: 9-3 TYPE: C

6. **You Make the Call—Situation 1**
Gary Fuller and his wife, Kelly Kimberly, have a dream of owning a successful restaurant. Three and a half years ago, Fuller was vice president of operations for a Cincinnati Bell affiliate; Kimberly was a public relations consultant. Now, they are considering a startup venture in Houston, Texas.

Early in their research, they uncovered some discouraging statistics about the restaurant industry: Profit margins run about 1 to 5 percent; one in three new restaurants don't last a year; and, because of the current economy, plans for new restaurants have been shelved by many existing companies. One industry consultant they contacted said the cost of setting up an average restaurant, like a diner, is around $300 per square foot—excluding property costs.

Source: Emily Lambert, "No Free Lunch," *Forbes,* Vol. 171, No. 12 (June 9, 2003), p. 154.

Question 1 How important will the location decision be to these two entrepreneurs? Why?
Question 2 What types of permits and zoning ordinances might they need to consider if they decide to pursue their dream?
Question 3 How could a presence on the Internet help with the success of this venture?

ANS:

1. Restaurants need customers and the "right" kind of customers to survive. Customer accessibility is always important to a restaurant. This means that the location decision may be the single decision that determines whether or not the entrepreneurs have a chance to be successful! Unless there are plans to operate a really unique restaurant that will attract customers from far away, then the restaurant is going to need to be where there is high traffic—either car or foot.
2. There will likely be a number of local permits to be obtained for this type of business. The local Health Department will most likely be involved fostering sanitary food preparation. If a new building is constructed, then a number of building permits will be needed. Certain areas may not be served this will also require a permit. Certain areas may not be zoned to permit the restaurant to operate. This will, of course, eliminate some sites from consideration.
3. The site can be used to generate excitement about dining at the restaurant and also communicate what kinds and assortments of foods are available. Also, the site can provide telephone numbers for reservations and maps for travel for those unfamiliar with the area. Any awards that the restaurant may receive can be publicized on the site.

REF: p. 201 OBJ: YMTC TYPE: C

7. **You Make the Call—Situation 2**

Estate Administrators and Liquidators is based in Sacramento, California, and is owned and operated by entrepreneur Sally Wheeler-Valine. Since 1990, the firm has served people seeking to sell the household goods of deceased friends or relatives.

The business auctions items at the deceased person's home, splitting the proceeds with the family. Any unsold items are taken back to the firm's store and sold, generating a commission based on the selling price.

To accommodate the large volume of merchandise she sells, Wheeler-Valine operates out of a new 13,000-squarefoot store. Business revenues climbed for several years, peaking in 1997. However, in 1999, revenues slumped drastically.

Source: Based on a story by Susan Hanson, "Store's Demise Blamed on Web Auctions," *Inc.*, July 2000, p. 41.

Question 1 What impact, if any, do you think that Internet-based businesses have had on Wheeler-Valine's business?
Question 2 In what way(s) could she use e-commerce to grow her business?
Question 3 How much presence on the Web, if any, do you think she should consider?
Question 4 What do you think will happen to this firm if it ignores the Internet?

ANS:

1. It would be easy to blame the drop in her firm's revenues on Internet competition, especially in light of comments Sally received from some of her old customers, saying they can more easily bid on the products they want through eBay than going to her auctions. However, there may be other issues that explain her problems. Since she travels to the home of the deceased to conduct the on-site sale, her expenses may be higher than normal and therefore her prices (the commission she gets) are probably high. This may be impacting demand for her services. She also takes all unsold items from the auctions back to her store for sale on consignment. The expense of maintaining the brick and mortar store has been substantial.
2. As noted in this chapter, the Internet offers different types of opportunities to the entrepreneur. For example, one can use the Internet for e-commerce by providing information to existing customers and potential new customers. Sally might want to consider a Web site, which would be a source of information for people who are seeking out on-site auctions that they might attend as buyers. She might also use the Internet as a means to locate those individuals who would like to have an estate auction conducted by someone like Sally.
3. Sally did get "her feet wet" on the Web by selling a few bowls, figurines, and vases on eBay, but she was not impressed with the results. The time required to prepare photos and descriptions to post alongside her offerings, plus the effort to respond to prospective buyers' e-mail inquires, was more trouble than she thought it was worth. However, providing a web site for informational purposes might end up being the full extent of her presence on the web.
4. To completely ignore the Internet would be a mistake. The greater issue is to decide the degree of online presence she wants. Sally needs to find someone to show her how the business can benefit, which would be likely to get her excited about its potential for her business.

   Concluding Note The business Estate Administrators was first opened in 1990. The plummet in sales was apparently too much for the firm to continue operations as they were, and Sally apparently didn't have a desire to establish an Internet site, so the business closed in 2000. One analyst says this was the result of Internet competition, or it may be that her prices were too high.

REF: p. 201 OBJ: YMTC TYPE: C

8. **You Make the Call—Situation 3**

A business incubator rents space to a number of small firms that are just beginning operations or are fairly new. In addition to supplying space, the incubator provides a receptionist, computer, conference room, fax machine, and copy machine. It also offers management counseling and assists new businesses in getting reduced advertising rates and reduced legal fees. One client of the incubator is a jewelry repair, cleaning, and remounting service that does work on a contract basis for pawn shops and jewelry stores. Another is a home health-care company that employs a staff of nurses to visit the homes of elderly people who need daily care but who cannot afford or are not yet ready to go to a nursing home.

Question 1 Evaluate each of the services offered by the incubator in terms of its usefulness to these two businesses. Which of the two businesses seems to be a better fit for the incubator? Why?

Question 2 If rental costs for incubator space were similar to rental costs for space outside the incubator, would the benefits of the services offered seem to favor location in the incubator? Why or why not?

ANS:

1. Assuming the receptionist answers the telephone, this service can be of value to both businesses. Having someone answer the telephone is usually superior to using an answering machine. It seems unlikely that either business would derive much benefit from use of the conference room or fax machine. No doubt the copy machine would have its advantages. Also, the computer might be useful for billing, maintaining customer records, and so on. The greatest potential advantage would seem to lie in the management counseling that is available. If it is of good quality, it could be of immense value in helping these businesses get off to a good start. The jewelry business may be basically the work of a tradesperson. Therefore, the home health-care firm would probably be the better fit.
2. The services make this location advantageous, particularly for the home health-care company.

REF: p. 201-202 OBJ: YMTC TYPE: C

9. **You Make the Call—Situation 4**

Entrepreneur Karen Moore wants to start a catering and decorating business to bring in money to help support her two young children. Moore is a single parent; she works in the banking industry but has always had the desire to start a business. She enjoys decorating for friends' parties and is frequently told, "You should do this professionally. You have such good taste, and you are so nice to people."

Moore has decided to take this advice but is unsure whether she should locate in a commercial site or in her home, which is in rural central Texas. She is leaning toward locating at home because she wants more time with her children. However, she is concerned that the home-based location is too far away from the city, where most of her potential customers live.

Initially, her services would include planning for wedding receptions and other special events, designing flower arrangements, decorating the sites, and even cooking and serving meals.

Question 1 What do you see as potential problems with locating Moore's new business at home?

Question 2 What do you see as the major benefits for Moore of a home-based business?

Question 3 How could Moore use technology to help her operate a home-based business?

ANS:

1. One of the drawbacks of operating a business from the home is the potential conflict between business demands and parental responsibilities. For example, Moore's children may find it difficult to understand why their mother turns her attention away from them whenever the phone rings. Creating a sense of spatial and nonspatial boundaries may help with this. Home-based businesses also find that it is difficult to maintain an appropriate business image, but this could be minimized in Moore's case if she establishes a professional image in all phone contact with clients and schedules consultations on-site (rather than at the home) whenever possible. Home-based businesses must also consider legal restrictions (e.g., zoning ordinances) since these can present a hurdle to the entrepreneur—an unlikely impediment in Moore's case since she lives in a rural location. Finally, Moore will need to consider the location decision in general if her home is so far away from her target market that it makes business contact impractical.
2. One of the obvious benefits to a home-based business in this case is that it would permit Moore to spend more time with her children, which is important to her. Beyond this, locating at home would also reduce costs significantly by eliminating the need to rent office space. This is very important when the entrepreneur is starting the business "on a shoestring" and does not have an established client base to get revenues flowing quickly, as appears to be the case in this situation.

3. Advancements in technology help to blur the perceptual distinctions between home-based and other businesses. Personal computers, fax machines, e-mail, voice mail, and other technological tools are sure to prove helpful in this situation. Moore should be certain to obtain a personal computer to keep track of business receipts and disbursements and establish an e-mail address to maintain contact with current and potential clients. At little additional cost, she could also purchase Internet access and post a Web site to promote her business and provide information (e.g., available services and prices) that customer would find helpful.

REF: p. 202 OBJ: YMTC TYPE: C

10. **You Make the Call—Situation 5**

Sam Doster is struggling to make ends meet or at least get them closer together. After retiring from a military career, he completed his business degree at a local college and, with the encouragement and support of his parents, started a travel agency. Deregulation of the airline industry and the events of 9/11 have severely reduced his agency's cash flows. Sam is considering closing the agency's office to reduce overhead costs and moving entirely to an internet-based business that he could operate from his home.

Question 1 What are the advantages for Sam in moving to an internet-based business at home?

Question 2 How will moving to internet -based business affect the level of customer service for the type of business that Sam is operating?

ANS:

1. Electronic commerce benefits a startup in a number of ways. Basically, it offers the new firm the opportunity to compete with bigger businesses on a more level playing field. Limited resources frequently restrict the ability of small firms to reach beyond local markets. Confined to their brick-and-mortar world, small firms typically serve a restricted geographic area. But the Internet blurs geographic boundaries. E-commerce allows any business access to customers almost anywhere. The Internet is a great equalizer, giving small firms a presence comparable to that of the giants in the marketplace.

   An e-commerce operation can help Sam with cash flow problems by compressing the sales cycle—that is, reducing the time between receiving an order and converting the sale to cash. E-commerce systems can be designed to generate an order, authorize a credit card purchase, and contact a supplier and shipper in a matter of minutes, all without human assistance. The shorter cycle translates into quicker payments from customers and improved cash flows to the business.

2. E-commerce enables small firms to build on one of their greatest strengths—customer relationships. The Internet has brought new life and technology to bear on the old-fashioned notion of customer service. Sam will need to become proficient in **Electronic Customer Relationship Marketing (eCRM).** A typical eCRM system allows an e-commerce firm to integrate data from Web sites, call centers, sales force reports, and other customer contact points, with the goal of building customer loyalty.

REF: p. 202 OBJ: YMTC TYPE: C

Correlation Table for Chapter 10—The Financial Plan Part 1: Projecting Financial Requirements

	Learning Objectives	Question Type	Definition Define new term, recall facts	Concept Understand or relate concepts	Application Apply knowledge, analyze data
1	Describe the purpose and content of the income statement, the balance sheet, and the cash flow statement.	T/F	1,2,3,4,7,8,9,10, 14	5,11,12,13,15	6
		MC	1,11,13,23	2,3,4,5,6,7,8,9, 10,12,14,15,16, 22,24,27.28	17,18,19,20,21, 25,26
		ES	1,2		
2	Forecast a new venture's profitability.	T/F		16,17,18,19,20	
		MC	29,37	30,31,32,33,34, 35,36,	
		ES		3	
3	Determine asset requirements, evaluate financial sources, and estimate cash flows for a new venture.	T/F	25	21,22,23,24,26, 27,28,29,30	
		MC		38,39,41,42,43, 44,45,46	40,47,48
		ES		5	4
4	Explain the importance of using good judgment when making projections.	T/F			
		MC	50	49	
		ES			
	You Make the Call	ES		7,9	6,8

Total Number of Test Questions: 89 (30 True/False; 50 Multiple-Choice; 9 Essay)

Chapter 10—The Financial Plan: Part 1

TRUE/FALSE

1. The income statement shows a firm's financial position on a specific date.

   ANS: F
   The income statement indicates the amount of profits generated by a firm *over a given period of time*, often one year.

   REF: p. 205 OBJ: 10-1 TYPE: D

2. The income statement shows the profit or loss from a firm's operations over a given period of time.

   ANS: T REF: p. 205 OBJ: 10-1 TYPE: D

3. The income statement answers the question: "How profitable is the business?"

   ANS: T REF: p. 205 OBJ: 10-1 TYPE: D

4. The balance sheet shows a firm's assets, liabilities, and owners' equity at a specific point in time.

   ANS: T REF: p. 208 OBJ: 10-1 TYPE: D

5. Total assets less outstanding debt must always equal ownership equity.

   ANS: T REF: p. 208 OBJ: 10-1 TYPE: C

6. Jan Woodring is considering investing in a business. To see the firm's financial position over a period of time, she should look at its balance sheet.

   ANS: F
   An income statement reflects the firm's position *over a period of time*, whereas a balance sheet provides a snapshot of a firm's financial position *at a given point in time*.

   REF: p. 205 OBJ: 10-1 TYPE: A

7. Accounts payable consist of payments due from a firm's customers.

   ANS: F
   It is accounts *receivable* that consist of payments due from a firm's customers.

   REF: p. 209 OBJ: 10-1 TYPE: D

8. Inventory is a relatively permanent asset that is intended for use in the business rather than for sale.

   ANS: F
   Inventory consists of the raw materials and products held by the firm for eventual sale, so this is not a permanent asset in any way.

REF: p. 209 OBJ: 10-1 TYPE: D

9. Accounts payable, accrued expenses, 5-year notes payable, and 90-day notes are short-term liabilities.

ANS: F
Short-term liabilities would not include 5-year notes payable because debt due in more than 12 months is considered *long-term* debt.

REF: p. 211 OBJ: 10-1 TYPE: D

10. The money that owners invest in the business is called *owners' equity.*

ANS: T REF: p. 211 OBJ: 10-1 TYPE: D

11. The major difference between cash-basis accounting and accrual-basis accounting lies in when the firm recognizes revenue and profits.

ANS: T REF: p. 213 OBJ: 10-1 TYPE: C

12. A new business needs to manage cash flows carefully because if a firm runs out of cash, it is out of business.

ANS: T REF: p. 213 OBJ: 10-1 TYPE: C

13. Entrepreneurs should learn how to compute and interpret cash flows, because a business can fail from lack of cash flows even if it is profitable.

ANS: T REF: p. 213 OBJ: 10-1 TYPE: C

14. Cash flows that investors either provide to or receive from the business are called *cash flows from owners' equity.*

ANS: F
These are called *cash flows from financing*, not *cash flows from owners' equity.*

REF: p. 216 OBJ: 10-1 TYPE: D

15. If entrepreneurs are to calculate the small firm's cash flows from assets, they should ask what causes the cash flows within their business to occur.

ANS: T REF: p. 213 OBJ: 10-1 TYPE: C

16. Financial projections are just a management frill.

ANS: F
Financial projections are not just a management frill—they stand at the heart of effective management.

REF: p. 217 OBJ: 10-2 TYPE: C

17. A profitable company does not necessarily have positive cash flows.

ANS: T REF: p. 212 OBJ: 10-2 TYPE: C

18. Profits reward owners for investing in a company, but they do little to promote future growth.

ANS: F
Profits are a primary source of financing to support future growth.

REF: p. 218 OBJ: 10-2 TYPE: C

19. A small business owner can calculate the interest expense of the company for each year by multiplying the interest rate by the amount of debt outstanding.

ANS: T REF: p. 219 OBJ: 10-2 TYPE: C

20. In a real-world situation, an entrepreneur should project the profits of a new company one to three years into the future.

ANS: F
The textbook recommends that an entrepreneur project profits three to five years into the future.

REF: p. 219 OBJ: 10-2 TYPE: C

21. The entrepreneur has great control over a new venture, making it easier to estimate capital requirements.

ANS: F
The uncertainties surrounding an entirely new venture makes estimating capital requirements difficult.

REF: p. 217 OBJ: 10-3 TYPE: C

22. High-tech ventures usually require more initial financing than service businesses.

ANS: T REF: p. 219 OBJ: 10-3 TYPE: C

23. A firm's distribution network is the primary driving force behind future asset needs.

ANS: F
The firm's sales are the primary driving force behind future asset needs.

REF: p. 221 OBJ: 10-3 TYPE: C

24. Ratio analysis is a useful approach to estimating asset requirements.

ANS: T REF: p. 221 OBJ: 10-3 TYPE: C

25. Liquidity represents the degree to which a firm can meet maturing short-term debt obligations with available working capital.

ANS: T REF: p. 223 OBJ: 10-3 TYPE: D

26. A common weakness in small business financing is the disproportionately small investment in fixed assets relative to current assets.

ANS: F
A common weakness in small business financing is the disproportionately small investment in *current* assets relative to *fixed* assets.

REF: p. 223 OBJ: 10-3 TYPE: C

27. A conventional measure of a firm's liquidity is a comparison of current assets to current liabilities.

ANS: T REF: p. 223 OBJ: 10-3 TYPE: C

28. Equity capital is derived only from sources external to the firm.

ANS: F
Equity capital can come from internal (e.g., profits from operations) and external (e.g., investor) sources.

REF: p. 224 OBJ: 10-3 TYPE: C

29. Total asset requirements must equal total sources of financing.

ANS: T REF: p. 224 OBJ: 10-3 TYPE: C

30. If a new venture's projected profit margins do not substantially exceed the reported profit margins of comparable businesses, investors are likely to doubt these projections.

ANS: F
Profit margin projections are suspect if they greatly exceed or fall far below industry norms.

REF: p. 227 OBJ: 10-3 TYPE: C

MULTIPLE CHOICE

1. The _____ shows the results of a firm's operations over a period of time, usually one year.
   a. income statement
   b. balance sheet
   c. statement of cash flow
   d. statement of financial position

ANS: A REF: p. 205 OBJ: 10-1 TYPE: D

2. Earnings before taxes are computed by deducting the firm's financing costs from its ______ income.
   a. total
   b. projected
   c. net
   d. operating

ANS: D REF: p. 205 OBJ: 10-1 TYPE: C

3. An example of a current asset is
   a. land.
   b. inventories.
   c. equipment.
   d. buildings.

ANS: B REF: p. 208 OBJ: 10-1 TYPE: C

4. An example of a current asset is
   a. equipment.
   b. land.
   c. leased property.
   d. accounts receivable.

ANS: D REF: p. 208 OBJ: 10-1 TYPE: C

5. Net working capital includes
   a. accounts receivable.
   b. leased property.
   c. stockholders' equity.
   d. equipment.

ANS: A REF: p. 215 OBJ: 10-1 TYPE: C

6. Assets that are relatively liquid are classified as
   a. current assets.
   b. fixed assets.
   c. short-term assets.
   d. other assets.

ANS: A REF: p. 208 OBJ: 10-1 TYPE: C

7. An example of a fixed asset is
   a. a delivery truck for sale by an automotive dealer.
   b. inventory.
   c. a delivery truck used by a grocer to deliver merchandise to customers.
   d. short-term investments in stock.

ANS: C REF: p. 209 OBJ: 10-1 TYPE: C

8. Fixed assets include
   a. land.
   b. copyrights.
   c. contingency funds.
   d. goodwill.

ANS: A REF: p. 209 OBJ: 10-1 TYPE: C

9. *Other assets* include
   a. land.
   b. machinery.
   c. contingency funds.
   d. goodwill.

ANS: D REF: p. 210 OBJ: 10-1 TYPE: C

10. *Other assets* would include all of the following *except*
   a. startup costs.
   b. patents.
   c. copyrights.
   d. inventories.

ANS: D REF: p. 210 OBJ: 10-1 TYPE: C

11. The amount of the business owners' initial investment, owners' later investment in the business, and retained earnings comprise
   a. debt capital.
   b. accrued expenses.
   c. owners' long-term debt.
   d. owners' equity capital.

ANS: D REF: p. 211 OBJ: 10-1 TYPE: D

12. Though often assumed to be the same, profits shown on a company's income statement are *not* the same as its
   a. owners' total compensation.
   b. financial performance.
   c. cash flows.
   d. taxable income.

ANS: C REF: p. 213 OBJ: 10-1 TYPE: C

13. The _____ shows all cash receipts and payments involved in operating the business and managing its financial activities.
   a. income statement
   b. balance sheet
   c. cash flow statement
   d. statement of financial position

ANS: C REF: p. 212 OBJ: 10-1 TYPE: D

14. The major distinction between cash-basis and accrual-basis accounting is that the
    a. cash method is easier to use.
    b. cash method matches revenue and expenses better.
    c. point of recognition of revenue and expenses is different.
    d. cash method involves less record keeping.

ANS: C REF: p. 213 OBJ: 10-1 TYPE: C

15. Which of the following is *not* included on a cash flow statement?
    a. Collections from customers
    b. Payments to suppliers
    c. Cash tax payments
    d. Existing fixed assets such as machinery

ANS: D REF: p. 215 OBJ: 10-1 TYPE: C

16. Which of the following does *not* increase or decrease cash flows from assets?
    a. The firm's after-tax cash flows from operations
    b. Changes in working capital
    c. Changes in personal income tax regulations
    d. Changes in fixed assets and other long-term assets

ANS: C REF: p. 213 OBJ: 10-1 TYPE: C

17. Mike Prinz has noticed that his operating income is decreasing yet he has managed to keep his operating expenses from increasing and sales are increasing. What is happening to cause the change in operating income?
    a. His receivables are increasing.
    b. His liabilities are increasing.
    c. His cost of goods is increasing.
    d. His gross profit is decreasing.

ANS: C REF: p. 219 OBJ: 10-1 TYPE: A

18. The "bottom line" of the income statement is affected by all of the following EXCEPT:
    a. cost of good sold
    b. dividends paid to owners
    c. general and administrative costs
    d. marketing expenses

ANS: B REF: p. 207 OBJ: 10-1 TYPE: A

19. Current assets include all of the following EXCEPT
    a. accounts payable
    b. accounts receivable
    c. cash
    d. inventories

ANS: A REF: p. 208 OBJ: 10-1 TYPE: A

20. An increase in assets on the balance sheet will result in
    a. an increase in ownership equity or outstanding debt.
    b. a decrease in ownership equity or outstanding debt.
    c. a decrease in ownership equity and an increase in outstanding debt.
    d. an increase in ownership equity and a decrease in outstanding debt.

ANS: A REF: p. 209 OBJ: 10-1 TYPE: A

21. Which of the following factors affect the size of a firm's cash reservoir?
    a. the volume of sales
    b. cash receipts
    c. cash payments
    d. all of these

ANS: D REF: p. 209 OBJ: 10-1 TYPE: A

22. The value of a depreciable asset
    a. is constant over time.
    b. increases with each use of the asset.
    c. decreases over time.
    d. increases over time.

ANS: C REF: p. 209 OBJ: 10-1 TYPE: C

23. Raw materials and products held by the firm for sale constitute ________.
    a. accounts payable.
    b. accounts receivable.
    c. cost of goods.
    d. inventories.

ANS: D REF: p. 209 OBJ: 10-1 TYPE: D

24. Cumulative depreciation expense is shown on the
    a. balance sheet.
    b. cash-flow statement.
    c. income statement.
    d. all of these.

ANS: A REF: p. 210 OBJ: 10-1 TYPE: C

25. A two year-old asset has a depreciable life of 10 years. Its initial purchase cost was $450,000 and it is depreciated by 10 percent annually. What is the remaining depreciable value of the asset?
    a. $ 0.00
    b. $90,000
    c. $200,000
    d. $360,000

ANS: D REF: p. 210 OBJ: 10-1 TYPE: A

26. A five year-old asset has a remaining depreciable value of $75,000. It has been depreciated at five percent per year. How many years remain before its depreciated value will be $0.
    a. 5
    b. 10
    c. 15
    d. 20

ANS: A REF: p. 210 OBJ: 10-1 TYPE: A

27. The cash flow statement measures cash flows on
   a. an annual basis.
   b. an accrual basis.
   c. a cash-basis.
   d. a normalized basis.

ANS: C REF: p. 213 OBJ: 10-1 TYPE: C

28. The cash flow statement reflects cash flows from
   a. operating activities.
   b. investment activities.
   c. financing activities.
   d. all of these.

ANS: D REF: p. 214 OBJ: 10-1 TYPE: C

29. Projected financial statements are also known as
   a. adjusted financial statements.
   b. pro forma financial statements.
   c. "predicting the unpredictable."
   d. cost of goods to be sold.

ANS: B REF: p. 217 OBJ: 10-2 TYPE: D

30. Pro forma financial statements can answer the following question:
   a. How profitable can the firm be, given past sales and expense relationships?
   b. How much and what type of financing has been used in the firms operations?
   c. If projected sales and sales-expense relationships are accurate, how profitable will the firm be?
   d. Has the firm been doing a good job of managing its cash flows?

ANS: C REF: p. 217 OBJ: 10-2 TYPE: C

31. The computation of cost of goods sold and operating expenses is based on all of the following *except*
   a. the cost of goods sold.
   b. general and administrative expenses.
   c. the firm's interest expense.
   d. depreciation expenses.

ANS: C REF: p. 218 OBJ: 10-2 TYPE: C

32. Essential elements in the forecasting of profits include all of the following EXCEPT
   a. amount of sales levels.
   b. cost of goods and operating expenses.
   c. additional owner equity.
   d. interest expense.

ANS: C REF: p. 218-219 OBJ: 10-2 TYPE: C

33. The first step in projecting the firm's income involves calculating
    a. the interest expense for each year.
    b. estimated income taxes.
    c. total cost of goods sold.
    d. sales projections.

ANS: D REF: p. 218 OBJ: 10-2 TYPE: C

34. A company's net income depends on all of the following *except*
    a. amount of sales.
    b. cost of goods sold.
    c. interest expenses and taxes.
    d. inventory estimates.

ANS: D REF: p. 218 OBJ: 10-2 TYPE: C

35. Operating expenses include
    a. marketing-related expenses.
    b. the cost for independent dealers to prepare for the distribution of the product.
    c. interest on all loans.
    d. income taxes.

ANS: A REF: p. 218 OBJ: 10-2 TYPE: C

36. A startup typically experiences losses for a period of time, frequently as long as
    a. one year.
    b. 2-3 years.
    c. 3-5 years.
    d. 5-10 years.

ANS: B REF: p. 219 OBJ: 10-2 TYPE: C

37. A startup typically does not become profitable or breakeven for
    a. the first year.
    b. two to three years.
    c. four to six years.
    d. six to eight years.

ANS: B REF: p. 219 OBJ: 10-2 TYPE: D

38. When forecasting capital requirements for a proposed venture, the analyst should consider
    a. the investment needed for startup, since capital needs for future growth can be assessed later.
    b. personal expenses, especially when the entrepreneur receives no income from other sources.
    c. only the most optimistic scenario for the business.

d. only the most pessimistic scenario for the business.

ANS: B REF: p. 221 OBJ: 10-3 TYPE: C

39. A primary driving force of future asset needs is
    a. investments.
    b. sales.
    c. external equity.
    d. internal equity.

ANS: B REF: p. 221 OBJ: 10-3 TYPE: C

40. If a retailer's estimated sales are $1 million and assets in the firm's industry tend to run about 25 percent of sales, the retailer should maintain assets of
    a. $250,000.
    b. $500,000.
    c. $4,000,000.
    d. $25,000,000.

ANS: A REF: p. 222 OBJ: 10-3 TYPE: A

41. The projection of the financing needed by a new business should *not* be based on
    a. the firm's anticipated sales volume.
    b. anticipated regularity of cash receipts.
    c. predicted regularity of cash payments.
    d. estimates of the fixed assets held by the startup's strongest competitor.

ANS: D REF: p. 217 OBJ: 10-3 TYPE: C

42. A common weakness in small business financing is
    a. the disproportionately large investment in liquid assets.
    b. the disproportionately small investment in liquid assets.
    c. the disproportionately large investment in personal savings relative to debt financing.
    d. the disproportionately small investment in personal savings relative to debt financing.

ANS: B REF: p. 223 OBJ: 10-3 TYPE: C

43. The liquidity of a firm is
    a. often measured by a ratio of current assets to current liabilities.
    b. not important to a company's financial health.
    c. the ability of the firm to sell its products quickly.
    d. a measurement of spontaneous financing.

ANS: A REF: p. 223 OBJ: 10-3 TYPE: C

44. The owners of small firms have a tendency to ________ the amount of capital their business requires.
   a. downplay
   b. ignore
   c. overestimate
   d. underestimate

ANS: D REF: p. 227 OBJ: 10-3 TYPE: C

45. A common weakness in small business financing is
   a. too much owner financing.
   b. too much debt financing.
   c. too much investment in fixed assets.
   d. too much investment in current assets.

ANS: C REF: p. 223 OBJ: 10-3 TYPE: C

46. Retained profits represent
   a. spontaneous financing.
   b. external equity.
   c. internal equity.
   d. sweat equity.

ANS: C REF: p. 224 OBJ: 10-3 TYPE: C

47. If a firm's current ratio improves from 1.5 to 2.0, what has likely happened?
   a. Current liabilities have decreased.
   b. Fixed assets have increased.
   c. Ownership equity has increased
   d. Long-term debt has decreased.

ANS: A REF: p. 225 OBJ: 10-3 TYPE: A

48. If a firm's current ratio ________, its liquidity ________.
   a. increases. increases
   b. increases, decreases
   c. decreases, increases
   d. increases, remains the same

ANS: A REF: p. 223 OBJ: 10-3 TYPE: A

49. Operating profit margins of expanding businesses tend to suffer in the short run because
   a. variable operating costs increase.
   b. fixed operating costs increase.
   c. economies of scale increase costs.
   d. additional investment capital costs are always higher

ANS: B REF: p. 227 OBJ: 10-4 TYPE: C

50. A _______ shows the level that sales must reach before profitability is achieved.
   a. break-even case
   b. gross margin case
   c. most likely (base case)
   d. sales-to-profit case

ANS: A REF: p. 228 OBJ: 10-4 TYPE: D

ESSAY

1. Name and define three categories of assets.

ANS:
Current assets are relatively liquid assets. Sometimes called working capital, they include cash, inventory, accounts receivable, and prepaid expenses. Fixed assets are relatively permanent assets used in production and operation of the business. They include machinery and equipment, buildings, and land. Other assets include organizational costs and intangible assets like patents, copyrights, and goodwill.

REF: p. 208 OBJ: 10-1 TYPE: D

2. The textbook identifies a number of sources of current debt. Name these sources and describe the nature of each.

ANS:
Current debt (or short-term liabilities) involves borrowed money that must be repaid within 12 months. The sources of current debt are as follows:

- Accounts payable-the credit extended by suppliers to a firm when it purchases inventories.
- Accrued expenses-short-term liabilities that have been incurred but not yet paid (e.g., work performed for which payment has not been made).
- Short-term notes-cash amounts borrowed from a bank, or other lending source, for a short period of time (e.g., 90 days).

REF: p. 210 OBJ: 10-1 TYPE: D

3. What four variables drive the amount of profit a company earns?

ANS:
The four variables are the amount of sales, the cost of goods sold and operating expenses, the interest expense on borrowed funds, and taxes, which usually increase as the amount of income increases.

REF: p. 218 OBJ: 10-2 TYPE: C

4. What are the principles that govern the firm's financing?

ANS:
Several principles should guide the process of financing the new venture.

- Firms have greater financial requirements as necessary assets increase.
- Management should be certain to maintain an appropriate degree of liquidity.
- The amount of equity provided by owners places a ceiling on the amount of debt that can be used.
- As the firm grows, it is likely to take on short-term (or "spontaneous") debt.
- Firms can raise equity internally (e.g., from retained earnings) or externally (e.g., from the initial and subsequent investment of the owners).

REF: p. 223 OBJ: 10-3 TYPE: C

5. List the textbook's practical suggestions to guide financial forecasting.

ANS:
Several suggestions may help the entrepreneur make better financial forecasts, including the following:

- Don't make overly optimistic projections—be factual and conservative.
- Beware of the "hockey stick" problem—i.e., do not forecast flat sales that suddenly take off.
- Spell out the details of any marketing plan.
- List the assumptions underlying all projections.
- Use industry—specific comparison data to validate forecasts.
- Do not deviate far from industry comparisons.
- Check pro forma projections against actual results at least once a month.

REF: p. 227 OBJ: 10-3 TYPE: C

6. **You Make the Call—Situation 1**
The Donahoo Furniture Sales Company was formed on December 31, 2004, with $1,000,000 in equity plus $500,000 in long-term debt. On January 1, 2005, all of the firm's capital was held in cash. The following transactions occurred during January 2005.
   - January 2: Donahoo purchased $1,000,000 worth of furniture for resale. It paid $500,000 in cash and financed the balance using trade credit that required payment in 60 days.
   - January 3: Donahoo sold $250,000 worth of furniture that it had paid $200,000 to acquire. The entire sale was on credit terms of net 90 days.
   - January 15: Donahoo purchased more furniture for $200,000. This time, it used trade credit for the entire amount of the purchase, with credit terms of net 60 days.
   - January 31: Donahoo sold $500,000 worth of furniture, for which it had paid $400,000. The furniture was sold for 10 percent cash down, with the remainder payable in 90 days. In addition, the firm paid a cash dividend of $100,000 to its stockholders and paid off $250,000 of its long-term debt.

Question 1 What did Donahoo's balance sheet look like at the outset of the firm's life?
Question 2 What did the firm's balance sheet look like after each transaction?
Question 3 Ignoring taxes, determine how much income Donahoo earned during January. Prepare an income statement for the month. Recognize an interest expense of 1 percent for the month (12 percent annually).

ANS:

1. Donahoo's balance sheet at the outset of the firm's life:

Date	Change in Assets	Balance Sheet: Assets		Balance Sheet: Debt + Equity		Change in Debt + Equity
1-Jan	Plus $1,500	Cash	$1,500	Debt	$ 500	Plus $500
				Equity	1,000	Plus $1,000
		Total	$1,500	Total	$1,500	

2. The firm's balance sheet after each transaction:

Date	Change in Assets	Assets		Debt + Equity		Change in Debt + Equity
2-Jan		Cash	$1,000	Accts	$ 500	

Date	Change in Assets	Assets		Debt + Equity		Change in Debt + Equity
				payable		
	Less $500	Inventory	1,000	Debt	500	Plus $500
	Plus $1,000	Total	$2,000	Equity	1,000	
				Total	$2,000	
	Change in Assets	Assets		Debt + Equity		Change in Debt + Equity
3-Jan		Cash	$1,000	Payables	$ 500	
	Plus $250	Receivables	250	Debt	500	
	Less $200	Inventory	800	Equity	1,050	Plus $50
	Plus $50		$2,050		$2,050	
Date	Change in Assets	Assets		Debt + Equity		Change in Debt + Equity
15-Jan		Cash	$1,000	Payables	$ 700	
		Receivables	250	Debt	500	Plus $200
	Plus $200	Inventory	1,000	Equity	1,050	
			$2,250		$2,250	
	Change in Assets	Assets		Debt + Equity		Change in Debt + Equity
31-Jan	Cash sale: + $50			Payables	$ 700	
	Reduce debt: -$250	Cash	$ 700	Debt	250	
	Dividend: -$100			Equity	1,050	Plus $50
	Total cash -$300				$2,000	
	Plus $450	Receivables	700			
	Less $400	Inventory	600			
			$2,000			

3. Income Donahoo earned during January:

	January 3	January 31	Jan 1 – Jan 31
Revenues	$ 250	$ 500	$ 750
Cost of goods sold	(200)	(400)	(600)
Gross profits/operating	$ 50	$ 100	$ 150

profits			
Interest expense (1%/month)	--	--	(5)
Net Income	$ 50	$ 100	$ 145

4. Donahoo's cash flow for the month of January:

Beginning cash (January 1)	$ 1,500
Ending cash (January 31)	700
Net change in cash	$ (800)

Free cash flow Operating Perspective	
Operating income	$ 150
Depreciation Expense	---
EBITDA	$ 150
Change in current assets	
Cash	$ (800)
Accounts receivable	700
Inventory	600
Change in current assets	$ 500
Change in accounts payable	700
Change in net working capital	$ (200)
Free cash flow (operating)	$ 350

Free cash flows Financing perspective		
Dividends		$ 100
Debt retirement		250
Interest expense	$ 5	
Change in accounts payable	(5)	
Interest paid		---
Free cash flow		$ 350

REF: p. 226 OBJ: YMTC TYPE: A

7. **You Make the Call—Situation 2**
At the beginning of 2005, Mary Abrahams purchased a small business, the Turpen Company, whose income statement and balance sheets are shown below.

Income Statement for the Turpen Company for 2005

Sales revenue		$175,000
Cost of goods sold		105,000
Gross profit		$ 70,000
Operating expenses:		
Depreciation	$ 5,000	
Administrative expenses	20,000	
Selling expenses	26,000	
Total operating expenses		$ 51,000
Operating income		$ 19,000
Interest expense		3,000
Earnings before taxes		$ 16,000
Taxes		8,000
Net income		$ 8,000

Balance Sheets for the Turpen Company for 2004 and 2005

	2004	2005
Assets		
Current assets:		
Cash	$ 8,000	$ 10,000
Accounts receivable	15,000	20,000
Inventories	22,000	25,000
Total current assets	$45,000	$ 55,000
Fixed assets:		
Gross fixed assets	$50,000	$ 55,000
Accumulated depreciation	15,000	20,000
Total fixed assets	$35,000	$ 35,000
Other assets	12,000	10,000
TOTAL ASSETS	$92,000	$100,000
Debt (Liabilities) and Equity		
Current debt:		
Accounts payable	$10,000	$ 12,000
Accruals	7,000	8,000
Short-term notes	5,000	5,000
Total current debt	$22,000	$ 25,000
Long-term debt	15,000	15,000
Total debt	$37,000	$ 40,000
Equity	$55,000	$60,000
TOTAL DEBT AND EQUITY	$92,000	$100,000

The firm has been profitable, but Abrahams has been disappointed by the lack of cash flows. She had hoped to have about $10,000 a year available for personal living expenses. However, there never seems to be much cash available for purposes other than business needs. Abrahams has asked you to examine the financial statements and explain why, although they show profits, she does not have any discretionary cash for personal needs. She observed, "I thought that I could take the profits and add depreciation to find out how much cash I was generating. However, that doesn't seem to be the case. What's happening?"

Question 1 Given the information provided by the financial statements, what would you tell Abrahams? (As part of your answer, calculate the firm's cash flows.)
Question 2 How would you describe the cash flow pattern for the Turpen Company?

ANS:

1. Explain to Ms. Abrahams that her equation for determining cash flows (profits + depreciation), although correct once in a while, can be very misleading. The cash flows can be better determined as follows:

<u>Firm's cash flows:</u>	
Operating income	$19,000
Depreciation	5,000
Earnings before interest, taxes, and depreciation	$24,000
Cash taxes	8,000
After-tax cash flows from operations	$16,000
Change in net working capital:	
Change in current assets	$10,000

Change in non-interest bearing short-term debt	3,000
Change in net working capital	$7,000
Investment in fixed assets	($5,000)
Decrease in other assets	2,000
Firm's cash flows:	$6,000
Financing cash flows:	
Interest	$3,000
Dividends	3,000
Financing cash flows	$6,000

Thus, the Turpen Company generated $6,000 in cash flows, which were used to pay dividends and interest to investors. Also, we should notice that of the $6,000 that was paid to investors, $2,000 came from a reduction in cash balances. If the cash had not been reduced, there would have been only $4,000 available to the investors. In short, there is no money available for Rose.

2. The primary sources of cash are (a) income plus depreciation (a noncash charge) and (b) increasing short-term borrowings in the form of accounts payable and accruals. The primary uses are (a) increased investments in accounts receivable, inventories, and fixed assets and (b) payment of dividends.

REF: p. 216 OBJ: YMTC TYPE: C

8. **You Make the Call—Situation 3**
Cameron Products, Inc., used as an example in chapter 10, is an actual firm (although some of the facts were changed to maintain confidentiality). Kate Lynn bought the firm from its founding owners and moved its operations to her hometown. Although she estimated the firm's asset needs and financing requirements, she cannot be certain that these projections will be realized. The figures merely represent the most likely case. Lynn also made some projections that she considers to be the worst-case and best-case sales and profit figures. If things do not go well, the firm might have sales of only $200,000 in its first year. However, if the potential of the business is realized, Lynn believes that sales could be as high as $325,000. If she needs any additional financing beyond the existing line of credit, she could conceivably borrow another $5,000 in short-term debt from the bank by pledging some personal investments. Any additional financing would need to come from Lynn herself, thereby increasing her equity stake in the business.
Source: Personal conversation with Kate Lynn. (Numbers are hypothetical.)

Question If all of Cameron Products' other relationships hold, how will Lynn's worst-case and best-case projections affect the income statement and balance sheet in the first year?

ANS:

$150,000 in Sales
Cameron Products, Inc.
Projected Balance Sheet at Year End

Assets:		
Cash	$ 7,500	
Accounts receivable	15,000	
Inventories	37,500	
Total current assets		$ 60,000
Fixed assets (machinery)		50,000
Total assets		$ 110,000
Debt:		

Accounts payable	$ 12,000	
Accruals	6,000	
Credit line	2,000	
Total current liabilities		$ 20,000
Long-term debt		35,000
Total debt		$ 55,000
Equity:		
Common stock	$ 40,000	
Retained earnings	15,000	
Total equity		$ 55,000
Total debt and equity		$ 110,000

$400,000 in Sales
Cameron Products, Inc.
Projected Balance Sheet at Year End

Assets:		
Cash $ 20,000		
Accounts receivable	40,000	
Inventories	100,000	
Total current assets		$ 160,000
Fixed assets (machinery)		50,000
Total assets		$ 210,000
Debt:		
Accounts payable	$ 32,000	
Accruals	16,000	
Credit line	20,000	
Total current liabilities		$ 68,000
Long-term debt		35,000
Total debt		$ 103,000
Equity:		
Common stock	$ 47,000	
Retained earnings	60,000	
Total equity		$ 107,000
Total debt and equity		$ 210,000

REF: p. 225 OBJ: YMTC TYPE: A

9. **You Make the Call—Situation 4**
Bremerhaven Holdings, Inc. has asked that you determine next year's asset requirements for its one year-old start-up business. It has furnished you with the following information:

Projected sales: $800,000 last year; sales are forecast to increase 12% next year.
Depreciation: $7,500 annually
Cash: 9%
Gross fixed assets: $85,000
Accounts receivable: 8%
Inventories: 32%

Question 1. Using the percentage of sales method, calculate the total assets that Bremerhaven will need to support the firm's activities in the coming year. Be sure to show all calculations in your answer.

ANS:
Calculations

		Year 1	Year 2
Sales		$ 800,000	$ 896,000
Assets	**Assumptions**		
Cash	9%	$ 72,000	$ 80,640
Accounts receivable	8%	64,000	71,680
Inventories	32%	256,000	286,720
Total current assets		392,000	$ 439,040
Gross fixed assets		85,000	85,000
Accumulated depreciation		7,500	15,000
Net fixed assets		77,500	70,000
TOTAL ASSETS		$ 469,500	$ 509,040

REF: p. 225 OBJ: YMTC TYPE: A

Correlation Table for Chapter 11—The Financial Plan, Part 2: Finding Sources of Funds

	Learning Objectives	Question Type	Definition Define new term, recall facts	Concept Understand or relate concepts	Application Apply knowledge, analyze data
1	Describe how the nature of a firm affects its financing sources.	T/F		1,2,3,4,5,6,7	
		MC	3	1,2,4,6,7	5,8
		ES			
2	Evaluate the choice between debt financing and equity financing.	T/F		8,9,10,11,12,13, 14,15	
		MC		9,11,12,13,14	10,15,16
		ES		1,2	
3	Identify the typical sources of financing used at the outset of a new venture.	T/F		16,17	
		MC		17,18,19	
		ES		3	
4	Discuss the basic process for acquiring and structuring a bank loan.	T/F	18,19,20		
		MC	22	20,21,23,24,25, 26,27,28,29	
		ES		4	
5	Explain how business relationships can be used to finance a small firm.	T/F	22	21	
		MC		30,31,32	
		ES			
6	Describe the two types of private equity investors that offer financing to small firms.	T/F	23,24	25	
		MC	34,36	33,35	
		ES			
7	Distinguish among the different government loan programs available to small companies.	T/F		26,27,28	
		MC	39	37,38	
		ES			
8	Explain when large companies and public stock offerings can be a source of financing.	T/F	29	30	
		MC		40	
		ES		5	
	You Make the Call	ES		6,7,8,9	

Total Number of Test Questions: 79 (30 True/False; 40 Multiple-Choice; 9 Essay)

Chapter 11—The Financial Plan: Part 2

TRUE/FALSE

1. The basic factors that determine how a firm is financed include the following: the firm's past economic performance, the nature of its assets, the maturity of the firm, and the personal preferences of owner(s) with respect to the marketing mix.

   ANS: F
   The basic factors that determine how a firm is financed are: the firm's *economic potential*, the nature of its assets, the maturity of the firm, and the personal preferences of owner(s) with respect to the *debt-equity* mix.

   REF: p. 237 OBJ: 11-1 TYPE: C

2. A firm with potential for large profits has many more possible sources of financing than does a firm that offer only unattractive returns, but high growth potential does not seem to have a similar effect on financing options.

   ANS: F
   A firm with potential for large profits *and high growth* has many more possible sources of financing than does a firm that offers only unattractive returns.

   REF: p. 237 OBJ: 11-1 TYPE: C

3. Most startup investors limit their investing to firms that offer potentially high returns within a one-to-three-year period.

   ANS: F
   Most startup investors limit their investing to firms that offer potentially high returns within a five-to-ten-year period.

   REF: p. 237 OBJ: 11-1 TYPE: C

4. The age of a company has little impact on the types of financing available to it.

   ANS: F
   The age of a company has a direct bearing on the types of financing available to it.

   REF: p. 237 OBJ: 11-1 TYPE: C

5. Venture capitalists restrict their investment in startup companies.

   ANS: T REF: p. 238 OBJ: 11-1 TYPE: C

6. Assets such as the quality of a firm's employees are considered tangible in nature and thus have substantial value as collateral.

ANS: F
Assets such as goodwill, research and development, and even the quality of a firm's employees are considered *in*tangible in nature and thus have little value as collateral

REF: p. 238 OBJ: 11-1 TYPE: C

7. For every firm, there is a "right" answer to the question of balancing debt and equity, and it is important that the small business owner find that balance.

ANS: F
There is no right or wrong answer when it comes to choosing between debt and equity.

REF: p. 239 OBJ: 11-1 TYPE: C

8. Borrowing money rather than issuing common stock increases the potential for higher rates of return to owners.

ANS: T REF: p. 242 OBJ: 11-2 TYPE: C

9. Borrowing allows owners to retain voting control of the company.

ANS: T REF: p. 242 OBJ: 11-2 TYPE: C

10. If a firm finances with equity rather than with debt, it will bear no interest expense and thus yield greater net income.

ANS: T REF: p. 242 OBJ: 11-2 TYPE: C

11. Generally, as long as a firm's operating income return on its assets in greater than the cost of debt, the owners' return on equity investment will decrease as the firm uses more debt.

ANS: F
As long as a firm's operating income return on its assets in greater than the cost of debt, the owners' return on equity investment will actually increase as the firm uses more debt.

REF: p. 242 OBJ: 11-2 TYPE: C

12. A small business should limit the amount of debt it takes on because debt can add to the firm's risk.

ANS: T REF: p. 242 OBJ: 11-2 TYPE: C

13. Use of debt financing increases potential returns when a company is performing well, but it also increases the possibility of lower-even negative-returns if the company does not attain its goals in a given year.

ANS: T REF: p. 242 OBJ: 11-2 TYPE: C

14. Small business owners sometimes accept higher levels of debt because doing so permits them to retain all of the stock and full ownership.

ANS: T REF: p. 242 OBJ: 11-2 TYPE: C

15. To retain control and avoid accountability to those with a minority equity position in the firm, small business owners are often reluctant to give away any of the company's ownership.

ANS: T REF: p. 242 OBJ: 11-2 TYPE: C

16. Approximately one-half of the financing for startups comes from personal savings.

ANS: F
Approximately three-fourths of the financing for startups comes from personal savings, with the remainder coming from family, friends, or partners.

REF: p. 243 OBJ: 11-3 TYPE: C

17. One potential problem with acquiring funds from friends and relatives is that they might feel that they have the right to interfere in the management of the business.

ANS: T REF: p. 245 OBJ: 11-3 TYPE: C

18. Lines of credit are legal obligations to provide capital.

ANS: F
Lines of credit are *informal agreements* to provide capital.

REF: p. 248 OBJ: 11-4 TYPE: D

19. A chattel mortgage is a loan for which real property, such as land or a building, serves as collateral.

ANS: F
This is a *real estate* mortgage. A chattel mortgage is secured by inventory or other movable property.

REF: p. 248 OBJ: 11-4 TYPE: D

20. The five Cs of credit are character, capacity, capital, conditions, and collateral.

ANS: T REF: p. 249 OBJ: 11-4 TYPE: D

21. Both wholesalers and equipment manufacturers/suppliers can be used as sources of funds.

ANS: T REF: p. 253 OBJ: 11-5 TYPE: C

22. Asset-based lending is a type of financing secured by assets such as receivables, inventory, or both.

ANS: T REF: p. 254 OBJ: 11-5 TYPE: D

23. Capital financing with no established marketplace is financing from commercial banks.

ANS: F
Capital financing with no established marketplace is financing from *business angels*.

REF: p. 254 OBJ: 11-6 TYPE: D

24. Commercial investors are sometimes called *business angels.*

ANS: F
This term sometimes applied to *individual* investors, not *commercial* investors.

REF: p. 254 OBJ: 11-6 TYPE: D

25. Around 5% of the business plans reviewed by venture capitalists are funded.

ANS: F
Fewer than 1% of the business plans reviewed by venture capitalists are funded.

REF: p. 255 OBJ: 11-6 TYPE: C

26. Small Business Administration loans include guaranty loans and loans directly from the SBA.

ANS: F
The Small Business Administration assists in small business in obtaining funding through loans only through intermediaries.

REF: p. 257 OBJ: 11-7 TYPE: C

27. Qualified small businesses that cannot obtain business loans through normal lending channels can get loans directly from the SBA through its **7(a) Loan Guaranty Program**.

ANS: F REF: p. 257 OBJ: 11-7 TYPE: C

28. State and local governments are becoming less involved in financing new businesses.

ANS: F
Federal, state, and local governments have allocated *increased* amounts of money to finance new businesses.

REF: p. 256 OBJ: 11-7 TYPE: C

29. Private placement is the selling of stock only to selected individuals.

ANS: T REF: p. 258 OBJ: 11-8 TYPE: D

30. The public sale of a firm's common stock is regulated by the Securities and Exchange Commission.

ANS: T REF: p. 258 OBJ: 11-8 TYPE: C

MULTIPLE CHOICE

1. Compared to firms that provide a good lifestyle for the owner but little in the way of attractive returns, a firm with potential for high growth and large profits has ________ possible sources of financing.
   a. fewer
   b. about the same number of
   c. more

d. many more

ANS: D REF: p. 237 OBJ: 11-1 TYPE: C

2. Most of those who invest in startups limit their investing to firms with potentially high returns in a ________ period.
   a. 6-12 month
   b. 1-2 year
   c. 3-5 year
   d. 5-10 year

ANS: D REF: p. 237 OBJ: 11-1 TYPE: C

3. When entrepreneurs "bootstrap" their financing, this means that they are
   a. enhancing the "corporate image" of their enterprise by the way they raise capital.
   b. depending on their own initiative to come up with the capital necessary to start up and grow.
   c. subordinating future capital formation to short-term financial performance.
   d. waiting to establish a reputation in the marketplace before raising the bulk of their capital.

ANS: B REF: p. 238 OBJ: 11-1 TYPE: D

4. Typical venture capitalists invest approximately ____ of their investment in later-stage businesses.
   a. one-fourth
   b. one-half
   c. three-fourths
   d. nearly all

ANS: C REF: p. 238 OBJ: 11-1 TYPE: C

5. When bankers look for evidence of whether a business will be able to repay a loan, they usually base their assessment of this on
   a. what the firm has done in the past.
   b. what the owner says the firm will do in the future.
   c. the opinion of investment analysts.
   d. the business plan of the enterprise.

ANS: A REF: p. 238 OBJ: 11-1 TYPE: A

6. When it comes to financing a company, a banker looks at two kinds of assets:
   a. direct and indirect.
   b. tangible and intangible.
   c. those founded upon past performance and those depending on future performance.
   d. industry-specific and firm-specific.

ANS: B REF: p. 238 OBJ: 11-1 TYPE: C

7. When it comes to choosing between debt and equity financing,
   a. there is always a right or wrong answer.
   b. there is never a right or wrong answer.
   c. there will never be a way to tell whether the small business owner made a wise decision.
   d. the decision should always be market-driven.

ANS: B REF: p. 239 OBJ: 11-1 TYPE: C

8. The return on the owner's investment (equity) is a better measure of performance than
   a. the return on assets ratio.
   b. the current ratio.
   c. the quick ratio.
   d. the absolute dollar amount of income.

   ANS: D REF: p. 240 OBJ: 11-1 TYPE: A

9. Issuing stock rather than increasing debt does *not*
   a. limit the potential rate of return to owners.
   b. dilute owners' voting control.
   c. reduce financial risk.
   d. limit the firm's capacity to meet its financial obligations.

   ANS: D REF: p. 242 OBJ: 11-2 TYPE: C

10. Louise Piper plans to sell stock in her company in order to raise capital. One of the benefits of issuing stock as a source of funds is
    a. reduced risk to the enterprise.
    b. sharing success potential.
    c. confidentiality.
    d. periodic reporting requirements.

    ANS: A REF: p. 242 OBJ: 11-2 TYPE: A

11. Drawbacks of selling stock as a source of funds include
    a. enhanced corporate image.
    b. loss of voting control of the company.
    c. future financing.
    d. estate planning.

    ANS: B REF: p. 242 OBJ: 11-2 TYPE: C

12. If a firm finances with equity rather than debt, net income will be greater because
    a. equity financing almost always leads to better firm performance than debt financing.
    b. the terms of equity financing are more stable than the terms of debt financing.
    c. this impacts asset selection for the better.
    d. there is no interest expense.

    ANS: D REF: p. 240 OBJ: 11-2 TYPE: C

13. Equity investors cannot demand more than
    a. those who have invested debt in the enterprise.
    b. what is earned.
    c. anticipated future financing.
    d. established cash flows.

    ANS: B REF: p. 242 OBJ: 11-2 TYPE: C

14. One of the factors that influences the choice between debt and equity is the
    a. returns anticipated from the enterprise.
    b. risk of nationalization.
    c. degree of control the owners hope to retain.
    d. state of the owners' estate plan.

ANS: C REF: p. 242 OBJ: 11-2 TYPE: C

15. To retain control over his business, an entrepreneur should seek initially to secure ______ financing.
    a. debt
    b. equity
    c. internal
    d. asset

ANS: A REF: p. 242 OBJ: 11-2 TYPE: A

16. If the firm's rate of return on its assets is _______than the cost of borrowing, then the owners' rate of return on equity will _______ as the firm uses ______ debt
    a. greater, increase, less
    b. greater, decrease, more
    c. greater, increase, more
    d. less, increase, more

ANS: C REF: p. 241 OBJ: 11-2 TYPE: A

17. Though not as common as using personal savings, one of the more often used sources of financing is
    a. asset-based lenders.
    b. personal charge card accounts.
    c. wealthy individuals.
    d. venture capitalists.

ANS: B REF: p. 246 OBJ: 11-3 TYPE: C

18. One of the major sources of early financing is
    a. family members.
    b. commercial banks.
    c. business suppliers.
    d. asset-based lenders.

ANS: A REF: p. 245 OBJ: 11-3 TYPE: C

19. Prospective entrepreneurs will usually acquire their initial financing from
    a. venture capitalists.
    b. personal savings.
    c. wealthy individuals.
    d. the securities market.

ANS: B REF: p. 244 OBJ: 11-3 TYPE: C

20. A loan covenant is very unlikely to require
    a. provision of timely and complete information.
    b. salary limitations.
    c. a personal guarantee.
    d. a fixed business strategy.

ANS: D REF: p. 251 OBJ: 11-4 TYPE: C

21. A marketing campaign would be mostly likely financed by
    a. a commercial bank.
    b. an owner.
    c. an outside investor.
    d. the SBA.

ANS: B REF: p. 245 OBJ: 11-4 TYPE: C

22. A line of credit is the ________ amount of credit a bank will provide a borrower at any one time.

a. average
b. annual
c. maximum
d. minimum

ANS: C REF: p. 248 OBJ: 11-4 TYPE: D

23. A _______ mortgage would likely be used to secure financing for mobile construction office.
a. chattel
b. real estate
c. revolving
d. term

ANS: A REF: p. 248 OBJ: 11-4 TYPE: C

24. Term loans are generally used to finance equipment with a useful life ________ the loan's term.
a. equal to
b. longer than
c. less than one-half
d. greater than one-half

ANS: A REF: p. 248 OBJ: 11-4 TYPE: C

25. Pro forma statements required by bankers include all of the following EXCEPT
a. balance sheets
b. cash flow statements
c. income statements
d. personal financial statements

ANS: D REF: p. 249 OBJ: 11-4 TYPE: C

26. Lenders tend to view buyouts favorably because the acquired business has all of the following EXCEPT:
a. a credit history
b. existing assets
c. a customer base
d. seller financing

ANS: D REF: p. 253 OBJ: 11-4 TYPE: C

27. LIBOR is________________ the prime rate.
a. approximately equal to
b. considerably higher than
c. considerably lower than
d. a lagging indicator of

ANS: C REF: p. 251 OBJ: 11-4 TYPE: C

28. A balloon payment
a. is an upfront payment to obtain a loan.
b. is due when a loan comes due.
c. may be due at any time during the term of a loan.
d. is used to lift (remove) a loan covenant.

ANS: B REF: p. 251 OBJ: 11-4 TYPE: C

29. If Bill Bailey, owner of Cherokee Communications, had violated the covenants of his loan agreement,
a. the loan payments would have been automatically rescheduled.
b. the loan interest rate would have increased to maximum legal rate.
c. the borrower's liability would have become unlimited.
d. the lender could have declared the loan due in full immediately.

ANS: D REF: p. 252 OBJ: 11-4 TYPE: C

30. A primary source of financing for most smaller companies is
a. trade credit.
b. long-term bank loans.
c. mortgages.

d. asset-based notes.

ANS: A REF: p. 253 OBJ: 11-5 TYPE: C

31. Instead of borrowing money from suppliers to purchase equipment, an increasing number of small businesses are
   a. obtaining trade credit instead.
   b. making these purchases outright.
   c. choosing to lease the equipment.
   d. opting to streamline assembly processes to reduce expenditures.

ANS: C REF: p. 253 OBJ: 11-5 TYPE: C

32. The assets most commonly used for security by asset-based lending companies are
   a. land and buildings.
   b. accounts receivable and inventory.
   c. equipment and buildings.
   d. inventory and equipment.

ANS: B REF: p. 254 OBJ: 11-5 TYPE: C

33. The traditional way to locate business angels is through
   a. contact with business associates, accountants, and lawyers.
   b. formal angel networks or clubs.
   c. advertisements in magazines.
   d. contact with friends and relatives.

ANS: A REF: p. 254 OBJ: 11-6 TYPE: C

34. Venture capital companies
   a. provide investment support to young businesses.
   b. provide for the financing needs of large companies only.
   c. are corporations or partnerships that operate as liquidation groups.
   d. no longer operate in the U.S. market.

ANS: A REF: p. 255 OBJ: 11-6 TYPE: D

35. Business angels provide
   a. asset-based loans.
   b. factoring.
   c. informal venture capital.
   d. trade credit.

ANS: C REF: p. 254 OBJ: 11-6 TYPE: C

36. How likely is the typical startup to succeed in getting funded by a venture capitalist?
   a. Very unlikely (1-2 percent)
   b. Unlikely (10-20 percent)
   c. Likely (60-75 percent)
   d. Very likely (90 percent)

ANS: A REF: p. 255 OBJ: 11-6 TYPE: D

37. Guaranty loans are
   a. made by private lenders.
   b. guaranteed up to 50 percent by the SBA.
   c. made through foreign banks.
   d. limited to $100,000.

ANS: A REF: p. 257 OBJ: 11-7 TYPE: C

38. The federal government provides funds to small businesses through
   a. venture capital companies.
   b. the Small Business Administration.
   c. business angels.
   d. the Securities and Exchange Commission.

ANS: B REF: p. 256 OBJ: 11-7 TYPE: C

39. Small business investment companies (SBICs)
   a. are licensed and regulated by the Federal Trade Commission.
   b. may lend funds or supply equity funds.
   c. obtain part of their capital from local governments at attractive interest rates.
   d. provide only short-term financing.

ANS: B REF: p. 257 OBJ: 11-7 TYPE: D

40. Private placement
   a. is the sale of capital stock to selected individuals.
   b. is the sale of capital stock to investment bankers.
   c. requires compliance with all securities laws.
   d. maintains the ownership control of the original owners.

ANS: A REF: p. 258 OBJ: 11-8 TYPE: C

ESSAY

1. What are the four basic factors that determine *how* a firm is financed?

ANS:
The four basic factors that determine how a firm is financed are:
- The firm's economic potential
- The nature of the firm's assets
- The maturity of the firm
- The personal preferences of the owner(s) with respect to the tradeoffs between debt and equity

REF: p. 237 OBJ: 11-2 TYPE: C

2. What are the tradeoffs between profitability, risk, and control that should be considered when choosing between debt and equity?

ANS:
Borrowing money rather than issuing common stock increases the potential for higher rates of return to the owners. Taking on debt instead of issuing stock also allows the owner(s) to retain voting control of the company. However, debt represents a fixed obligation to repay and a schedule for repayment and thus increases the risk of the firm. Owners who decide to issue stock instead of increasing debt will proportionately reduce the risk of the firm, but they will also limit their potential for returns and give up some voting control. There are clearly tradeoffs between the two options.

REF: p. 239-242 OBJ: 11-2 TYPE: C

3. What sources of funds are available to businesses?

ANS:
Major sources of equity financing are personal savings, family and friends, other individual investors (including business angels), venture capitalists, and the sale of securities. Major sources of debt financing are commercial banks, government-sponsored programs, business suppliers, asset-based lenders, equipment loans, community-based financial institutions, and individual investors.

REF: p. 243 OBJ: 11-3 TYPE: C

4. What are the "five C's of credit"?

ANS:
The "five C's of credit" are:

- The borrower's *character*
- The borrower's *capacity* to repay the loan
- The *capital* being invested in the venture by the borrower
- The *conditions* of the industry and economy
- The *collateral* available to secure the loan

REF: p. 249 OBJ: 11-4 TYPE: C

5. List two methods of selling common stock, and discuss each method.

ANS:
One way to sell common stock is through private placement, in which the firm's stock is sold to selected individuals, usually the firm's employees, the owner's acquaintances, members of the local community, customers, and suppliers. Some small firms make their stock available to the general public in what is called an initial public offering (IPO). The reason often cited for a public sale is the need for additional working capital.

REF: p. 258 OBJ: 11-8 TYPE: C

6. **You Make the Call—Situation 1**
David Bernstein needs help financing his Lodi, New Jersey–based Access Direct Inc., a six-year-old $3.5 million company. “We’re ready to get to the next level,” says Bernstein. “But we’re not sure which way to go.” Access Direct spruces up and then sells used computer equipment for corporations; it is looking for up to $2 million in order to expand. “Venture capitalists, individual investors, or banks,” says Bernstein, who owns the company with four partners, “we’ve thought about them all.”

Question 1 What is your impression of Bernstein’s perspective on raising capital to “get to the next level”?

Question 2 What advice would you offer Bernstein as to both appropriate and inappropriate sources of financing in his situation?

ANS:

1. Bernstein gives the impression that he is looking to a wide variety of sources. However, typically, anything that is of interest to one type of investor will not be of interest to another. For example, what a bank would be interested in would not be of interest to a venture capitalist. Bernstein needs to clarify exactly what he needs and then focus on sources that are a good fit for that need.
2. If Bernstein is looking to finance assets that can be used as collateral for a loan, then a bank or an asset lender might have an interest. However, if $2 million in debt would overload the company's debt position, then he needs to find equity financing. To be an attractive investment for private equity investors, he must demonstrate that the investors have a chance to earn substantial rates of return—70% or more per year—and be able to cash out in five to seven years. If he cannot do that, then he will need to rely on friends and family to help with the financing, or he may just have to limit the expansion to the firm's ability to finance the growth internally.

REF: p. 261 OBJ: YMTC TYPE: C

7. **You Make the Call—Situation 2**
Carter Dalton is well on his way to starting a new venture—Max, Inc. He has projected a need for $350,000 in initial capital. He plans to invest $150,000 himself and either borrow the additional $200,000 or find a partner who will buy stock in the company. If Dalton borrows the money, the interest rate will be 6 percent. If, on the other hand, another equity investor is found, he expects to have to give up 60 percent of the company's stock. Dalton has forecasted earnings of about 16 percent in operating income on the firm's total assets.

Question 1 Compare the two financing options in terms of projected return on the owner's equity investment. Ignore any effect from income taxes.

Question 2 What if Dalton is wrong and the company earns only 4 percent in operating income on total assets?

Question 3 What should Dalton consider in choosing a source of financing?

ANS:
1. Compare the two financing options in terms of projected return on the owner's equity investment. Ignore any effect from income taxes.

   Owner's return on equity investment = Net income ÷ Owner's investment

   If equity is issued:
   Owner's return on equity investment =
   ($350,000 x 18%) ÷ $350,000 = 18%

   If debt is issued:
   Owner's return on equity investment =
   ([$350,000 x 18%] – [$200,000 x 12%]) ÷ $150,000 = 26%

2. If equity is issued:
   Owner's return on equity investment = ($350,000 x 5%) ÷ $350,000 = 5%
   If debt is issued:
   Owner's return on equity investment =
   ([$350,000 x 5%] – [$200,000 x 12%]) ÷ $150,000 = -4.3%

3. He has to compare the firm's expected return on its assets with the interest rate. As a general rule, as long as a firm's return on its assets is greater than the cost of the debt (interest rate), the owner's return on equity investment will be increased. Stegemoller hopes to earn 18 percent on its assets but pay only a 12-percent interest rate for debt financing. Using debt therefore increases the owners' opportunity to enhance the rate of return on their investment.

REF: p. 261 OBJ: YMTC TYPE: C

8. **You Make the Call—Situation 3**
Steve Peplin is the president of Talan Products, a metal stamper based in Cleveland. Peplin has a long-term relationship with his banker. But recently his firm ran into financial difficulty, and the bank is demanding that Peplin personally guarantee 100 percent of the company's loans. Peplin would prefer not to do so, but isn't sure that he has a choice.
Source: "Hands On," *Inc.*, Vol. 25, No. 8 (August 2003), p. 50.

Question 1 Should Peplin be surprised by the bank's demand for a personal guarantee? Why or why not?
Question 2 What would you advise Peplin to do?

ANS:
1. Peplin should not be surprised that the bank wants him to personally guarantee the loan. Rarely do banks make loans to small businesses without the owner personally guarantee the loan, much less when the firm is having financial difficulty.
2. Accept the need to personally guarantee the loan, and then over deliver on his promises to be in a better position to have the guarantee removed at some point in the future.

REF: p. 261 OBJ: YMTC TYPE: C

9. **You Make the Call—Situation 4**
James Ridings's firm, Craftmade International, Inc., sells ceiling fans. Originally, Ridings was a sales representative for a company that sold plumbing supplies. When the company added ceiling fans to its line, Ridings developed a number of customers who bought the fans. Some time later, when the firm eliminated the ceiling fans, Ridings had customers and nothing to sell them. Consequently, in 1997, he became partners with James Ivins, a sales representative for a firm that imported ceiling fans. They scraped together $30,000 and bought 800 fans from Taiwan, which were quickly sold. Encouraged, Ridings raised $45,000 to buy more fans. Again, they sold quickly. By the end of the first year, Ridings and Ivins had putt together a sales force of 15 persons and were selling 3,000 fans per month. By 1999, the two men had started designing their own high-quality and high-profit-margin fans. Sales had grown to $10 million, and the firm was profitable. However, while the firm's sales were increasing at 50 percent per year, a problem developed: The firm ran into cash problems. At one critical point, Ridings had to persuade a supplier to accept stock in lieu of payment on a $224,000 order. Another time, Ridings and Ivins had to approach 16 bankers within a matter of a few days before finding someone who would loan them $100,000 to pay their bills.

Question 1 Craftmade International, Inc. is a successful firm when it comes to growing, but what are its owners overlooking?
Question 2 What steps would you suggest to Ridings and Ivins to solve their problems?

ANS:
1. While the company is growing, it requires an increased line of credit to finance its working capital. Since they failed to estimate actual cash needs in the future period, the owners failed to arrange a line of credit in advance.
2. Because banks extend credit only when they are well informed, Ridings and Ivins should plan how much cash the business will need in the future. They should then ask the bank in advance to extend credit, in order to have the maximum amount of credit when the company needs to borrow.

REF: p. 0 OBJ: YMTC TYPE: C

Correlation Table for Chapter 12—The Harvest Plan

	Learning Objectives	Question Type	Definition Define new term, recall facts	Concept Understand or relate concepts	Application Apply knowledge, analyze data
1	Explain the importance of having a harvest, or exit, plan.	T/F	1	2,3,4	
		MC	1	2,3	
		ES			
2	Describe the options available for harvesting.	T/F		5,6,7,8,9,10,11, 12,13,14,15,16, 17,18,19,20	
		MC		4,5,6,7,8,9,10.12, 13,14,15,16,17, 18,19,20,21,22, 23,24	11,25
		ES		1,2,3,4	
3	Explain the issues in valuing a firm that is being harvested and deciding on the method of payment.	T/F		21,22,23,24	
		MC	27	26,28,29,30,31	
		ES			
4	Provide advice on developing an effective harvest plan.	T/F		25,26,27,28,29, 30	
		MC		32,33,34,35,36, 37, 38,39,40	
		ES		5	
	You Make the Call	ES		6,7,8,9	

Total Number of Test Questions: 78 (30 True/False; 40 Multiple-Choice; 8 Essay)

Chapter 12—The Harvest Plan

TRUE/FALSE

1. Harvesting is the method entrepreneurs and investors use to grow their firms.

   ANS: F
   Harvesting is the method entrepreneurs and investors use to exit a business and, hopefully, reap the value of their investment in the firm.

   REF: p. 265 OBJ: 12-1 TYPE: D

2. Many entrepreneurs successfully grow their firms, but fail to develop an effective exit plan.

   ANS: T REF: p. 265 OBJ: 12-1 TYPE: C

3. Many entrepreneurs who founded companies in the 1970s and 1980s are finding it increasingly difficult to harvest their businesses.

   ANS: F
   In recent times, there have been an unprecedented number of opportunities for entrepreneurs to sell their firms. In the last few years, investors have been actively buying firms in the same industry and then consolidating them into a single, larger company.

   REF: p. 265 OBJ: 12-1 TYPE: C

4. Harvesting encompasses more than just selling and leaving a business.

   ANS: T REF: p. 265 OBJ: 12-1 TYPE: C

5. As in any exit strategy, the sale of a firm is solely about determining the value of a company.

   ANS: F
   The sale of a firm is concerned with how to value a company, but it also considers how to structure the sale.

   REF: p. 266 OBJ: 12-2 TYPE: C

6. An employee buyer is most interested in the firm as a stand-alone, cash-generating business.

   ANS: F
   The employee buyer is primarily interested in the firm as a means of *preserving jobs.*

   REF: p. 267 OBJ: 12-2 TYPE: C

7. A strategic buyer is most interested in the stand-alone, cash-generating potential of a business.

   ANS: F

A strategic buyer is most interested in the *synergies* that can be achieved via an acquisition.

REF: p. 267 OBJ: 12-2 TYPE: C

8. In earlier years, the leveraged buyout became synonymous with the bust-up leveraged buyout.

ANS: T REF: p. 267 OBJ: 12-2 TYPE: C

9. More recently, the bust-up leveraged buyout was replaced with the build-up leveraged buyout.

ANS: T REF: p. 267 OBJ: 12-2 TYPE: C

10. The build-up leveraged buyout is typically used in industries that are dominated by large firms.

ANS: F
The build-up leveraged buyout is typically used in industries that are dominated by small business, such as funeral services and automobile dealerships.

REF: p. 267 OBJ: 12-2 TYPE: C

11. Employee stock ownership plans provide a way for employees with stock in a firm to cash out their ownership position.

ANS: F
Employee stock ownership plans provide a way for the *owners of a business* to cash out their ownership position.

REF: p. 268 OBJ: 12-2 TYPE: C

12. Most businesses with ESOPs are large, and eventually all of them become publicly traded.

ANS: F
Most businesses with ESOPs are small, and only a handful of them have ever been publicly traded.

REF: p. 269 OBJ: 12-2 TYPE: C

13. The boost to employee motivation and effort that results from ownership will vary significantly from firm to firm.

ANS: T REF: p. 269 OBJ: 12-2 TYPE: C

14. Since future growth usually requires great cash inflows, owners who decide to harvest a value-creating firm by withdrawing cash flows should accelerate the process as much as possible.

ANS: F
The cash flow withdrawal process can be immediate if the owners simply sold off the assets of the firm and ceased business operations; however, this option would not make sense for a value-creating firm (i.e., one that earns attractive rates of return for its investors), since the firm's rate of return exceeds the investors' opportunity cost of funds.

REF: p. 269 OBJ: 12-2 TYPE: C

15. One of the drawbacks of harvesting by withdrawing cash flows is that the owner must seek out a buyer for the eventual sale of the business.

ANS: F
Not having to seek out a buyer for the business is one of the *advantages* of harvesting via free cash flow withdrawal; the other is the retaining of control.

REF: p. 269 OBJ: 12-2 TYPE: C

16. For the entrepreneur who is simply tired of the day-to-day operations of the business, siphoning off cash flows over time may require too much patience.

ANS: T REF: p. 270 OBJ: 12-2 TYPE: C

17. Many entrepreneurs consider an initial public offering to be the "holy grail" of their career, even though most do not really understand the process.

ANS: T REF: p. 270 OBJ: 12-2 TYPE: C

18. One of the reasons for going public to raise equity capital is to create a liquid market for the company's stock.

ANS: T REF: p. 271 OBJ: 12-2 TYPE: C

19. With an initial public offering, the entrepreneur's goals and motivations are likely to be very different from those of the investment banker.

ANS: T REF: p. 271 OBJ: 12-2 TYPE: C

20. With a private equity placement, the firm's equity is sold in public equity markets, but the transaction is handled by a private investment banker.

ANS: F
With a private equity placement, *private equity capital* is infused to help a family-controlled firm transfer ownership from one generation to the next and eventually to outside investors, while at the same time providing growth capital.

REF: p. 273 OBJ: 12-2 TYPE: C

21. More often than not, buyers and sellers base the harvest value of a company on the observed market value of a comparable firm relative to its earnings.

ANS: T REF: p. 275, reference 590 OBJ: 12-3 TYPE: C

22. Harvesting owners can be paid in cash or in stock of the acquiring firm, with stock generally being preferred over cash.

ANS: F
Harvesting owners can be paid in cash or in stock of the acquiring firm, with cash generally being preferred over stock.

REF: p. 275 OBJ: 12-3 TYPE: C

23. Owing to the precision of the formulas that guide practice, many think of business valuation as an exact science.

ANS: F
Business valuation is part science and part art—there is no precise formula for determining the price of a private company.

REF: p. 275 OBJ: 12-3 TYPE: C

24. Entrepreneurs who accept stock in payment for the sale of their businesses are usually pleased with the results because they escape a significant tax burden.

ANS: F
Entrepreneurs who accept stock in payment for the sale of their businesses do avoid some unfavorable tax consequences, but overall they are frequently *disappointed* with the outcome.

REF: p. 275 OBJ: 12-3 TYPE: C

25. Entrepreneurs frequently do not appreciate the difficulty of selling or exiting a business.

ANS: T REF: p. 276 OBJ: 12-4 TYPE: C

26. Investors always think ahead about how to exit an enterprise, but the entrepreneur should not have this focus since the business will perform better if it is managed with day-to-day operations in mind.

ANS: F
Investors are always concerned with how to exit an enterprise, and entrepreneurs need to have a similar mind-set, especially when they are planning an IPO.

REF: p. 276 OBJ: 12-4 TYPE: C

27. The opportunity to exit a business is triggered by an interested seller.

ANS: F
The opportunity to exit a business is triggered by the availability of a willing and interested *buyer*, not just an interested seller.

REF: p. 276 OBJ: 12-4 TYPE: C

28. Entrepreneurs often do not make good employees.

ANS: T REF: p. 277 OBJ: 12-4 TYPE: C

29. Entrepreneurs should think very carefully about their motives for exiting a business and what they plan to do after the harvest.

ANS: T REF: p. 279 OBJ: 12-4 TYPE: C

30. Many entrepreneurs have a sense of gratitude for the benefits they have received from living in a capitalist system, so they feel the need to give something back to society, both with their time and with their money.

ANS: T REF: p. 281 OBJ: 12-4 TYPE: C

MULTIPLE CHOICE

1. Harvesting refers to
   a. starting a business.
   b. managing the growth of a business.
   c. exiting a business.
   d. diversifying a business.

   ANS: C REF: p. 265 OBJ: 12-1 TYPE: D

2. Exiting or harvesting encompasses
   a. merely selling and leaving a business.
   b. the creation of future options.
   c. the establishment of a benchmark for firm risk.
   d. capturing future profitability.

   ANS: B REF: p. 265 OBJ: 12-1 TYPE: C

3. The availability of exit options is an important determinant of the appeal of the firm to
   a. suppliers.
   b. investors.
   c. the employees of the company.
   d. the management of the company.

   ANS: B REF: p. 266 OBJ: 12-1 TYPE: C

4. Which of the following is *not* one of the common harvest strategies used by small businesses?
   a. Releasing the firm's cash flows to its owners
   b. Offering stock to the public in an IPO
   c. Completing a private placement of a stock
   d. Inviting a friendly takeover

   ANS: D REF: p. 266 OBJ: 12-2 TYPE: C

5. The different types of transactions involving small businesses are
   a. strategic, financial, and employee acquisitions.
   b. financial, employee, and internal acquisitions.
   c. strategic, internal, and financial acquisitions.
   d. internal, external, and complex acquisitions.

   ANS: A REF: p. 267 OBJ: 12-2 TYPE: C

6. Strategic buyers evaluate acquisition candidates according to the
   a. stand-along, cash-generating potential of a target business.
   b. synergies they think the target business will create.
   c. potential of the target business to preserve employment.
   d. quality of the business strategy of the target firm.

   ANS: B REF: p. 267 OBJ: 12-2 TYPE: C

7. In earlier years, leveraged buyouts became synonymous with the ________ LBO.
   a. bust-up
   c. owner-financed

b. build-up d. publicly-funded

ANS: A REF: p. 267 OBJ: 12-2 TYPE: C

8. A build-up leveraged buyout involves
   a. developing the business to make it an attractive takeover target.
   b. acquiring businesses that occupy a higher level in the market channel.
   c. a longer time horizon than a bust-up leveraged buyout.
   d. constructing a larger enterprise to be taken public via an IPO.

   ANS: D REF: p. 267 OBJ: 12-2 TYPE: C

9. An employee stock ownership plan represents
   a. a good way for a business founder to build his/her position in the company.
   b. an opportunity for employees to acquire an ownership interest in their company.
   c. a harvest method of choice.
   d. an effort to ease investor concerns.

   ANS: B REF: p. 268 OBJ: 12-2 TYPE: C

10. The mere fact that a firm is earning high rates of return on the firm's asset indicates that
    a. the firm is worth more as a going concern than as a dead one.
    b. downsizing is likely to be an economically sound option for the business.
    c. it is time to start growing the business again.
    d. it might be wise to further limit the cash flows returned to investors.

    ANS: A REF: p. 269 OBJ: 12-2 TYPE: C

11. Matt Townsend owns a car dealership that is very profitable. Since he plans to retire in 5-10 years, Townsend has decided to retain ownership for now, but without continuing to grow the business. This change would also allow him to invest for retirement some of the cash that the business is now generating. Which of the following harvesting methods does this illustrate?
    a. A delayed sellout
    b. A strategy to release the firm's free cash flows to the owners
    c. Offering stock to the public through an IPO
    d. Issuing a private placement of stock

    ANS: B REF: p. 269 OBJ: 12-2 TYPE: A

12. From the owner's perspective, which of the following would be considered an advantage of harvesting via withdrawal of cash flows from the firm?
    a. Retaining control
    b. Preserving cash for later reinvestment
    c. Greater latitude in seeking out a buyer for the firm
    d. Increasing long-term returns from the business

    ANS: A REF: p. 269 OBJ: 12-2 TYPE: C

13. Going public can be beneficial to a firm by helping it
    a. create a liquid currency to fund future acquisitions.
    b. avoid becoming a takeover target in the future.
    c. erect a shield against the fluctuations of the stock market.
    d. offer better compensation packages to attract superior management talent.

ANS: A REF: p. 271 OBJ: 12-2 TYPE: C

14. Having publicly traded stock can be beneficial to owners in that a public market offers
    a. greater liquidity.
    b. protection against an unwanted harvest.
    c. insight into how to improve the performance of the firm.
    d. a justification for refusing requests for ESOP options.

ANS: A REF: p. 271 OBJ: 12-2 TYPE: C

15. Which of the following steps in the IPO process precedes the others?
    a. Audit the last three years of financial statements
    b. Draft a registration statement
    c. Explain IPO attributes to potential investors
    d. Decide upon a price for the business

ANS: A REF: p. 271 OBJ: 12-2 TYPE: C

16. The IPO process may be one of the most ____________ experiences of an entrepreneur's life.
    a. exhilarating, frustrating, and exhausting
    b. frustrating, tempting, and exhausting
    c. tempting, exhausting, and exhilarating
    d. encouraging and nerve-wrecking

ANS: A REF: p. 271 OBJ: 12-2 TYPE: C

17. According to an *Inc.* survey, how much time did CEOs who participated in public offerings spend on those offerings (on average)?
    a. 14 hours per week over 3 and a half months
    b. 21 hours per week over 3 and a half months
    c. 33 hours per week over 4 and a half months
    d. 47 hours per week over 4 and a half months

ANS: C REF: p. 271 OBJ: 12-2 TYPE: C

18. Regarding IPOs, the primary motivation of the issuing firm and that of the investment banker are
    a. the same-maximizing the price of the firm.
    b. similar-completing the sale.
    c. very different because they are compensated for different outcomes.
    d. impossible to know since every deal is structured differently.

ANS: C REF: p. 271 OBJ: 12-2 TYPE: C

19. When surveyed about transfers of ownership within a family-owned firm, most entrepreneurs indicated that the transfer had been or would be financed by
    a. seller financing.
    b. third-party financing.
    c. gift.
    d. the acquirer's personal financing.

ANS: C REF: p. 273 OBJ: 12-2 TYPE: C

20. The owner of a hardware store has agreed to sell his business to another local hardware store owner. The purchaser would likely be described as a sale to a _________ buyer.
    a. competing
    c. financial

b. employee
d. strategic

ANS: D REF: p. 267 OBJ: 12-2 TYPE: C

21. ____________ acquisitions are not popular among many small business owners.
a. Competing
b. Employee
c. Financial
d. Strategic

ANS: C REF: p. 267 OBJ: 12-2 TYPE: C

22. A leveraged buyout involves a high level of _______ financing.
a. debt
b. equity
c. strategic
d. unsecured

ANS: A REF: p. 267 OBJ: 12-2 TYPE: C

23. The most immediate goal of a company once it becomes highly leveraged is to
a. make an operating profit.
b. purchase additional assets.
c. restructure its logistics systems.
d. service the debt.

ANS: D REF: p. 267 OBJ: 12-2 TYPE: C

24. Harvesting a business by releasing the cash flows as dividends creates the worst tax disadvantage for _______.
a. C-corporation shareholders
b. partnerships
c. S-corporation shareholders
d. sole proprietors

ANS: A REF: p. 270 OBJ: 12-2 TYPE: C

25. The sale of Linda Bush's company, SafeRent, Inc., to First American Corporation is an example of
a. a sale to a corporate buyer.
b. a sale to a financial buyer.
c. a sale to a strategic buyer.
d. an employee buyout.

ANS: C REF: p. 272 OBJ: 12-2 TYPE: A

26. Which of the following is a very important question to ask as a firm moves toward a harvest?
a. Why do the owners want to harvest?
b. What is the value of the firm?
c. Does the firm have a leadership succession plan in the event that the firm sells?
d. Will the owners change their minds?

ANS: B REF: p. 273 OBJ: 12-3 TYPE: C

27. The value of privately held companies will usually be estimated based on
a. net income.
b. EBITDA.
c. operating income.
d. market capitalization.

ANS: B REF: p. 0 OBJ: 12-3 TYPE: D

28. Which of the following best characterizes business valuation?
a. Valuation is almost a perfect science.
b. Since there are so many intangibles, valuation is mostly an art.
c. The buyer determines the value of a business.
d. Negotiation skills play an important part in valuation.

ANS: D REF: p. 275 OBJ: 12-3 TYPE: C

29. Harvesting owners generally prefer ________ over ________.
    a. cash, stock
    b. debt, equity
    c. equity, debt
    d. stock, cash

ANS: A REF: p. 275 OBJ: 12-3 TYPE: C

30. The value of a business is determined by
    a. what the owner believes the business is worth.
    b. what a valuation formula determines its worth is to the owner.
    c. what a valuation formula determines its worth is to the buyer.
    d. what a buyer with the cash is prepared to pay.

ANS: D REF: p. 275 OBJ: 12-3 TYPE: C

31. The median percentage of ownership by a firm's officers and directors ______ in the 10 years following an IPO.
    a. declines
    b. increases
    c. remains steady
    d. increases sharply, then steadily decreases

ANS: A REF: p. 271 OBJ: 12-3 TYPE: C

32. In a harvest situation, the exiting owners are usually paid in cash or
    a. tangible assets.
    b. imputed goodwill.
    c. favorable publicity.
    d. stock.

ANS: D REF: p. 276 OBJ: 12-4 TYPE: C

33. Uncertainties accompanying an impending sale of a business often
    a. lead to lower employee morale.
    b. attract the attention of the Securities and Exchange Commission.
    c. cause the deal to fall through.
    d. increase costs from added legal services.

ANS: A REF: p. 276 OBJ: 12-4 TYPE: C

34. Which of the following are always concerned about how to exit a business?
    a. Investors
    b. Entrepreneurs
    c. Employees of the firm
    d. Investment bankers

ANS: A REF: p. 276 OBJ: 12-4 TYPE: C

35. Running a public company requires
    a. accounting records that satisfy the founder's personal accountant.
    b. a board of directors that can keep the business out of bankruptcy.
    c. managing the firm toward a track record of successful performance.
    d. a focus on a long-term exit strategy.

ANS: C REF: p. 276 OBJ: 12-4 TYPE: C

36. After harvesting, many entrepreneurs experience conflicts that are ___________ in nature.
    a. financial
    c. emotional

b. practical
d. tactical

ANS: C REF: p. 277 OBJ: 12-4 TYPE: C

37. Post-harvest entrepreneurs may become disillusioned when they realize their sense of identity
   a. was associated with the quest for wealth.
   b. derived from interactions with employees.
   c. was intertwined with their business.
   d. does not return after joining in social or charitable work.

ANS: C REF: p. 279 OBJ: 12-4 TYPE: C

38. Which of the following is a key question that an entrepreneur must address in anticipation of post-harvest life?
   a. How can I increase my passion for the harvest process?
   b. Will I experience serious regrets over the decision to harvest my investment in the company?
   c. Will I still be respected as a leader in the company?
   d. What will my legacy be within the company?

ANS: B REF: p. 280 OBJ: 12-4 TYPE: C

39. The effects of the harvesting process include
   a. a reduction in time and energy.
   b. an increased managerial focus.
   c. an increase in momentum.
   d. poor performance.

ANS: D REF: p. 276 OBJ: 12-4 TYPE: C

40. Planning for an IPO requires
   a. maintaining an accounting process that cleanly separates the business from the entrepreneur's personal life.
   b. selecting a strong board of directors that can and will offer valuable business advice.
   c. managing the firm so as to produce a successful track record of performance.
   d. all of these

ANS: D REF: p. 276 OBJ: 12-4 TYPE: C

ESSAY

1. List and briefly explain the four basic harvest strategies for the small business.

ANS:
Selling the firm involves transferring ownership of the business to a willing and able buyer.
Releasing the firm's cash flows to its owners involves the orderly withdrawal of the owner's investment in the firm, rather than reinvesting this excess capital for the future growth of the firm.
Offering stock to the public through an IPO is used primarily as a way to raise additional capital to finance company growth, but it is also used as a way to harvest the owner's investment.
Issuing a private placement of the firm's stock entails the infusion of private equity capital to help a family-controlled firm transfer ownership from one generation to the next and eventually to outside investors, while at the same time providing growth capital.

REF: p. 266 OBJ: 12-2 TYPE: C

2. List the three basic types of acquisitions and identify the purpose of each.

ANS:
Strategic acquisitions are focused on synergy formation.
Financial acquisitions look primarily to the firm's stand-alone, cash-generating potential.
Employee acquisitions are designed to preserve employment.

REF: p. 267 OBJ: 12-2 TYPE: C

3. According to Lisa D. Stein, vice president of Solomon Smith Barney, what are the most important reasons for going public?

ANS:
- To raise capital to repay certain outstanding debt
- To strengthen the company's balance sheet to support future growth
- To create a source of capital that can be selectively accessed in the future to fund growth
- To create a liquid currency to fund future acquisitions
- To create a liquid market for the company's stock
- To broaden the company's stockholder base
- To create ongoing interest in the company and its continued development

REF: p. 270 OBJ: 12-2 TYPE: C

4. Outline the steps in the IPO process.

ANS:
- Step 1: Decide to go public.
- Step 2: Audit the last three years of the firm's financial statements.
- Step 3: Select an investment banker to guide the IPO process.
- Step 4: Draft a registration statement and submit it for review by the SEC.
- Step 5: Respond to the SEC's comments and issues a prospectus.
- Step 6: Spend 10-15 days "on the road," explaining the firm's attributes to investors.
- Step 7: On the day before the offering is released, decide upon a final price.
- Step 8: Offer the stock to the public and see how it is received.

REF: p. 271 OBJ: 12-2 TYPE: C

5. What are the personal issues an entrepreneur will face in post-harvest life?

ANS:
There are really two key questions that an entrepreneur must address in anticipation of post-harvest life. First, will the entrepreneur have serious regrets over the decision to harvest the business? Since the business is an integral part of the lives of entrepreneurs, exiting the enterprise can be a very emotional experience. In reality, they may not realize how intensely their personal identify is intertwined with the business until after the harvest has been implemented. This emotional turbulence may lead to unproductive, even destructive behavior.

The Second question concerns what will become of the entrepreneur's passion after adjusting to the "easy life" after exiting the business. Or, stated succinctly, what's next? Since entrepreneurs tend to be strongly purpose-driven, life after the harvest is not likely to be fulfilling without finding a new purpose in life. Often, this means giving back to the community through worthy charitable causes or institutions.

REF: p. 279 OBJ: 12-4 TYPE: C

6. **You Make the Call—Situation 1**

Bill and Francis Waugh founded Casa Bonita. They started with a single fast-food Mexican restaurant in Abilene, Texas. At the time, they both worked seven days a week. From that small beginning, they expanded to 84 profitable restaurants located in Texas, Oklahoma, Arkansas, and Colorado. Over the years, other restaurant owners expressed an interest in buying the firm; however, the Waughs were not interested in selling. Then an English firm, Unigate Limited, offered them $32 million for the business and said Bill could remain the firm's CEO. The Waughs were attracted by the idea of having $32 million in liquid assets. They flew to London to close the deal. On the flight home, however, Bill began having doubts about their decision to sell the business. He thought, "We spent 15 years of our lives getting the business where we wanted it, and we've lost it." After their plane landed in New York, they spent the night and then flew back to London the next day. They offered the buyers $1 million to cancel the contract, but Unigate's management declined the offer. The Waughs flew home disappointed.

Question 1 How could the Waughs be disappointed with $32 million?
Question 2 What should the Waughs have done to avoid this situation?
Question 3 What advice would you offer Bill about continuing to work for the business under the new owners?

ANS:

1. When this story is told to students, they find it difficult to believe that anyone could have remorse with $32 million in the bank. But to the Waughs, especially Bill, he felt that he lost the foundation for much that he was about and did. The Waughs simply had not thought carefully enough about what was most important to them. They probably had mistaken impressions about what it would be like to have the "good life." The journey is what is important, not the final outcome.
2. As already suggested, they should have given more thought to what really mattered to them. They also could have talked to others who had been through the process, which they did after the fact.
3. He should expect that things will change. Most likely, the new owners will have different values and will run the company differently than he did, which indeed happened. So he should not have held onto rigid expectations about what it would be like after the sale; otherwise, he would be disappointed, which he was.

REF: p. 279 OBJ: YMTC TYPE: C

7. **You Make the Call—Situation 2**

Ed and Barbara Bonneau started their wholesale sunglass distribution firm 30 years ago with $1,000 of their own money and $5,000 borrowed from a country banker in Ed's hometown. The firm grew quickly, selling sunglasses and reading glasses to such companies as Wal-Mart, Eckerd Drugs, and Phar-Mor. In addition, the Bonneaus enjoyed using the company to do good things. For example, they had a company chaplain, who was available when employees were having family problems, such as a death in the family. Although the company had done well, the market had matured recently and profit margins narrowed significantly. Wal-Mart, for example, was insisting on better terms, which meant significantly lower profits for the Bonneaus. Previously, Ed had set the prices that he needed to make a good return on his investment. Now, the buyers had consolidated, and they had the power. Ed didn't enjoy running the company as much as he had in the past, and he was finding greater pleasure in other activities; for instance, he served on a local hospital board and was actively involved in church activities.

Just as Ed and Barbara began to think about selling the company, they were contacted by a financial buyer, who wanted to use their firm as a platform and then buy up several sunglass companies. After negotiations, the Bonneaus sold their firm for about $20 million. In addition, Ed received a retainer fee for serving as a consultant to the buyer. Also, the Bonneaus' son-in-law, who was part of the company's management team, was named the new chief operating officer.

Question 1 Do you agree with the Bonneaus' decision to sell? Why or why not?
Question 2 Why did the buyers retain Ed as a consultant? (In answering this question, you might consider the quote by Bonneau in the chapter 12.)
Question 3 Do you see any problem with having the Bonneaus' son-in-law become the new chief operating officer?

ANS:

1. The Bonneaus were becoming less and less interested in the business. It was no longer fun for them, which suggested that they needed a change. Also, it was time to sell so that someone else with deeper pockets could consolidate several firms in the same business and gain power in dealing with the larger customers, such as Wal-Mart.
2. It was intended as a de facto non-compete agreement.
3. It placed Bonneau and his son-in-law in an awkward position. The son-in-law was having to negotiate from the perspective of the new chief operating officer after the sale, so he had certain needs. Bonneau, on the other hand, was negotiating from the perspective of someone who would be exiting the firm. There were some conflicts of interest as a result.

REF: p. 277 OBJ: YMTC TYPE: C

8. **You Make the Call—Situation 3**

At age 63, Michael Lipper sold his firm to Reuters. His assessment of the sale follows:

One of the reasons we sold our business to Reuters was because we knew we probably couldn't manage the technology of the future by ourselves. Any entrepreneur who builds a business for as long as I have would be dishonest if he did not suffer a certain sadness [from selling]. If [Reuters] make a wonderful success out of this, there may be some ego pain. If they muck it up, they've damaged our name and hurt our people.

Lois Silverman co-founded CRA Managed Care (now known as Concentra Managed Care). When the firm went public in 1995, Silverman's stake was over $10 million. After taking Concentra public, Silverman gave up all involvement in day-to-day operations. Along with 12 other successful businesswomen, she formed the not-for-profit Commonwealth Institute, to help women entrepreneurs set up boards and secure capital. She also became involved with a newspaper called *Women's Business*. She later told this story:

> *The other day a man said to me on a golf course, "I hope I hit this ball, because since I've left my business, I don't know what to do with myself." And I said to myself, "I'm so lucky."*

Question 1 Compare the people in the above true stories in terms of their feelings about exiting their firms.

Question 2 What might explain the difference between those who have positive feelings about cashing out and those who do not?

ANS:
1. Lipper understood that there would be some emotional stress after selling his firm, but he also understood that a time might come when someone else could do more with the business than he was able to do. Thus, his emotions were balanced with the reality of the situation. Siverman avoided any emotional problems by having other priorities that gave meaning to her life apart from the company. The golfer clearly was emotionally distressed by not having other interests that made a difference to someone. Golfing did not provide an adequate foundation for a positive self-image.

REF: p. 277 OBJ: YMTC TYPE: C

9. **You Make the Call—Situation 5**

Craigen Corporation was sold to a financial buyer, who financed the purchase as a leveraged buyout (LBO). The company's financial structure before and after the sale is as follows

	Before the Sale	**After the Sale**
Current liabilities	$ 3,433,532	$11,018,041
Long-term liabilities	1,350,000	47,720,878
Deferred income taxes	569,736	1,742,165
Total liabilities	$ 5,353,268	$60,481,084
Equity	12,948,456	6,789,340
Total liabilities and equity	$18,301,724	$67,270,424

Question 1 The before-sale and after-sale numbers differ significantly—the total debt and equity increased from $18.3 million to $67.3 million. In the typical LBO, what would cause this increase?

ANS:
1. The increase in value for a LBO typically is the result of changing from historical accounting numbers to numbers that reflect the firm's current value to the buyer. In other words, the founders of the company had invested just over $18 million in the firm during their years of ownership, up to the point of the acquisition. However, the buyer believed the business was worth over $67 million.

REF: p. 273 OBJ: YMTC TYPE: C

Correlation Table for Chapter 13—Customer Relationships: The Key Ingredient

	Learning Objectives	Question Type	Definition Define new term, recall facts	Concept Understand or relate concepts	Application Apply knowledge, analyze data
1	Define customer relationship management (CRM) and explain its importance to a small firm.	T/F	1,2,3,5	4	
		MC		1,2	
		ES			
2	Discuss the significance of providing extraordinary customer service.	T/F	8	6,7,9	
		MC		3,4,5	6
		ES			
3	Illustrate how technology, such as the Internet, can improve customer relationships.	T/F	10,11,12	13	
		MC	8	7,9	
		ES			
4	Describe the techniques for creating a customer profile.	T/F	14,15,16		
		MC		10	11,12,13
		ES			
5	Explain how consumers are decision makers and why this is important to understanding customer relationships.	T/F	17,18	19,20,20,21,22, 23,24,25	
		MC	15,17	14,15	16,18,19,20,21, 22
		ES			
6	Describe certain psychological influences on consumer behavior.	T/F	26,27,29	30,31,32	28
		MC	23,24		25,25,27,28,29, 30,31,32
		ES			
7	Describe certain sociological influences on consumer behavior.	T/F	34,35	33	
		MC	33,34	36	35,37,38,39,40
		ES			
	You Make the Call	ES		1,2,3,4	

Total Number of Test Questions: 79 (35 True/False; 40 Multiple-Choice; 4 Essay)

Chapter 13—Customer Relationships: The Key Ingredient

TRUE/FALSE

1. Customer relationship management means the different things to different people.

   ANS: T REF: p. 287 OBJ: 13-1 TYPE: D

2. The goals of a CRM program for most small firms are the complete customization of products and/or services to fit individual customer needs.

   ANS: F REF: p. 287 OBJ: 13-1 TYPE: D

3. The central message of every CRM program is "Court customers for a one-time sale."

   ANS: F REF: p. 287 OBJ: 13-1 TYPE: D

4. Buying or developing CRM software leads to higher customer retention.

   ANS: F REF: p. 288 OBJ: 13-1 TYPE: C

5. There must be a company-wide commitment to CRM concept if CRM is to be productive.

   ANS: T REF: p. 288 OBJ: 13-1 TYPE: D

6. Superior customer service translates directly to customer loyalty.

   ANS: F
   Superior customer service leads to customer satisfaction, and it is customer satisfaction that leads most directly to customer loyalty.

   REF: p. 289 OBJ: 13-2 TYPE: C

7. Customer satisfaction is all about providing extraordinary services to the buyer.

   ANS: F
   A number of factors contribute to customer satisfaction, including basic elements that consumers expect in a product, general support services (e.g., customer assistance), a recovery process for counteracting bad experiences, and extraordinary services (e.g., customization).

   REF: p. 289 OBJ: 13-2 TYPE: C

8. "Boo-boo research" refers to that part of any customer loyalty program that reaches out to lost customers to learn why they took their business elsewhere.

   ANS: T REF: p. 290 OBJ: 13-2 TYPE: D

9. Regardless of the nature of the business, providing exceptional customer service can give small firms a competitive edge.

ANS: T REF: p. 290 OBJ: 13-2 TYPE: C

10. Long-term transactional relationships with customers are fostered by good information.

ANS: T REF: p. 294 OBJ: 13-3 TYPE: D

11. The ability to enjoy one-on-one contact with customers has always been a competitive advantage for large firms.

ANS: F REF: p. 294 OBJ: 13-3 TYPE: D

12. Sales endeavors generate the second largest amount of customer contact.

ANS: F
Deciding which marketing activity should get initial CRM support is not always easy. However, the sales department is a popular place to start, because sales endeavors generate the greatest amount of customer contact.

REF: p. 294 OBJ: 13-3 TYPE: D

13. Lack of in-house expertise is a major justification for using outside CRM services.

ANS: T REF: p. 295 OBJ: 13-3 TYPE: C

14. Mac McConnell, owner of the Artful Framer Gallery in Plantation, Florida. reworked his business based on the results of a survey showed that price was a top priority and quality was last. He added a low end line and made inexpensive framing his specialty.

ANS: F REF: p. 296 OBJ: 13-4 TYPE: D

15. Customer profiles are limited to demographic variables such as age, gender, and marital status.

ANS: F REF: p. 295 OBJ: 13-4 TYPE: D

16. Customer profiles primarily reflect demographic variables such as age, gender, and marital status, but they can also include behavioral, psychological, and sociological information.

ANS: T REF: p. 295 OBJ: 13-4 TYPE: D

17. A consumer's recognition of a problem can be characterized as routine if the problem occurs infrequently, evolves over time, and requires much thought by the individual.

ANS: F
Some problems are routine conditions of depletion; however, those problems that arise infrequently and evolve over time are not routine in nature.

REF: p. 297 OBJ: 13-5 TYPE: D

18. Evoked sets are features or characteristics of products or services that are used to compare brands.

ANS: F
Features or characteristics of products or services that are used to compare brands are referred to as *evaluation criteria*, whereas an *evoked set* is a group of brands that a consumer is both aware of and willing to consider as a solution to a purchase problem.

REF: p. 297 OBJ: 13-5 TYPE: D

19. Small businesses must strive to recognize cognitive dissonance among their customers and to manage it effectively.

ANS: T REF: p. 297 OBJ: 13-5 TYPE: C

20. An evoked set is a group of brands that a consumer is aware of but unwilling to consider as a solution to a purchase problem.

ANS: F REF: p. 297 OBJ: 13-5 TYPE: C

21. An evoked set is a group of brands that a consumer is both aware of and willing to consider as a solution to a purchase problem.

ANS: T REF: p. 297 OBJ: 13-5 TYPE: C

22. In the information search and evaluation stage, the firm's principal objective is to establish evaluative criteria.

ANS: F REF: p. 297 OBJ: 13-5 TYPE: C

23. A brand gains market awareness once it becomes part of consumers' evoked sets.

ANS: F REF: p. 297 OBJ: 13-5 TYPE: C

24. Post-purchase dissonance has been shown to be unrelated to customer satisfaction because it occurs after customers have satisfied their needs.

ANS: F REF: p. 298 OBJ: 13-5 TYPE: C

25. Post-purchase dissonance and consumer complaints are both directly related to customer satisfaction.

ANS: T REF: p. 298 OBJ: 13-5 TYPE: C

26. An investigation of culture with a narrow definitional boundary (e.g., by age, geographic location, etc.) is called perceptual categorization.

ANS: F
Perceptual categorization is a process by which things that are similar are perceived as belonging together.

REF: p. 299 OBJ: 13-6 TYPE: D

27. Attitudes have an indirect impact on consumer behavior.

ANS: F
Attitudes *directly* impact behavior, acting as an obstacle or a catalyst in bringing a customer to a product.

REF: p. 300 OBJ: 13-6 TYPE: D

28. Consumer needs can be completely satisfied by proper customer relationship management.

ANS: F REF: p. 298 OBJ: 13-6 TYPE: A

29. Attitudes are forces that organize and give direction to the tension caused by unsatisfied needs.

ANS: F REF: p. 300 OBJ: 13-6 TYPE: D

30. Three classes of needs—social, psychological, and spiritual—cannot be connected to behavior through motivations.

ANS: F REF: p. 298 OBJ: 13-6 TYPE: C

31. Marketers create needs that offer unique motivations to consumers.

ANS: F REF: p. 300 OBJ: 13-6 TYPE: C

32. A marketer must determine which motivations the consumer will perceive as acceptable in a given situation.

ANS: T REF: p. 300 OBJ: 13-6 TYPE: C

33. Similar to a caste system, a genuine social class system does not allow for upward mobility.

ANS: F
A social class system is unlike a caste system in that only the former provides for upward mobility.

REF: p. 301 OBJ: 13-7 TYPE: C

34. Every group to which an individual belongs is a reference group for that consumer.

ANS: F
A reference group refers to those that which an individual allows to influence his or her behavior; group membership is not a requirement.

REF: p. 302 OBJ: 13-7 TYPE: D

35. In general, opinion leaders are considered to be knowledgeable, visible, and exposed to mass media.

ANS: T REF: p. 302 OBJ: 13-7 TYPE: D

MULTIPLE CHOICE

1. Which of the following is *not* a focus of modern CRM?
   a. Customers rather than products
   c. All channels and media involved in the

b. Changes in processes, systems, and culture
marketing effort
d. Reductions in transactional relationships

ANS: D REF: p. 287 OBJ: 13-1 TYPE: C

2. Economic benefits associated with maintaining relationships with current customers include:
   a. Acquisition costs for new customers are huge.
   b. New customers spend more money than long-time customers.
   c. Order processing costs are lower for new customers.
   d. All of these.

ANS: A REF: p. 288 OBJ: 13-1 TYPE: C

3. The basic ideas forming the foundation of customer loyalty for small firms include the notion that
   a. superior customer service will almost always lead directly to customer satisfaction.
   b. customer satisfaction demands customer loyalty.
   c. small firms possess great potential for providing superior customer service.
   d. customer satisfaction is "the name of the game" for such businesses.

ANS: C REF: p. 289 OBJ: 13-2 TYPE: C

4. Which of the following is *not* one of the suggestions for developing extraordinary customer service?
   a. Naming names
   b. Customer care
   c. Keeping in touch
   d. "Bamboo research"

ANS: D REF: p. 289 OBJ: 13-2 TYPE: C

5. Most customer service problems are identified by
   a. personal observation.
   b. outside consultants.
   c. customer complaints.
   d. entries in a suggestion box.

ANS: C REF: p. 292 OBJ: 13-2 TYPE: C

6. Offering to relaunder a customer's shirt at no charge to add additional starch is an example of which key element in attaining customer satisfaction?
   a. basic benefits
   b. general support services
   c. a recovery process
   d. extraordinary services

ANS: C REF: p. 289 OBJ: 13-2 TYPE: A

7. Long-term transactional relationships with customers are fostered by
   a. directed advertising.
   c. good information.

b. focused discounts.
d. all of these.

ANS: C REF: p. 294 OBJ: 13-3 TYPE: C

8. Software packages containing __________ tools are available to assist in supporting customer contacts.
   a. word-processing,
   b. spreadsheet
   c. database
   d. all of these

ANS: D REF: p. 294 OBJ: 13-3 TYPE: D

9. According to Forrester Research, almost ______ percent of small to mid-sized businesses with fewer than 1,000 employees are interested in outsourcing some type of application.
   a. 20
   b. 45
   c. 60
   d. 85

ANS: C REF: p. 295 OBJ: 13-3 TYPE: C

10. In a very small business, the customer profiles maintained in the entrepreneur's _______ often constitute the firm's CRM "database."
   a. computer
   b. card file
   c. head
   d. shoe box

ANS: C REF: p. 295 OBJ: 13-4 TYPE: C

11. In which category of a customer profile would a customer's shirt size most likely be stored?
   a. Customer contacts
   b. Descriptive information
   c. Responses to marketing stimuli
   d. Transactions

ANS: B REF: p. 295 OBJ: 13-4 TYPE: A

12. Information taken from warranty cards would be stored in which category of a customer profile?
   a. Customer contacts
   b. Descriptive information
   c. Responses to marketing stimuli
   d. Transactions

ANS: A REF: p. 295 OBJ: 13-4 TYPE: A

13. A customer's use of a discount coupon would most likely be recorded in which category of her customer profile?
   a. Customer contacts
   b. Descriptive information
   c. Responses to marketing stimuli
   d. Transactions

ANS: C REF: p. 295 OBJ: 13-4 TYPE: A

14. All of the following are stages of consumer decision making *except*

a. post-purchase evaluation.
b. purchase decision.
c. problem recognition.
d. perceptual categorization.

ANS: D REF: p. 296 OBJ: 13-5 TYPE: C

15. According to consumer information-processing theory, _____ is the final stage through which consumers progress.
a. purchase decision
b. cognitive dissonance
c. post-purchase evaluation
d. evaluative categorization

ANS: C REF: p. 297 OBJ: 13-5 TYPE: D

16. Mary Adams, an independent sales contractor, recently expressed her concern about having to travel extensively in her car each day to see clients. Specifically, Adams realized that the time she spent in her car was hindering her ability to be in continuous contact with important clients. She believes the purchase of a cellular phone would allow her more freedom to conduct business outside of the office. Adams has just proceeded through the _____ stage of consumer decision making.
a. purchase evaluation
b. evaluative categorization
c. problem recognition
d. cognitive dissonance

ANS: C REF: p. 297 OBJ: 13-5 TYPE: A

17. The tension that occurs immediately following a purchase is referred to as
a. cognitive dissonance.
b. post-purchase satisfaction.
c. cognitive assessment.
d. post-decisional distress.

ANS: A REF: p. 298 OBJ: 13-5 TYPE: D

18. Maurice has come to the conclusion that he needs increase his earning power. He is in the ________ stage of the consumer decision making process.
a. information search and evaluation
b. problem recognition
c. post-purchase evaluation
d. purchase decision

ANS: B REF: p. 297 OBJ: 13-5 TYPE: A

19. Linda is considering several colleges at which to finish her engineering teaching degree. She is in the ________ stage of the consumer decision making process.
a. information search and evaluation
c. post-purchase evaluation

b. problem recognition
d. purchase decision

ANS: A REF: p. 297 OBJ: 13-5 TYPE: A

20. Sara has decided to make an offer on a particular house. She is in the ________ stage of the consumer decision making process.
a. information search and evaluation
b. problem recognition
c. post-purchase evaluation
d. purchase decision

ANS: D REF: p. 297 OBJ: 13-5 TYPE: A

21. Josh is concerned that the snacks he bought are the ones that his friends will enjoy when they come over to watch the game. He is in the ________ stage of the consumer decision making process.
a. information search and evaluation
b. problem recognition
c. post-purchase evaluation
d. purchase decision

ANS: C REF: p. 297 OBJ: 13-5 TYPE: A

22. Even though it is available, Bob never purchases bottled water when he is thirsty. Bob's behavior indicates that bottled water
a. does not meet Bob's evaluative criteria.
b. increases Bob's cognitive dissonance.
c. is not included in Bob's evoked set.
d. decreases Bob's perceptual categorization.

ANS: C REF: p. 297 OBJ: 13-5 TYPE: A

23. Individual processes that ultimately give meaning to stimuli that confront consumers are known as
a. perceptions.
b. motivations.
c. attitudes.
d. opinions.

ANS: A REF: p. 298 OBJ: 13-6 TYPE: D

24. An enduring opinion that is based on a combination of knowledge, feeling, and behavioral tendency is referred to as
a. a motivation.
b. a perception.
c. an attitude.
d. a cognition.

ANS: C REF: p. 300 OBJ: 13-6 TYPE: D

25. Buying an expensive set of underwear is most likely an attempt to satisfy which category of need?
a. physiological
b. psychological
c. spiritual
d. social

ANS: A REF: p. 298 OBJ: 13-6 TYPE: A

26. Attending a wedding is most likely an attempt to satisfy which category of need?
a. physiological
b. psychological
c. spiritual
d. social

ANS: D REF: p. 298 OBJ: 13-6 TYPE: A

27. Working out at the gym is most likely an attempt to satisfy which category of need?
a. physiological
b. psychological
c. spiritual
d. social

ANS: A REF: p. 298 OBJ: 13-6 TYPE: A

28. Attending a prayer breakfast is most likely an attempt to satisfy which category of need?
a. physiological
b. psychological
c. spiritual
d. social

ANS: C REF: p. 298 OBJ: 13-6 TYPE: A

29. Juan's belief that all diet sodas taste awful is an example of
a. cognitive dissonance.
b. an evoked set.
c. perceptual categorization.
d. unilateral indifference.

ANS: C REF: p. 299 OBJ: 13-6 TYPE: A

30. A firm's packaging of its product to closely resemble similar competing products is an attempt to take advantage of
a. cognitive dissonance.
b. need conflicts.
c. perceptual categorization.
d. problem evaluation.

ANS: C REF: p. 299 OBJ: 13-6 TYPE: A

31. The reason that a group of uniformed people walking down the street playing musical instruments is recognized as a band is the result of
a. characteristic profiling.
b. evaluative criteria.
c. perceptual categorization.
d. problem recognition.

ANS: C REF: p. 299 OBJ: 13-6 TYPE: A

32. June has always believed that the grocery store nearby doesn't have fresh produce. This ________ may cause her to avoid the local store and shop at a store across town.
a. attitude
c. motivation

b. cognitive dissonance
d. perceptual categorization

ANS: A REF: p. 300 OBJ: 13-6 TYPE: A

33. Divisions in society with different levels of social prestige are called
    a. reference groups.
    b. cultures.
    c. social classes.
    d. perceptual categories.

ANS: C REF: p. 301 OBJ: 13-7 TYPE: D

34. Groups that an individual allows to influence his or her behavior are known as
    a. reference groups.
    b. referral groups.
    c. perceptual groups.
    d. associate groups.

ANS: A REF: p. 302 OBJ: 13-7 TYPE: D

35. Erin Withers, a typical consumer, often purchases goods and services because she feels her family and fellow workers will approve of these items. Family and co-workers are _____ for this consumer.
    a. reference groups
    b. referral groups
    c. perceptual groups
    d. opinion leaders

ANS: A REF: p. 302 OBJ: 13-7 TYPE: A

36. In general, a person can be an opinion leader, even if he or she is not
    a. knowledgeable.
    b. visible.
    c. exposed to the mass media.
    d. a nationally recognized public figure.

ANS: D REF: p. 302 OBJ: 13-7 TYPE: C

37. Kwan's desire for the spicy food of his homeland is the result of which sociological influence?
    a. culture
    b. opinion leaders
    c. reference groups
    d. social class

ANS: A REF: p. 300 OBJ: 13-7 TYPE: A

38. Your mother prompting you to "act your age" is the result of which sociological influence?
    a. culture
    c. reference groups

b. opinion leaders
d. social class

ANS: C REF: p. 302 OBJ: 13-7 TYPE: A

39. Your mother prompting you to "act like a lady (gentleman)" is the result of which sociological influence?
a. culture
b. opinion leaders
c. reference groups
d. social class

ANS: D REF: p. 301 OBJ: 13-7 TYPE: A

40. Nikita's decision to buy her shoes at same shop that her favorite professor patronizes is the result of which sociological influence?
a. culture
b. opinion leaders
c. reference groups
d. social class

ANS: B REF: p. 302 OBJ: 13-7 TYPE: A

ESSAY

1. **You Make the Call—Situation 1**
Jeremy Shepherd is the founder of PearlParadise.com, in Santa Monica, California. His jewelry business recognizes the importance of ensuring that customers keep them coming back.
However, Shepherd is uncertain as to which customer retention techniques he should use to develop a strong foundation of repeat customers. PearlParadise.com's Web site has the software capabilities to support customer interaction.
Source: Melissa Campanelli, "Happy Returns," www.entrepreneur.com/mag/article/0,1539,312420,00.htm, January 2004.

Question 1 What customer loyalty techniques would you recommend to Shepherd?
Question 2 What information would be appropriate to collect about customers in a database?
Question 3 What specific computer-based communication could be used to achieve Shepherd's goal?

ANS:
1. Superior delivery and after the sale service are the two most important loyalty techniques for Shepherd. It encourages repeat business with a "Pearl Points" program. In this program each order earns several "Pearl Points" coupon cards which can be used for later purchases.
2. Almost any demographic information would be helpful to build a customer database as well as past purchasing behavior with their business and other suppliers. Special personal dates such as a spouse's birthday or anniversary would be useful in creating a CRM program.
3. Shepherd includes an option for visitors to the web site to fill out a very short questionnaire. It asks, "What type of pearls are you most interested in?" and "What price ranges are you most interested in?", as well as a few questions about the web site. There is a place for the visitor to enter their name.

   PearlParadise.com also uses an opt-in customer database used to offer special sales to its repeat customers. Sheppard can send an e-mail message out to customers in the database to inform them of a special inventory of pearls. **Note:** One Mother's Day he offered this type of special and sold out of nearly 100 pearl strands within a matter of hours.

REF: p. 294 OBJ: YMTC TYPE: C

2. **You Make the Call—Situation 2**
Paul Layer is the owner of Aspen Funeral Alternatives in Albuquerque, New Mexico. Aspen is located in a converted restaurant with fluorescent lights, and its chapel has chairs, not pews. "It looks more like your insurance company or local business office, rather than a funeral home," Layer says.
Aspen has adopted a strategy of discounted prices for funeral products and services. Its Web site (http://www.aspenfuneral.com) promotes low-cost alternatives with no fancy facilities, no limousines, and no hearses. A general price list, covering Aspen's professional services, use of its facilities, and caskets, is posted on the site.
Sources: Lorrie Grant, "Funeral Stores Sell Inevitable in Style," *USAToday*, May 30, 2001, p. 3B; and http://www.aspenfuneral.com, June 8, 2004.

Question 1 What psychological concepts of consumer behavior are relevant to marketing this service? Be specific.
Question 2 How can the stages of consumer decision making be applied to a person's decision to use a particular funeral home?
Question 3 What types of CRM could be used by this type of business?

ANS:
1. Every psychological—and sociological—concept discussed in the chapter can be tied to this type service. For example, a family's attitude toward death and eternity can determine the type of funeral service purchased. How elaborate should it be? This business has positioned its appeal as a low cost alternative which may or may not be what certain customers (client's family) wants or needs. Perception of how a funeral arranged by this firm will "look" to others may be a major consideration.
2. This type of product (service) is typically an unsought good—meaning most purchases are not made in advance of the need. However, the funeral industry has marketed a Pre-Need program for many years. Pre-Planning is also promoted by Aspen. Their web site provides a Pre Planning Form which can be submitted to them. There is no cost for this service.

   The Information Search and Evaluation stage is a critical one for Aspen's success simply because there is usually not much time after Stage 1 , before Stage 3 must be completed.
3. The Pre Planning Form is one effort to create some information that could be used in a CRM effort. The form requests information such as the person's telephone number, address, marital status, occupation and disposition preference—burial, cremation, etc.

REF: p. 298,296,294 OBJ: YMTC TYPE: C

3. **You Make the Call—Situation 3**
In the late 1990s, entrepreneur Neil Peterson was traveling in Europe when he observed what to him was a new way to own a car. It was called car sharing. Under this concept, the customer doesn't buy a car outright but uses the vehicle as a person would a timeshare property. The concept isn't totally new to the United States but hasn't yet caught on. Peterson has big plans. He wants to bring the car sharing concept to large U.S. cities. His research, based on American Automobile Association data, showed that the average cost of owning or leasing a new car, including insurance, is around $625 a month. He believes the average car-sharing member will pay only $100 a month.
Source: Kortney Stringer, "How Do You Change Consumer Behavior?" http://www.entrepreneur.com/Your_Business/YB_PrintArticle/ 0,2361,310457,00.html, June 7, 2004.

Question 1 What sociological issues may have an impact on the success of this venture?
Question 2 In which consumer decision-making stage do you believe Peterson's potential customers will be located? Why?

ANS:

1. The ingrained behavior of the American culture, as it relates to the automobile, is the single most important sociological issue Peterson must face. Americans have a love affair with their cars and the idea of sharing this love with someone else is difficult to accept.

2. Most of Peterson's potential customers will probably be in Stage 2. They will understand they have a transportation problem but will need to be convinced that Peterson's solution is viable to them.

   Note: Mr. Peterson started Flexcar in Seattle in 1999 with five vehicles. He attempted to market his car sharing concept as liberating by using such slogans as "Why buy wheels when you can borrow them?" He pushed the price advantage over other options. Success was slow coming but began to arrive when Peterson discovered that a better market niche was business and people looking for second cars. Check out the web site www.flexcar.com to see how he is doing.

REF: p. 298, 296 OBJ: YMTC TYPE: C

4. **You Make the Call—Situation 4**

Paul McKinney is the owner and operator of a small restaurant located in the downtown area of Oklahoma City, Oklahoma. McKinney is a college graduate with a major in accounting. His ability to analyze and control costs has been a major factor in keeping his five-year-old venture out of the red. The restaurant is located in an old but newly remodeled downtown building. His business is based on high volume and low overhead. However, space limitations permit seating of only 25 to 30 people at one time. McKinney feels that customers stay too long after they've finished their meals, thereby tying up seating. He has considered using a small flashing light at each table to remind customers that it is time to move on. He realizes that this method may be too obvious and may create customer dissatisfaction.

Question 1 What is your opinion of McKinney's proposed flashing light system?
Question 2 What other suggestions can you make to help increase turnover? Why are your ideas better?
Question 3 What kinds of sociological factors may bear on customers' patronage of this restaurant?

ANS:

1. It is a terrible idea! McKinney's concern that the method is too obvious and may create customer dissatisfaction is well founded. About the only system that might be worse would be one that sent an electrical shock through the customer's chair.

2. McKinney must use less obvious tactics to open up more seating. A couple of ideas that might help are the following:

   - Provide the customer with the check immediately on completion of the meal. It may help if servers offer to take payments to the cashier.
   - Remove plates and dishes from customers' tables immediately after the meal.
   - Clean and set the table for the next customers as soon as the earlier customers leave.

3. Of the sociological factors mentioned in the chapter, those that affect patterns of attitudes and consumer behavior among larger groups (i.e., culture and social class) may have the greatest impact in this case. Culture is tightly embedded within a society and thus exerts a strong, but subtle, influence on consumer responses. McKinney should consider whether the prevailing culture in his area would accept the use of a flashing light without strong and negative reactions. He should recognize that his background in accounting and interest in cost control might emphasize a time consciousness that his customers do not appreciate, so the idea might seem good to him but could lead to a significant loss of business. Better to have lingering patrons than none at all!

   McKinney should also recognize the influence of social class on consumer response. For example, if his customers tend to come from a social class that emphasizes social connection and network building, then the flashing light is more likely to be offensive because it stifles an important feature of their life in the community. In contrast, a "blue collar" crowd may view the light as an amusing feature of eating in his restaurant since they are accustomed to punching a time clock at work.

REF: p. 298-302 OBJ: YMTC TYPE: C

Correlation Table for Chapter 14—Product and Supply Chain Management

	Learning Objectives	Question Type	Definition Define new term, recall facts	Concept Understand or relate concepts	Application Apply knowledge, analyze data
1	Explain the challenges associated with growth in a small firm.	T/F			
		MC			
		ES		1	
2	Explain the role of innovation in a firm's growth.	T/F		1,2	
		MC	1	2,3,4,5,6,7,8	
		ES			
3	Identify stages in the product life cycle and the new product development process.	T/F		3,4,5,6,7,8	
		MC	10,12	9,11,13,14,15,16, 17,18,	
		ES			
4	Describe the building of a firm's total product.	T/F	10,11	9,12,13,14,15	
		MC	19	21,23,24,25,26	20,22
		ES			
5	Explain product strategy and the alternatives available to small businesses.	T/F		16	17,18
		MC		27,28,32	29,30,31
		ES		2	
6	Describe the legal environment affecting product decisions.	T/F	19,23,24	20,21,22	
		MC	33,37	34,36,38	35
		ES	3		
7	Explain the importance of supply chain management.	T/F	26,27	25,28,29	
		MC	39,40,42	41	43
		ES			
8	Specify the major considerations in structuring a distribution channel.	T/F	33,34,35	30,31,32	
		MC		44,45,46,47,48,	49,50
		ES		4	
	You Make the Call	ES		5,6,7,8	

Total Number of Test Questions: 92 (35 True/False; 50 Multiple-Choice; 7 Essay)

Chapter 14—Product and Supply Chain Management

TRUE/FALSE

1. It is important that small firms gain a competitive advantage, which cannot be quickly imitated.

   ANS: T REF: p. 310 OBJ: 14-2 TYPE: C

2. According to the textbook's three-stage model of the life cycle of a competitive advantage, firms can exploit a competitive advantage during the "develop" stage.

   ANS: F
   It is during the *deploy* stage that a firm can capitalize on its competitive advantage.

   REF: p. 310 OBJ: 14-2 TYPE: C

3. Strategies for goods marketing and services marketing are essentially identical.

   ANS: F
   Strategies for the marketing of goods and services are not the same—they differ along a number of dimensions (e.g., tangibility, standardization, and perishability).

   REF: p. 318 OBJ: 14-3 TYPE: C

4. Despite the limited resources of a typical small business, this type of firm should formalize the product development process.

   ANS: T REF: p. 312 OBJ: 14-3 TYPE: C

5. In the business analysis stage of the product development process, every new-product idea must be carefully analyzed in terms of several financial considerations.

   ANS: T REF: p. 313 OBJ: 14-3 TYPE: C

6. Considering the business analysis stage of the product development process, a product that is completely new to a small firm should not be added to the product mix, in most cases, unless it is consistent with—or somehow related to—the existing product mix.

   ANS: T REF: p. 313 OBJ: 14-3 TYPE: C

7. It is generally easier and more beneficial for a small business to develop products that are similar to those of competitors, rather than attempt to offer a sufficiently different product.

   ANS: F
   Given that strong competition in a market can make the introduction of a new product difficult, it is best for a small firm to offer a product that is sufficiently different from competitors' products or that is in a cost and price bracket where it can avoid direct competition.

   REF: p. 313 OBJ: 14-3 TYPE: C

8. Product testing is the last step in the product development process.

ANS: T REF: p. 313 OBJ: 14-3 TYPE: C

9. A major, explicit responsibility of marketing is to transform a basic product into a total product offering.

ANS: T REF: p. 314 OBJ: 14-4 TYPE: C

10. A brand includes only the verbal identification of a product.

ANS: F
A brand is a means of identifying a product—verbally and/or symbolically.

REF: p. 314 OBJ: 14-4 TYPE: D

11. Trademark and service mark are legal terms indicating the exclusive right to use a brand.

ANS: T REF: p. 316 OBJ: 14-4 TYPE: D

12. Packaging is a significant tool for increasing the value of the total product by creating a distinctive impression.

ANS: T REF: p. 316 OBJ: 14-4 TYPE: C

13. Innovative packaging is frequently a deciding factor for consumers.

ANS: T REF: p. 316 OBJ: 14-4 TYPE: C

14. Labeling information should be limited to minimum legal requirements.

ANS: F
Labeling information should *go beyond* the specified minimum legal requirements.

REF: p. 316 OBJ: 14-4 TYPE: C

15. In order to be enforceable, warranties must be in writing.

ANS: F
The warranty may be written or unwritten.

REF: p. 317 OBJ: 14-4 TYPE: C

16. There are six categories of product strategy alternatives for small businesses.

ANS: T REF: p. 319 OBJ: 14-5 TYPE: C

17. If a firm extends a janitorial cleanser from the industrial market to reach the home market, it is following a one product/multiple markets strategy.

ANS: T REF: p. 319 OBJ: 14-5 TYPE: A

18. To balance out seasonal use, some sporting goods firms manufacture both snow skis and water skis. This should provide a useful hedge against volatile shifts in market demand.

ANS: T REF: p. 323 OBJ: 14-5 TYPE: A

19. According to the Nutrition Labeling and Education Act of 1990, food products addressed must have a standard nutrition label, listing the amount of calories, fat, salt, and nutrients contained.

ANS: T REF: p. 320 OBJ: 14-6 TYPE: D

20. The four primary means firms can use to protect their tangible assets are trademarks, patents, copyrights, and trade dress.

ANS: T REF: p. 321 OBJ: 14-6 TYPE: C

21. Given the complexity of the task, entrepreneurs must use an attorney to conduct a trademark search.

ANS: F
The task is complex, but an entrepreneur can conduct the trademark search personally by using the Trademark Search Library of the United States Patent and Trade Office.

REF: p. 321 OBJ: 14-6 TYPE: C

22. A trademark registered today will remain effective for 5 years and may be renewed for an additional 5 years.

ANS: F
By law, a trademark registered today will remain effective for *10* years and may be renewed for an additional *10* years.

REF: p. 321 OBJ: 14-6 TYPE: C

23. A utility patent covers the appearance of a product and everything that is an inseparable part of the product.

ANS: F
It is a *design* patent (not a *utility* patent) that covers the appearance of a product and everything that is an inseparable part of the product.

REF: p. 321 OBJ: 14-6 TYPE: D

24. Trade dress describes those elements of a firm's distinctive operating image that are not specifically protected under a trademark, patent, or copyright.

ANS: T REF: p. 322 OBJ: 14-6 TYPE: D

25. Entrepreneurs often regard distribution as the most glamorous marketing activity.

ANS: F
Entrepreneurs often regard distribution as the *least* glamorous marketing activity.

REF: p. 322 OBJ: 14-7 TYPE: C

26. The term *channel management* is synonymous with the term *logistics*.

ANS: F
The activities involved in physically moving products are called *physical distribution* or *logistics*.

REF: p. 322 OBJ: 14-7 TYPE: D

27. Distribution includes both the physical movement of products and the establishment of intermediary relationships to guide and support the movement of products.

ANS: T REF: p. 323 OBJ: 14-7 TYPE: D

28. Distribution is essential for tangible goods, but not for intangible goods.

ANS: F
Distribution is essential for both tangible and intangible goods.

REF: p. 322 OBJ: 14-7 TYPE: C

29. A *direct channel* of distribution is one that involves no intermediaries.

ANS: T REF: p. 323 OBJ: 14-7 TYPE: C

30. Analysis of competitors' channels is a valuable source of information to a small business that is structuring its own distribution system.

ANS: T REF: p. 323 OBJ: 14-8 TYPE: C

31. The three main considerations in structuring a channel of distribution are cost, coverage, and control.

ANS: T REF: p. 324 OBJ: 14-8 TYPE: C

32. Physical distribution of products includes only transportation.

ANS: F
Transportation is the *main* component of physical distribution—additional components include storage, materials handling, delivery terms, and inventory handling.

REF: p. 325 OBJ: 14-8 TYPE: C

33. Shippers that own their own means of transport are called common carriers.

ANS: F
Shippers that own their own means of transport are called *private* carriers.

REF: p. 325 OBJ: 14-8 TYPE: D

34. Delivery terms specify which party pays the freight costs, selects carriers, bears the risk of damage, and selects the modes of transport.

ANS: T REF: p. 326 OBJ: 14-8 TYPE: D

35. F.O.B. origin, freight collect, is a delivery term that shifts all responsibility for freight costs to the buyer.

ANS: T REF: p. 326 OBJ: 14-8 TYPE: D

MULTIPLE CHOICE

1. Sustainable competitive advantage is
   a. rarely appreciated by the firm's owners.
   b. of little consequence to profitability.
   c. an idealized position that is unachievable in reality.
   d. a value-creating industry position that is likely to endure over time.

ANS: D REF: p. 310 OBJ: 14-2 TYPE: D

2. A firm's competitive advantage will *never*
   a. last forever.
   b. be duplicated by competitors.
   c. lead to superior performance.
   d. cost as much to develop as anticipated.

ANS: A REF: p. 310 OBJ: 14-2 TYPE: C

3. The competitive advantage life cycle has three stages, including the __________ stage.
   a. determination
   b. distill
   c. decline
   d. delimit

ANS: C REF: p. 310 OBJ: 14-2 TYPE: C

4. Joe Kott has established a successful formed cement products business by developing an inventory control method and delivery service that gets products to construction sites faster than his rivals. If Kott continues to improve this system and stay ahead of his competitors, it can be a source of
   a. sustainable competitive advantage.
   b. total quality management.
   c. business process reengineering.
   d. competitive adjustment.

ANS: A REF: p. 310 OBJ: 14-2 TYPE: C

5. If a small firm is to maintain its performance over time, it is essential to
   a. produce a continuous stream of competitive advantages.

b. extend the competitive advantage of the firm.
c. replicate the strategies that have led to success in the past.
d. retain the personnel who made the firm successful in the first place.

ANS: A REF: p. 310 OBJ: 14-2 TYPE: C

6. To maintain it performance, the small business must launch a new competitive advantage
   a. and keep that competitive advantage alive.
   b. and make adjustments to that competitive advantage over time.
   c. that rival firms can see and respond to.
   d. before the current strategy has run its course.

ANS: D REF: p. 311 OBJ: 14-2 TYPE: C

7. For small businesses, one growing threat to sustainable competitive advantage is a lack of
   a. available new technology.
   b. government support.
   c. legal planning.
   d. new product development.

ANS: C REF: p. 310 OBJ: 14-2 TYPE: C

8. Sustainable competitive advantage can be achieved only when the entrepreneur
   a. is quick to copy the approaches taken by rivals firms that are successful.
   b. combines environmental potentials with organizational capabilities to create customer value.
   c. has a deep understanding of the latest technologies available to the firm.
   d. is committed to employment independence.

ANS: B REF: p. 310 OBJ: 14-2 TYPE: C

9. Marketing strategies for goods and services vary because of differences in all of the following characteristics *except*
   a. perishability.
   b. standardization.
   c. consumer appeal.
   d. tangibility.

ANS: C REF: p. 318 OBJ: 14-3 TYPE: C

10. The collection of product lines within a firm's ownership and control is referred to as the
    a. product depth.
    b. product accumulation.
    c. product line consistency.
    d. product mix.

ANS: D REF: p. 318 OBJ: 14-3 TYPE: D

11. All of the following are stages in a formal product development process *except*
    a. business analysis.
    b. idea accumulation.
    c. product testing.
    d. product conceptualization.

ANS: D REF: p. 312 OBJ: 14-3 TYPE: C

12. The initial stage in a formal product development process is the _____ stage.
    a. business analysis
    b. idea accumulation
    c. product testing
    d. total product development

ANS: B REF: p. 313 OBJ: 14-3 TYPE: D

13. All of the following are legitimate sources of new product ideas within the framework of a formal product development process *except*
    a. business personnel.
    b. customer requests or suggestions.
    c. government-owned patents.
    d. competitor-owned patents.

ANS: D REF: p. 313 OBJ: 14-3 TYPE: C

14. Every new product must be carefully analyzed in terms of financial considerations in the _____ stage of the product development process.
    a. business analysis
    b. idea accumulation
    c. product testing
    d. total product development

ANS: A REF: p. 313 OBJ: 14-3 TYPE: C

15. Key factors to consider when conducting the business analysis phase of the new product development process include all of the following *except*
    a. cost of development and introduction.
    b. total product development.
    c. available personnel and facilities.
    d. the product's relationship to existing product lines.

ANS: B REF: p. 313 OBJ: 14-3 TYPE: C

16. The _____ stage of the product development process entails planning for branding, packaging, and other supporting efforts such as pricing and promotion.
    a. business analysis
    b. idea accumulation
    c. product conceptualization
    d. total product development

ANS: D REF: p. 314 OBJ: 14-3 TYPE: C

17. All of the following are appropriate vehicles for testing a product in the product development process *except*
    a. laboratory tests.
    b. limited market field tests.
    c. purchase simulations.
    d. tests of the physical product.

ANS: C REF: p. 313 OBJ: 14-3 TYPE: C

18. A small firm can try to increase sales of an existing product by all of the following *except*
    a. convincing nonusers in the market to become customers.
    b. persuading current customers to use more of the product.
    c. alerting current customers to new uses for the product.
    d. emphasizing diversification.

ANS: D REF: p. 313 OBJ: 14-3 TYPE: C

19. A verbal or symbolic means of identifying a product is referred to as a
    a. brand.
    b. trademark.
    c. service mark.
    d. trade dress.

ANS: A REF: p. 314 OBJ: 14-4 TYPE: D

20. An entrepreneur opened a small business producing high-quality paper products. She decided to place a multicolored pine tree on all product boxes and on the sign outside the facilities, to symbolize the business. This symbol is an example of
    a. a brand.
    b. a trademark.
    c. a service mark.
    d. trade dress.

ANS: A REF: p. 314 OBJ: 14-4 TYPE: A

21. Important rules of thumb in naming a product include all of the following *except*
    a. choosing a descriptive name.

b. selecting a name that is easy to pronounce and remember.
c. selecting a name that can be used appropriately for only a single product line.
d. using a name that can have legal protection.

ANS: C REF: p. 314 OBJ: 14-4 TYPE: C

22. The name Xerox is a
a. generic label.
b. brand.
c. trade dress.
d. copyrighted designation.

ANS: B REF: p. 314 OBJ: 14-4 TYPE: A

23. Explicit functions of packaging include all of the following *except*
a. increasing the quality of the total product.
b. distinguishing the product from competitors' products.
c. influencing customers.
d. protecting the product.

ANS: A REF: p. 316 OBJ: 14-4 TYPE: C

24. Which of the following is *not* true with respect to labeling?
a. It shows the product brand.
b. It is an informative tool for consumers.
c. It should include only the minimum legal requirements.
d. It should emphasize brand visibility.

ANS: C REF: p. 316 OBJ: 14-4 TYPE: C

25. Effective evaluation of warranty policies should focus on all of the following *except*
a. legal implications.
b. service capability.
c. customer perceptions.
d. former practices.

ANS: D REF: p. 317 OBJ: 14-4 TYPE: C

26. Warranties are important for products
a. that are relatively inexpensive.
b. that are frequently purchased.
c. that are relatively complex to repair.
d. regardless of how they are positioned in the market.

ANS: C REF: p. 317 OBJ: 14-4 TYPE: C

27. All of the following are product strategy alternatives *except*
    a. multiple products strategies.
    b. one product strategies.
    c. product market strategies.
    d. modified product strategies.

ANS: C REF: p. 319 OBJ: 14-5 TYPE: C

28. In general, the most appropriate and effective product strategy to use in the initial stage of a small business is the _____ product strategy.
    a. one product/one market
    b. one product/multiple markets
    c. multiple products/one market
    d. multiple products/multiple markets

ANS: A REF: p. 319 OBJ: 14-5 TYPE: C

29. Technologies Limited, a small producer of closed-circuit, handheld radio communication devices marketed to contractors (walkie-talkies), wants to expand. Using its knowledge of communication technologies, it developed a cellular-based phone system designed for contractors. Technologies Limited is employing a _____ product strategy.
    a. multiple products/one market
    b. multiple products/multiple markets
    c. modified product/one market
    d. modified product/multiple markets

ANS: A REF: p. 319 OBJ: 14-5 TYPE: A

30. Auto Shine is introducing an improved version of its existing car wax targeted at luxury car owners. The firm has decided to leave the original product in the mix and aim the new product at the original target market. Auto Shine is employing a _____ product strategy.
    a. multiple products/one market
    b. multiple products/multiple markets
    c. modified product/one market
    d. modified product/multiple markets

ANS: C REF: p. 319 OBJ: 14-5 TYPE: A

31. Written Instruments, a maker of plastic ballpoint pens targeted at school-aged children, decided to market an additional line of pens. However, this small business was concerned that the introduction of a new ballpoint pen would reduce sales of the existing product in its current market niche. Therefore, Written Instruments created a high-quality, felt-tip pen targeted at business executives in order to expand sales. This company was employing a _____ product strategy.
    a. multiple products/one market
    b. multiple products/multiple markets
    c. one product/multiple markets

d. modified product/multiple markets

ANS: B REF: p. 319 OBJ: 14-5 TYPE: A

32. A product strategy that includes a new product that is quite different from existing products
    a. can be very risky.
    b. is often used by small businesses.
    c. will likely determine the future direction of the firm.
    d. is encouraged, as long as it represents no more than half of the firm's product offerings.

ANS: A REF: p. 319 OBJ: 14-5 TYPE: C

33. A legal term indicating the exclusive right of a firm to use a brand to identify a product is a
    a. copy mark.
    b. trademark.
    c. service mark.
    d. trade dress.

ANS: B REF: p. 321 OBJ: 14-6 TYPE: D

34. Small businesses can protect their intangible assets by means of any of the following *except*
    a. trademarks.
    b. patents.
    c. copyrights.
    d. formal redress.

ANS: D REF: p. 321 OBJ: 14-6 TYPE: C

35. The United States Patent and Trade Office rejected Microsoft's 1990 effort to gain exclusive rights to the name *Windows*. This decision illustrates the fact that
    a. copyright protection has its limits.
    b. design patents do not cover computer software applications.
    c. trade dress will not cover the "look and feel" of a product, as Microsoft claimed.
    d. common-law rights do not always justify trademark protection over a generic term.

ANS: D REF: p. 321 OBJ: 14-6 TYPE: A

36. A copyright provides protection for the duration of the creator's life, plus
    a. 25 years.
    b. 70 years.
    c. 75 years.
    d. 100 years.

ANS: B REF: p. 321 OBJ: 14-6 TYPE: C

37. The distinctive operating image of a product, including features such as size, shape, color or color combinations, texture, graphics, or even particular sales techniques, can be protected
    a. by copyright.
    b. by patent.
    c. as trade dress.
    d. as a registered concept.

ANS: C REF: p. 322 OBJ: 14-6 TYPE: D

38. A *copyright notice* should include
    a. the symbol (c).
    b. the date the work was published.
    c. the name of the copyright owner's company.
    d. a listing of all other copyrights held by the owner.

ANS: A REF: p. 322 OBJ: 14-6 TYPE: C

39. Both the physical movement of products and the establishment of intermediary relationships to guide and support the movement of the products are included in
    a. distribution.
    b. logistics.
    c. middlemen.
    d. channels.

ANS: A REF: p. 322 OBJ: 14-7 TYPE: D

40. ____________ encompasses both the physical movement of products and the establishment of intermediary relationships.
    a. Logistics
    b. Distribution
    c. Physical distribution
    d. Marketing management

ANS: B REF: p. 322 OBJ: 14-7 TYPE: D

41. Intermediaries exist because
    a. they can perform the distribution function better than the producer or user of the product.
    b. they reach geographic areas with much less expense.
    c. risk levels are low.
    d. customer needs are highly specialized.

ANS: A REF: p. 323 OBJ: 14-7 TYPE: C

42. When a small firm operates with more than one channel of distribution, it is said to be using
    a. multiple distribution.
    b. dual distribution.

c. channel integration.
d. intermediary replication

ANS: B REF: p. 324 OBJ: 14-7 TYPE: D

43. Seasons Greetings, a small manufacturer of holiday greeting cards, sells its product through independent retailers and mail-order marketing. Seasons Greetings is relying on
a. a direct channel of distribution.
b. an indirect channel of distribution.
c. a dual distribution channel.
d. a multiple-outlet distribution channel.

ANS: C REF: p. 324 OBJ: 14-7 TYPE: A

44. The three considerations in building a channel of distribution are
a. cost, coverage, and control.
b. cost, coverage, and compatibility.
c. coverage, control, and compatibility.
d. cost, control, and compatibility.

ANS: A REF: p. 324 OBJ: 14-8 TYPE: C

45. Small businesses are encouraged to view distribution costs as
a. prohibitive.
b. sunk costs.
c. an investment.
d. necessary evils.

ANS: C REF: p. 324 OBJ: 14-8 TYPE: C

46. The scope of physical distribution covers all of the following *except*
a. transportation.
b. inventory management.
c. materials handling.
d. final assembly.

ANS: D REF: p. 325 OBJ: 14-8 TYPE: C

47. When the channel system uses ______, the storage function is transferred to the intermediary.
a. agents
b. brokers
c. common carriers
d. merchant middlemen or wholesalers

ANS: D REF: p. 325 OBJ: 14-8 TYPE: C

48. Available types of transportation intermediaries include all of the following *except*
    a. common carriers.
    b. public carriers.
    c. private carriers.
    d. contract carriers.

ANS: B REF: p. 325 OBJ: 14-8 TYPE: C

49. Import Properties, a small firm that imports trade goods from South America, ships purchased goods on one of two company-owned vessels. Import Properties operates as a
    a. common carrier.
    b. public carrier.
    c. private carrier.
    d. contract carrier.

ANS: C REF: p. 325 OBJ: 14-8 TYPE: A

50. Bovine Ice Cream is a small frozen-dairy business that engages in contractual agreements with transportation intermediaries in order to move its products from its manufacturing facility to distant markets. Bovine Ice Cream is employing _____ for its shipping needs.
    a. common carriers
    b. public carriers
    c. private carriers
    d. contract carriers

ANS: D REF: p. 325 OBJ: 14-8 TYPE: A

ESSAY

1. How can a successfully growing firm fall into a "growth trap"?

ANS:
Successful growth seldom occurs on its own. Many factors—including financing—must be considered and managed carefully. When a firm experiences rapid growth in sales volume, the firm's income statements will generally reflect growing profits. However, rapid growth in sales and profits may be hazardous to the firm's cash flows. A "growth trap" can occur, because growth tends to soak up additional cash more rapidly than such cash is generated in the form of additional profits.

REF: p. 307-308 OBJ: 14-1 TYPE: C

2. Name the six categories of major product strategies.

ANS:
One product/one market
One product/multiple markets
Modified product/one market
Modified product/multiple markets

Multiple products/one market
Multiple products/multiple markets

REF: p. 319 OBJ: 14-5 TYPE: C

3. Briefly describe a trademark.

ANS:
A trademark is a legal term indicating the exclusive right to use brand names and brand marks that have been given legal protection. A word or symbol that identifies a product can be a trademark.

REF: p. 321 OBJ: 14-6 TYPE: D

4. List and briefly comment on the three main considerations in constructing a channel of distribution.

ANS:
The three main considerations in building a channel of distribution are costs, coverage, and control.

- *Costs* are always a major consideration. The distribution decision should be viewed as an investment. What return on investment can be obtained from one alternative as compared to another?
- A channel of distribution must achieve the desired market *coverage*. The merchandise must be at the right place at the right time, in good condition, and in the correct quantities.
- There is obviously more *control* in a direct channel of distribution. With indirect channels, products may not be marketed as intended.

REF: p. 323 OBJ: 14-8 TYPE: C

5. **You Make the Call—Situation 1**
Linda McMahan was getting numerous compliments on a handbag she carried to The University of Texas events. She had purchased the handbag, which carried the UT name, at a local store but felt the quality of the bag was poor. She and her sister-in-law, Sue Craft McMahan, decided to become partners and produce and sell high-end handbags emblazoned with the college logo.
The pair designed four different types of bags—a large totebag, a smaller bag, a crescent-shaped handbag, and a "bolder" game-day bag—all marked with The University of Texas emblem. Early responses to the product line were overwhelming. They've now set their sights on other big-name schools.
Source: Nichole L. Torros, "Smells Like School Spirit," *Entrepreneur*, December 2003, p. 132.

Question 1 What problems, if any, do you see with the use of the university's brand?
Question 2 What strategy should they pursue to obtain cooperation from the university?
Question 3 What distribution options are likely to be used?

ANS:
1. The university will most likely have copyright and trademark protection on any name, design, or slogan uniquely associated with them. Therefore, any use of a name or unique design will create problems unless McMahan gets permission from the university, which will likely come in the form of licensing

2. She may want to sell the university on the value her products by showing how they will add to the image of the university or most likely she will need to show them how they can profit from a licensing fee or other financial arrangement
3. She can probably use the local store(s) or even create an Internet site for ordering. Many stadiums and arenas have shops where products of this kind can be sold.

REF: p. 314 OBJ: YMTC TYPE: C

6. **You Make the Call—Situation 2**
John Kowalski, of Aliquippa, Pennsylvania, is the man behind the Load Hog, a device that enables pickup truck beds to function like dump trucks. The Load Hog evolved from a product originally introduced by an Australian importer back in 1992. After years of product development by Kowalski, the Load Hog, with a price tag of $350,000, exhibits virtually no trace of the Australian product.
Kowalski and his wife, Carol, have promoted the Load Hog to truck dealers as an after-market product. They have exhibited at outdoor-vehicle and specialty-equipment shows and have sold around 400 of the units by mail order. More recently, they have launched a Web site (http://www.loadhog.com).
Source: Leigh Buchanan, "Pickup Artist," *Inc.*, Vol. 23, No. 8 (June 2001), pp. 68–73.

Question 1 Do you think there may be other channels of distribution that Kowalski might use? If so, what are they?
Question 2 What other related products might be added to the product mix?
Question 3 What do you think about the choice of the name for the device?

ANS:

1. There are definitely other channel alternatives for this product. Kowalski could establish a relationship with distributors throughout the country who could handle his product as well as other truck accessory items. These distributors could be shops that would handle installation work, which could be very appealing to many non-technical customers (even though the Web site advertises "easy installation"). Check out the Instructions page on the Web site! At some point in time he may want to consider distribution with the major auto parts chains, since many of their customers have trucks.
2. Kowalski has already added several other related products. Through his Web site, you can order hitches and Load Hog Wearables. Any specialized product for trucks is a possibility. Later on, the firm may want to enter other markets with their products, such as the fleet market.
3. The name is pretty neat! It qualifies well on each of the five naming rules discussed in the chapter. Rule #5 regarding use on several product lines of a similar nature may be the only questionable characteristic. Only time will tell if it can be used on all new product items.

REF: p. 323 OBJ: YMTC TYPE: C

7. **You Make the Call—Situation 3**
Kim Hodges operates a 3-year-old furniture company named Metallika in Waco, Texas. Does the name sound familiar? According to a lawyer for the heavy-metal rock band Metallica, it sounds too familiar. In a letter to Hodges, the lawyer wrote, "Specifically, we need you to change the name of your business to a name that does not include the terms Metallika, Metalika, Metallica, Metalica, or any name, term, logo, domain name or vanity telephone number similar thereto."
The lawyer said if Hodges chooses not to change the name of his company, they might sue for damages, company profits, and attorneys' fees.

Source: Mike Copeland, "Metallika Rocked by Metallica," *Waco Tribune Herald*, December 9, 2000, p. 1A.

Question 1 What course of action would you recommend to Hodges?
Question 2 What can Hodges say in defense of the name he chose for his furniture business?

ANS:
1. It might be best for Hodges to get a lawyer to write a few letters to the lawyer representing the rock band to see if they might examine their demands and back off. If this didn't work, one might suggest that Hodges strongly consider changing the name.
2. One defense he may have is that he had the name first (if, in fact, he did). Or he may contend that there has not been, and will not be, any confusion in the minds of the public between the products of his company and the rock band. Also, there may be some defense based upon the market area he serves—it is local and is thus not likely to infringe on the market of the rock band. *(These are only ideas and not legal advice. See a lawyer for all legal advice.)*

REF: p. 315 OBJ: YMTC TYPE: C

8. **You Make the Call—Situation 4**

Rance Swensen believes that his small company's products will always sell in the market as they have in the past. They are good, sturdy products but their designs are becoming obviously dated to everybody except Rance. A curious phenomena that Rance has observed is that while product sales are currently still rising, profits are declining.

Question 1 What could you tell Rance about the product life cycle that would explain this phenomena and the danger it poses to the future success of the firm?
Question 2 Why is the product life cycle important to small business managers?

ANS:
1. An important concept underlying sound product strategy is the product life cycle, which visualizes the sales and profits of a product from the time it is introduced until it is no longer on the market. The **product life cycle** provides a detailed picture of what happens to an *individual* product's or service's sales and profits; it has a shape similar to that of the competitive advantage life cycle. Progressing through the product life cycle takes on the characteristics of a roller-coaster ride, which is the way many entrepreneurs describe their experiences with the life cycles of their products. The initial stages are characterized by a slow and, ideally, upward movement. The stay at the top is exciting but relatively brief. Then, suddenly, the decline begins, and downward movement is rapid. The introductory stage is dominated by losses, with profits peaking in the growth stage.
2. The product life cycle concept is important to the small business manager for three reasons. First, it helps the entrepreneur to understand that promotion, pricing, and distribution policies should all be adjusted to reflect a product's position on the curve. Second, it highlights the importance of rejuvenating product lines, whenever possible, before they die. Third, it is a continuing reminder that the natural life cycle of a product follows the classic sigmoid curve—a tilted S-shaped curve describing the time line of life itself—and, therefore, that innovation is necessary for a firm's survival. According to Charles Handy, author of *The Age of Paradox*, the best time to begin a new curve is before the existing curve of the product life cycle peaks.

REF: p. 312 OBJ: YMTC TYPE: C

Correlation Table for Chapter 15—Pricing and Credit Decisions

	Learning Objectives	Question Type	Definition Define new term, recall facts	Concept Understand or relate concepts	Application Apply knowledge, analyze data
1	Discuss the role of cost and demand factors in setting a price.	T/F	6	1,2,3,4,5,7	
		MC	1,4,5,10,11,12	2,3,8,9	6,7
		ES		1	
2	Apply break-even analysis and markup pricing.	T/F	11	8,9,10,12	
		MC	13,16	14,15,17	18,19,20
		ES			2
3	Identify specific pricing strategies.	T/F	14,17,18	13,15,16,19,20, 21	
		MC	21,25	22,27,28	23,24,26
		ES		3	
4	Explain the benefits of credit, factors that affect credit extension, and types of credit.	T/F	26,27	22,23,24,25,28, 29	
		MC	32,33,34	29,30,31,35,36, 37,40,41,42	38,39
		ES	4		
5	Describe the activities involved in managing credit.	T/F	34,35	30,31,32,33	
		MC	45,46,50	43,44,47,48,49	
		ES			1
	You Make the Call	ES		6,7,8,9	

Total Number of Test Questions: 94 (35 True/False; 50 Multiple-Choice; 9 Essay)

Chapter 15—Pricing and Credit Decisions

TRUE/FALSE

1. Because small businesses are small by definition, pricing and credit considerations are relatively unimportant to their overall performance.

   ANS: F
   Pricing and credit decisions are vital to small businesses because they affect both revenues and cash flow.

   REF: p. 331 OBJ: TYPE: C

2. Sound pricing practices begin with knowing product costs.

   ANS: T REF: p. 332 OBJ: 15-1 TYPE: C

3. Because the method takes into consideration both fixed and variable costs, average pricing is always an appropriate pricing approach for small businesses.

   ANS: F
   Although fixed and variable costs do not behave in the same way, small businesses often treat them identically—this average pricing approach is thus a dangerous one.

   REF: p. 333 OBJ: 15-1 TYPE: C

4. Under certain conditions, pricing at less than total costs makes sense as a long-term strategy.

   ANS: F
   Pricing at less than total cost can be sustained only over the *short* term, and even then this will work only under certain circumstances.

   REF: p. 333 OBJ: 15-1 TYPE: C

5. The competitive advantage of a firm will affect consumers' demand for its product.

   ANS: T REF: p. 333 OBJ: 15-1 TYPE: C

6. Prestige pricing (setting a high price to convey an image of high quality or uniqueness) is a pricing tactic that reflects competitive advantage.

   ANS: T REF: p. 334 OBJ: 15-1 TYPE: D

7. When customers know very little about product characteristics, they often use product category as an indicator of quality.

   ANS: F
   When customers know very little about product characteristics, they often use *price* as an indicator of quality.

REF: p. 334 OBJ: 15-1 TYPE: C

8. In conducting a comprehensive break-even analysis, a firm must examine both its revenue-cost relationships and sales forecasts.

ANS: T REF: p. 335 OBJ: 15-2 TYPE: C

9. The objective of developing sales forecasts for a break-even analysis is to determine the quantity at which the product, with an assumed price, will generate enough revenue to start earning a profit.

ANS: F
This is the objective of *examining cost and revenue relationships*, not developing sales forecasting.

REF: p. 335 OBJ: 15-2 TYPE: C

10. In conducting a break-even analysis, it is important for the entrepreneur to realize that demand for a product always decreases as its price increases.

ANS: F
Demand *typically* decreases as price increases, but this is not always the case.

REF: p. 336 OBJ: 15-2 TYPE: C

11. Markup pricing is a cost-plus method of pricing that arrives at a markup percentage high enough to cover operating expenses, subsequent price reductions, and desired profit levels.

ANS: T REF: p. 336 OBJ: 15-2 TYPE: D

12. Markups may be expressed as a percentage of either the firm's cost or the industry-standard cost.

ANS: F
Markups may be expressed as a percentage of either cost or the selling price of the product/service.

REF: p. 337 OBJ: 15-2 TYPE: C

13. Break-even analysis is an accurate tool for pricing because it points directly to the correct price for a given product.

ANS: F
Break-even analysis may not be as accurate as it seems, so this should be viewed only as a tool for pricing and should not be used by itself to determine the final price.

REF: p. 337 OBJ: 15-3 TYPE: C

14. With a skimming price strategy, prices for products or services are set lower than normal, long-range market prices in order to gain more rapid market acceptance or to increase market share.

ANS: F
It is a *penetration* price strategy that sets lower than normal, long-range market prices in order to gain more rapid market acceptance or to increase market share.

REF: p. 338 OBJ: 15-3 TYPE: D

15. A penetration price strategy is most practical when there exists little threat of short-term competition in the market or when startup costs must be recovered rapidly.

ANS: F
It is a *skimming* price strategy that is most practical when there is little threat of short-term competition in the market or when startup costs must be recovered rapidly.

REF: p. 338 OBJ: 15-3 TYPE: C

16. A small business in competition with larger firms is seldom in a position to function as a price leader.

ANS: T REF: p. 338 OBJ: 15-3 TYPE: C

17. Sellers using a practice called dynamic pricing set prices based on those of market leaders.

ANS: F
Dynamic pricing refers to a practice of setting prices higher after gauging a customer's financial means and desire for the product or service.

REF: p. 338 OBJ: 15-3 TYPE: D

18. Price lining refers to the systematic determination of the right price for a product or service.

ANS: F
A price lining strategy determines several distinct prices at which similar items of retail merchandise are offered for sale.

REF: p. 339 OBJ: 15-3 TYPE: D

19. The policy of pricing on the basis of what the traffic will bear will work only for nonstandardized products in markets in which little or no competition exists.

ANS: T REF: p. 339 OBJ: 15-3 TYPE: C

20. Under certain circumstances, local, state, and federal laws must be considered in setting prices in a small business.

ANS: T REF: p. 339 OBJ: 15-3 TYPE: C

21. When a small business markets a line of products, some of which may compete with one another, pricing decisions must take into account the effects of a single product price on the rest of the line.

ANS: T REF: p. 339 OBJ: 15-3 TYPE: C

22. Sellers often decide to offer credit to borrowers because it helps with the exchange of purchased items.

ANS: F
Better service and greater convenience when exchanging items is a benefit to the borrower, but not to the seller.

REF: p. 340 OBJ: 15-4 TYPE: C

23. One of the benefits of extending credit to borrowers is that doing so provides better records of purchases on credit billing statements.

ANS: T REF: p. 340 OBJ: 15-4 TYPE: C

24. Because it is a standard practice in many types of businesses, credit selling often cannot be avoided.

ANS: T REF: p. 340 OBJ: 15-4 TYPE: C

25. By allowing credit sales a seller is following a risk-free practice to increase profits.

ANS: F
Although a seller always hopes to increase profits by allowing credit sales, this is not a risk-free practice.

REF: p. 340 OBJ: 15-4 TYPE: C

26. Trade credit is extended by businesses to consumers purchasing large volumes of products.

ANS: F
Trade credit is extended by *nonfinancial firms* (e.g., manufacturers and wholesalers) to *other businesses* that are also consumers of the firm's products/services.

REF: p. 342 OBJ: 15-4 TYPE: D

27. An installment account is a typical trade credit agreement.

ANS: F
An installment account is not a trade credit; it is a vehicle for long-term consumer credit.

REF: p. 342 OBJ: 15-4 TYPE: D

28. Bank credit cards are widely accepted by retailers who desire to offer credit but do not have their own credit cards.

ANS: T REF: p. 342 OBJ: 15-4 TYPE: C

29. In many lines of business, trade credit terms are so firmly set by tradition that a unique policy is difficult for a small firm to implement.

ANS: T REF: p. 343 OBJ: 15-4 TYPE: C

30. Credit management should be implemented in a business when high levels of bad debt arise and should continue throughout the credit cycle until the level of bad debt is rectified.

ANS: F
Credit management should precede the first credit sale, starting with the initial screening of credit applicants.

REF: p. 343 OBJ: 15-5 TYPE: C

31. Every applicant is credit worthy to some degree.

ANS: T REF: p. 344 OBJ: 15-5 TYPE: C

32. An important source of credit information is the customer's previous credit history.

ANS: T REF: p. 344 OBJ: 15-5 TYPE: C

33. Trade-credit agencies collect credit information on business firms and consumers in a given area.

ANS: F
Trade-credit agencies collect credit information on business firms, but not consumers.

REF: p. 344 OBJ: 15-5 TYPE: C

34. The primary purposes of the Equal Credit Opportunity Act are to inform consumers about terms of a credit agreement and to require creditors to specify how finance charges are computed.

ANS: F
These are the primary purposes of the federal Consumer Credit Protection Act. The Equal Credit Opportunity Act ensures that all consumers are given an equal chance to obtain credit.

REF: p. 348 OBJ: 15-5 TYPE: D

35. The Consumer Credit Protection Act requires that the finance charge for credit be stated as an annual percentage rate and that creditors specify the procedures used for correcting billing mistakes.

ANS: T REF: p. 347 OBJ: 15-5 TYPE: D

MULTIPLE CHOICE

1. The seller's measure of what he or she is willing to receive in exchange for transferring ownership or use of a product or service is known as
   a. credit.
   b. average pricing.
   c. demand.
   d. price.

ANS: D REF: p. 331 OBJ: 15-1 TYPE: D

2. The total sales revenue of a small business is a direct reflection of
   a. sales volume and credit terms.
   b. price and credit terms.
   c. price and expenses.
   d. sales volume and price.

ANS: D REF: p. 331 OBJ: 15-1 TYPE: C

3. Will's business will not be successful unless it charges a price for its products that covers its
   a. total variable cost.
   b. total cost.
   c. total fixed cost.
   d. total cost and some margin of profit.

ANS: D REF: p. 332 OBJ: 15-1 TYPE: C

4. Costs incurred by a firm in actually producing a product (e.g., materials, machinery, etc.) are considered to be a part of
   a. general overhead expenses.
   b. costs of manufacturing.
   c. cost of goods sold.
   d. manufacturing overhead expenses.

ANS: C REF: p. 3332 OBJ: 15-1 TYPE: D

5. Marie will account for the costs incurred by a her firm in producing its products (e.g., materials, machinery, etc.) as a part of its
   a. general overhead expenses.
   b. costs of manufacturing.
   c. cost of goods sold.
   d. manufacturing overhead expenses.

ANS: C REF: p. 332 OBJ: 15-1 TYPE: D

6. Active Feet, a small manufacturer of shoes, hired an additional vice-president and purchased a barrel of synthetic rubber used to make shoe soles. These two expenses should be considered a (an) _____ and a (an) _____, respectively.
   a. selling cost/cost of goods sold
   b. overhead cost/cost of goods sold
   c. selling cost/overhead cost
   d. overhead cost/selling cost

ANS: B REF: p. 332 OBJ: 15-1 TYPE: A

7. Hollywood Amusement, a small independent movie theater, decreased the price of admission from $5 to $4. Prior to the price decrease, the business sold 1,000 tickets each month. After the price decrease, it experienced ticket sales of 1,500 a month. If the change in sales is attributable only to the change in price, Hollywood Amusement faces ____ for its movie tickets.
   a. inelastic demand
   b. constant demand
   c. variable demand
   d. elastic demand

ANS: D REF: p. 333 OBJ: 15-1 TYPE: A

8. In general, products that are consumed in fixed amounts have
   a. inelastic demand.
   b. constant demand.
   c. variable demand.
   d. elastic demand.

ANS: A REF: p. 333 OBJ: 15-1 TYPE: C

9. In general, products that are consumed in different amounts have
   a. inelastic demand.
   b. constant demand.
   c. variable demand.
   d. elastic demand.

ANS: D REF: p. 333 OBJ: 15-1 TYPE: C

10. A pricing tactic whereby a firm sets a high price to convey an image of high quality or uniqueness is known as
    a. skimming pricing.
    b. penetration pricing.
    c. variable pricing.
    d. prestige pricing.

ANS: D REF: p. 334 OBJ: 15-1 TYPE: D

11. The salesman told Todd that the high price of the dealerships' automobiles was indicative of their high quality. The dealership is using a ________ pricing strategy.
    a. skimming
    b. penetration
    c. variable
    d. prestige

ANS: D REF: p. 334 OBJ: 15-1 TYPE: D

12. A competitor would likely use a _______ pricing strategy for a gaming console intended to compete directly with Sony's Playstation gaming console.
    a. follow-the-leader
    b. penetration
    c. variable
    d. prestige

ANS: A REF: p. 338 OBJ: 15-1 TYPE: D

13. Juan is using ________ when he systematically compares various cost and revenue estimates in order to determine the acceptability of alternative prices.
    a. break-even analysis
    b. price lining
    c. cost functioning
    d. demand functioning

ANS: A REF: p. 335 OBJ: 15-2 TYPE: D

14. A comprehensive break-even analysis entails
    a. examining revenue-cost relationships and establishing sales forecasts.
    b. analyzing marketing strategy.
    c. the use of comparison pricing.
    d. approximations of debits and credits.

ANS: A REF: p. 335 OBJ: 15-2 TYPE: C

15. Within the framework of a break-even analysis, an examination of _____ is conducted to determine the quantity at which the product, with an assumed price, will generate enough revenue to start earning a profit.
    a. costs
    b. revenues
    c. sales forecasts
    d. costs and revenue

ANS: D REF: p. 335 OBJ: 15-2 TYPE: C

16. Nina should use ___________ if she must cover operating expenses, subsequent price reductions, and achieve a desired profit level.
    a. markup pricing.
    b. price lining.
    c. break-even pricing.
    d. cost-based pricing.

ANS: A REF: p. 336 OBJ: 15-2 TYPE: D

17. Markup pricing may be expressed in terms of a percentage of either the _____ or the cost.
    a. quantity
    b. operating expenses
    c. selling price
    d. estimated expenses

ANS: C REF: p. 337 OBJ: 15-2 TYPE: C

18. Fine Framings, a small framing shop, uses markup pricing to arrive at a final selling price. The firm sells its frames at a price of $10, given a $6 unit cost. Fine Framings' markup on the selling price is _____, and its markup on cost is _____.
   a. 66.66%, 40%
   b. 40%, 66.66%
   c. 40%, 60%
   d. 55%, 45%

ANS: B REF: p. 337 OBJ: 15-2 TYPE: A

19. Clock Tickers, a small retailer of a quality alarm clock, sells its product for $180. If Clock Tickers adheres to pricing based on a 35% markup of cost, the firm's product costs are approximately
   a. $63.
   b. $98.
   c. $133.
   d. $155.

ANS: C REF: p. 337 OBJ: 15-2 TYPE: A

20. The Widget Company sells 1,000 widgets annually at a price of $35 each. If the company's pricing policies adhere to a 40% markup of selling price, the *cost* of each widget is
   a. $14.
   b. $21.
   c. $28.
   d. $32.

ANS: B REF: p. 337 OBJ: 15-2 TYPE: A

21. Gomez is pricing his products at a lower than normal, long-range market price in order to gain more rapid market acceptance. He is using a __________ strategy.
   a. variable pricing
   b. skimming price
   c. penetration pricing
   d. price lining

ANS: C REF: p. 338 OBJ: 15-3 TYPE: D

22. All of the following are reasons for implementing a penetration pricing strategy *except*
   a. to gain rapid market acceptance.
   b. to discourage new competitors' entry into the market.
   c. to rapidly recover startup costs.
   d. to increase existing market share.

ANS: C REF: p. 338 OBJ: 15-3 TYPE: C

23. Colorful Concoctions, a maker of children's crayons, decided to price its boxes of crayons below the long-term market price. The firm agreed to reduce its profit margin from 30 percent to 5 percent in the short-term in order to increase market share and discourage other firms from entering the crayon market. Colorful Concoctions was implementing a
    a. variable pricing strategy.
    b. skimming price strategy.
    c. penetration pricing strategy.
    d. price lining strategy.

ANS: C REF: p. 338 OBJ: 15-3 TYPE: A

24. Natural Well, a local supplier of natural bottled water, initially sold its product at a premium price of $4 because the company believed consumers would view the bottled water as a prestige item. The company decided that when startup costs had been fully recovered and competition became imminent, the company would reduce the price to a more reasonable $1. Natural Well is implementing a
    a. variable pricing strategy.
    b. skimming price strategy.
    c. penetration pricing strategy.
    d. price lining strategy.

ANS: B REF: p. 338 OBJ: 15-3 TYPE: A

25. Setting prices for products or services using a particular competitor as a model of reference is known as a
    a. variable pricing strategy.
    b. flexible pricing strategy.
    c. follow-the-leader pricing strategy.
    d. price lining strategy.

ANS: C REF: p. 338 OBJ: 15-3 TYPE: D

26. Hollywood Entertainment analyzed its customer base to ascertain the characteristics of customer segments and understand special market conditions. The independent movie theater found that senior citizens thought the current $5 admission price was too high and that most consumers preferred to go to the movies after 6:00 p.m. To strengthen ticket demand, Hollywood Entertainment began offering $3.50 tickets to all seniors and $4 tickets for all movies starting before 6:00 p.m. Hollywood Entertainment was employing a
    a. variable pricing strategy.
    b. flexible pricing strategy.
    c. price lining strategy.
    d. differentiated pricing strategy.

ANS: A REF: p. 338 OBJ: 15-3 TYPE: A

27. Within the context of a price lining strategy, the inventory level of the different lines depends directly on the _______ of the store's customers.
    a. product awareness
    b. personal demographics

c. credit worthiness
d. income level and buying desires

ANS: D REF: p. 339 OBJ: 15-3 TYPE: C

28. Which one of the following is *not* true with respect to pricing in a small business?
   a. Continual price adjustments can be both costly to the seller and confusing to buyers.
   b. In some situations, local, state, and federal laws must be considered when setting prices.
   c. Conducted properly, price determination is an exact science.
   d. Systems of discounts are often used to adjust prices to meet a variety of market needs.

ANS: C REF: p. 339 OBJ: 15-3 TYPE: C

29. The major objective of a firm in granting credit is
   a. generating consumer goodwill.
   b. reducing bad debt risk.
   c. expanding sales.
   d. promoting the business.

ANS: C REF: p. 340 OBJ: 15-4 TYPE: C

30. Benefits of credit to sellers include all of the following *except*
   a. creating a closer association with the customers.
   b. smoothing out sales peaks and valleys.
   c. providing a tool for competitive advantage.
   d. sustaining long-term sales, even if these exceed the buying power of the customer.

ANS: D REF: p. 340 OBJ: 15-4 TYPE: C

31. Credit sales ______ the amount of working capital needed by the business doing the selling.
   a. augment
   b. decrease
   c. increase
   d. offset

ANS: C REF: p. 340 OBJ: 15-4 TYPE: C

32. Credit granted by retailers to final consumers who purchase for personal or family use is referred to as
   a. trade credit.
   b. personal credit.
   c. open credit.
   d. consumer credit.

ANS: D REF: p. 342 OBJ: 15-4 TYPE: D

33. With ______, the customer obtains possession of goods or services when they are purchased, with payment due when billed at a later date.

a. an open charge account
b. an installment account
c. a revolving account
d. a selective account

ANS: A REF: p. 342 OBJ: 15-4 TYPE: D

34. Credit cards are usually based on a ____________ account system.
a. an open charge
b. an installment
c. a revolving
d. a selective

ANS: C REF: p. 342 OBJ: 15-4 TYPE: D

35. Which of the following is true with respect to installment accounts?
a. A down payment is normally required.
b. Large purchases are usually not covered by this form of credit.
c. By law, finance charges cannot exceed 20 percent of the purchase price.
d. Short-term consumer credit is provided.

ANS: A REF: p. 342 OBJ: 15-4 TYPE: C

36. Which of the following is true with respect to revolving charge accounts?
a. A down payment is normally required.
b. Charged purchases may not exceed the credit limit.
c. A fixed amount must be paid monthly, regardless of the outstanding balance.
d. Finance charges increase as the outstanding balance increases.

ANS: B REF: p. 342 OBJ: 15-4 TYPE: C

37. If Hillary wants to purchase refrigerator on credit. If she uses an installment plan, which of the following is most likely to occur?
a. She will be required to make a down payment.
b. She will not be charged taxes.
c. By law, finance charges on her account cannot exceed 20 percent of the purchase price.
d. She will not get a discounted price on her purchase.

ANS: A REF: p. 342 OBJ: 15-4 TYPE: C

38. Quality Cars, an independent used-car dealership, utilizes long-term consumer credit in its business. Typically, consumers are allowed to place a 15 percent down payment on an automobile. Then, over a period of 48 months, the consumer is allowed to make payments on the balance of the account, which includes compound interest of 2 percent monthly on the unpaid portion. Quality Cars is employing _____ in its business.
a. open charge accounts

b. installment accounts
c. revolving accounts
d. selective accounts

ANS: B REF: p. 342 OBJ: 15-4 TYPE: A

39. Handyman Hardware, a small community-based store, offers its consumers the option of using credit. Creditworthy individuals are able to use the "HH Credit Card" for all purchases up to a credit limit of $1,000. Consumers are required to pay at least 20 percent of their outstanding balance at the end of each month. A two percent finance charge is assessed on the unpaid balance at the end of each billing cycle. Handyman Hardware is employing _____ in its business.
a. open charge accounts
b. installment accounts
c. revolving charge accounts
d. selective accounts

ANS: C REF: p. 342 OBJ: 15-4 TYPE: A

40. The basic types of credit cards include all of the following *except*
a. entertainment credit cards.
b. retailer credit cards.
c. bank credit cards.
d. collective establishment credit cards.

ANS: D REF: p. 342-343 OBJ: 15-4 TYPE: C

41. A trade credit bill of $80,000 with terms of sale of 2/5, net 30 means the buyer saves _______ if the bill is paid within the discount period.
a. $400
b. $1,600
c. $2,500
d. $4,000

ANS: B REF: p. 343 OBJ: 15-4 TYPE: C

42. How much discount will a buyer receive if the buyer pays a trade credit bill of $60,000 with terms of sale of 2/5, net 30 on the net due date?
a. $0
b. $500
c. $1200
d. $3,000

ANS: A REF: p. 343 OBJ: 15-4 TYPE: C

43. Major steps in a formal, comprehensive credit management system for a small business include all of the following *except*

a. aging accounts receivable.
b. evaluating the credit of applicants.
c. establishing effective billing and collection procedures.
d. maintaining the credit history of customers to whom credit is extended.

ANS: D REF: p. 343-347 OBJ: 15-5 TYPE: C

44. Which of the following is a good source of consumer credit information?
a. Trade-credit agencies
b. The Federal Credit Reporting Agency
c. Third-party reports
d. Credit bureaus

ANS: D REF: p. 345 OBJ: 15-5 TYPE: C

45. Information Express is a privately owned and operated organization that collects credit information on business firms. After the organization analyzes and evaluates the data, it makes credit ratings available to client companies for a fee. Information Express is a
a. credit collection agency.
b. trade-credit agency.
c. financial credit agency.
d. credit bureau.

ANS: B REF: p. 345 OBJ: 15-5 TYPE: A

46. CarePair, a small business specializing in making and distributing hospital gowns to medical facilities, often sells its product on credit. The company maintains a ledger that divides accounts receivable into age categories based on the length of time they have been outstanding. Receivables 1-6 months old are deemed grade A (regular business); 7-12, grade B (overdue business); and 13-24, grade C (delinquent business); those accounts receivable over 24 months old are turned over to a collection agency. CarePair is relying on _____ to keep track of accounts receivable.
a. a collection categorization
b. an aging schedule
c. a delinquent adjustment schedule
d. a financial credit schedule

ANS: B REF: p. 345 OBJ: 15-5 TYPE: A

47. Which of the following statements is true of credit bureaus?
a. They act as third-party underwriters of credit to companies which then offer this to customers.
b. They provide a likely scenario of future use/misuse of credit.
c. They profile members' credit experiences specifically with non-profit organizations.
d. They collect credit information and offer it only to member businesses.

ANS: D REF: p. 345 OBJ: 15-5 TYPE: C

48. Slow-paying credit accounts
    a. almost always help to build goodwill with customers.
    b. yield advantages from carry-over effects.
    c. tie up the seller's working capital.
    d. are rarely a problem for small businesses.

ANS: C REF: p. 346 OBJ: 15-5 TYPE: C

49. All of the following are acceptable options available to entrepreneurs attempting to collect delinquent accounts receivable *except*
    a. written reminders.
    b. personal contacts.
    c. telephone calls to a customer's employer.
    d. referrals to collection agencies or attorneys.

ANS: C REF: p. 347 OBJ: 15-5 TYPE: C

50. One of the primary purposes of the federal Consumer Credit Protection Act is to
    a. require creditors to specify how finance charges are computed.
    b. grant certain rights to credit applicants regarding credit reports.
    c. inform consumers about all forms of credit available to them.
    d. specify what information a customer's employer can release about him/her.

ANS: A REF: p. 347 OBJ: 15-5 TYPE: D

ESSAY

1. Explain what is meant by elastic demand and inelastic demand. Use products to illustrate each type of demand.

   ANS:
   The extent to which a change in price affects the quantity demanded is called the elasticity of demand. The change in total revenue as the price is increased or decreased is the gauge of elasticity. For example, if the price is raised and total revenue goes up, demand is inelastic. If the price is lowered and the total revenue goes up, demand is elastic. Luxury products, such as jewelry, have elastic demand. Products that are considered necessities, such as salt, have inelastic demand.

   REF: p. 333 OBJ: 15-1 TYPE: C

2. What would be the break-even point if a firm set a unit selling price of $100 when total fixed costs were $100,000 and variable costs per unit were $80? Draw a graph that depicts the break-even point.

   ANS:
   5,000 units.

   REF: p. 335 OBJ: 15-2 TYPE: A

3. Contrast penetration price and skimming price strategies.

ANS:
Penetration pricing involves pricing products or services lower than the normal, long-range market price. The purpose is to gain more rapid market acceptance or to increase existing market share.

Skimming pricing sets prices at very high levels for a limited period for the purpose of recovering startup costs rapidly or when there is little threat of short-term competition.

REF: p. 338 OBJ: 15-3 TYPE: C

4. List and describe the major types of consumer credit.

ANS:
The three major types of consumer credit are the following:
- Open charge accounts–customers obtain possession of goods at the time of purchase, with payment due when billed.
- Installment accounts–long-term consumer credit that requires a down payment and typically allows a repayment period of 12 to 60 months.
- Revolving charge accounts–seller grants a customer a line of credit, and charged purchases may not exceed it.

REF: p. 342 OBJ: 15-4 TYPE: D

5. Assume you are responsible for managing accounts receivable in a small business. What are some of the methods you would use?

ANS:
Answers will vary from student to student. However, the following list contains items that could be discussed in their answers.
- Analyze credit information on customers from credit bureaus.
- Use an aging schedule to forecast cash conversion rates.
- Use periodic billing statements.
- Establish adequate records and collection procedures.
- Compute a bad-debt ratio.
- Follow credit regulations and rules.

REF: p. 343-347 OBJ: 15-5 TYPE: A

6. **You Make the Call—Situation 1**
Steve Jones is the 35-year-old owner of a highly competitive small business, which supplies temporary office help. Like most businesspeople, he is always looking for ways to increase profit. However, the nature of his competition makes it very difficult to raise prices for the temps' services, while reducing their wages makes recruiting difficult. Jones has, nevertheless, found an area—bad debts—in which improvement should increase profits. A friend and business consultant met with Jones to advise him on credit management policies. Jones was pleased to get this friend's advice, as bad debts were costing him about 2 percent of sales. Currently, Jones has no system for managing credit.

Question 1 What advice would you give Jones regarding the screening of new credit customers?

Question 2 What action should Jones take to encourage current credit customers to pay their debts? Be specific.

Question 3 Jones has considered eliminating credit sales. What are the possible consequences of this decision?

ANS:

1. Jones should investigate clients, when possible, prior to supplying them with temporary help. If a new client's needs are immediate, help could be supplied and the credit investigation begun concurrently. Banks and trade-credit agencies would be possible sources of credit information. Jones must be careful not to offend new clients, but at the same time he must realize that the credit check is simply a good business practice.

   A client application form could be used to obtain relevant information for the credit evaluation. Jones might also offer a discount for services paid for in cash.

2. The most important step is to provide timely billing. Most credit customers will pay their bills on time if they receive proper notification and verification. Jones could offer a higher discount for credit customers who pay early and/or on time. He could also devise a formal procedure with timely step-by-step collection actions.

3. The loss of business is the most obvious consequence of eliminating credit. Many businesses are set up to make payments on credit, and requiring payment in cash is an inconvenience to them.

   On the other hand, by eliminating credit sales, Jones can eliminate the loss of 2 percent of sales revenue, which could amount to more than the gross revenue lost as a result of the new policy.

REF: p. 349 OBJ: YMTC TYPE: C

7. **You Make the Call—Situation 2**

Tom Anderson started his records storage business in the New York metropolitan area in 1991. His differentiation strategy was to offer competitive prices while providing state-of-the-art technology, easy access to his warehouse, and, of course, great service.

After opening the business, Anderson learned that most potential customers had already signed long-term storage contracts with competitors. These contracts included a removal fee for each box permanently removed from the storage company's warehouse, making it difficult for customers to consider switching.

Anderson believes that the survival of his company hinges on his view of what the essence of his business is. In other words, is he operating a storage company or a real estate business? He is convinced that he must answer this question before making any decision regarding pricing strategy.

Question 1 What do you think Anderson means when he asks, "Is my business storage or real estate?" Why do you think he feels a need to ask this question prior to developing a pricing strategy?

Question 2 What pricing strategy would be effective in combating the existing contractual relationships between potential customers and competitors?

Question 3 Assuming that business costs would allow Anderson to lower prices, what problems do you see with this approach?

Question 4 Do you believe his business could benefit from offering credit to customers? Why or why not?

ANS:

1. Anderson is probably asking whether he should be pricing the space (a real estate view) or is he pricing the service (a storage company). The answer to this question may impact his promotion and other elements of his marketing effort, but it is not really an issue right now. He needs to evaluate his costs, both fixed and variable, and equate these relationships to what demand levels he believes he can achieve.
2. Anderson should consider a combination of a penetration and variable pricing strategy. Some of his customers need a concession on price to reflect the removal fee they would have to pay to switch to Anderson's storage business. The penetration pricing strategy will enable him to price lower than he normally will to gain more rapid market acceptance.
3. The main problem with lowering prices is the expectation that the strategy creates in the minds of consumers. That is why a temporary reduction has to be clearly communicated as a discounted price, not a price expected to last forever.
4. Every firm should evaluate a credit system to decide if the benefits discussed in this chapter will apply to their situation. It may be a standard practice in his industry and therefore difficult to avoid. There is a cost associated with credit, and this must be balanced against the potential increase in sales revenue related to offering credit.

REF: p. 349-350 OBJ: YMTC TYPE: C

8. **You Make the Call—Situation 3**
Paul Bowlin owns and operates a tree removal, pruning, and spraying business in a large metropolitan area with a population of approximately 200,000. The business started in 1975 and has grown to the point where Bowlin uses one and sometimes two crews, with four or five employees on each crew. Pricing has always been an important tool in gaining business, but Bowlin realizes that there are ways to entice customers other than quoting the lowest price. For example, he provides careful cleanup of branches and leaves, takes out stumps below ground level, and waits until a customer is completely satisfied before taking payment. At the same time, he realizes his bids for tree removal jobs must cover his costs. In this industry, Bowlin faces intense price competition from operators with more sophisticated wood-processing equipment, such as chip grinders. Therefore, he is always open to suggestions about pricing strategy.

Question 1 What would the nature of this industry suggest about the elasticity of demand affecting Bowlin's pricing?
Question 2 What types of costs should Bowlin evaluate when he is determining his break-even point?
Question 3 What pricing strategies could Bowlin adopt to further his long-term success in this market?
Question 4 How can the high quality of Bowlin's work be used to justify somewhat higher price quotes?

ANS:
1. The nature of this industry is such that service is not standardized. There are large differences in the services that can be provided. In other words, this service can be distinguished from other tree removal and pruning businesses. This means that demand can be very inelastic within a certain range. There is the opportunity to distinguish the services in such a way that small price increases will cause little resistance from customers and thereby result in increasing total revenues.
2. The types of costs Bowlin must evaluate are the same as in any other business—fixed and variable costs. For Bowlin, fixed costs may include such items as chain saws, tools, pick-up trucks, and insurance. Variable costs would include gasoline and labor costs.

3. A variable pricing strategy will be required in this type of business because no two jobs will be exactly the same. Bowlin may also want to consider flexible pricing to reflect special market conditions such as distant locations and adverse weather conditions.

4. Bowlin might consider some degree of prestige pricing for certain high-income customers, which could successfully convey an image of high quality or uniqueness. This approach could work well if certain customers associate quality with price.

REF: p. 350 OBJ: YMTC TYPE: C

9. **You Make the Call—Situation 4**

Mom's Monogram is a small firm that manufactures and imprints monogramming designs for jackets, caps, tee shirts, and other articles of clothing. The business has been in operation for two years. In the first year, sales reached $50,000. The next year, sales raced up to $300,000. Pricing of the firm's services has been based on a straight, cost-plus approach. Success has spawned plans to double plant size and equipment. The owners have never spent money on advertising and believe that the expansion will double sales within the next three years. They plan to continue pricing their services using markup pricing.

Question 1 What problems may be encountered by this business if it continues to use markup pricing?
Question 2 How can the firm's total costs be analyzed to ascertain the appropriate pricing strategy?
Question 3 What types of discounts might be offered to customers of Mom's Monogram? Be specific.

ANS:

1. If Mom's Monogram ignores demand, it may either price too high or forgo revenues that could have been earned in a market that could support higher prices.

2. The firm's total costs should be analyzed to identify those that are fixed and those that are variable. Only then can break-even analysis be applied to the costs associated with the proposed plant and equipment expenditure.

3. Several types of discounts could be offered. Mom's Monogram should base its choice of which to offer on the reason for giving the discount. Consider the following options:

   - A quantity discount could be offered to encourage customers to buy more.
   - A trade discount could be offered to shift some marketing costs (for example, cut back on delivery service).
   - A cash discount could be offered to encourage credit customers to pay early.
   - A seasonal discount could be offered to encourage customers to stock early.

REF: p. 0 OBJ: YMTC TYPE: C

Correlation Table for Chapter 16—Promotional Planning

	Learning Objectives	Question Type	Definition Define new term, recall facts	Concept Understand or relate concepts	Application Apply knowledge, analyze data
1	Describe the communication process and the factors determining a promotional mix.	T/F	2	1,3,4	5
		MC		1,2,3,4	
		ES			
2	Explain methods of determining the appropriate level of promotional expenditure.	T/F		6,7,8,9	
		MC		5,7,8,9,10,11	6,12
		ES		1	
3	Describe personal selling activities.	T/F	10,11	12,13,14,16,17, 18	15
		MC	13	14,16,17,18,19, 22,23,24,26,27	15,20,21,25
		ES		2,3	
4	Identify advertising options for a small business.	T/F	21,22,23,30	19,20,24,25,26, 27,28,29,31,32, 33,34	
		MC	28,36,39	29,30,32,33,34, 35,37,38,40,41, 42	31
		ES		4	
5	Discuss the use of sales promotional tools.	T/F	35,40	36,37,38,39,41, 42	
		MC	43,47	44,45,48,49	46,50
		ES		5	
	You Make the Call	ES		6,7,8,9	

Total Number of Test Questions: 101 (42 True/False; 50 Multiple-Choice; 9 Essay)

Chapter 16—Promotional Planning

TRUE/FALSE

1. The way small businesses communicate with their customers is completely different from the way family members communicate with one another.

   ANS: F
   There are many similarities between the way small businesses communicate with their customers and the way, for example, that parents would communicate with a daughter (as depicted in Figure 16-1).

   REF: p. 354 OBJ: 16-1 TYPE: C

2. Every communication has a receiver, a source, and a channel through which the message is passed.

   ANS: T REF: p. 353 OBJ: 16-1 TYPE: D

3. According to the textbook, promotion is based on communication.

   ANS: T REF: p. 354 OBJ: 16-1 TYPE: C

4. The promotional mix is influenced by three major factors: the geographical nature of the market to be reached, customer income, and the target market.

   ANS: F
   The promotional mix is influenced by three major factors: the geographical nature of the market to be reached, the size of the promotional budget, and the product's characteristics.

   REF: p. 354 OBJ: 16-1 TYPE: C

5. Personal selling is an effective method for promoting products such as razor blades.

   ANS: F
   A widely dispersed market generally requires mass coverage through advertising, in contrast to the more costly contact of individuals through personal selling.

   REF: p. 354 OBJ: 16-1 TYPE: A

6. When estimating sales promotion expenditures, it is usually a good idea to consider all four methods of budgeting funds for small business.

   ANS: T REF: p. 355 OBJ: 16-2 TYPE: C

7. The best approach to promotional funding is allocating what can be spared.

   ANS: F
   Such an approach to promotional spending should be avoided because it ignores promotional goals.

REF: p. 355 OBJ: 16-2 TYPE: C

8. The approach called *spending as much as the competition does* can lead the firm to copy the mistakes of rival firms, as well as their successes.

ANS: T REF: p. 355 OBJ: 16-2 TYPE: C

9. In estimating promotional expenses, a small business should start by assessing what it will take to do the job.

ANS: T REF: p. 355 OBJ: 16-2 TYPE: C

10. Personal selling is promotion that is delivered in a one-on-one environment.

ANS: T REF: p. 355 OBJ: 16-3 TYPE: D

11. Prospecting is the ongoing search for new customers.

ANS: T REF: p. 356 OBJ: 16-3 TYPE: D

12. Inquiries by a potential customer that do not lead to a sale can still create what is known as a "promising prospect."

ANS: F
These inquiries can create what is called a "hot prospect."

REF: p. 357 OBJ: 16-3 TYPE: C

13. A "canned" sales talk is successful with most buyers.

ANS: F
A "canned" sales talk will *not* succeed with most buyers.

REF: p. 358 OBJ: 16-3 TYPE: C

14. In relationship selling, a salesperson must exhibit professional etiquette in all contacts with customers, since this will determine the success of the sale.

ANS: F
It is true that professional etiquette is of great importance in making a sale, but so are other factors (e.g., good appearance and a pleasant personality).

REF: p. 358 OBJ: 16-3 TYPE: C

15. During sales presentations, a salesperson should never admit product weaknesses to a potential customer.

ANS: F
In a sales situation, high ethical standards are of utmost importance if a salesperson is to create customer goodwill.

REF: p. 358 OBJ: 16-3 TYPE: A

16. A salesperson can help to build goodwill by understanding the customer's point of view.

ANS: T REF: p. 358 OBJ: 16-3 TYPE: C

17. One problem with motivating salespeople is that the entrepreneur's goals and a salesperson's goals may differ.

ANS: T REF: p. 358 OBJ: 16-3 TYPE: C

18. Straight salaries are best for motivating salespeople because of the financial security salaries provide.

ANS: F
Straight salaries may actually *reduce* the motivation of salespeople precisely because of the financial security salaries provide.

REF: p. 359 OBJ: 16-3 TYPE: C

19. Advertising is one type of personal selling technique.

ANS: F
Advertising is the *impersonal* presentation of an idea, not personal selling per se.

REF: p. 359 OBJ: 16-4 TYPE: C

20. Advertising seeks to sell by informing, persuading, and reminding customers of the existence or superiority of a firm's product or service.

ANS: T REF: p. 359 OBJ: 16-4 TYPE: C

21. Institutional advertising is primarily concerned with a company and its reputation.

ANS: T REF: p. 359 OBJ: 16-4 TYPE: D

22. Product advertising makes potential customers aware of a particular product or service and their need for it.

ANS: T REF: p. 359 OBJ: 16-4 TYPE: D

23. Product advertising is intended to keep the public conscious of the company and its good reputation.

ANS: F
It is *institutional* advertising that is intended to keep the public conscious of the company and its good reputation.

REF: p. 359 OBJ: 16-4 TYPE: D

24. Only institutions such as universities use institutional advertising.

ANS: F
Other organizations (e.g., small firms) can also use institutional advertising.

REF: p. 359 OBJ: 16-4 TYPE: C

25. The majority of small business advertising is institutional advertising.

ANS: F
The majority of small business advertising is *product* advertising.

REF: p. 359 OBJ: 16-4 TYPE: C

26. The type of advertising used should be based on the nature of the business, industry practice, available media, and the firm's objectives.

ANS: T REF: p. 359 OBJ: 16-4 TYPE: C

27. Most small businesses create their own promotional messages.

ANS: F
Most small businesses rely on others (e.g., advertising agencies, suppliers, trade associations, advertising media) to create their promotional messages.

REF: p. 359 OBJ: 16-4 TYPE: C

28. Advertising agencies can furnish small firms with design, artwork, and copy for specific advertisements or commercials.

ANS: T REF: p. 360 OBJ: 16-4 TYPE: C

29. Advertising on the World Wide Web is still too new and untested to challenge traditional media for promotional dollars.

ANS: F
With color graphics, two-way information exchanges, video streaming, and 24-hour availability, Web advertising is challenging traditional media for promotional dollars.

REF: p. 360 OBJ: 16-4 TYPE: C

30. A Web site is a location on the World Wide Web where users can find information about a firm and its products.

ANS: T REF: p. 360 OBJ: 16-4 TYPE: D

31. E-mail promotion provides a low-cost way to pinpoint customers and achieve response rates higher than those for banner ads.

ANS: T REF: p. 361 OBJ: 16-4 TYPE: C

32. The effectiveness of *banner ads* is obvious—that's why they are so prevalent on the Internet.

ANS: F

The effectiveness of this form of advertising is not yet clear, but these ads may work well with a targeted campaign.

REF: p. 361 OBJ: 16-4 TYPE: C

33. Most of the domain names that were once available for dot.coms have been taken.

ANS: F
Contrary to general opinion, plenty of domain names are still available.

REF: p. 363 OBJ: 16-4 TYPE: C

34. Unlike in traditional retailing where customers are demanding and first impressions are important, e-commerce firms do not have to worry about initial communications, since bad first impressions can be overcome with follow-up contacts and high-quality Web designs.

ANS: F
First impressions are important in the e-commerce world since potential customers can move on to other sites with a mere click of a mouse.

REF: p. 363 OBJ: 16-4 TYPE: C

35. Sales promotion refers to promotional techniques other than personal selling or advertising.

ANS: T REF: p. 366 OBJ: 16-5 TYPE: D

36. Advertising is considered to be part of sales promotion.

ANS: F
Advertising is *not* considered to be part of sales promotion.

REF: p. 366 OBJ: 16-5 TYPE: C

37. Trade show groups claim that the cost of an exhibit is less than one-fourth the cost of a sales call.

ANS: T REF: p. 368 OBJ: 16-5 TYPE: C

38. Trade shows are accurately profiled as "free advertising."

ANS: F
Trade show exhibits are more cost-effective that advertising, but they are *not free*.

REF: p. 368 OBJ: 16-5 TYPE: C

39. Regular contacts with news media are required if publicity programs are to be effective.

ANS: T REF: p. 368 OBJ: 16-5 TYPE: C

40. Publicity is accurately described as free advertising.

ANS: F

Although publicity is often considered to be free advertising, this type of promotion is not always free (e.g., consider charges for representation in school yearbooks and with community athletic programs.)

REF: p. 368 OBJ: 16-5 TYPE: D

41. Both wholesalers and retailers can utilize sales promotion tools to increase sales.

ANS: T REF: p. 368 OBJ: 16-5 TYPE: C

42. Joining with another firm to promote products is a form of strategic alliance.

ANS: T REF: p. 369 OBJ: 16-5 TYPE: C

MULTIPLE CHOICE

1. Which of the following is *not* part of the communication process?
   a. Source
   b. Message
   c. Perception
   d. Channel

ANS: C REF: p. 353 OBJ: 16-1 TYPE: C

2. A promotional mix is influenced by the following three major factors:
   a. Geography of the market, the size of the promotional budget, and product characteristics.
   b. Geography of the market, retailer market, and product characteristics.
   c. The firm's target customers, product characteristics, and budget requirements.
   d. The firm's target customers, market size, and product characteristics.

ANS: A REF: p. 354 OBJ: 16-1 TYPE: C

3. A widely dispersed market favors which of the promotional methods?
   a. Personal selling
   b. Sales promotion
   c. Personal promotion
   d. Advertising

ANS: D REF: p. 354 OBJ: 16-1 TYPE: C

4. Which of the following is one of the basic promotional methods?
   a. Advertising
   b. Provisional selling
   c. Sales enhancement
   d. Expansive communication

ANS: A REF: p. 354 OBJ: 16-1 TYPE: C

5. Promotional funds are determined according to past experience in which of the following methods?
   a. Spending as much as the competition
   b. What can be spared
   c. Percentage of sales
   d. Forecasted industry standard

ANS: C REF: p. 355 OBJ: 16-2 TYPE: C

6. Inspiring Toys, a small manufacturer of educational toys, is formulating a budget for next year's promotional activities. The company decides to budget $40,000 for promotional expenses (5 percent of the current year's $800,000 in sales). Inspiring Toys is using the _____ method of budgeting.
   a. spending as much as the competition
   b. what it will take to do the job
   c. percentage of sales
   d. what can be spared

ANS: C REF: p. 355 OBJ: 16-2 TYPE: A

7. The major problem with the _____ method of determining promotional expenditures is the tendency to spend more when sales are increasing and less when they are declining.
   a. percentage of sales
   b. what it will take to do the job
   c. sales plus
   d. what can be spared

ANS: A REF: p. 355 OBJ: 16-2 TYPE: C

8. Which of the following does *not* describe a method of determining promotional expenditures?
   a. Matching industry forecasts
   b. Spending as much as the competition
   c. What can be spared
   d. What it will take to do the job

ANS: A REF: p. 355 OBJ: 16-2 TYPE: C

9. A widely used piecemeal approach to determining the level of promotional expenditures is
   a. expert opinion.
   b. what can be spared.
   c. what the market will bear.
   d. cost plus.

ANS: B REF: p. 355 OBJ: 16-2 TYPE: C

10. The preferred method of determining promotional expenditures is
    a. percentage of sales.
    b. what it will take to do the job.
    c. cost plus.
    d. what can be spared.

ANS: B REF: p. 355 OBJ: 16-2 TYPE: C

11. The "spending as much as the competition" method
    a. can be used to duplicate the promotional efforts of close competitors.
    b. should never be used.
    c. depends on past experiences.
    d. should be used to introduce a unique, new product.

ANS: A REF: p. 355 OBJ: 16-2 TYPE: C

12. Mini Makers, a small manufacturer of action figures, is formulating a budget for next year's promotional activities. The company decides to budget $50,000 for promotional expenses (an amount equal to its nearest competitor's allotment.) Mini Makers is using the _____ method of budgeting.
    a. spending as much as the competition
    b. what it will take to do the job
    c. percentage of sales
    d. what can be spared

    ANS: A REF: p. 355 OBJ: 16-2 TYPE: A

13. _____ is a promotion delivered in a one-on-one environment.
    a. Personal selling
    b. Sales promotion
    c. Personal promotion
    d. Advertising

    ANS: A REF: p. 355 OBJ: 16-3 TYPE: D

14. Personal selling is widely used in
    a. retail establishments only.
    b. wholesale and retail establishments only.
    c. service establishments only.
    d. retail, wholesale, and service establishments.

    ANS: D REF: p. 355 OBJ: 16-3 TYPE: C

15. Mary White, a sales representative for a small cleaning business, asks current customers for names of friends, customers, and other businesses that might be interested in the company's cleaning services. White is relying on _____ to identify potential customers.
    a. customer-initiated contacts
    b. marketer-initiated contacts
    c. impersonal referrals
    d. personal referrals

    ANS: D REF: p. 356 OBJ: 16-3 TYPE: A

16. Which of the following is *not* a technique for prospecting?
    a. Impersonal referrals
    b. Personal referrals
    c. Public records
    d. Agency-initiated contacts

    ANS: D REF: p. 356 OBJ: 16-3 TYPE: C

17. The two major steps in preparing for a sales presentation are
    a. advertising and practicing.
    b. prospecting and practicing.
    c. publicity and prospecting.
    d. exhibits and prospecting.

    ANS: B REF: p. 356 OBJ: 16-3 TYPE: C

18. Media publications, public records, and directories are sources of

a. impersonal referrals.
b. marketer-initiated contacts.
c. personal referrals.
d. customer-initiated contacts.

ANS: A REF: p. 356 OBJ: 16-3 TYPE: C

19. Telephone calls and mail surveys are examples of
a. impersonal referrals.
b. marketer-initiated contacts.
c. personal referrals.
d. customer-initiated contacts.

ANS: B REF: p. 356 OBJ: 16-3 TYPE: C

20. Will Thompson is a salesperson for a small appliance store. In an attempt to locate potential new customers, he decides to mail a survey to residents in selected neighborhoods. Those individuals who return completed surveys will receive a phone call from Thompson about the store's products and current "deals." Thompson is gaining knowledge of potential customers through
a. customer-initiated contacts.
b. marketer-initiated contacts.
c. impersonal referrals.
d. personal referrals.

ANS: B REF: p. 356 OBJ: 16-3 TYPE: A

21. A salesperson at Carpet Warehouse searches public records of new building permits to identify potential customers for new carpets. This salesperson is relying on _____ to identify sales prospects.
a. customer-initiated contacts
b. marketer-initiated contacts
c. impersonal referrals
d. personal referrals

ANS: C REF: p. 356 OBJ: 16-3 TYPE: A

22. Customer objections can be categorized as relating to
a. product and price.
b. need and sequence.
c. source and pitch.
d. timing and sequence.

ANS: A REF: p. 357 OBJ: 16-3 TYPE: C

23. Which approach can be used to handle a customer's objections?
a. Showing what a delay might cost
b. Hearing the prospect out
c. Using the boomerang technique
d. Using the "Yes, but" response

ANS: C REF: p. 357 OBJ: 16-3 TYPE: C

24. Using the boomerang technique to respond to a prospect's objection involves

a. listening to the objection.
b. turning a valid objection into a valid reason to buy.
c. responding with "Yes, but."
d. admitting faults and apologizing

ANS: B REF: p. 357 OBJ: 16-3 TYPE: C

25. Aaron Michels, a corporate account salesperson for Software Etc., is conducting a sales presentation for a potential new customer. Following the presentation, the prospective client states that her firm already uses a competing product. Intuitively, Mr. Michels replies, "In that case, I'm certain that you are now ready to upgrade to the best product available." Mr. Michels's response is an example of using
    a. the boomerang technique.
    b. admitting and counterbalancing.
    c. the "Yes, but" approach.
    d. comparisons.

    ANS: A REF: p. 357 OBJ: 16-3 TYPE: A

26. An example of a nonfinancial reward that may motivate a salesperson is
    a. personal recognition.
    b. compensation.
    c. a bonus plan.
    d. a stock plan.

    ANS: A REF: p. 358 OBJ: 16-3 TYPE: C

27. Which is the compensation plan best suited for salespersons in a small business?
    a. Straight salary plan
    b. Strictly commissions-on-sales plan
    c. Combination of salary and commissions, with the salary representing the larger portion
    d. Combination of salary and commissions, with the commissions representing the larger portion

    ANS: C REF: p. 359 OBJ: 16-3 TYPE: C

28. The two basic types of advertising are ______, which makes potential customers aware of products and their need for them, and ______, which conveys an idea about the firm that produces the product.
    a. institutional, product
    b. product, institutional
    c. product, publicity
    d. specialty, publicity

    ANS: B REF: p. 359 OBJ: 16-4 TYPE: D

29. Small firms may restrict their advertising by
    a. media channel.
    b. customers' perceptions of products offered.
    c. customer type.
    d. business category.

    ANS: C REF: p. 360 OBJ: 16-4 TYPE: C

30. The right combination of advertising media depends on

a. the type of business.
b. customer income.
c. the ad agency.
d. the class of the customer.

ANS: A REF: p. 360 OBJ: 16-4 TYPE: C

31. Before meeting with media representatives, a small business manager should
   a. perform a statistical analysis of the market.
   b. consult different banks for loan rates.
   c. learn about the strengths and weaknesses of each advertising medium.
   d. create the message.

   ANS: C REF: p. 360 OBJ: 16-4 TYPE: A

32. Which of the following is *not* one of the services ad agencies provide?
   a. Furnishing design and artwork
   b. Evaluating the effectiveness of different advertising appeals
   c. Analyzing the balance of a firm's marketing mix
   d. Advising on sales promotions

   ANS: C REF: p. 360 OBJ: 16-4 TYPE: C

33. Outside sources that may assist in formulating and carrying out promotional programs include
   a. marketing coaches.
   b. professional associations.
   c. the advertising media.
   d. trade representatives.

   ANS: C REF: p. 359 OBJ: 16-4 TYPE: C

34. Advertising via the Web is appealing because this medium
   a. has demonstrated that it is effective in attracting potential customers.
   b. offers an intense one-way transfer of information.
   c. is available 24 hours a day.
   d. is a reliable way of getting a firm's message out.

   ANS: C REF: p. 361 OBJ: 16-4 TYPE: C

35. The basic methods of Web promotion include
   a. customer targeting.
   b. Web site replication.
   c. creating banner ads and pop-ups.
   d. establishing Web page "thumbprints."

   ANS: C REF: p. 361 OBJ: 16-4 TYPE: C

36. A Web site is
   a. a location on the Web where users can find information about a company and its products.
   b. an essential tool in today's business environment.
   c. usually too expensive for small businesses to support.
   d. often difficult for customers to find, and therefore of little use to reaching a market.

   ANS: A REF: p. 361 OBJ: 16-4 TYPE: D

37. Internet advertising is already facing an obstacle because
    a. viewers are reluctant to respond to banner ad images that pass by so quickly.
    b. a viewer can install ad-blocking software on his or her computer.
    c. it lacks scale efficiencies, given that few companies are choosing to advertise on this medium.
    d. of legislation that is intended to restrict use of the Internet.

ANS: B REF: p. 362 OBJ: 16-4 TYPE: C

38. Which of the following is *not* one of the critical startup tasks involved in the preparation of the successful launch of a dot.com site?
    a. Creating and registering a site name
    b. Building a user-friendly site
    c. Promoting the firm's site
    d. Identifying a target market

ANS: D REF: p. 362 OBJ: 16-4 TYPE: C

39. The nonprofit corporation currently overseeing the global Internet is called the
    a. Global Internet Management Corporation.
    b. International Office for Internet Oversight.
    c. International Public Internet Corporation.
    d. Internet Corporation for Assigned Names and Numbers.

ANS: D REF: p. 363 OBJ: 16-4 TYPE: D

40. One of the biggest reasons Web sites fail to retain customers is
    a. privacy concerns.
    b. pure and simple boredom.
    c. slow downloading.
    d. the poor performance of Web-based businesses in order fulfillment.

ANS: C REF: p. 365 OBJ: 16-4 TYPE: C

41. One of the ways that a company can promote its online business is by
    a. placing banner ads on its site.
    b. offering rebates that can be applied toward future purchases on the site.
    c. making sure that the Web site is accessed by Internet search engines.
    d. germ marketing.

ANS: C REF: p. 365 OBJ: 16-4 TYPE: C

42. Which of the following is one of the ways an online business can submit a Web site to search engines?
    a. Employing search engine submission hardware
    b. By calling 1-800-ENGINES
    c. Using a paid submission service
    d. Requesting such services from the Small Business Administration

ANS: C REF: p. 366 OBJ: 16-4 TYPE: C

43. _____ serves as an inducement to buy a certain product while typically offering value to recipients.
    a. A sales promotion

b. A specialty trade show
c. Advertising
d. Specialty advertising

ANS: A REF: p. 366 OBJ: 16-5 TYPE: D

44. Which of the following is *not* considered a sales promotion tool?
a. Coupons
b. Newspaper ads
c. Premiums
d. Point-of-purchase displays

ANS: B REF: p. 367 OBJ: 16-5 TYPE: C

45. The most widely used specialty item is the
a. calendar.
b. pen.
c. lighter.
d. key chain.

ANS: A REF: p. 367 OBJ: 16-5 TYPE: C

46. John Frye, a small business manager, is interested in creating more company goodwill. Which of the following promotional tools should he use?
a. Publicity program
b. Trade show exhibit
c. Contest
d. Specialties

ANS: D REF: p. 367 OBJ: 16-5 TYPE: A

47. Specialties are promotional tools that can
a. create goodwill for the company.
b. prevent price competition.
c. allow customers to sample the product.
d. cast doubt on the products offered by competitors.

ANS: A REF: p. 367 OBJ: 16-5 TYPE: D

48. The "lasting medium" is a term that refers to which of the following?
a. Contests
b. Sampling
c. Specialties
d. Free merchandise

ANS: C REF: p. 367 OBJ: 16-5 TYPE: C

49. Hands-on experience with a product is possible with
a. coupons.
b. trade show exhibits.
c. specialty promotions.
d. personal selling.

ANS: B REF: p. 367 OBJ: 16-5 TYPE: C

50. Anne Dunne owns a small business dealing with industrial products. She currently uses personal selling extensively, but she wants to reduce her cost without losing exposure. Which promotional tool should she use?
    a. Specialties
    b. Coupons
    c. Contests
    d. Trade show exhibits

    ANS: D REF: p. 368 OBJ: 16-5 TYPE: A

ESSAY

1. List and briefly explain the four common methods of earmarking funds for promotion.

   ANS:

   - *Percentage of sales.* A company's own past sales experiences are evaluated to establish the firm's promotion/sales ratio.
   - *What can be spared.* Promotional budgeting is based on spending what is left over when all other activities have been funded.
   - *Spending as much as the competition.* This method studies competitors and allocates funds at a level close to theirs.
   - *What it will take to do the job.* This method analyzes the market and promotional alternatives to determine the amount of funds required to do the job.

   REF: p. 355 OBJ: 16-2 TYPE: C

2. List five techniques for responding to customers' objections.

   ANS:
   - *Direct denial*: Follow denial by giving facts to back up the denial.
   - *Boomerang technique*: Turn the valid objection into a valid reason to buy.
   - *Indirect denial*: Follow an expression of concern about the prospect's objection with a denial.
     Compensation method: Admit to agreeing with the objection and then proceed to show compensating advantages.
   - *Pass-up method*: Acknowledge the concern expressed by the prospect and then move on.

   REF: p. 357 OBJ: 16-3 TYPE: C

3. What are the advantages and disadvantages of using salary and commission as methods of compensating salespeople?

   ANS:
   Security for the salesperson is the greatest advantage of a salary plan. However, a straight salary tends to restrict the salesperson's earning ability and can even promote laziness. On the other hand, when a salesperson is compensated with salary, the firm can more easily require that person to perform nonselling activities.

A commission plan serves as a strong incentive to the sales force "no sale, no income." A commission plan also helps with a firm's cash flow problems because payment is not made until sales revenue begins to come in. A 100 percent commission plan may not help the salesperson's morale, however, if sales are slow.

REF: p. 358 OBJ: 16-3 TYPE: C

4. What are the specific services that an advertising agency can provide?

ANS:

- Furnishing design, artwork, and copy for specific advertisements and/or commercials
- Evaluating and recommending the advertising media with the greatest "pulling power"
- Evaluating the effectiveness of different advertising appeals
- Advising on sales promotions and merchandise displays
- Conducting market-sampling studies to evaluate product acceptance or determining the sales potential of a specific geographic region
- Furnishing mailing lists

REF: p. 360 OBJ: 16-4 TYPE: C

5. List three sales promotional tools discussed in the textbook and briefly explain the unique characteristics of each.

ANS:
These methods are as follows:
- *Specialties* are sales promotion items with enduring nature and tangible value.
- *Publicity* is a less costly form of sales promotion that is almost "free" but can be unfavorable.
- *Trade show exhibits* are product demonstrations that provide hands-on experience with a product.

REF: p. 367 OBJ: 16-5 TYPE: C

6. **You Make the Call—Situation 1**
The driving force behind Cannon Arp's new business was several bad experiences with his car—two speeding tickets and four minor fender-benders. Consequently, his insurance rates more than doubled, which resulted in Arp's idea to design and sell a bumper sticker that read "To Report Bad Driving, Call My Parents at . . . ." With a $200 investment, Arp printed 15,000 of the stickers, which contain space to write in the appropriate telephone number. He is now planning a promotion to support his strategy of distribution through auto parts stores.

Question 1 What role, if any, should personal selling have in Arp's total promotional plan?
Question 2 Arp is considering advertising in magazines. What do you think about this medium for promoting his product?
Question 3 Of what value might publicity be for selling Arp's stickers? Be specific.

ANS:
Situation 1

1. Arp could reap dividends from personal selling to certain institutional customers. Schools and certain civic groups that often promote safe driving could be profitable targets. On a broader scale, Arp might contact nationwide auto clubs that could be interested in his concept.
2. Arp actually advertised in magazines and concluded they were a waste of his money. Many magazines reach audiences with broad demographic profiles. If Arp were to use a magazine, it would have to be selected carefully to provide exposure to the appropriate target market.
3. Publicity actually proved to be beneficial to Arp's selling. After several radio stations interviewed him, there was heavy demand from parents who heard the programs. In one single two-month period following this exposure, he filled 5,000 orders!

REF: p. 355, 359 OBJ: YMTC TYPE: C

7. **You Make the Call—Situation 2**
Cheree Moore owns and operates a small business that supplies delicatessens with bulk containers of ready-made salads. When served in salad bars, the salads appear to have been freshly prepared from scratch at the delicatessen. Moore wants additional promotional exposure for her products and is considering using her fleet of trucks as rolling billboards. If the strategy is successful, she may even attempt to lease space on other trucks. Moore is concerned about the cost-effectiveness of the idea and whether the public will even notice the advertisements. She also wonders whether the image of her salad products might be hurt by this advertising medium.

Question 1 What suggestions can you offer that would help Moore make this decision?
Question 2 How could Moore go about determining the cost-effectiveness of this strategy?
Question 3 What additional factors should Moore evaluate before advertising on trucks?

ANS:
1. If the advertisements are of high quality and colorful, they should be attention-getting. The firm actually used full-scale ads covering the entire side of the trucks (9 ft. by 48 ft.). The image concern is an important consideration but should not be a problem for this product. It is likely that Moore will want to avoid some trucking companies—those from insecticides or animal product companies, for example.
2. Moore offered a trucking firm approximately $1,500 for the privilege to advertise on 25 of its trucks for three years. Using these cost figures, some exposure data provided by the American Trucking Association, and a reference showing that 90 percent of survey respondents notice truck advertising, Moore estimated that she is paying only 21 cents per thousand exposures.
3. One concern is a legal one. Does the Department of Transportation allow this type of advertising on the trucks it regulates? With certain restrictions, Moore's ads were acceptable to the department's Bureau of Motor Carrier Safety.

   Moore also had to evaluate whether the trucks would be traveling into markets where the salad products were not distributed. In fact, Moore received calls from people who had seen the truck advertising but could not find the product.

REF: p. 359 OBJ: YMTC TYPE: C

8. **You Make the Call—Situation 3**
Corinna Lathan is co-founder and CEO of AnthroTronix, which is currently located in the business incubator at the University of Maryland. Founded in July 1999, the company is a human factors engineering firm committed to optimizing interactions between people and technology.

With co-founder Jack M. Vice, Lathan is developing a Muppet-like robot for use as a therapeutic tool with children with speech, learning, and physical disabilities. The robot has been tested at a Maryland hospital, where the medical director says the kids using the device have shown measurable improvement. Here's how the robot, named JesterBot, works:

A child puts on leg- or armbands and a hat embedded with radio transceivers and sensors. By waving a hand, say, or nodding her head, she sends out radio signals that are interpreted by a central processing unit in the JesterBot. During exercises, the JesterBot can gauge a child's range of motion, while electronically reporting the results of the session to a therapist via a data port hooked up to a PC.

To launch the product, the company needs additional funding, which it hopes to get soon.

Source: Nicole Ridgway, "Robo-Therapy," *Forbes*, Vol. 167, No. 11 (March 14, 2001), p. 216.

Question 1 When the product is ready to launch, what kinds of promotion should the company use? Why?
Question 2 What techniques might this firm use to set the promotional budget?
Question 3 In what way, if any, could Internet promotion help this business?

ANS:

1. Lathan and her company will need to consider very specialized forms of promotion, since the audience is very concentrated. For example, a direct marketing campaign focusing on private and public educational facilities that work with disabled children would be an option. To reach this market, however, she will need to exhibit at the appropriate trade shows.
2. Each of the techniques discussed in the chapter would apply in this situation.
3. The Internet will likely be the best place for Lathan to promote her product. Do a word search using *JesterBot* and you will see a number of articles and entries related to her product. She may also link up with educational organizations already on the Web and gain hits to her site from visitors to their sites.

REF: p. 360 OBJ: YMTC TYPE: C

9. **You Make the Call—Situation 4**

Phil Damiani and Kenny Lee own and operate the Ooof Ball Company in Media, Pennsylvania. For four years, they have been establishing a market for their bouncy medicine ball, which is promoted as "building muscle while improving coordination." Their promotional task is continually handicapped by a minimal ad budget and an unproven product. Both Dimiani and Lee believe that their major challenge is to bring the product into the public eye and get people talking about it.

Question 1 What promotional techniques might be appropriate for this situation? Why?
Question 2 How important would a trade show exhibit be to this promotional effort?
Question 3 Do you believe word-of-mouth advertising would be important to this product? Why or why not?

ANS:

1. Each of the following promotional methods is a possibility for this venture at this stage: personal selling, publicity, trade show exhibits, specialties, direct mail (to distributors), magazines, and word of mouth.
2. A trade show exhibit aimed at distributors would be an excellent method of promoting this product. This approach would allow potential distributors to try the product, and it would also allow the entrepreneurs to personally answer questions.

3. Word-of-mouth advertising is always important, but in this circumstance it is especially needed, since the limited promotional budget precludes other mass communication techniques. It would be critical to identify distributors who are likely opinion leaders for their peers.

REF: p. 366 OBJ: YMTC TYPE: C

Correlation Table for Chapter 17—Global Marketing

	Learning Objectives	Question Type	Definition Define new term, recall facts	Concept Understand or relate concepts	Application Apply knowledge, analyze data
1	Describe the potential of small firms as global enterprises.	T/F		1,2,3,4	
		MC	2,3	1,4,5,6	7
		ES			
2	Identify the basic forces prompting small firms to engage in global expansion.	T/F	14,15	5,6,8,9,10,11,12, 13,16,17,18,19	7
		MC	16	8,9,10,11,12,13, 14,15,17,18,19, 20,21,23,25,26, 28,29,30,31	22,24,27
		ES		1	
3	Identify and compare strategy options for global businesses.	T/F	21,23,25,28,29	20,22,24,26,27, 30,31	
		MC	33,34,35,36,37, 39,40	32	38
		ES		2	
4	Explain the challenges that global enterprises face.	T/F	33	32,34	
		MC	42	43,44	41
		ES	3		
5	Recognize the sources of assistance available to support international business efforts.	T/F		35	
		MC	46,48,49	45,47	50
		ES	5	4	
	You Make the Call	ES		6,7,8	9

Total Number of Test Questions: 94 (35 True/False; 50 Multiple-Choice; 9 Essay)

Chapter 17—Global Marketing

TRUE/FALSE

1. International dissimilarities in language and culture, business practices, and government regulations are fading over time.

   ANS: T REF: p. 373 OBJ: TYPE: C

2. The *2004 Index of Economic Freedom* has reported that per capita income around the world is rising, but there is no discernable change in levels of economic freedom.

   ANS: F
   The *2004 Index of Economic Freedom* has reported that economic freedom continues to grow worldwide, which has had a positive impact on per capita income around the globe.

   REF: p. 373 OBJ: TYPE: C

3. Internationalization is increasing among large firms, but this has not been the trend with small businesses in recent years.

   ANS: F
   Recent startups and even the small of businesses are internationalizing at an increasing rate.

   REF: p. 373 OBJ: 17-1 TYPE: C

4. The U.S. Department of Commerce publishes *A Guide to Exporting*, which outlines some of the important questions entrepreneurs should consider when deciding whether a firm is ready for the challenges of global business.

   ANS: T REF: p. 374 OBJ: 17-1 TYPE: C

5. In the past, most American entrepreneurs started their businesses with the home market in mind and with no interest in ever penetrating international markets.

   ANS: F
   At one time, entrepreneurs in the U.S. were content to position their startups for the home market, but they also looked forward to the day when international sales might materialize.

   REF: p. 375 OBJ: 17-2 TYPE: C

6. The interest in international markets dates back at least as far as the 1200s when Marco Polo traveled to China to trade western goods for Oriental silk and spices.

   ANS: T REF: p. 375 OBJ: 17-2 TYPE: C

7. These days, the rival on the other side of the street from a firm may be a minor threat compared to an online competitor on the other side of the globe.

   ANS: T REF: p. 375 OBJ: 17-2 TYPE: A

8. Some of the motivations fostering international expansion by small businesses are tried and true, but new motivations are also emerging as the global economy takes form.

   ANS: T REF: p. 376 OBJ: 17-2 TYPE: C

9. More than 75 percent of the world's population lives outside of the United States.

   ANS: F
   Actually, more than 95 percent of the world's population lives outside of the U.S.

   REF: p. 376 OBJ: 17-2 TYPE: C

10. Today, companies tend to focus on developed countries as they search out international markets.

    ANS: F
    This was true in the past, but today companies are paying greater attention to emerging markets, where income and buying power are growing rapidly.

    REF: p. 376 OBJ: 17-2 TYPE: C

11. Taken together, China and India account for nearly 30 percent of the world's 4 billion inhabitants.

    ANS: F
    These two countries account for nearly *40* percent of the world's *6* billion inhabitants.

    REF: p. 376 OBJ: 17-2 TYPE: C

12. In the past, firms tended to introduce new products in the United States first and then sell them in other developed nations, giving no attention to less-advanced countries because of their weak consumer purchasing power.

    ANS: F
    While new products were usually introduced in the United States first, firms would later sell these goods in less-advanced country markets as the home market declined.

    REF: p. 377 OBJ: 17-2 TYPE: C

13. Efforts to exploit the competitive advantage of specialized products across international markets may be more important to small businesses than to their large competitors.

    ANS: T REF: p. 378 OBJ: 17-2 TYPE: C

14. Experience curve efficiencies refers to the savings that arise from spreading activity across more units of output and from acquiring more specialize plants, equipment, and employees.

    ANS: F

These gains are the result of *economies of scale*, not experience curve efficiencies.

REF: p. 379 OBJ: 17-2 TYPE: D

15. Learning effects are the direct result of economies of scale in operations.

ANS: F
Learning effects occur when an employee gains insight from experience, which leads to improved work performance.

REF: p. 379 OBJ: 17-2 TYPE: D

16. Startups that are based on complex technologies are more likely to gain benefits from learning effects and economies of scale.

ANS: T REF: p. 379 OBJ: 17-2 TYPE: C

17. Increasingly, small firms are going global in search of skilled labor.

ANS: T REF: p. 379 OBJ: 17-2 TYPE: C

18. The unique features of a local environment can yield benefits to small firms locating there.

ANS: T REF: p. 381 OBJ: 17-2 TYPE: C

19. Increasingly, small firms find that they must locate their operations abroad if they are to keep their contracts as suppliers to large companies.

ANS: T REF: p. 381 OBJ: 17-2 TYPE: C

20. Most small firms choose to go global first by exporting.

ANS: T REF: p. 382 OBJ: 17-3 TYPE: C

21. Trade missions can provide a useful means for a firm to explore the potential for international business.

ANS: T REF: p. 383 OBJ: 17-3 TYPE: D

22. In some cases, selling in international markets can actually be helpful to domestic operations.

ANS: T REF: p. 383 OBJ: 17-3 TYPE: C

23. Exporting involves the purchase of goods in the home country made by manufacturers in other countries.

ANS: F
This is actually *importing*, since exporting involves the sale of products produced at home to customers in another country.

REF: p. 383 OBJ: 17-3 TYPE: D

24. The Internet has been helpful to small firm operations in the United States, but there are too few customers with Internet access in foreign markets to make this a powerful tool for going global.

ANS: F
The Internet has fueled vigorous growth in export activity, and small firms see this medium as a powerful tool for increasing their international visibility and for connecting with customers that were previously beyond their reach.

REF: p. 383 OBJ: 17-3 TYPE: C

25. Importing is the "flip side" of exporting.

ANS: T REF: p. 383 OBJ: 17-3 TYPE: D

26. It is clear that a small firm can generate the greatest financial returns using international licensing strategies when these efforts involve the company's products.

ANS: F
Small businesses tend to think of *products* when they explore international licensing options, but licensing *intangible assets* (e.g., proprietary technologies, copyrights, and trademarks) may offer even greater potential returns.

REF: p. 385 OBJ: 17-3 TYPE: C

27. International firms often have to deal with the problem of counterfeit goods, but foreign licensing can help to shield the small business from this threat.

ANS: T REF: p. 385 OBJ: 17-3 TYPE: C

28. International franchising is essentially an alternative form of exporting.

ANS: F
International franchising is actually a variation on the *licensing* theme.

REF: p. 385 OBJ: 17-3 TYPE: D

29. Small firms are able to share risks and pool resources by using international strategic alliances.

ANS: T REF: p. 385 OBJ: 17-3 TYPE: D

30. Small businesses have many options when they choose to go global, but it is not a good idea for such firms to establish a sales or production facility abroad because of the resources this requires.

ANS: F
A small business with advanced global aspirations may choose to establish a foreign presence in its own strategic markets, especially if it has a developed international customer base.

REF: p. 386 OBJ: 17-3 TYPE: C

31. Small firms can successfully open an overseas sales office, but this should only be done when sales in the local market are great enough to justify this expensive move.

ANS: T REF: p. 386 OBJ: 17-3 TYPE: C

32. Fortunately, small international businesses do not face trivial problems, such as content restrictions in television advertising, which allows these firms to focus their resources on greater risks, such as the government takeover of the firm's private assets.

ANS: F
These are trivial and very serious political risks, respectively, but they both are risks that small firms face nonetheless.

REF: p. 386 OBJ: 17-4 TYPE: C

33. Economic risk is very different from political risk; indeed, these forms of risk are unrelated to one another.

ANS: F
Economic risk and political risk are related. For example, political moves that impact the exchange rates of a country's currency create economic risk for firms operating there.

REF: p. 387 OBJ: 17-4 TYPE: D

34. International business will never be as easy as doing business at home.

ANS: T REF: p. 388 OBJ: 17-4 TYPE: C

35. Perhaps the easiest way to break into international markets is to use a trade intermediary.

ANS: T REF: p. 391 OBJ: 17-5 TYPE: C

MULTIPLE CHOICE

1. One of the documented effects of increased economic freedom is
   a. stable demand for goods and services.
   b. greater acceptance from other economically-free nations.
   c. increased prosperity.
   d. rising government approval ratings.

ANS: C REF: p. 373 OBJ: TYPE: C

2. When a small firm is launched with cross-border activities in mind, some would say the business
   a. is internationally diverse.
   b. has been "born global."
   c. is sure to succeed.
   d. has no choice but to move forward with plans for internationalization.

ANS: B REF: p. 373 OBJ: 17-1 TYPE: D

3. Salvatore intended from the start that his small pasta firm would sell its products in overseas market, some would say the business
   a. was intentionally internationally diverse.

b. was sure to succeed.
c. was "born global."
d. had no choice but to move forward with plans for internationalization.

ANS: C REF: p. 373 OBJ: 17-1 TYPE: D

4. One of the reasons that entrepreneurs today are focusing more on international business is that
   a. global communications are now possible.
   b. they are likely to have experience with operations in foreign nations.
   c. technologies today are sophisticated, expensive to develop, and quickly replaced.
   d. global involvement brings a dimension of prestige to the firm's reputation.

ANS: C REF: p. 373 OBJ: 17-1 TYPE: C

5. Because technologies are becoming increasingly sophisticated, expensive, and short-lived,
   a. it is more important than ever to recover R&D costs quickly by expanding the market globally.
   b. entrepreneurs struggle to compete in high-end technologies used in fast-paced markets.
   c. only large corporations should attempt to compete in cutting-edge, high-tech industries.
   d. the pace of innovation has started to show signs of deceleration.

ANS: A REF: p. 373 OBJ: 17-1 TYPE: C

6. When a small business owner is thinking of going global, he or she should first decide whether
   a. the firm has the necessary "deep pockets" to follow through.
   b. domestic operations are capable of subsidizing overseas operations.
   c. the firm has the technology necessary to get into the international game.
   d. the company is up to the task.

ANS: D REF: p. 374 OBJ: 17-1 TYPE: C

7. Tariffs are
   a. taxes charged on exported goods.
   b. taxes charged on imported goods.
   c. duties charged on exported goods.
   d. duties charged on imported.

ANS: B REF: p. 375 OBJ: 17-1 TYPE: D

8. Trade integrations such as the North American Free Trade Agreement and the European Union are established to
   a. facilitate social integration of disparate countries.
   b. reduce or eliminate tariffs and trade restrictions.
   c. protect trade relationships with non-member nations.
   d. satisfy the demands of organized labor.

ANS: B REF: p. 375 OBJ: 17-2 TYPE: C

9. The established motivations behind global expansion include all of the following, *except*
   a. promoting the independence of the enterprise.
   b. gaining access to resources.
   c. expanding markets.
   d. cutting costs.

ANS: A REF: p. 376 OBJ: 17-2 TYPE: C

10. Which of the following is one of the emerging motivations driving global expansion?
    a. Expanding the market
    b. Creating a satisfying way of life
    c. Making the most of experience
    d. Reducing costs

ANS: C REF: p. 379 OBJ: 17-2 TYPE: C

11. Seeking to extend the product life cycle by expanding into international markets has become a less effective strategy, in part, because
    a. customer preferences have become more similar around the world.
    b. international delivery systems cannot handle the variety of company distribution systems.
    c. income levels in many countries are insufficient to support this strategy.
    d. product life cycles have already been growing over the years.

ANS: A REF: p. 387 OBJ: 17-2 TYPE: C

12. Lee Marine's attempt to extend the product life cycle of older models of its boats by selling them in international markets has not been effective strategy, in part, because
    a. international delivery systems cannot handle the variety of company distribution systems.
    b. of the increasing similarity of customer preferences around the world.
    c. income levels in many countries are insufficient to support this strategy.
    d. product life cycles have already been growing over the years.

ANS: B REF: p. 387 OBJ: 17-2 TYPE: C

13. When it comes to expanding the market, an emerging motivation for going global is to
    a. take advantage of unique features of the local market.
    b. find buyers for highly specialized products.
    c. obtain tariff reductions.
    d. extend the product life cycle.

ANS: B REF: p. 378 OBJ: 17-2 TYPE: C

14. It is becoming clear that international markets are demanding
    a. the same products that are distributed to other national markets.
    b. differentiated products that satisfy their unique needs and interests.
    c. direct access to products sold elsewhere in the world.
    d. more expensive products and fewer inexpensive products.

ANS: B REF: p. 378 OBJ: 17-2 TYPE: C

15. When it comes to gaining access to resources, a traditional motivation for going global has been to
    a. take advantage of unique features of the local market.
    b. find raw materials.
    c. change the shape of the product life cycle.
    d. serve the local community through the business.

ANS: B REF: p. 379 OBJ: 17-2 TYPE: C

16. Economies of scale refers to

a. learning effects from manufacturing experience.
b. the incremental drop in costs that results from the doubling of output.
c. efficiencies that are most common in low-tech operations.
d. gains from the spreading of investment across more units of production.

ANS: D REF: p. 379 OBJ: 17-2 TYPE: D

17. Crumpton Industries reduced its unit costs when it expanded its productive capacity, indicating that it has benefited from
a. experience curve efficiencies.
b. learning effects.
c. economies of scale
d. economies of scope

ANS: C REF: p. 379 OBJ: 17-2 TYPE: C

18. Long production runs at Bayshore Industries have steadily reduced its unit costs, indicating that it has benefited from
a. experience curve efficiencies.
b. learning effects.
c. economies of scale.
d. economies of scope.

ANS: A REF: p. 379 OBJ: 17-2 TYPE: C

19. Newplant has the most experienced production employees and the lowest unit costs in its industry, indicating that it had benefited from
a. experience curve efficiencies.
b. learning effects.
c. economies of scale.
d. economies of scope.

ANS: B REF: p. 379 OBJ: 17-2 TYPE: C

20. Prior to the 1990s, startups considered going global
a. only after they had established a solid position in the domestic market.
b. early in the firm life cycle.
c. from the beginning because market growth in the United States had stagnated.
d. when they recognized the wealth of support the government provided to expand abroad.

ANS: A REF: p. 379 OBJ: 17-2 TYPE: C

21. Recent research has shown that globalizing early in a company's life tends to lead to
a. lower levels of firm risk.
b. a boost to the firm's reputation.
c. increased sales growth.
d. financial disaster.

ANS: C REF: p. 379 OBJ: 17-2 TYPE: C

22. When an American biotechnology startup establishes an office in Brazil to manage teams of biologists that search the rain forest to find new plants that may have undiscovered medicinal properties, the firm has globalized to

a. gain access to essential raw materials.
b. capitalize on special features of location.
c. expand its supply chain.
d. extend the life cycle of its products.

ANS: A REF: p. 379 OBJ: 17-2 TYPE: A

23. Increasingly, small businesses are expanding internationally to
a. obtain raw materials.
b. gain access to skilled labor.
c. create job opportunities for domestic employees.
d. take advantage of government incentives.

ANS: B REF: p. 379 OBJ: 17-2 TYPE: C

24. Considering the nature of its products, a cement fabricator that specializes in the manufacture of bird baths is likely to go global to
a. gain access to critical raw materials.
b. capitalize on special features of location.
c. obtain specialized human resources.
d. cut costs.

ANS: D REF: p. 381 OBJ: 17-2 TYPE: A

25. Regional free trade areas have been formed in order to
a. duplicate government regulatory systems.
b. reduce tariffs to increase trade.
c. coordinate the currencies of included countries.
d. accommodate the demands of organized labor.

ANS: B REF: p. 381 OBJ: 17-2 TYPE: C

26. The intent of the North American Free Trade Agreement (NAFTA) was to
a. duplicate government regulatory systems.
b. reduce tariffs to increase trade.
c. coordinate the currencies of included countries.
d. accommodate the demands of organized labor.

ANS: B REF: p. 381 OBJ: 17-2 TYPE: C

27. If a small business sets up a design studio in Milan, Italy to create its line of specialty apparel, it is going global to
a. expand its market.
b. take advantage of special features of location.
c. seek protection for its design patents.
d. obtain critical raw materials.

ANS: B REF: p. 381 OBJ: 17-2 TYPE: A

28. When it comes to cutting costs, an emerging motivation for going global is to
a. obtain tariff reductions.
b. find raw materials.
c. follow large client firms that locate abroad.

d. find suppliers offering highly specialized products.

ANS: A REF: p. 381 OBJ: 17-2 TYPE: C

29. For most small businesses, the primary motivation for going global is to
    a. develop new market opportunities.
    b. reduce the costs of doing business.
    c. gain access to resources that are important to the firm's operations.
    d. capitalize on special features of location.

ANS: A REF: p. 376 OBJ: 17-2 TYPE: C

30. Part of the appeal of forming a regional trade area is that companies can then
    a. gain access to more employees.
    b. benefit from locational features unrelated to costs.
    c. draw upon the advantages of a "fortress mentality."
    d. acquire the potential to expand into international markets.

ANS: B REF: p. 381 OBJ: 17-2 TYPE: C

31. For small businesses, the ultimate incentive to go global is the following:
    a. Purely domestic firms are less likely to stay in business over the long run.
    b. Government programs are available to ensure success of global firms, but not domestic ones.
    c. If you fail to seize an international market opportunity, someone else will.
    d. Research shows that global firms experience more consistent gains in profitability.

ANS: C REF: p. 382 OBJ: 17-2 TYPE: C

32. If an entrepreneur has decided to go global, the next step is to
    a. begin to hire employees with international experience.
    b. spend some time estimating the market potential of various countries.
    c. join a trade mission.
    d. plan a strategy that takes into account the potential of the firm.

ANS: D REF: p. 382 OBJ: 17-3 TYPE: C

33. The export strategy option involves
    a. the sale of goods from abroad in the home country.
    b. the sale of products produced in the home country to customers in another country.
    c. the purchase of the right to manufacture and sell a firm's product in overseas markets.
    d. the authorized use of intellectual property.

ANS: B REF: p. 382 OBJ: 17-3 TYPE: D

34. Importing can be described as the
    a. "flip side" of exporting.
    b. sale of products produced in the home country to customers in another country.
    c. purchase of the right to manufacture and sell a firm's product in overseas markets.
    d. authorized use of intellectual property.

ANS: A REF: p. 383 OBJ: 17-3 TYPE: D

35. With a foreign licensing strategy, the company purchasing the right to manufacture and sell a product in overseas markets is called the
    a. royalty receiver.
    b. licensor.
    c. licensee.
    d. license initiator.

ANS: C REF: p. 384 OBJ: 17-3 TYPE: D

36. With a foreign licensing strategy, the company granting the right to manufacture and sell a product in overseas markets is called the
    a. royalty receiver.
    b. licensor.
    c. licensee.
    d. license initiator.

ANS: B REF: p. 384 OBJ: 17-3 TYPE: D

37. International franchising is a variation on the theme of
    a. exporting.
    b. importing.
    c. foreign licensing.
    d. international strategic alliances.

ANS: C REF: p. 384 OBJ: 17-3 TYPE: D

38. John Berryhill is interested in joining with a large corporation in a cooperative venture to share risks and pool resources for his small auto parts manufacturing business, so the strategy option he is exploring could best be described as
    a. an international strategic alliance.
    b. exporting.
    c. importing.
    d. international cost shifting.

ANS: A REF: p. 385 OBJ: 17-3 TYPE: A

39. Forming from scratch a wholly owned subsidiary in another country is what can be most accurately described as
    a. a greenfield venture.
    b. a cross-border acquisition.
    c. an international transplant.
    d. a duplication strategy.

ANS: A REF: p. 386 OBJ: 17-3 TYPE: D

40. Crossborder Manufacturing USA has developed a new and wholly-owned subsidiary in another country that is most accurately described as
    a. a greenfield venture.
    b. a cross-border acquisition.
    c. an international transplant.
    d. a duplication strategy.

ANS: A REF: p. 386 OBJ: 17-3 TYPE: D

41. From a company-owned plant in Pakistan, Howard Eden manufactures specialty apparel items for his small business, Garments of Eden. Because of overseas operations of the U.S. military in the region, Eden fears that his plant may be sabotaged or that the local government may attempt to take over the facility. Specifically, his fears are about
    a. exchange rate risk.
    b. economic risk.
    c. societal risk.
    d. political risk.

    ANS: D REF: p. 386 OBJ: 17-4 TYPE: A

42. Economic risk refers to the
    a. risk that a startup will not generate the performance necessary to stay in business long term.
    b. potential for loss of capital in a business deal.
    c. probability that a government will change business conditions and hinder firm performance.
    d. chance that an entrepreneur will not be financially successful.

    ANS: C REF: p. 387 OBJ: 17-4 TYPE: D

43. When the exchange rate for a currency rises relative to that of another country, the rising currency
    a. has decreased in value relative to the other currency.
    b. has increased in value relative to the other currency.
    c. has been devalued by its government.
    d. reflects increased political risk in its home country.

    ANS: B REF: p. 387 OBJ: 17-4 TYPE: C

44. While not always true for small firms, large multinationals can deal with currency fluctuations by
    a. using forward contracts and foreign-currency options.
    b. locating all their plants in the country that offers the most advantageous exchange position.
    c. limiting sales in each country market to reduce exposure to any one currency.
    d. following the advice of the international sales manager.

    ANS: A REF: p. 388 OBJ: 17-4 TYPE: C

45. For the small business that wants to go global, one of the activities that is most fundamental to success abroad is
    a. avoiding rigid planning that will commit the firm's resources to a single plan of action.
    b. being sure to tap government programs that provide an incentive for international expansion.
    c. finding international markets that fit the company's unique potentials.
    d. figuring out which of the firm's competitors is capable of copying its strategy.

    ANS: C REF: p. 389 OBJ: 17-5 TYPE: C

46. When an entrepreneur joins an organized trip designed to introduce the company to interested international customers or potential strategic alliance partners, he/she has participated in a
    a. State Department initiative.
    b. trade mission.

c. economic freedom venture.
d. "go global" program.

ANS: B REF: p. 390 OBJ: 17-5 TYPE: D

47. Perhaps the greatest barrier to international expansion is
a. labor limitations.
b. financing.
c. trade restrictions.
d. a shortage of qualified trade intermediaries.

ANS: B REF: p. 392 OBJ: 17-5 TYPE: C

48. When a small business forges an agreement with a bank that consents to honor a draft or other demand for payment after goods are delivered internationally, the firm receives a
a. international invoice.
b. bill of lading.
c. letter of confirmation.
d. letter of credit.

ANS: D REF: p. 392 OBJ: 17-5 TYPE: D

49. Once a product has been shipped internationally and the title has been transferred, the exporter receives what is called a
a. international invoice.
b. bill of lading.
c. letter of confirmation.
d. letter of credit.

ANS: B REF: p. 392 OBJ: 17-5 TYPE: D

50. Peter Herring, a 32-year-old American, has decided to use set up an import/export business with friends in Thailand that he met in his MBA program. One good source of valuable information and advice about starting and maintaining the business would be the
a. Small Business Administration.
b. Office of Export Trade.
c. International Export Board.
d. Foreign Service Office.

ANS: A REF: p. 392 OBJ: 17-5 TYPE: A

ESSAY

1. Identify the four primary motivations that encourage entrepreneurs to go global and provide an example of a traditional motivation and an emerging motivation for each.

ANS:
- *Expanding markets.* A traditional motivation would be to expand the product life cycle of the firm's goods, but an emerging motivation is to find buyers for specialized products.
- *Cutting costs.* A traditional motivation would be to reduce labor and transportation costs, but an emerging motivation is to obtain tariff reductions.

- *Gaining access to resources.* A traditional motivation would be to find raw materials, but an emerging motivation is to obtain human resources.
- *Capitalizing on special features of location.* A traditional motivation would be to profit from unique locations (e.g., the flair for design of Italian artisans), but an emerging motivation is to follow large client firms that locate abroad.

REF: p. 375 OBJ: 17-2 TYPE: C

2. List and briefly describe the main strategy options for small firms that decide to go global.

ANS:
- *Exporting* involves the sale of products made in the home country to customers in another country.
- *Importing* involves selling goods from abroad in the firm's home market.
- *Foreign licensing* allows a company in another country to purchase the right to manufacture and sell a firm's products in overseas markets.
- *International franchising* is a variation of the foreign licensing strategy where the franchisor offers a standard package of products, systems, and management services to the franchisee, which provides capital, market insight, and hands-on management.
- *International strategic alliances* allows firms to share risks and pool resources as they enter a new market, matching the local partner's understanding of the target market (its culture, legal system, competitive conditions, etc.) with the technology or product knowledge of its alliance counterpart.
- *Establishing an international presence* involves a small business with advanced global aspirations that may choose to establish a foreign presence of its own in strategic markets, especially if that firm has already developed an international customer base using the strategies mentioned above. Most small companies start by locating a facility or sales office overseas. Two options include a cross-border acquisition and a greenfield startup.

REF: p. 382 OBJ: 17-3 TYPE: C

3. What is political risk?

ANS:
The political risk of a country refers to the potential for political forces there to negatively affect the performance of business enterprises operating within its borders. Often this is determined by the instability of a nation's government, which can create difficulties for companies operating within its borders. These problems can range from threats as trivial as new regulations restricting the content of television advertising to challenges with catastrophic consequences, such as a government takeover of private assets. Political risk can threaten access to an export market, require transfer of closely-held technologies, or determine the local content of manufactured goods.

REF: p. 386 OBJ: 17-4 TYPE: D

4. How should a small business go about analyzing international markets and planning a strategy to enter targeted markets? Identify specific sources of information in your answer.

ANS:

First, a small business should begin its research of foreign markets and entry strategy options by exhausting secondary sources of information, including government publications on how to locate and exploit global market opportunities. The Small Business Administration's Office of International Trade is a U.S. government agency responsible for helping small companies expand abroad. The international programs and services of the SBA are delivered through the U.S. Export Assistance Centers (USEACs.)

One excellent source of information about global marketing is *Opportunities in Exporting*, which is available on the Web site of the SBA Office of International Trade. Also available from the same source is the *SBA Guide to Exporting*, which provides an overview of export strategy that is useful for new and experienced exporters. This publication provides a nuts-and-bolts handbook to guide small firms through the complexities of going global, with chapters focused specifically on identifying markets, choosing an entry strategy, managing transactions, financing trade, arranging transportation, forming strategic alliances, and other important topics. This is essential reading for any small business owner with international ambitions.

Though not focused on small businesses alone, the International Trade Administration of the U.S. Department of Commerce maintains a Web site that supplies helpful insights about international expansion. Publications such as *World Trade Magazine* can also be helpful, providing timely, in-depth analyses of world trade markets and business issues. Beyond these resources, state and private organizations offer excellent sources of trade information, trade leads, and company databases. TradePort is one such source, offering information online to promote international trade with California-based companies.

Talking with someone who has lived or even just visited a potential foreign market can be a valuable way to learn about it. For example, conversations with international students at a local university can be very helpful. However, the best way to study a foreign market is to visit the country personally. A representative of a small firm can do this either as an individual or as a member of an organized group.

REF: p. 389 OBJ: 17-5 TYPE: C

5. Describe the role trade intermediaries play in assisting small businesses that choose to go global. Identify the types of trade intermediaries that are most useful to small businesses.

   ANS:
   Perhaps the easiest way to break into international markets is to use a trade intermediary, which is an agency that can distribute your product to international customers on a contract basis. These agencies can tap their established web of contacts as well as their local cultural and market expertise to distribute your product to local buyers. The intermediary can manage the entire export end of the business, taking care of everything except filling the orders.

   The following types of trade intermediaries are most likely to provide the services small businesses will require when they go global:

   - Export management companies
   - Export trading companies
   - Export agents, merchants, or remarketers
   - Piggyback marketers

   REF: p. 391 OBJ: 17-5 TYPE: D

6. **You Make the Call—Situation 1**

Bill Moss and several other small business owners joined a trade mission to China to explore market opportunities there. The group learned that China has a population of 1.3 billion and is the third-fastest-growing export market for small- and medium-sized U.S. firms. Average annual income for farmers in China is approximately $285 per person; typical urban income is about $827, with an average of $1,557 a year in more prosperous cities like Shanghai. In any given year, the Chinese software market grows by 30 percent and the number of Internet users quadruples. Furthermore, the demand for management consulting services is increasing, especially information technology consulting. Members of the group were surprised by the number of people who had cell phones and regularly surfed the Internet, especially in large urban centers such as Beijing, Shanghai, and Guangzhou. On the downside, they found that counterfeit goods (from clothing and leather goods to software and CDs) were readily available at a fraction of the cost of legitimate merchandise and that local merchants expressed an interest in doing business only with vendors with whom they had established relationships.

Sources: Data from http://www.china.org.cn/english/2002/Feb/26975.htm and http://www.china.org.cn/BAT/28231.htm.

Question 1 What types of businesses would prosper in China? Why?
Question 2 What are the challenges and risks associated with doing business in China?
Question 3 What steps should Moss take to address these challenges and risks in order to increase his chance of success in the market?

ANS:

1. China offers opportunities for small businesses that produce goods as well as those that provide services. Small manufacturers in certain high technology industries, including wireless telecommunications and computers, may find success in China. Large businesses tend to dominate the hardware side of telecommunications and computers, though, so small businesses may be successful by providing components, peripherals, or supporting equipment. This may be done by partnering with large firms with established brands or by selling these items directly to consumers. The demand for consulting services in China is high. Small businesses with knowledgeable employees who can provide consulting, training, or information technology services have numerous opportunities in the market. Since China is shifting further toward a free market economy and has even joined the World Trade Organization, Chinese firms (privately-owned and state-owned) are seeking greater understanding of Western business practices. Chinese firms are hiring Western firms for training and consultation.

2. Small companies doing business in China face a number of challenges and risks. While the potential upside of the Chinese market is its large size, the income levels in China are lower. Businesses must therefore consider the actual size of the potential market rather than the size of China's population. If producing or selling goods, particularly ones that are tied to brand image or brand names, the potential for counterfeiting must be recognized. Language and cultural differences pose additional problems. Business practices differ significantly in China, compared to the U.S. Another challenge, which is related to and complicated by language and cultural differences, is building relationships with key constituents (e.g., customers, government agencies, distributors, suppliers.) Guanxi (or connections) are close links between friends and relatives that have developed over many years. In many cases, these connections are critical to success when conducting business in China.

3. There are a number of approaches to addressing the language and cultural differences. The ideal way to bridge the language gap is to speak the language. Unless a company has employees who already speak Chinese, however, there may not be sufficient time to learn a new language before entering the market. Small businesses can hire translators or may hire new employees who speak Chinese. Education and training can help businesses and employees to understand cultural issues and differences. This is likely to make the employees more aware of such differences, but they may not be fully equipped to address these differences. Forming a strategic partnership with a Chinese firm may help overcome language and cultural barriers. In addition, partnerships can facilitate market entry if the chosen partner has already established relationships with distributors, target customers, and others needed to conduct business in China. Finding a partner and negotiating a partnership agreement, in itself, may prove a challenge for small businesses. However, small businesses can draw on their existing relationships with other businesses and governmental agencies that have already developed ties in China. One goal for Moss in forming such a partnership should be to begin to develop his own relationships with Chinese customers, suppliers, and distributors. He must also remember that patience is required for doing business in China. Results may not come immediately.

REF: p. 386 OBJ: YMTC TYPE: C

7. **You Make the Call—Situation 2**
Lynn Cooper owns and operates BFW, Inc., in Lexington, Kentucky, where she produces fiber-optic lights and headgear-mounted video cameras used for medical exams and surgery. She sees exporting as a means of increasing sales, but with just one employee, she wonders how best to handle the additional marketing and distribution exporting would require.

Question 1 What sources of information would be helpful to Cooper?
Question 2 Would you recommend that she consider using an international distributor? If so, what characteristics should she look for in a distributor?
Question 3 Do you think exporting is a feasible alternative for Cooper at this time? Why or why not?

ANS:
1. Cooper should consult three general sources of information. First, she should do some background research (consulting books and Internet resources) to learn the ins-and-outs of exporting. Taking this step will give her a rough idea of what is involved in distributing goods in foreign countries, what options are available to her as she goes international, and how much time and effort will be required to sell abroad. Second, she should contact the appropriate trade association(s) to learn more about potential demand and the specifics of required documentation, government clearances, etc. Finally, it would be helpful to talk with the owners of a few small firms (that do not compete with her own) that have added international sales to their operations. This will provide a practical view of the potentials and headaches involved in such expansion.

2. Using an international distributor is often beneficial for the novice exporter, and this is likely to be a good option for Cooper's business. However, it is imperative that Cooper consider several factors if she selects a distributor, including the following: cost of services, market coverage, flexibility in transportation and product handling, reputation and track record with other client firms, and knowledge of distribution systems in targeted international markets. It is rarely best to choose an international distributor merely because its services are the cheapest (though this is an important matter), but the exporter should make this decision looking across all relevant factors.

3. Exporting is probably a good idea for Cooper. From a rational perspective, her firm is likely to benefit from international sales as long as marginal revenue from these sales exceed marginal costs of offering the products abroad. However, several cautions should be heeded. For example, international business is complicated, so Cooper should be sure that she knows what she is getting into. If the added hassles of international expansion will take the pleasure out of overseeing her business, she should think twice about this option. Also, companies find it challenging to manage overseas operations where circumstances are more likely to be beyond their control. Is it wise for Cooper to start exporting now to promising markets abroad and jeopardize the reputation of the firm when an order is mishandled or contract misunderstandings arise? Missteps early on will not bode well for expanding business later on, especially when it comes to critical products such as the surgical equipment Cooper's firm supplies.

REF: p. 382 OBJ: YMTC TYPE: C

8. **You Make the Call—Situation 3**

Dr. Juldiz Afgazar, a native of the Republic of Kazakhstan, had been invited to spend a semester in the United States as a visiting scholar in entrepreneurial finance. Kazakhstan gained its independence from the former Soviet Union in 1991, and only after that were laws passed allowing citizens to own private businesses. Dr. Afgazar wanted to learn more about the free market economy of the United States to determine whether such a system could be implemented in Kazakhstan.

Prior to this visit to the United States, Dr. Afgazar had not traveled extensively outside her country. Although she enjoyed many aspects of U.S. culture, she was particularly impressed by the seemingly unlimited quantity and variety of goods and foods that were readily available. After a visit to a local restaurant's pizza buffet, she became an avid fan of American-style pizza! Dr. Afgazar found the crisp yeast crust, spicy tomato sauce, melted mozzarella cheese, and assortment of toppings to be a delicious combination. Pizza was an entirely new type of food for her, since it was not available in Kazakhstan. A true entrepreneur, Dr. Afgazar began to wonder if a pizza restaurant could be successful in her country.

Source: Developed by Elisabeth J. Teal of Northern Georgia College and State University, Dahlonega, Georgia, and Aigul N. Toxanova of Kokshetau Higher College of Management and Business, Kazakhstan.

Question 1 What obstacles would an entrepreneur have to overcome to establish a pizza restaurant in a country with a developing market-based economy, such as Kazakhstan?

Question 2 Is Dr. Afgazar's idea of developing a pizza restaurant in Kazakhstan ahead of its time? That is, do you think the economy of Kazakhstan is sufficiently developed to support a pizza restaurant?

Question 3 What methods could an entrepreneur use to evaluate the likelihood of success of a pizza restaurant in Kazakhstan?

ANS:

1. Since pizza restaurants do not currently exist in Kazakhstan, local entrepreneurs (including Afgazar) are unlikely to have the requisite expertise to start one. For example, pizza requires unique inputs and combinations of ingredients (specified by recipes), as well as special equipment (pans, ovens, etc.), and these features of the business will be completely unfamiliar to the entrepreneur and to those who might be hired to work in the new restaurant. Thus, the restaurant is not likely to work without a great deal of training, which can be costly. Established U.S. pizza franchises have not yet entered far more promising markets, so they are unlikely to be interested in supporting such a venture, so knowledge of the business must be cobbled together from wherever sources the entrepreneur can find.

Beyond initial concerns, several other questions arise. Is there sufficient market demand for a foreign food that is unknown to locals? How would the entrepreneur conduct inexpensive marketing research when potential customers do not even know what pizza looks like? Will the necessary ingredients and equipment be available to operate such a restaurant? What about the reliability of suppliers to the local market for required inputs? Will the perishability of ingredients be a problem? These issues and many others should be settled before making a decision to commence operations.

2. This is an important question. The primary issue here is whether the local market will be able to afford to buy pizza. In emerging markets, most people and do not have enough discretionary income to eat out, so exotic foods are financially out of reach to the majority of consumers. The obvious response is to reduce the price to make pizza affordable, but this cuts into profit margins where costs are already high (i.e., inputs will be costly to procure because the food is unique and thus its inputs are not readily available.)

3. To reduce risk exposure, Afgazar should concentrate on testing the market in small ways to get a feel for reactions in Kazakhstan. For example, she could begin by importing small quantities of the ingredients she would be likely to use in restaurant operations later. Then, she can make a few crude pizzas at home and invite friends to come and see if they like it. If the response is positive, she could make more pizzas at home and do taste tests by setting up a stand and handing out samples to those who pass by. If market reaction is favorable at that point, more sophisticated marketing research would be warranted. In addition to testing the market directly, Afgazar should assess demand indirectly by determining how well other restaurant operations in the area are doing. If restaurants in general are not thriving, the potential for success of a pizza restaurant may not be great.

REF: p. 381 OBJ: YMTC TYPE: C

9. **You Make the Call—Situation 4**

ChemiClean, a small specialty chemical company, sells private custom-label products globally to wholesalers, retailers, and dealers. Overseas sales have been slow and this year's profits have declined precipitously from the previous year. Duster's, one of the ChemiClean's largest overseas customers, placed an large order for wall-mounted hand soap dispensers with its logo imprinted on the dispenser's face. The customer is now complaining that the color of the logo on the delivered dispensers does not match the graphic standards used in its world-wide advertising campaigns. The customer is demanding that ChemiClean make a $100,000 adjustment and it will keep the dispensers. If ChemiClean makes the adjustment, it will make no profit on the sale. The sales manager has reviewed the customer's order and discovered that it contains no exact specification for the color of the Duster's logo.

Question 1 Is this a customer relations problem or an ethics problem for ChemiClean?
Question 2 Is Duster's request reasonable? Is it ethical?
Question 3 How should ChemiClean respond to Duster's demand for an adjustment?

ANS:

1. It is both. It is a consumer relations problem, because the artwork error created dissatisfaction for the customer. There is no doubt that repeat business with this client will be affected by any settlement—one way or the other. But it is also a matter of ethics. ChemiClean needs to decide what is fair in this case and determine what would lead to equitable treatment for the overseas client.

2. The reasonableness of this request is obviously a matter of judgment. Asking ChemiClean to cover 75% of the cost may seem like a heavy charge for a slight difference in color. On the other hand, ChemiClean perhaps has failed in its duty to maintain its quality and thus the delivered product was defective.

3. Accepting the proposal would contribute to good relations with the overseas client in the future, as well as doing what the client considers to be fair. For a small company, the cost may seem high, but a reputation for both fairness and quality in international markets can be built through such actions.

REF: p. 382 OBJ: YMTC TYPE: A

Correlation Table for Chapter 18—Professional Management in the Entrepreneurial Firm

	Learning Objectives	Question Type	Definition Define new term, recall facts	Concept Understand or relate concepts	Application Apply knowledge, analyze data
1	Discuss the entrepreneur's leadership role.	T/F		1	2,3
		MC	1,5,6,7,8,9	2,3,4	
		ES		1	
2	Explain the distinctive features of small firm management.	T/F	9,10,11,18	4,5,6,7,8,12,13, 14,15,19	
		MC	13,14,15,18,21, 25,26	10,11,12,16,17, 19,24	20,22,23
		ES		2	
3	Identify the managerial tasks of entrepreneurs.	T/F	25,26	16,17,20,21,22, 23,24	
		MC	38,39	27,28,29,31,32, 33,34,35,36	30,37
		ES		3	
4	Describe the problem of time pressure and suggest solutions.	T/F		27,28,29,30,31	
		MC	40	41	42
		ES		4	
5	Explain the various types of outside management assistance.	T/F	33,34	32,35	
		MC	43,45,46,47,50	49	44,48
		ES		5	
	You Make the Call	ES		6,7,8,9	

Total Number of Test Questions: 94 (35 True/False; 50 Multiple-Choice; 9 Essay)

Chapter 18—Professional Management in the Entrepreneurial Firm

TRUE/FALSE

1. By creating an environment that encourages personal interaction, the leader of a small firm can motivate employees and attract prospective employees.

   ANS: T REF: p. 399 OBJ: 18-1 TYPE: C

2. An automobile dealer wants to use the modern management concept of work teams. To do so, he should reduce direct supervision in the body shop.

   ANS: T REF: p. 401 OBJ: 18-1 TYPE: A

3. A florist began asking employees for their ideas about the business. This practice is a good illustration of empowerment.

   ANS: F
   Empowerment goes beyond the solicitation of employees' opinions and ideas, adding increased authority to act and make decisions on their own.

   REF: p. 400 OBJ: 18-1 TYPE: A

4. Entrepreneurs who are professional in their work are sometimes described as using an approach that is scientific in nature.

   ANS: T REF: p. 401 OBJ: 18-2 TYPE: C

5. Founders may fail to appreciate the value of good management practices.

   ANS: T REF: p. 401 OBJ: 18-2 TYPE: C

6. In small businesses, poor management is prevalent and inevitable.

   ANS: F
   In small businesses, poor management is neither universal nor inevitable.

   REF: p. 402 OBJ: 18-2 TYPE: C

7. A small business typically lacks the marketing research tools that big corporations have.

   ANS: T REF: p. 402 OBJ: 18-2 TYPE: C

8. The early growth stages of a new business involve significantly less change than that which occurs during the growth of a relative mature business.

   ANS: F

Changes involved in the early growth stages of a new business are *much more* extensive than those that occur with the growth of a relative mature business.

REF: p. 402 OBJ: 18-2 TYPE: C

9. Intermediate supervision, which occurs in Stage 3 of small business growth, involves the use of budgets, personnel policies, organizational charts, and computerization.

ANS: F
These features more accurately describe Stage 4, the stage of formal organization.

REF: p. 404 OBJ: 18-2 TYPE: D

10. When a firm reaches Stage 2 (player-coach) in its growth, the entrepreneur withdraws from personal participation in production, selling, writing checks, and record keeping.

ANS: F
In Stage 2, the entrepreneur engages extensively in these work activities.

REF: p. 403 OBJ: 18-2 TYPE: D

11. The intermediate supervision stage of business growth is a turning point because the entrepreneur must learn to rise above direct management and work through an intermediate level of managers.

ANS: T REF: p. 404 OBJ: 18-2 TYPE: D

12. The need for effective management becomes greater as the business expands.

ANS: T REF: p. 404 OBJ: 18-2 TYPE: C

13. Entrepreneurs who follow a win-win strategy are taking an approach that ensures that their own firm will achieve the outcomes that are best for their own firm.

ANS: F
Implementing a win-win strategy involves the identification of a solution that will satisfy at least the basic interests of both parties.

REF: p. 409 OBJ: 18-2 TYPE: C

14. For the manager, the control function is the same thing as the planning function.

ANS: F
The control function is a follow-up to planning, ensuring that the firm is functioning as intended.

REF: p. 407 OBJ: 18-2 TYPE: C

15. The last step in the control process is establishing standards.

ANS: F
The control process *begins* with the establishment of standards.

REF: p. 408 OBJ: 18-2 TYPE: C

16. Developing a plan for the firm helps the entrepreneur to think through the issues faced by the firm as well as providing a focus for the firm.

ANS: T REF: p. 405 OBJ: 18-3 TYPE: C

17. Owner-managers of small businesses typically overdo the amount of planning.

ANS: F
Small business managers tend to do less planning than would be ideal.

REF: p. 404 OBJ: 18-3 TYPE: C

18. As a firm moves from Stage 1 to Stage 4, the pattern of entrepreneurial activities changes in that the entrepreneur becomes less of a manager and more of a doer.

ANS: F
As a firm moves from Stage 1 to Stage 4, the pattern of entrepreneurial activities changes. The entrepreneur becomes less of a doer and more of a manager.

REF: p. 404 OBJ: 18-2 TYPE: D

19. In his study of the origin and evolution of new businesses, Amar V. Bhide found that entrepreneurs play different roles in starting businesses than they play in building what he calls long-lived firms.

ANS: T REF: p. 404 OBJ: 18-2 TYPE: C

20. Because they are used and tested constantly, naturally evolving organizational structures are as nearly perfect as one can hope for.

ANS: F
Unplanned structures are seldom perfect.

REF: p. 405 OBJ: 18-3 TYPE: C

21. Line organization uses a dual chain of command.

ANS: F
Line organization uses a single, specific chain of command.

REF: p. 405 OBJ: 18-3 TYPE: C

22. If staff specialists begin to give orders instead of being helpers, they destroy the unity of command.

ANS: T REF: p. 405 OBJ: 18-3 TYPE: C

23. An informal group can help or hinder the proper functioning of a business organization, even in a small firm.

ANS: T REF: p. 406 OBJ: 18-3 TYPE: C

24. The number of employees who can be supervised effectively by a capable manager is variable, depending on a number of factors.

ANS: T REF: p. 406 OBJ: 18-3 TYPE: C

25. Stewardship delegation focuses on results in judging the performance of a subordinate in carrying out assigned tasks.

ANS: T REF: p. 407 OBJ: 18-3 TYPE: D

26. Gofer delegation allows the subordinate substantial freedom in carrying out an assignment.

ANS: F
Gofer delegation refers to work assignments in which the supervisor-delegator controls the details of the task.

REF: p. 407 OBJ: 18-3 TYPE: D

27. Many owner-managers work from 60 to 80 hours a week.

ANS: T REF: p. 0409 OBJ: 18-4 TYPE: C

28. Despite the long work hours owner-managers put in, they can always work efficiently.

ANS: F
A frequent and unfortunate result of such a schedule is inefficient work performance.

REF: p. 410 OBJ: 18-4 TYPE: C

29. If the busy entrepreneur wants to keep a hand on the pulse of the business, he or she should continue to read technical or trade publications.

ANS: T REF: p. 410 OBJ: 18-4 TYPE: C

30. The greatest time saver is the effective use of time.

ANS: T REF: p. 410 OBJ: 18-4 TYPE: C

31. Preparing a daily written plan of activities is useful in deciding which tasks deserve highest priority.

ANS: T REF: p. 411 OBJ: 18-4 TYPE: C

32. There are now several hundred incubators in the United States, but the popularity of these facilities is decreasing.

ANS: F
The number of incubators in the United States is growing rapidly.

REF: p. 411 OBJ: 18-5 TYPE: C

33. A major goal of business incubators is to promote economic development by providing financial assistance to new businesses.

ANS: F
Business incubators offer space and managerial/clerical services to new businesses.

REF: p. 411 OBJ: 18-5 TYPE: D

34. The SCORE program offers entrepreneurs the opportunity to enroll in college courses.

ANS: F
In the SCORE program, retired executives provide free management advice to small business managers.

REF: p. 413 OBJ: 18-5 TYPE: D

35. Although management consultants can be helpful to business performance, they do not serve small businesses.

ANS: F
Management consultants serve both large and small businesses.

REF: p. 413 OBJ: 18-5 TYPE: C

MULTIPLE CHOICE

1. The number one challenge in a growing business according to Joshua Schechter, founder of Online Business Services, is
   a. overcoming inadequate resources.
   b. attracting management talent.
   c. transferring your entrepreneurial spirit.
   d. growth that creates a leadership vacuum.

ANS: C REF: p. 398 OBJ: 18-1 TYPE: D

2. Barry Ramirez demands that his employees immediately comply with his orders. His leadership style is typical of ________ leaders.
   a. authoritative
   b. coercive
   c. pacesetting
   d. affiliative

ANS: B REF: p. 400 OBJ: 18-1 TYPE: C

3. Linda Semmes sets high standards and expects excellence from her employees. Her leadership style is typical of ________ leaders.
   a. authoritative
   b. coercive
   c. pacesetting
   d. affiliative

ANS: C REF: p. 400 OBJ: 18-1 TYPE: C

4. Leadership in small firms is more _______ in comparison to the leadership in large corporations.
   a. haphazard

b. impersonal
c. personalized
d. more skillful

ANS: C REF: p. 400 OBJ: 18-1 TYPE: C

5. Harry Ramirez wishes to create greater enthusiasm among employees in his industrial distribution business. A widely used approach that he might take is
a. empowerment of employees.
b. formulating of policies.
c. establishment of control standards.
d. adoption of budgets.

ANS: A REF: p. 400 OBJ: 18-1 TYPE: A

6. Workers act on their own and to make decisions about the processes they're involved with are considered to be
a. empowered employees.
b. policy-capable subordinates.
c. work-team ready.
d. nascent managers.

ANS: A REF: p. 400 OBJ: 18-1 TYPE: A

7. Marcia Mendez, who runs a drapery business, has groups of employees who work in production and in installation. If she decides to use work teams as part of her leadership approach, she must increase
a. supervision.
b. compensation.
c. independence.
d. quality.

ANS: C REF: p. 401 OBJ: 18-1 TYPE: A

8. If Fran Fishburn, who runs a wholesale flower business, successfully creates properly functioning self-managed teams among her employees, her supervisors
a. will feel threatened by her leadership approach to teams.
b. will likely become fewer in number.
c. will likely attempt to delegate mundane tasks to the teams.
d. will need to maintain close supervision.

ANS: B REF: p. 401 OBJ: 18-1 TYPE: A

9. Roger Childers owns and runs a printing firm with twelve employees. As a result of his extensive personal interaction with these employees, Childers realizes that
a. the employees pretty well understand where the business is going.
b. a chain of command is unnecessary.
c. personnel policies would be overly restrictive.
d. marketing research is part of everyone's job.

ANS: A REF: p. 401 OBJ: 18-1 TYPE: A

10. The founder of a firm is least likely to be described as a
a. creative person.

b. good manager.
c. risk taker.
d. courageous person.

ANS: B REF: p. 401 OBJ: 18-2 TYPE: C

11. The founder of a firm is most likely to be described as a
a. creative person.
b. good manager.
c. low risk taker.
d. good organization member.

ANS: A REF: p. 401 OBJ: 18-2 TYPE: C

12. Less-than-professional management behavior on the part of an entrepreneur can
a. provide a spark to the business because of the spontaneity it introduces.
b. be interpreted as evidence of creativity.
c. act as a drag on business growth.
d. normally provide a competitive edge to the firm.

ANS: C REF: p. 402 OBJ: 18-2 TYPE: C

13. A bank loan officer believes that a particular small business loan applicant is a typical entrepreneur and, therefore, is
a. skilled in general management.
b. lacking in managerial expertise.
c. strongly oriented toward careful planning.
d. focused on financial management.

ANS: B REF: p. 402 OBJ: 18-2 TYPE: A

14. A small business operations manager is confronted with a quality problem. A typical small business handicap that will hamper his efforts to solve the problem is a lack of
a. time.
b. chain of command.
c. accounting data.
d. specialized staff assistance.

ANS: D REF: p. 402 OBJ: 18-2 TYPE: A

15. A corporate marketing executive is moving to a managerial position in a small firm, where she may logically expect to find
a. adequate financial resources and adequate staff.
b. inadequate financial resources and inadequate staff.
c. adequate financial resources and inadequate staff.
d. inadequate financial resources and adequate staff.

ANS: B REF: p. 402 OBJ: 18-2 TYPE: A

16. Which of the following is *not* a constraint on management in small firms?
a. Bureaucratic red tape
b. Lack of money
c. Limited managerial staff

d. Lack of marketing research talent

ANS: A REF: p. 402 OBJ: 18-2 TYPE: C

17. Which of the following would least concern a corporate manager considering joining a small firm?
    a. Lack of bureaucratic red tape
    b. Lack of money
    c. Limited managerial staff
    d. Lack of marketing research talent

ANS: A REF: p. 402 OBJ: 18-2 TYPE: C

18. Stage 1 in the growth of a business is characterized by
    a. entrepreneur as player-coach.
    b. multilayered organization.
    c. hands-off management practices.
    d. one-person operation.

ANS: D REF: p. 403 OBJ: 18-2 TYPE: D

19. Mario has just begun to personally supervise employees, his firm is in the stage of growth called
    a. one-person operation.
    b. intermediate supervision.
    c. player-coach.
    d. formal organization.

ANS: C REF: p. 403 OBJ: 18-2 TYPE: C

20. Susan Keller has seen her retail shop grow to the point that she has designated supervisors for the office and two selling areas. Her shop's stage of growth is called
    a. one-person operation.
    b. player-coach.
    c. intermediate supervision.
    d. formal organization.

ANS: C REF: p. 404 OBJ: 18-2 TYPE: A

21. The use of written policies, budgets, and job descriptions is most closely associated with which of the following stages of growth?
    a. One-person operation
    b. Player-coach
    c. Intermediate supervision
    d. Formal organization

ANS: D REF: p. 404 OBJ: 18-2 TYPE: D

22. A new business has been launched with four employees who work for the entrepreneur-owner. As the owner contemplates growth in sales and personnel, she realizes that the next step of growth will involve the special problem of
    a. intermediate supervision.
    b. formal policies.
    c. direct supervision.
    d. quality management.

ANS: A REF: p. 404 OBJ: 18-2 TYPE: A

23. As his small business prospers and grows from Stage 1 to Stage 4, Carlos Perez realizes that he also must grow by increasing his
    a. doing skills.
    b. advertising skills.
    c. managing skills.
    d. legal skills.

ANS: C REF: p. 404 OBJ: 18-2 TYPE: A

24. Controlling is the managerial function that involves the manager's
    a. thinking through issues confronting a firm and developing a plan to increase productivity.
    b. keeping track of performance and investigating when results are out of line.
    c. developing an atmosphere of cooperation and teamwork.
    d. keeping an optimum number of people under supervision.

ANS: B REF: p. 407 OBJ: 18-2 TYPE: C

25. A printing shop owner believes that his business is running rather haphazardly and wants to get it under control. The first step he should take is to
    a. increase inspection.
    b. set standards.
    c. take corrective action.
    d. draw up a strategic plan.

ANS: B REF: p. 408 OBJ: 18-2 TYPE: A

26. To improve control of operations, a shop owner wishes to measure performance at the process stage. The owner might
    a. inspect raw materials.
    b. use quality control.
    c. set sales quotas.
    d. improve personnel-selection methods.

ANS: B REF: p. 408 OBJ: 18-2 TYPE: A

27. The fact that the daily "brush fires" of doing business tend to push aside planning until it is forgotten is the message of
    a. Parkinson's law of planning.
    b. the Peter principle.
    c. the tyranny of the urgent.
    d. Murphy's law of strategic action.

ANS: C REF: p. 405 OBJ: 18-3 TYPE: C

28. A budget is an example of a
    a. policy.
    b. short-range plan.
    c. strategic plan.
    d. nonrecurring procedure.

ANS: B REF: p. 405 OBJ: 18-3 TYPE: C

29. A monthly production schedule is an example of a
    a. strategic plan.
    b. short-range plan.
    c. tactical plan.
    d. operational plan.

    ANS: B REF: p. 405 OBJ: 18-3 TYPE: C

30. The manager of a rapidly growing small business is unsure about where the business will be in 3 to 5 years. She should focus on
    a. business policies.
    b. procedures.
    c. budgets.
    d. strategic plans.

    ANS: D REF: p. 405 OBJ: 18-3 TYPE: A

31. The best feature of an organizational structure that evolves naturally is its
    a. economy.
    b. clarity.
    c. practicality.
    d. use of staff positions.

    ANS: C REF: p. 405 OBJ: 18-3 TYPE: C

32. In a line organization, each employee has
    a. one supervisor.
    b. two supervisors.
    c. three supervisors.
    d. an indefinite number of supervisors.

    ANS: A REF: p. 405 OBJ: 18-3 TYPE: C

33. For small businesses, the most likely form of organizational structure is
    a. functional.
    b. line.
    c. line-and-staff.
    d. committee.

    ANS: B REF: p. 45 OBJ: 18-3 TYPE: C

34. Frequent and flagrant disregard of the chain of command undermines the position of the
    a. founder.
    b. operative employee.
    c. staff specialist.
    d. bypassed manager.

    ANS: D REF: p. 405 OBJ: 18-3 TYPE: C

35. In a line-and-staff organization, which of the following is a line activity?
    a. Production
    b. Human resources management

c. Accounting
d. Legal work

ANS: A REF: p. 405 OBJ: 18-3 TYPE: C

36. In a line-and-staff organization, which of the following is a staff activity?
a. Production
b. Warehousing
c. Receiving
d. Human resource management

ANS: D REF: p. 405 OBJ: 18-3 TYPE: C

37. Faced with the challenge of recruiting, selecting, and compensating a growing number of employees, a small business owner is planning to hire a human resource manager. This owner is apparently going to establish
a. an informal organization.
b. a line-and-staff organization.
c. a Stage 2 organization.
d. a line organization.

ANS: B REF: p. 405 OBJ: 18-3 TYPE: A

38. The number of subordinates reporting to one superior constitutes that manager's
a. span of control.
b. informal organization.
c. organizational structure.
d. chain of command.

ANS: A REF: p. 405 OBJ: 18-3 TYPE: D

39. Which of the following refers to the fact that subordinates are to report to only one superior?
a. span of control.
b. informal organization.
c. formal organization
d. chain of command.

ANS: D REF: p. 405 OBJ: 18-3 TYPE: D

40. A busy owner-manager is trying to cope with the problem of excessive time pressure that requires her to work 60 to 70 hours per week. She should realize that this work schedule is
a. light, because 50 percent or more of all owner-managers work 80 hours or more per week.
b. fairly typical, because many owner-managers work this amount or more each week.
c. heavy, because more than one-half of all owner-managers work a normal 40 to 45 hour week.
d. unusually heavy, because most owner-entrepreneurs function as idea people, leaving the details to others and working only 20 to 30 hours per week on average.

ANS: B REF: p. 409 OBJ: 18-4 TYPE: A

41. The first step in planning and improving one's use of time should be
a. listing long-run objectives.
b. recording time spent on various activities during the day.

c. listing projects that need attention.
d. assigning priorities to unfinished tasks.

ANS: B REF: p. 410 OBJ: 18-4 TYPE: C

42. A survey of time usage has been recommended to a small business owner by a management consultant. This will provide the owner with a basis for improving the business by
a. classifying time spent according to functional areas of the business.
b. avoiding procrastination.
c. focusing attention on the most crucial tasks.
d. minimizing use of meetings.

ANS: C REF: p. 410 OBJ: 18-4 TYPE: A

43. Organizations that provide both space and management services to new businesses are
a. almost always funded solely by the government.
b. usually organized by Small Business Development Centers.
c. referred to as business incubators.
d. often put together by management consultants to create consulting opportunities.

ANS: C REF: p. 411 OBJ: 18-5 TYPE: D

44. Shirley Lessman is planning to launch a business and has been encouraged to start in a business incubator. This will give her access to
a. bank loans.
b. free rent.
c. prepaid insurance.
d. management counsel.

ANS: D REF: p. 411 OBJ: 18-5 TYPE: A

45. The consulting resources of universities are made available to small business firms by
a. student consulting team programs.
b. SCORE.
c. business incubators.
d. management consultants.

ANS: A REF: p. 412 OBJ: 18-5 TYPE: D

46. SCORE refers to
a. the grade assigned to a small firm by the SBA.
b. the management knowledge possessed by an entrepreneur.
c. a group of retired executives who act as consultants to small firms.
d. an alliance of small firms for the purpose of bidding on government contracts.

ANS: C REF: p. 413 OBJ: 18-5 TYPE: D

47. Small business service organizations that are patterned after the Agricultural Extension Service and are affiliated with universities are
a. student consulting team programs.
b. Small Business Development Centers.
c. business incubators.
d. SCORE.

ANS: B REF: p. 413 OBJ: 18-5 TYPE: D

48. As a farmer, Larry Rogers received assistance from the U.S. Agricultural Extension Service. Having sold the farm, he is planning to start a farm supply store and has been told that the federal government provides comparable help to small businesses through
   a. Small Business Development Centers (SBDCs.)
   b. the Service Corps of Retired Executives (SCORE.)
   c. sponsorship of student consulting team projects.
   d. New Business Incubators (NBIs.)

   ANS: A REF: p. 413 OBJ: 18-5 TYPE: A

49. Entrepreneurs can get management assistance from peers through
   a. outside consultants.
   b. SCORE advisors.
   c. volunteer work in the community.
   d. networking.

   ANS: D REF: p. 414 OBJ: 18-5 TYPE: C

50. The process of developing and engaging in mutually beneficial relationships with peers is
   a. networking.
   b. politicking.
   c. instrumental tying.
   d. effective connecting.

   ANS: A REF: p. 414 OBJ: 18-5 TYPE: D

ESSAY

1. Discuss the use of employee empowerment and self-managed work teams as leadership approaches.

   ANS:
   Through empowerment, a manager gives employees a share in the management of an operation. They are granted the freedom to make some decisions or to act more independently than they were previously able to. Most empowered employees sense a greater respect by management for their role and contribution and react favorably to such leadership. This type of leadership contrasts sharply with the more autocratic supervision popular a few decades ago. Empowerment should be contrasted with mere participation, which allows for employee input but does not necessarily give employees greater authority.

   To create self-managed work teams, management must reduce direct supervision. Typically, this also permits reduction in the number of first-level managers required. The work teams must take over a major part of the management of their own operation and must work together. They must also accept responsibility for results. This process is not without its complications, but it has been highly successful in many settings.

   REF: p. 400-401 OBJ: 18-1 TYPE: C

2. Discuss how well founders function as managers.

   ANS:

A founder's strengths often lie in a functional area such as product design or sales. As a consequence, founders often are weak managers. (There are exceptions, of course.) Those who create firms are not always good organization members. They may have entered into business for themselves because they disliked life in other bureaucratic organizations. It is easy for them to think of management precepts as secondary concerns.

REF: p. 401 OBJ: 18-2 TYPE: C

3. What conditions call for the use of a line-and-staff form of organization? Explain the relationship of this form to the principle of unity of command.

ANS:
Growth in size requires a change from line organization. Line organization is practical only in a very small firm. As specialized services and assistance are required, it becomes necessary to adopt a line-and-staff organization. The nature of specialized services can be illustrated in many ways (e.g., those provided by a human resource manager.)

If special assistants and specialized departments are permitted to issue orders, unity of command deteriorates. This is the reason that staff must function only as helpers or facilitators. By insisting that they retain this character, the entrepreneur can preserve unity of command in the business.

REF: p. 405 OBJ: 18-3 TYPE: C

4. Discuss the topic of delegation of authority in small business. Include in your discussion a definition of the term, manifestations of weakness in delegation, and benefits to be realized.

ANS:
Delegation of authority involves a superior granting to a subordinate the right to make certain types of choices or decisions. Poor delegation is a major limitation of many small businesses, whose founders or managers have not learned to use their subordinates efficiently. The need to clear everything with the boss, a bottleneck at the boss's office, and an exceptionally busy boss are all manifestations of weakness in delegation. To be meaningful, delegation must be stewardship delegation rather than "gofer" delegation, in which everything must be cleared with the delegator.

Delegation is necessary for growth. Among the specific benefits to be realized are the personal development of those to whom authority is delegated and lessening of the workload of the delegator, who can then turn to other more important tasks.

REF: p. 407 OBJ: 18-4 TYPE: C

5. Discuss the use of student consulting teams and SCORE consultants in small firms.

ANS:
Student consulting teams work with small businesses under the supervision of a faculty member of a college or university. Some student consulting teams have made great contributions to the small firms they served. However, these consultants are still learners themselves, and this limits the quality of their consultation

SCORE consultants are retired managerial and professional personnel. What they can offer depends on their experiential background and their ability. It is possible for a small business to gain outstanding talent if it is fortunate enough to obtain the services of an outstanding retired professional. The services of SCORE consultants are free, except for their out-of-pocket expenses.

REF: p. 413 OBJ: 18-5 TYPE: C

6. **You Make the Call—Situation 1**
In one small firm, the owner-manager and his management team use various methods to delegate decision making to employees at the operating level. New employees are trained thoroughly when they begin, but no supervisor monitors their work closely once they have learned their duties. Of course, help is available as needed, but no one is there on an hour-to-hour basis to make sure employees are functioning as needed and that they are avoiding mistakes.

Occasionally, all managers and supervisors leave for a day-long meeting and allow the operating employees to run the business by themselves. Job assignments are defined rather loosely. Management expects employees to assume responsibility and to take necessary action whenever they see that something needs to be done. When employees ask for direction, they are sometimes simply told to solve the problem in whatever way they think best.

Question 1 Is such a loosely organized firm likely to be as effective as a firm that defines jobs more precisely and monitors performance more closely? What are the advantages and the limitations of the managerial style described above?
Question 2 How might such managerial methods affect morale?
Question 3 Would you like to work for this company? Why or why not?

ANS:
1. This company's leadership philosophy is unusual in the extent to which it emphasizes individual responsibility. It has the potential for encouraging enthusiastic performance. Effectiveness cannot be assumed, however. Much depends on the quality of personnel and the extent to which they have learned to respond to such supervision. Such a management style is limited in that it would not work well with incompetent employees or with employees who had been conditioned to distrust management and to do as little as possible. Also, some individuals are less comfortable in a work environment that is loosely structured.

2. We believe that most students would respond positively and that most employees would also respond positively. This approach might not lead to high morale for the type of employees mentioned above, however. Also, management might try to stretch an employee beyond his or her abilities, and that can be discouraging.

3. The respondents' answers will indicate their supervisory preferences. Our prediction is that most will be favorable.

REF: p. 417 OBJ: YMTC TYPE: C

7. **You Make the Call—Situation 2**
A few years after successfully launching a new business, an entrepreneur found himself spending 16-hour days running from one appointment to another, negotiating with customers, drumming up new business, signing checks, and checking up as much as possible on his six employees. The founder realized that his own strength was in selling, but general managerial responsibilities were very time consuming and interfered with his sales efforts. He even slept in the office two nights a week.

Despite his hard work, however, he knew that employees weren't organized and that many problems existed. He lacked the time to set personnel policies or to draw up job descriptions for his six employees. One employee even took advantage of the laxity in supervision to skip work sometimes. Invoices were sent to customers late, and delivery schedules were sometimes missed. Fortunately, the business was profitable in spite of the numerous problems.

Question 1 Is this founder's problem one of time management or general managerial ability? Would it be feasible to engage a management consultant to help solve the firm's problems?

Question 2 If this founder asked you to recommend some type of outside management assistance, would you recommend a SCORE counselor, a student consulting team, a CPA firm, a management consultant, or some other type of assistance? Why?

Question 3 If you were asked to improve this firm's management system, what would be the first steps you would take? What would be your initial goal?

ANS:

1. A lack of general management skills must take at least some of the blame. Other firms run successfully with less frantic administrative activities. The situation appears ideal for analysis by a well-qualified management consultant. The entrepreneur is aware of the problem and concerned about solving it. However, he apparently lacks knowledge of how to deal with it. He should run to the nearest qualified consultant.

2. The answer will reflect the respondent's experience and bias. If the firm is strapped for cash, the entrepreneur could consider SCORE or a student consulting team. The quality of such services is unpredictable, however. The business is profitable and so may be able to pay for consulting services. A CPA firm may be able to offer management assistance or to recommend another source of qualified help.

3. Some steps would be to interview key members of the company, examine organization structure and responsibilities, evaluate qualifications of key personnel, look for gaps in staffing, and study the entrepreneur's administrative style. An initial goal might be to eliminate the owner's need to sleep in the office at night and to cut his 16-hour days to a more modest 12 to 14 hours.

   What Actually Happened: The entrepreneur hired a general manager, who was allowed to run the business. This freed the owner to reduce his working hours and also to devote more of his time to selling.

REF: p. 417 OBJ: YMTC TYPE: C

8. **You Make the Call—Situation 3**

After an inauspicious start in a spare bedroom in his home, an entrepreneur's business had flourished. He wondered if he had the necessary talent to ensure its continued success. The business had grown to 100 employees and then to 200 employees. When the business was small, the entrepreneur could figure out the solutions to problems on a case-by-case basis, but the problems were becoming increasingly complicated.

Question 1 What kinds of practices or procedures will this entrepreneur need to adopt to enable the business to continue to operate successfully?

Question 2 What resources might this entrepreneur use to get good feedback to help him assess his competence and understand the issues his growing business is facing?

ANS:

1. The entrepreneur needs to adopt some systematic methods of management to supplement his informal approach. Among these might be the following:

   a. Create an organization structure.
   b. Designate capable leasers for each segment.
   c. Give leaders sufficient authority for needed decisions.
   d. Establish some basic personnel policies.
   e. Create a planning and budgetary process.

f. Arrange systems and relationships for communicating.
g. Develop control methods including methods for quality control.

2. The entrepreneur can secure help from a number of sources. These may include the firms banker and/or CPA and/or attorney to the extent the firm has made such connections. Other sources of help include SCORE, consultants, student teams, possibly locating in a business incubator.

REF: p. 417 OBJ: YMTC TYPE: C

9. **You Make the Call—Situation 4**
An increasing number of Web sites promise entrepreneurs everything they need to run their businesses, including expert advice on management, finance, technology, and recruiting. The owner of a local bakery (selling mostly specialty breads and cookies) senses a need for advice concerning his business operations. The business does little more than break even, but the owner believes it could be much more profitable. Using the Internet to get the expertise he needs seems to be an economical approach, and he has started reading the information available at http://www.allbusiness.com.

Question 1 How effective do you think this or similar Web sites will be in helping this business owner?
Question 2 What other types of managerial assistance would be practical for such a business?

ANS:
1. The Web site given is a well-organized one that offers a great deal of information on a number of topics. It was considered by Inc. magazine to be one of the 10 best general-interest small-business offerings. Several Inc. staffers gave it the following review:

> **www.allbusiness.com** All singin', all dancin', Allbusiness.com covers finance, human resources, sales and marketing, and office services, among other things. However, our CEO evaluators tell us that this Web powerhouse tries too much to be all things to all CEOs. Despite its easy-to-use design and good organization, it ends up being overwhelming in scope. Among its useful amenities: a "virtual file cabinet," in which you can store documents or Web tools. There are also handy links to the site's numerous partners and informal alliances: Lawyers.com (legal advice), Barnesandnoble.com (books), Onsale.com (auctions), Atyouroffice.com (office supplies), etc.

The limitation of this type of help is that it does not provide a diagnosis or evaluation of the particular firm as a consultant might do. It is somewhat like going to the library and learning about what might help. An advantage of the Web site, on the other hand, is that it provides anonymity if the owner has questions that may be embarrassing to ask. He can also participate in chat sessions and/or ask questions.

2. A SCORE counselor or a team of college students would provide the most economical assistance. Depending upon the location, a small business development center or college-based entrepreneurial center may have resources of the type needed. And, of course, local management consultants might also be available, as well as a CPA firm in some cases.

REF: p. 0 OBJ: YMTC TYPE: C

Correlation Table for Chapter 19—Managing Human Resources

	Learning Objectives	Question Type	Definition Define new term, recall facts	Concept Understand or relate concepts	Application Apply knowledge, analyze data
1	Explain the importance of employee recruitment and list some sources that can be useful in finding suitable applicants.	T/F	11	1,2,3,4,5,6,7,8, 9,10,12,13	
		MC	2	1,5,6,7,8,9,10	3,4,11,12
		ES		1	
2	Identify the steps to take in evaluating job applicants.	T/F		14,15,16,	
		MC		13,15,16	14,17,18,19,20
		ES		2	
3	Describe the role of training for both managerial and nonmanagerial employees in a small firm.	T/F	19,22	17,18,20,21	
		MC	23,25	21,22,37,28,29, 30	24,26
		ES		3	
4	Explain the various types of compensation plans, including the use of incentive plans.	T/F		23,24,25,26,27, 28,29	
		MC	40,41	31,32,35,36,37, 38	33,34,39,42
		ES		4	
5	Discuss the human resource issues of employee leasing, legal protection, labor unions, and the formalizing of employer–employee relationships.	T/F		30,31,32,34,35	
		MC		43,44,45,48,49	46,47,50
		ES		5	
	You Make the Call	ES		6,7,8,9	

Total Number of Test Questions: 93 (35 True/False; 50 Multiple-Choice; 8 Essay)

Chapter 19—Managing Human Resources

TRUE/FALSE

1. Personnel programs are the same for small companies as for Wal-Mart or Sears, just on a much smaller scale.

   ANS: F
   Small businesses cannot duplicate the personnel programs of such industry giants, but they can adopt approaches that work best for small firms.

   REF: p. 421 OBJ: TYPE: C

2. A small firm should act aggressively in recruiting, taking the initiative in locating applicants.

   ANS: T REF: p. 422 OBJ: 19-1 TYPE: C

3. Small firms need to identify their distinctive advantages if they are to recruit outstanding prospects successfully, especially those seeking technical positions.

   ANS: F
   Competition for well-qualified business talent requires small firms to identify their distinctive advantages when recruiting outstanding prospects, *especially those seeking managerial and professional positions.*

   REF: p. 422 OBJ: 19-1 TYPE: C

4. Small firms suffer a recruiting handicap because of the ability of large companies to offer more freedom on the job.

   ANS: F
   In reality, small firms can structure the work environment to offer personnel greater freedom than they would have in a larger business.

   REF: p. 422 OBJ: 19-1 TYPE: C

5. A firm may receive unsolicited applications from qualified applicants.

   ANS: T REF: p. 423 OBJ: 19-1 TYPE: C

6. Private employment agencies administer the various state unemployment insurance programs.

   ANS: F
   It is *public* employment offices that administer the various state unemployment insurance programs, and these offer employment assistance to small businesses at no cost.

   REF: p. 423 OBJ: 19-1 TYPE: C

7. The fee charged by a private employment agency is usually paid by the applicant.

ANS: F
This is sometimes the case; however, the firm is usually responsible for the agency fee if the applicant is highly qualified.

REF: p. 423 OBJ: 19-1 TYPE: C

8. Employee referrals provide a rich source of good applicants for many small firms.

ANS: T REF: p. 423 OBJ: 19-1 TYPE: C

9. Because help-wanted advertising tends to be ineffective, most well-managed organizations reject this method of recruitment.

ANS: F
Although some have questioned the effectiveness of help-wanted advertising, many well-managed organizations recruit in this way.

REF: p. 422 OBJ: 19-1 TYPE: C

10. Temporary help agencies are good sources of employees when extensive training is required.

ANS: F
Staffing with temporary employees is less practical when extensive training is required.

REF: p. 423 OBJ: 19-1 TYPE: C

11. A *job description* refers to a listing of the knowledge, skills, abilities, and other characteristics necessary to perform a job.

ANS: F
A *job description* refers to an outline, or summary, of the work to be performed.

REF: p. 424 OBJ: 19-1 TYPE: D

12. The balance of the U.S. workforce is rapidly shifting toward higher proportions of women, older workers, and racial minorities.

ANS: T REF: p. 424 OBJ: 19-1 TYPE: C

13. In small firms, a professional's versatility and flexibility may be more important than technical competence.

ANS: T REF: p. 424 OBJ: 19-1 TYPE: C

14. Though time spent on interviewing and other phases of the selection process helps to address the immediate need of finding suitable employees, the long-term benefits of this investment are trivial.

ANS: F
Time spent on interviewing and other phases of the selection process can save time and money later on.

REF: p. 425 OBJ: 19-2 TYPE: C

15. It is now illegal for employers to arrange for background investigations of job applicants.

ANS: F
Employees can legally arrange for background investigations of job applicants, and such checks may help to avoid the serious consequences of a hiring mistake.

REF: p. 426 OBJ: 19-2 TYPE: C

16. The possibility of being sued makes employers reluctant to give a full and candid report on former employees.

ANS: T REF: p. 426 OBJ: 19-2 TYPE: C

17. Obviously, training helps prepare a new recruit to perform the duties for which he or she has been hired.

ANS: T REF: p. 427 OBJ: 19-3 TYPE: C

18. A good training program enhances morale and helps in recruitment.

ANS: T REF: p. 427 OBJ: 19-3 TYPE: C

19. Orientation refers to instructions given during the interview with an applicant.

ANS: F
Orientation begins with an individual's first two or three days on the job and can be used to help new employees get settled into their new positions.

REF: p. 427 OBJ: 19-3 TYPE: D

20. A small business can facilitate the orientation process by providing an employee handbook, which outlines the company's practices and procedures.

ANS: T REF: p. 427 OBJ: 19-3 TYPE: C

21. The small firm should concentrate its training on nonmanagerial employees, recognizing that development of managers is beyond its range of expertise.

ANS: F
Small firms have a particularly strong need to develop managerial and professional employees.

REF: p. 428 OBJ: 19-3 TYPE: C

22. Job instruction training is characterized by six easy steps.

ANS: F
Job instruction training involves *four* steps: (1) prepare employees, (2) present the operations, (3) try out performance, and (4) follow up.

REF: p. 429 OBJ: 19-3 TYPE: D

23. Small firms can offer several nonfinancial incentives that appeal to both managerial and nonmanagerial employees.

ANS: T REF: p. 428 OBJ: 19-4 TYPE: C

24. Small firms must be roughly competitive in wage or salary levels in order to attract well-qualified personnel.

ANS: T REF: p. 430 OBJ: 19-4 TYPE: C

25. A sales commission compensation plan is a type of time-based compensation system.

ANS: F
A sales commission compensation plan is a type of *incentive* system.

REF: p. 430 OBJ: 19-4 TYPE: C

26. Profit sharing provides a more direct work incentive in small firms than it does in large firms.

ANS: T REF: p. 431 OBJ: 19-4 TYPE: C

27. Fringe benefits are expensive, amounting to more than 40 percent of payroll expense for many small firms.

ANS: T REF: p. 431 OBJ: 19-4 TYPE: C

28. Small businesses cannot offer cafeteria plans because they are too difficult to implement.

ANS: F
Cafeteria plans do indeed involve a great deal of detailed paperwork; nonetheless, small firms can still manage to offer these programs with the support of outside help (e.g., consultants, payroll accounting services, insurance companies.)

REF: p. 431 OBJ: 19-4 TYPE: C

29. Employee stock ownership plans have become popular but still carry many tax disadvantages.

ANS: F
It is the tax advantages of employee stock ownership plans that have made these such a popular option.

REF: p. 432 OBJ: 19-4 TYPE: C

30. Companies that lease employees to small businesses charge a fee of 1 to 5 percent of payroll.

ANS: T REF: p. 432 OBJ: 19-5 TYPE: C

31. Since leasing companies typically employ hundreds or thousands of people, they can afford to offer benefits superior to those offered by the typical small firm.

ANS: T REF: p. 432 OBJ: 19-5 TYPE: C

32. Unions typically concentrate their primary attention on small companies, where their influence is most needed.

ANS: F
Unions typically focus their attention on large companies.

REF: p. 433 OBJ: 19-5 TYPE: C

33. By following enlightened personnel policies, small firms can reduce the likelihood of unionization.

ANS: T REF: p. 433 OBJ: 19-5 TYPE: C

34. As a firm grows, it experiences pressure to formalize its personnel policies and procedures.

ANS: T REF: p. 433 OBJ: 19-5 TYPE: C

35. In a small business, a human resource manager is generally desirable when employee morale is satisfactory and the labor turnover is extremely low.

ANS: F
Conditions such as unsatisfactory employee morale and high labor turnover are favorable to the decision to appoint a human resource manager.

REF: p. 434 OBJ: 19-5 TYPE: C

MULTIPLE CHOICE

1. In many small businesses, the importance of people shows up in the direct relationship between the attitude of its salespeople and
   a. inventory growth.
   b. sales revenue.
   c. gross profits.
   d. growth of the product line.

ANS: B REF: p. 421 OBJ: 19-1 TYPE: C

2. In his study of good-to-great companies, Jim Collins found that the great companies first
   a. "got the bus out of the barn."
   b. "took the bus to the right mechanics."
   c. "got the right people on the bus."
   d. "got the bus in high gear early on."

ANS: C REF: p. 421 OBJ: 19-1 TYPE: D

3. Tom Clancy is experiencing difficulty in recruiting competent technicians for his business. One way to increase the attractiveness of his small business is by using
   a. flexible work schedules.
   b. job descriptions.
   c. performance testing.
   d. private employment agencies.

ANS: A REF: p. 422 OBJ: 19-1 TYPE: A

4. A small business owner wishes to persuade a highly qualified applicant (a business school graduate) to consider a position with his firm carefully, even though the applicant has also had offers from large corporations. The owner should most strongly emphasize the
   a. family atmosphere.
   b. retirement program.
   c. potential for greater freedom of personnel to structure their job duties.
   d. long history of the firm.

ANS: C REF: p. 422 OBJ: 19-1 TYPE: A

5. Small firms compete with large firms for qualified personnel, but they have several potential advantages over large firms in attracting personnel, including which of the following?
   a. Recognizing individual contributions
   b. Offering standardized work scheduling as a possible lure
   c. Allowing any employee to influence the overall direction of the firm
   d. Providing greater bonuses

ANS: D REF: p. 422 OBJ: 19-1 TYPE: C

6. If qualified walk-ins cannot be hired immediately, their applications should be
   a. destroyed.
   b. sent to other firms.
   c. kept on file.
   d. turned over to a private employment agency.

ANS: C REF: p. 423 OBJ: 19-1 TYPE: C

7. Secondary and trade schools are a likely source of
   a. managers.
   b. personnel to fill positions requiring no specific work experiences.
   c. accountants.
   d. high-potential employees.

ANS: B REF: p. 423 OBJ: 19-1 TYPE: C

8. An employer who hires an employee through a public employment office pays the employment office a fee of
   a. nothing—this is a free service.
   b. one month's salary.
   c. one-tenth of the employee's yearly salary.
   d. $250, the standard amount.

ANS: A REF: p. 423 OBJ: 19-1 TYPE: C

9. In seeking personnel for key positions, small firms sometimes turn to recruiting specialists called
   a. temporary help agencies.
   b. leasing companies.
   c. attorneys.
   d. headhunters.

ANS: D REF: p. 423 OBJ: 19-1 TYPE: C

10. In seeking personnel for non-critical positions, small firms sometimes turn to
   a. temporary help agencies.
   b. leasing companies.
   c. attorneys.
   d. headhunters.

   ANS: A REF: p. 423 OBJ: 19-1 TYPE: C

11. To obtain a replacement for an employee taking short-term leave under provisions of the Family Leave Act, an employer might most appropriately use
   a. public employment agencies.
   b. employee referrals.
   c. help-wanted advertising.
   d. temporary help agencies.

   ANS: D REF: p. 423 OBJ: 19-1 TYPE: A

12. Susan Williams wants to know the various tasks to be performed by a new employee before she looks for applicants. She should first
   a. examine production data for current employees.
   b. prepare a job description.
   c. consult the United States Employment Service.
   d. hire a temporary employee.

   ANS: B REF: p. 424 OBJ: 19-1 TYPE: A

13. Which of the following is a legal basis for selecting employees?
   a. Gender
   b. Age
   c. Education
   d. Disabilities

   ANS: C REF: p. 425 OBJ: 19-2 TYPE: C

14. The owner of a small automobile garage has been advised to use an application form in evaluating applicants. This will be most useful in discovering
   a. arrest records.
   b. general background information.
   c. physical disabilities.
   d. religious orientation.

   ANS: B REF: p. 426 OBJ: 19-2 TYPE: A

15. During an interview, an employer
   a. can evaluate the appearance, job knowledge, intelligence, and personality of the applicant.
   b. can judge an applicant without any further research.
   c. should do most of the talking.
   d. should find out whether a young woman plans to stay home with her children when they are born.

   ANS: A REF: p. 426 OBJ: 19-2 TYPE: C

16. Which of the following is *not* a recommended way to evaluate applicants for a position?
    a. Have them fill out an application form
    b. Conduct an interview
    c. Check references
    d. Hire a private investigator to follow the applicant and observe his or her behavior

    ANS: D REF: p. 425 OBJ: 19-2 TYPE: C

17. Karl Milgram is concerned that many employees who successfully passed their employment test later perform poorly on the job. He believes the employment test lacks
    a. applicability
    b. interpretability.
    c. reliability.
    d. validity.

    ANS: D REF: p. 427 OBJ: 19-2 TYPE: A

18. The Americans with Disabilities Act requires employers to make _______ adaptations to facilitate the employment of individuals protected by the act.
    a. specific
    b. minimal
    c. reasonable
    d. verifiable

    ANS: C REF: p. 427 OBJ: 19-2 TYPE: A

19. Karen Garcia is seeking references' comments on applicants for jobs with her business. The former employers and other parties she calls seem reluctant to do more than verify dates of employment. A probable reason for their reluctance is that
    a. records for former employees are filed away and not readily available.
    b. the former employer may plan to recall the employee and wants to avoid losing her to another employer.
    c. respondents may fear litigation by former employees who fail to get jobs they seek.
    d. requests of this kind simply take too much time for large company personnel departments.

    ANS: C REF: p. 426 OBJ: 19-2 TYPE: A

20. The owner of a small sporting goods store wants to avoid hiring drug users. He checks with his attorney and finds that
    a. drug testing before hiring is legal.
    b. drug usage is considered a disability and is not grounds for rejection.
    c. no economical tests are available to check for drug usage.
    d. the Americans with Disabilities Act of 1990 flatly prohibits drug testing for jobs in private businesses.

    ANS: A REF: p. 427 OBJ: 19-2 TYPE: A

21. Orientation applies most specifically to training given
    a. during the employment review.
    b. after selection, but prior to reporting for work.
    c. during the first two or three days on the job.
    d. during the first year of employment.

ANS: C REF: p. 427 OBJ: 19-3 TYPE: C

22. New employees benefit most from orientation when it is given
    a. during the employment review.
    b. after selection, but prior to reporting for work.
    c. during the first two or three days on the job.
    d. during the first year of employment.

ANS: C REF: p. 427 OBJ: 19-3 TYPE: C

23. Explaining company procedures and company policies should be part of
    a. initial or "basic" training.
    b. supervisory training.
    c. orientation.
    d. job instruction training.

ANS: C REF: p. 427 OBJ: 19-3 TYPE: D

24. Helen Garbo, owner of a travel agency, is concerned about the length of time needed for employees to get adjusted to the business and to become sure of their own roles in the business. She should first evaluate the firm's
    a. on-the-job training.
    b. management development efforts.
    c. quality training program.
    d. orientation sessions.

ANS: D REF: p. 428 OBJ: 19-3 TYPE: A

25. A systematic step-by-step method for on-the-job training of non-managerial employees is known as
    a. On-the-Job Training.
    b. Employee Development Training.
    c. Job Instruction Training.
    d. Intensive Job Orientation.

ANS: C REF: p. 428 OBJ: 19-3 TYPE: D

26. The owner of an industrial distribution company has attended a seminar on quality management and is determined to improve quality performance. This owner should recognize which of the following about training employees in quality?
    a. Quality training can teach employees about the importance of quality and ways to produce high-quality work.
    b. Direct supervisory one-on-one instruction is the only training procedure that shows consistent results.
    c. Quality training gradually raises quality consciousness but must be pursued for two or three years before significant improvements can be detected.
    d. Quality performance and workmanship are not good topics for training because careful work habits must be developed, if they are ever developed, on a personal basis over many years.

ANS: A REF: p. 428 OBJ: 19-3 TYPE: A

27. Quality management is concerned with all of the following *except*
    a. machines.

b. materials and measurements.
c. human performance.
d. the architectural design of facilities.

ANS: D REF: p. 428 OBJ: 19-3 TYPE: C

28. In establishing a management training program, Mark Russell should be consider all of the following factors *except*
a. The need for training.
b. A plan for training.
c. The timetable for training,
d. The design of the training facilities.

ANS: D REF: p. 428 OBJ: 19-3 TYPE: C

29. Managerial and professional employees in small businesses need training so that
a. individuals are developed to replace the founder in the case of a hostile takeover.
b. they can adequately carry out their assigned responsibilities.
c. outplacement services would be easier to set up.
d. available tax benefits for the company can be realized.

ANS: B REF: p. 428 OBJ: 19-3 TYPE: C

30. A primary consideration in training professional and managerial personnel is
a. counseling employees regarding their need for training.
b. how much the training will cost in terms of fringe benefits.
c. whether employees are too valuable in their present jobs to be changed.
d. whether the union will allow it.

ANS: A REF: p. 428 OBJ: 19-3 TYPE: C

31. Which of the following plays the central role in attracting and motivating employees?
a. Flexible work duties
b. Job sharing arrangements
c. Compensation
d. Vacation benefits

ANS: C REF: p. 430 OBJ: 19-4 TYPE: C

32. A compensation system based on time is most appropriate for jobs in which
a. performance is not easy to measure.
b. responsibilities are difficult to understand.
c. fringe benefits are an important part of the compensation offered.
d. commissions make up a significant portion of compensation received.

ANS: A REF: p. 430 OBJ: 19-4 TYPE: C

33. Kevin Chang believes that the nature of his business operations makes measurement of performance almost impossible. Therefore, he wants to pay employees on the basis of hours worked. The compensation system he should use is a
a. profit-sharing plan.
b. time-based compensation system.
c. commission system.

d. differential piece rate system.

ANS: B REF: p. 430 OBJ: 19-4 TYPE: A

34. Charlie Colson wants to pay employees on the basis of the individual number of units they produce. The compensation system he should use is a
a. profit-sharing plan.
b. standard hourly system.
c. commission system.
d. piece work system.

ANS: D REF: p. 430 OBJ: 19-4 TYPE: A

35. Management and other key personnel "get a piece of the action" through
a. fringe benefits.
b. time-based compensation.
c. profit sharing.
d. tax benefits.

ANS: C REF: p. 431 OBJ: 19-4 TYPE: C

36. Keys to developing effective bonus plans include all of the following EXCEPT
a. Setting attainable goals.
b. Including employees in planning.
c. Keep updating the goals.
d. Discontinuing the bonus plan periodically.

ANS: D REF: p. 431 OBJ: 19-4 TYPE: C

37. Profit-sharing plans
a. provide a more direct incentive in small firms than in large firms.
b. are practically impossible to use successfully in small firms.
c. are similar to individual incentive plans in their motivational effect.
d. are an expensive fringe benefit for small firms, costing 40 percent of payroll.

ANS: A REF: p. 431 OBJ: 19-4 TYPE: C

38. Fringe benefits include
a. hourly wages and overtime pay.
b. commissions and bonuses.
c. health insurance.
d. profit-sharing plans.

ANS: C REF: p. 431 OBJ: 19-4 TYPE: C

39. As part of preparing a business plan, Grace Wang wishes to show the cost of fringe benefits as a percentage of payroll costs. She should use the following percentage:
a. 40 percent.
b. 25 percent.
c. 15 percent.
d. 5 percent.

ANS: A REF: p. 431 OBJ: 19-4 TYPE: A

40. The cost of fringe benefits ___________ the cost of salary and wage payments.
    a. is less than half of
    b. is double
    c. is equal to
    d. considerably exceeds

ANS: A REF: p. 431 OBJ: 19-4 TYPE: D

41. Small firms give employees a share of ownership in the business through
    a. group incentive plans.
    b. profit plans.
    c. employee stock ownership plans.
    d. action-sharing plans.

ANS: C REF: p. 432 OBJ: 19-4 TYPE: D

42. The owner of a video rental business wishes to allow employees to own part of the business. She can do this by using
    a. a profit plan.
    b. a Keogh plan.
    c. an ESOP (employee stock ownership plan.)
    d. a fully vested pension plan.

ANS: C REF: p. 432 OBJ: 19-4 TYPE: A

43. Companies that lease employees to small businesses
    a. do not charge for their services.
    b. charge from 25 to 50 percent of payroll.
    c. take over personnel paperwork.
    d. lease only highly trained personnel.

ANS: C REF: p. 432 OBJ: 19-5 TYPE: C

44. Leasing employees is a good alternative for small businesses because
    a. leasing companies take care of much of the personnel paperwork.
    b. leasing companies decide who gets promoted.
    c. leasing companies charge the employees, not the small business.
    d. small companies that use leasing companies are exempt from regulations such as the Americans with Disabilities Act.

ANS: A REF: p. 432 OBJ: 19-5 TYPE: C

45. One of the disadvantages of leasing employees is that
    a. the leasing company determines who gets promoted.
    b. some leasing companies have run into financial trouble, leaving the small businesses liable for unpaid claims.
    c. benefits are not as good for the employees, although the firm saves money.
    d. the company receiving the employee loses control of his or her career path.

ANS: B REF: p. 432 OBJ: 19-5 TYPE: C

46. James Sandberg is investigating the advantages of employee leasing. It appears that the greatest benefit will be to free him and his firm from

a. the need for extensive training.
b. fringe benefit costs.
c. concern about disciplinary action.
d. excessive paperwork.

ANS: D REF: p. 432 OBJ: 19-5 TYPE: A

47. A small electrical contractor with nine employees hears that they would like to join a union. This contractor realizes that the firm
    a. must follow the bargaining pattern set by large contractors.
    b. can lawfully refuse to negotiate.
    c. must negotiate if a majority of employees decide to unionize.
    d. must deduct union dues from employees' paychecks.

    ANS: C REF: p. 433 OBJ: 19-5 TYPE: A

48. When employer-employee relationships in a small firm are compared with those in a large firm, it is found that
    a. the relationships are less formal in the large firm.
    b. the large firm concentrates more on production and the small firm is more interested in personnel.
    c. the small firm makes less use of formal personnel policies.
    d. personnel policy changes are implemented more quickly in the large firm than in the small firm.

    ANS: C REF: p. 433 OBJ: 19-5 TYPE: C

49. Which of the following conditions is most likely to encourage the appointment of a human resource manager?
    a. Labor turnover rate is low.
    b. Competition for personnel is low.
    c. Employees are represented by a union.
    d. There are 35 employees in the firm.

    ANS: C REF: p. 434 OBJ: 19-5 TYPE: C

50. The owner of a growing business wonders when to hire a human resource manager. The most likely time would be when
    a. labor turnover rate is low.
    b. total employment exceeds 100.
    c. employees are not unionized.
    d. morale is high.

    ANS: B REF: p. 434 OBJ: 19-5 TYPE: A

ESSAY

1. Explain the strengths of each of the following as a source of employees: (a) walk-ins, (b) schools, (c) public employment offices, (d) private employment agencies, (e) executive search firms, (f) employee referrals, (g) Internet recruiting, (h) help-wanted advertising, and (i) temporary help agencies.

   ANS:

a. Unsolicited applicants are sometimes qualified, and the cost of recruiting them is zero. There is, of course, a selection cost involved in talking with them, but some minimum time must be given as a matter of good public relations.
b. Schools are good sources of "raw material." For the most part, applicants recruited from schools require extensive training or on-the-job experience, but the employer can obtain necessary basic talent from this source.
c. Public employment offices provide applicants without cost to the employer. A frequent limitation, of course, is the type of manpower or quality level that is available through this source.
d. Private employment agencies are a good source of applicants with specific skills, such as accountants, computer operators, or managers. In *some* cases, the firm may not even be charged a fee for the service provided by the agency.
e. Executive search firms are effective for filling key positions in the firm, but the cost of these services is high, rendering this option impractical for small businesses (except those trying to move up to the next level.)
f. Employee referrals produce good-quality applicants if the firm's current employees are well qualified. Current employees typically only recommend personnel who would not embarrass them.
g. Internet recruiting is becoming more popular, owing to the efficiency of this approach in matching qualified applicants with potential employers.
h. Help-wanted advertising permits businesses to go after the type of personnel they need and to stir up interest on the part of qualified applicants who may not be listed with employment agencies.
i. Temporary help agencies can provide workers to small businesses as these firms adjust to fluctuations that are seasonal in nature or those that are due to absences from illness or vacation.

REF: p. 422-423 OBJ: 19-1 TYPE: C

2. What are the weaknesses of interviewing, and how can interviewing be used effectively in selecting employees?

ANS:
One of the major weaknesses of the interviewing process is that unskilled interviewers may think they are infallible judges of human nature. Interviewers must also be careful to avoid questions that conflict with the law.

Interviewing can be made more effective by following guidelines that have been found to facilitate the process:

- Decide on questions to ask before starting the interview.
- Conduct the interview in a quiet atmosphere.
- Give your entire attention to the applicant.
- Put the applicant at ease.
- Never argue.
- Keep the conversation at a level comfortable for the applicant.
- Listen attentively.
- Look for qualities that are important to the job.
- Try to avoid being influenced by the applicant's trivial mannerisms or features.

REF: p. 425 OBJ: 19-2 TYPE: C

3. Explain the nature of orientation programs and why they are needed.

ANS:
Orientation programs consist of training given during the first two or three days of employment. They include instruction not only about job duties but also about company policies, procedures, and benefits. They also acquaint the newcomer with personnel and the physical layout of the office or other facilities.

New employees are very sensitive when they begin a job. Orientation presents a valuable opportunity to help them start off on the right foot. The employer has the employee's attention in an unusual way and can use the orientation to lay the foundation for a long-term commitment or, inadvertently, to create feelings of alienation.

REF: p. 427 OBJ: 19-3 TYPE: C

4. Discuss the use of compensation and incentives in recruiting employees for small businesses.

ANS:
Except in very unusual situations, small firms must be roughly competitive with larger firms in financial remuneration. If the small firm pays substantially less than competitors, it will have difficulty obtaining comparable talent. To some extent, of course, weaknesses in the area of salaries might be offset by strengths in other areas (e.g., commission systems, bonus and profit sharing plans, fringe benefits, and employee stock ownership plans.) However, employers are viewed as attractive to potential applicants only to the degree that they can offer competitive rates.

In the area of nonfinancial incentives, small firms have the potential for superiority. They can offer applicants an escape from bureaucracy and red tape. They may offer applicants the opportunity to perform challenging work, as well as the opportunity to obtain diversified experience quickly. These are meaningful incentives if the firm is strong and growing and knows where it is going.

REF: p. 430 OBJ: 19-4 TYPE: C

5. Point out the advantages to a small business of leasing employees.

ANS:
Although long-term leasing of employees is relatively new, it offers some obvious advantages. By using this system, an employer avoids the red tape and paperwork associated with employment. For a fee of 1 to 5 percent of payroll, a leasing company will write paychecks, pay payroll taxes, and file necessary reports with government agencies. Also, the leasing company has more employees and can sometimes provide better fringe benefits than the small firm can provide.

REF: p. 432 OBJ: 19-5 TYPE: C

6. **You Make the Call—Situation 1**

The following is an account of one employee's introduction to a new job:

It was my first job out of high school. After receiving a physical exam and a pamphlet on benefits, I was told by the manager about the dangers involved in the job. But it was the old-timers who explained what was really expected of me. The company management never told me about the work environment or the unspoken rules. The old-timers let me know where to sleep and which supervisors to avoid. They told me how much work I was supposed to do and which shop steward to see if I had a problem.

Question 1 To what extent should a small firm use "old-timers" to help introduce new employees to the workplace? Is it inevitable that newcomers will look to old-timers to find out how things really work?

Question 2 How would you rate this firm's orientation effort? What are its strengths and weaknesses?

Question 3 Assume that this firm has fewer than 75 employees and no human resource manager. Could it possibly provide more extensive orientation than that described here? How? What low-cost improvements, if any, would you recommend?

ANS:

1. Old-timers will always have some input into the orientation process. Their association with newcomers in the workplace makes it inevitable. If the quality of management is good, the old-timers should reflect loyalty to the employer and exert a positive influence—in contrast to the situation reported here. However, management should not abdicate its own responsibility for providing a sound orientation by assuming that it will occur automatically as new employees interact with others.
2. On the plus side, this firm does have some orientation—a pamphlet and a warning. Unfortunately, this orientation is so minimal that it cannot be considered adequate. It is little wonder that the old-timers taught the newcomer how to avoid work!
3. Small size need not preclude proper orientation. Some manager—perhaps the owner-manager—should spend time going over the company history and the new employee's role. A supervisor should have a checklist of information to cover. And a trustworthy senior employee might be assigned to answer questions and help the newcomer as needed.

REF: p. 427 OBJ: YMTC TYPE: C

7. **You Make the Call—Situation 2**

Technical Products, Inc., distributes 15 percent of its profits quarterly to its eight employees. This money is invested for their benefit in a retirement plan and is fully vested after five years. An employee, therefore, has a claim to the retirement fund even if he or she leaves the company after five years of service. The employees range in age from 25 to 59 and have worked for the company from 3 to 27 years. They seem to have recognized the value of the program. However, younger employees sometimes express a preference for cash over retirement benefits.

Question 1 What are the most important reasons for structuring the profit-sharing plan as a retirement program?

Question 2 What is the probable motivational impact of this compensation system?

Question 3 How will an employee's age affect the appeal of this plan? What other factors are likely to strengthen or lessen its motivational value? Should it be changed in any way?

ANS:

1. This encourages longevity. At a minimum, employees have an incentive to stay for five years. A good retirement program helps provide retirement income for employees, many of whom have difficulty saving a portion of their paychecks.
2. The amount of profit is not stated. The larger the profit, the greater the motivation. Since only eight employees are involved, their own contributions to earning this profit should be clear, and this should provide strong personal motivation. The immediate effect on effort might be greater if the money were paid out immediately. However, the program looks attractive and should motivate employees to stay with this company.

3. Younger people think less about retirement, so the plan will probably have less effect on them. The amount of the profits and the extent to which profits depend on the input of employees will affect the plan's motivational value. The company's periodic communication about the program can also keep it in the minds of employees and affect the way it is perceived. There is no obvious need for change, but employees might be given the option of taking a portion of the profits in cash.

REF: p. 430 OBJ: YMTC TYPE: C

8. **You Make the Call—Situation 3**

Alibek Iskakov recently opened a small cafe, called Oasis, in Kokshetau, a city in Kazakhstan. The cafe, which is quite small, has seating for 20 customers and employs 7 people. Iskakov, the owner, has no experience in the restaurant business but has three years' experience in retailing and managing. He believes this experience will help him make intelligent decisions concerning management of the cafe. Iskakov oversees operations and assists wherever needed.

Zhanna Suleymenova was hired by Iskakov as an accountant and assistant manager. He hired her to be sure someone would always be at the cafe. He expects her to do the accounting and to make suggestions that will help him operate the cafe efficiently. She is the key person in the operation, with sound accounting experience and a little food service experience. The other employees are two cooks, two waitresses (who double as hostesses and bartenders), and a dishwasher.

Thus far, the cafe's operations have not run smoothly.

Source: This case was prepared by Dr. Aigul N. Toxanova and Yuliya L. Tkacheva, Kokshetau Institute of Economics and Management, Kokshetau, Kazakhstan.

Question 1 What is the most obvious weakness in the human resource management of this small cafe?
Question 2 Given that the restaurant has just opened, is it overstaffed or understaffed?

ANS:

1. One obvious weakness is the lack of any substantial restaurant experience on the part of the owner. Even Zhanna Suleymenova, the assistant manager, has only very limited food service experience. As a result, it is not surprising that operations do not yet run smoothly. We do not know about the background and work experience of other personnel, but there is no indication that the operation is benefiting from the business insights of any of these additional employees.
2. We must remember that this is a very small cafe, with space for only 20 customers. For such a small restaurant, the staff seems to be too large. Seemingly, one cook and one waitress should be adequate for such a small clientele. It is unlikely that all seating would be occupied at the same moment.

   It would also seem logical that the owner and assistant manager could perform non-supervisory duties while the restaurant is getting started. In fact, one supervisor/host(ess) should be adequate. (Perhaps they are each working only on a part-time basis.)

REF: p. 434 OBJ: YMTC TYPE: C

9. **You Make the Call—Situation 4**

Frank Wheat's small construction business in Gulf Shores, Alabama is rapidly expanding due to the tremendous amount of storm damage wrought by Hurricane Ivan. Based on his previous experience with reconstruction after Hurricane Frederick, Frank believes there will be a steady amount of contract construction work for several years to come. Gulf Shores was in the middle of a sustained construction boom when the hurricane struck and repairing the damage will only add to an already superheated demand for residential and commercial buildings. Frank's firm is also experiencing high turnover of its skilled tradespeople as other firms compete for scare available labor. It has become increasingly difficult to hire and retain qualified personnel.

Frank has asked you for help in deciding whether or not to hire a full-time human resource manager.

Question 1 What advice would you give Frank about the need for a human resource manager in his firm?

Question 2 What conditions exist that would favor the appointment of human resource manager?

ANS:

1. A firm with only a few employees cannot afford a full-time specialist to deal with personnel problems. Some of the more involved human resource techniques used in large businesses may be far too complicated for small businesses. As a small firm grows in size, however, its personnel problems will increase in both number and complexity. The point at which it becomes logical to hire a human resource manager cannot be specified precisely. In view of the increased overhead cost, the owner-manager of a growing business must decide whether circumstances would make it profitable to employ a personnel specialist. Hiring a part-time human resource manager—a retired personnel manager, for example—is a possible first step in some instances.
2. Conditions such as the following favor the appointment of a human resource manager in a small business:

    • There are a substantial number of employees (100 or more is suggested as a guide).
    • Employees are represented by a union.
    • The labor turnover rate is high.
    • The need for skilled or professional personnel creates problems in recruitment or selection.
    • Supervisors or operative employees require considerable training.
    • Employee morale is unsatisfactory.
    • Competition for personnel is keen.

REF: p. 434 OBJ: YMTC TYPE: C

Correlation Table for Chapter 20—Managing Operations

	Learning Objectives	Question Type	**Definition** Define new term, recall facts	**Concept** Understand or relate concepts	**Application** Apply knowledge, analyze data
1	Explain the key elements of total quality management (TQM) programs.	T/F	2,4,7,9	1,3,5,6,8,10,12	11
		MC	1,8,9,11,15	2,4,13,14	3,5,6,7,12
		ES		1,2	
2	Discuss the nature of the operations process for both products and services.	T/F	15,18,20,21	13,14,16,17,19	
		MC	27,29,30,31,32	17,20,21,22,23, 24,25	16,18,19,26,28, 33,34
		ES		4	3
3	Explain how reengineering and other methods of work improvement can increase productivity and make a firm more competitive.	T/F	26,28,29	22,23,24,25,27	
		MC	35,36,42,43	37,38,41	39,40
		ES		5	
4	Discuss the importance of purchasing and the nature of key purchasing policies.	T/F	32	30,31,33	
		MC		44,45,46,47	
		ES			
5	Describe ways to control inventory and minimize inventory costs.	T/F		34,35	
		MC		48,49,50,51	
		ES			
	You Make the Call	ES		6,7,8,9	

Total Number of Test Questions: 95 (35 True/False; 51 Multiple-Choice; 9 Essay)

Chapter 20—Managing Operations

TRUE/FALSE

1. Quality performance can be a particularly powerful competitive weapon for small businesses.

   ANS: T REF: p. 439 OBJ: TYPE: C

2. The term *quality* may be defined as the manufacture of products that are free of defects.

   ANS: F
   Quality is best defined as the totality of features and characteristics of a product or service that impacts the firm's ability to satisfy stated or implied needs.

   REF: p. 439 OBJ: 20-1 TYPE: D

3. Because some foreign markets are not accustomed to high quality goods and services, small firms in the U.S. are finding that an emphasis on quality is much more important to being competitive in the American market than in overseas markets.

   ANS: F
   International competition is increasingly turning on quality differences, for large and small firms.

   REF: p. 439 OBJ: 20-1 TYPE: C

4. Total quality management refers specifically to management of the process of manufacturing.

   ANS: F
   The focus of total quality management is an all-encompassing, quality-focused management approach to providing products and/or services that satisfy customer requirements.

   REF: p. 440 OBJ: 20-1 TYPE: D

5. In order to achieve market success, a firm merely needs to concentrate on either providing an excellent product/service or devising an insightful marketing strategy.

   ANS: F
   As suggested by the customer-oriented philosophy, a firm must also pursue customer satisfaction if it is to be successful.

   REF: p. 440 OBJ: 20-1 TYPE: C

6. A genuine concern for customer needs and customer satisfaction is a powerful force that energizes the total quality management effort of a small business.

   ANS: T REF: p. 441 OBJ: 20-1 TYPE: C

7. Benchmarking is a quality system that requires each worker to maintain a quality record at his or her workplace.

   ANS: F
   Benchmarking is the process of identifying the best products, services, and practices of other businesses, carefully studying those examples, and using any insights gained to improve one's own operations.

   REF: p. 442 OBJ: 20-1 TYPE: D

8. Though it is not really related to quality, employee performance is an important factor to the small business.

   ANS: F
   In most organizations, employee performance is a critical quality variable.

   REF: p. 442 OBJ: 20-1 TYPE: C

9. A quality circle is a group of inspectors who use statistical quality control methods.

   ANS: F
   Quality circles involve small groups of *employees* who meet periodically to discuss quality problems.

   REF: p. 442 OBJ: 20-1 TYPE: D

10. One hundred percent inspection of products prior to shipment to customers could theoretically eliminate all defective items.

    ANS: T REF: p. 443 OBJ: 20-1 TYPE: C

11. Measuring the weight of boxes of candy during a production process is an example of attribute inspection.

    ANS: F
    This is an example of *variable* inspection.

    REF: p. 443 OBJ: 20-1 TYPE: A

12. Statistical analysis makes it possible to determine tolerance limits that allow for inherent variation due to chance.

    ANS: T REF: p. 443 OBJ: 20-1 TYPE: C

13. Even a service firm has an operations process.

    ANS: T REF: p. 445 OBJ: 20-2 TYPE: C

14. Raw materials represent one input into the operations process.

    ANS: T REF: p. 445 OBJ: 20-2 TYPE: C

15. The operations process is concerned with the conversion of inputs into products or services.

ANS: T REF: p. 445 OBJ: 20-2 TYPE: D

16. Service establishments are exempt from setting quality standards, since their product is intangible and thus cannot be measured.

ANS: F
Quality standards are *more difficult* to set (and product quality more difficult to evaluate) in service operations, but this does not discount the need to undertake these efforts.

REF: p. 446 OBJ: 20-2 TYPE: C

17. Job shops in manufacturing use specialized equipment.

ANS: F
Job shops in manufacturing use *general-purpose* equipment.

REF: p. 447 OBJ: 20-2 TYPE: C

18. Batch manufacturing is another name for repetitive manufacturing.

ANS: F
Batch manufacturing involves more variety (and less volume) than repetitive manufacturing.

REF: p. 447 OBJ: 20-2 TYPE: D

19. Because manufacturing firms are so closely tied to their customers, they are limited in their ability to hold that which they offer over in the form of inventory.

ANS: F
It is *service* firms that are closely tied to their customers, and thus they are limited in their ability to produce services and hold them in inventory for customers.

REF: p. 448 OBJ: 20-2 TYPE: C

20. The maintenance function is intended to correct equipment failures and to prevent breakdowns from occurring.

ANS: T REF: p. 448 OBJ: 20-2 TYPE: D

21. Preventive maintenance is intended to reduce the occurrence of human injury.

ANS: T REF: p. 448 OBJ: 20-2 TYPE: D

22. High productivity and excellence in quality are conflicting goals.

ANS: F
Quality improvements, automation, and other improvements in operations methods are all routes to increased productivity.

REF: p. 449 OBJ: 20-3 TYPE: C

23. Michael Hammer and James Champy are noted for their advocacy of reengineering.

ANS: T REF: p. 449 OBJ: 20-3 TYPE: C

24. Improving productivity for an overall operation involves analysis of machine set up and groups initiatives.

ANS: F
Improving productivity for an overall operation involves the analysis of work flow, equipment, tooling, layout, working conditions, and individual jobs.

REF: p. 450 OBJ: 20-3 TYPE: C

25. The techniques used to measure work in an effort to set valid performance standards include motion study and time study.

ANS: T REF: p. 451 OBJ: 20-3 TYPE: C

26. The work measurement method that determines the fewest motions necessary to complete a job is called *time study*.

ANS: F
This is called *motion study*.

REF: p. 451 OBJ: 20-3 TYPE: D

27. Applying the laws of motion economy can often make work easier and more efficient.

ANS: T REF: p. 451 OBJ: 20-3 TYPE: C

28. The laws of motion economy provide managers with the basic guidelines for increasing efficiencies in the movement of physical goods.

ANS: F
The laws of motion economy are guidelines for increasing the efficiency of human movement and tool design.

REF: p. 451 OBJ: 20-3 TYPE: D

29. Work methods cannot be analyzed for service or merchandising firms as well as for manufacturers.

ANS: F
Work methods can be analyzed for service or merchandising firms as well as for manufacturers.

REF: p. 451 OBJ: 20-3 TYPE: D

30. Purchasing activities are used to obtain materials, merchandise, equipment, and services to meet production and marketing goals.

ANS: T REF: p. 451 OBJ: 20-4 TYPE: C

31. Making components is preferable to buying them from an outside vendor when using idle plant capacity would boost production efficiency, in-house production would protect a secret design, or the firm can reduce the cost of investment by purchasing equipment that will soon be obsolete.

    ANS: F
    The firm should consider *buying* components if doing so would shift the risk of equipment obsolescence to outside vendors.

    REF: p. 452 OBJ: 20-4 TYPE: C

32. A firm engages in outsourcing only when it procures components from outside the home country.

    ANS: F
    Outsourcing occurs when one firm buys products or services from another, even if both firms are from the same country.

    REF: p. 452 OBJ: 20-4 TYPE: D

33. The most significant factors to consider when selecting a supplier are price and quality.

    ANS: T REF: p. 454 OBJ: 20-4 TYPE: C

34. Both purchasing and inventory management share the same objective.

    ANS: T REF: p. 455 OBJ: 20-5 TYPE: C

35. Just-in-time inventory systems note that firms should select suppliers immediately before they need to use the inputs those vendors will provide.

    ANS: F
    Just-in-time inventory systems are used to minimize inventory, which has little to do with the timing of the supplier selection decision.

    REF: p. 457 OBJ: 20-5 TYPE: C

MULTIPLE CHOICE

1. Quality is defined by the American Society for Quality Control as
    a. the characteristics of a product or service that affect its ability to satisfy the needs of customers.
    b. a series of activities designed to create excellence in a product or service.
    c. a special rank designated for manufactured products that have less than one defect per hundred.
    d. any output that meets the specific standards of a society.

    ANS: A REF: p. 439 OBJ: 20-1 TYPE: D

2. One of the essential elements of successful quality management is
    a. customer focus.
    b. a supportive organizational structure.
    c. appropriate expectations.

d. a stable management team.

ANS: A REF: p. 440 OBJ: 20-1 TYPE: C

3. A manager of a small plumbing company is thinking about installing a total quality management (TQM) program. If TQM is installed, the manager should be aware that
   a. costs cannot be allowed to limit quality goals.
   b. quality must become a very important goal of the business.
   c. ISO 9000 will be the controlling criterion.
   d. reengineering is the most direct route to effective TQM.

   ANS: B REF: p. 440 OBJ: 20-1 TYPE: A

4. The ultimate judge of product quality is
   a. the customer.
   b. W. Edwards Deming.
   c. the owner of the business.
   d. the American Society for Quality Control.

   ANS: A REF: p. 440 OBJ: 20-1 TYPE: C

5. After attending a total quality management (TQM) seminar, a small business owner decides that her firm has a good customer focus and adequate tools and techniques. To be assured of a really strong quality program, however, she knows that she must now establish the proper
   a. statistical quality control.
   b. benchmarking.
   c. marketing research.
   d. organizational culture.

   ANS: D REF: p. 442 OBJ: 20-1 TYPE: A

6. A restaurant owner wants to analyze the competition and adopt any competitive practices that create superior quality. To accomplish this, the owner should use
   a. control charts.
   b. attribute inspection.
   c. benchmarking.
   d. ISO 9000.

   ANS: C REF: p. 442 OBJ: 20-1 TYPE: A

7. A transportation director is using ___________ when she analyzes the competition and uses the insights gained to improve quality internally.
   a. control charts.
   b. attribute inspection.
   c. benchmarking.
   d. ISO 9000.

   ANS: C REF: p. 442 OBJ: 20-1 TYPE: A

8. Quality circles consist of
   a. small groups of employees who meet periodically to discuss quality problems.
   b. managers of several companies who meet annually to give prizes for best quality achievement.

c. leaders of labor unions who meet monthly to discuss the employees' work environment.
d. whistle-blowers within the company who wish to voice complaints.

ANS: A REF: p. 442 OBJ: 20-1 TYPE: D

9. Ben is a member of a small group of employees who meet periodically to discuss quality problems. He is a member of a(n) ___________.
a. control group
b. quality achievement forum
c. quality circle
d. focus group

ANS: C REF: p. 442 OBJ: 20-1 TYPE: D

10. An issue in setting inspection standards and procedures is
a. design tolerances.
b. attribute allowances.
c. reduction of momentary disruptions.
d. achieving production closure.

ANS: A REF: p. 443 OBJ: 20-1 TYPE: C

11. An inspection plan that judges products as acceptable or unacceptable, good or bad, is known as
a. a 100 percent inspection plan.
b. an attribute inspection.
c. a variable inspection.
d. an inspection sampling plan.

ANS: B REF: p. 443 OBJ: 20-1 TYPE: D

12. The owner of a small manufacturing plant wants inspectors to check the width and length of a product (within specified tolerances) during the production process. This calls for
a. an attribute inspection.
b. a work sampling inspection.
c. a 100 percent inspection plan.
d. a variable inspection.

ANS: D REF: p. 443 OBJ: 20-1 TYPE: A

13. Quality management is applicable to
a. manufacturing but not service businesses.
b. service but not manufacturing businesses.
c. both service and manufacturing businesses.
d. neither service nor manufacturing businesses.

ANS: C REF: p. 445 OBJ: 20-1 TYPE: C

14. A control chart is used as part of a
a. statistical process control plan.
b. 100 percent inspection plan.
c. traditional inspection plan.
d. reengineering plan.

ANS: A REF: p. 444 OBJ: 20-1 TYPE: C

15. By conforming to ISO 9000, a small manufacturing firm should achieve improvements in
    a. sales to Wal-Mart.
    b. export sales.
    c. product design.
    d. quality of incoming raw materials.

    ANS: B REF: p. 444 OBJ: 20-1 TYPE: A

16. The owner of a hair-styling salon is studying quality management materials that refer to outputs. He should understand that one example of an output in this business is the
    a. process of washing and styling hair.
    b. combs and scissors.
    c. customer's trimmed and styled hair.
    d. labor of an employee in serving a customer.

    ANS: C REF: p. 445 OBJ: 20-2 TYPE: A

17. The operations process is found in
    a. manufacturing but not service businesses.
    b. service but not manufacturing businesses.
    c. neither service nor manufacturing businesses.
    d. both service and manufacturing businesses.

    ANS: D REF: p. 447 OBJ: 20-2 TYPE: C

18. In a printing plant's production process, ink constitutes
    a. an input.
    b. a throughput.
    c. an output.
    d. a process.

    ANS: A REF: p. 445 OBJ: 20-2 TYPE: A

19. In a printing plant's production process, a printed book constitutes
    a. an input.
    b. a throughput.
    c. an output.
    d. a process.

    ANS: C REF: p. 445 OBJ: 20-2 TYPE: A

20. Manufacturing operations are generally characterized by
    a. little customer contact and intangible products.
    b. measurable productivity and intangible products.
    c. measurable productivity and little customer contact.
    d. tangible products and measurable productivity.

    ANS: D REF: p. 447 OBJ: 20-2 TYPE: C

21. Manufacturing and service operations differ in which one of the following ways?
    a. Productivity is harder to measure in manufacturing.
    b. It is harder to build inventory in manufacturing.

c. It is harder to establish quality standards in services.
d. Service operations involve less contact with customers.

ANS: C REF: p. 448 OBJ: 20-2 TYPE: C

22. Job shops are most closely related to
a. short production runs.
b. long production runs.
c. special-purpose equipment.
d. standardized products.

ANS: A REF: p. 447 OBJ: 20-2 TYPE: C

23. Repetitive operations in manufacturing use
a. general-purpose machines.
b. job-order schedules.
c. highly specialized equipment.
d. short production runs.

ANS: C REF: p. 447 OBJ: 20-2 TYPE: C

24. A forklift is an example of a
a. general-purpose machine.
b. operationally-induced machine.
c. highly specialized equipment.
d. short-lived asset.

ANS: A REF: p. 448 OBJ: 20-2 TYPE: C

25. A powerful workstation computer for 3-D graphical product design is an example of a
a. general-purpose machine.
b. operationally-induced machine.
c. highly specialized equipment.
d. short-lived asset.

ANS: C REF: p. 448 OBJ: 20-2 TYPE: C

26. Resource Recovery Systems, a waste-recycling business, stresses maintenance of equipment in order to
a. avoid interruptions in the company's recycling operations.
b. meet OSHA requirements.
c. reduce skyrocketing costs.
d. utilize otherwise idle labor.

ANS: A REF: p. 448 OBJ: 20-2 TYPE: A

27. The plant maintenance function includes
a. repairs, but not inspections.
b. inspections, but not repairs.
c. both repairs and inspections.
d. neither inspections nor repairs.

ANS: C REF: p. 448 OBJ: 20-2 TYPE: D

28. A plant maintenance foreman would likely be responsible for

a. repairs, but not inspections.
b. inspections, but not repairs.
c. both repairs and inspections.
d. neither inspections nor repairs.

ANS: C REF: p. 448 OBJ: 20-2 TYPE: A

29. The corrective plant maintenance function includes
a. inspection of equipment and replacement of worn parts.
b. minor and major repairs following equipment breakdowns.
c. lubrication of equipment.
d. housekeeping.

ANS: B REF: p. 448 OBJ: 20-2 TYPE: D

30. Inspections of equipment is part of
a. production control.
b. supervising and follow-up.
c. scheduling and dispatching.
d. preventive maintenance.

ANS: D REF: p. 448 OBJ: 20-2 TYPE: D

31. Maintenance that includes inspections and other activities needed to prevent machine breakdowns is called
a. corrective maintenance.
b. full-scale maintenance.
c. preventive maintenance.
d. partial maintenance.

ANS: C REF: p. 449 OBJ: 20-2 TYPE: D

32. Maintenance that is intended to restore equipment or a facility to good condition is called
a. corrective maintenance.
b. full-scale maintenance.
c. preventive maintenance.
d. partial maintenance.

ANS: A REF: p. 449 OBJ: 20-2 TYPE: D

33. The owner of a small printing plant wishes to begin a preventive maintenance program. The owner should make plans for
a. contracting with an outside firm for major repair services.
b. hiring millwrights.
c. periodic equipment inspections.
d. installing process control charts.

ANS: C REF: p. 448 OBJ: 20-2 TYPE: A

34. The owner of a small bakery arranged a schedule for periodic inspections of equipment used in the bakery. The owner is establishing a system of
a. reengineering.
b. quality management.

c. preventive maintenance.
d. benchmarking.

ANS: C REF: p. 448 OBJ: 20-2 TYPE: A

35. The efficiency with which inputs are transformed into outputs is a definition of
a. input/output production.
b. in/out transformation.
c. quality production.
d. productivity.

ANS: D REF: p. 449 OBJ: 20-3 TYPE: D

36. Mark is more efficient in transforming his inputs into outputs than Joe. Mark's _________ is higher than Joe's.
a. input/output production
b. in/out transformation
c. quantity of production
d. productivity

ANS: D REF: p. 449 OBJ: 20-3 TYPE: D

37. Productivity improvements
a. are most likely in service operations.
b. may be enhanced by quality improvements.
c. are the result of a firm's doing less with more.
d. are dependent on the standard of living.

ANS: B REF: p. 449 OBJ: 20-3 TYPE: C

38. Michael Hammer and James Champy popularized an approach to management called
a. TQM.
b. reengineering.
c. continuous quality improvement.
d. work sampling.

ANS: B REF: p. 449 OBJ: 20-3 TYPE: C

39. The owner of a diesel engine business is planning on attending a seminar on reengineering. The owner should realize that the seminar will probably feature
a. benchmarking.
b. attribute inspection.
c. ISO 9000.
d. analysis of basic processes.

ANS: D REF: p. 450 OBJ: 20-3 TYPE: A

40. The owner of an automotive service center wishes to improve the business through reengineering. To do so, the owner should concentrate on the
a. basic processes of the business.
b. laws of motion economy.
c. use of time and motion study.
d. application of statistical process control.

ANS: A REF: p. 450 OBJ: 20-3 TYPE: A

41. Jim's primary focus is on reengineering his workplace. His activities will eventually
    a. find the proper time required for each work activity.
    b. establish the standard cost for each work activity.
    c. increase the quality level of products.
    d. create substantial improvements in operations.

ANS: D REF: p. 450 OBJ: 20-3 TYPE: C

42. Work methods can be analyzed for
    a. service firms.
    b. merchandising firms.
    c. manufacturers.
    d. all of these answers.

ANS: D REF: p. 451 OBJ: 20-3 TYPE: D

43. The laws of motion economy are useful to managers in improving
    a. under-used facilities
    b. off-schedule arrivals
    c. repetitive operations.
    d. variations in shipping departures.

ANS: C REF: p. 451 OBJ: 20-3 TYPE: D

44. A firms should decide to make components (as opposed to buying them) when
    a. it is considering adding plant capacity.
    b. this decision would allow the firm to protect a secret design.
    c. transportation costs are not a concern.
    d. the quality demands of the firm's customers are low.

ANS: B REF: p. 452 OBJ: 20-4 TYPE: C

45. A firm should decide to buy components from a supplier (as opposed to making them)
    a. when it has excess plant capacity.
    b. when it will require greater flexibility on the firm's part to accommodate the supplier.
    c. if product quality would be the same (regardless of the firm's decision.)
    d. if the risk of equipment obsolescence can be transferred to the supplier.

ANS: D REF: p. 452 OBJ: 20-4 TYPE: C

46. Activities easily outsourced by small businesses include
    a. payroll administration.
    b. research and development.
    c. quality control.
    d. top-level decision making.

ANS: A REF: p. 452 OBJ: 20-4 TYPE: C

47. Good relationships with suppliers is important, but they are especially important for
    a. large businesses.
    b. small businesses.

c. medium-sized business.
d. labor-intensive businesses.

ANS: B REF: p. 454 OBJ: 20-4 TYPE: C

48. The ABC method of inventory management is founded on the notion that
a. some inputs are more valuable or more critical to the firm's operations than others.
b. inventory costs should be cut to an absolute minimum by reducing inventory on hand.
c. a firm should know its economic order quantity at all times.
d. the cost of placing an order is a fixed cost.

ANS: A REF: p. 456 OBJ: 20-5 TYPE: C

49. A "C" class item in a system that uses the ABC method of inventory management is
a. critical.
b. noncritical.
c. most valuable.
d. least valuable.

ANS: B REF: p. 456 OBJ: 20-5 TYPE: C

50. An "A" class item in the ABC method of inventory management is a ______ item.
a. critical
b. noncritical
c. most valuable
d. least valuable

ANS: A REF: p. 456 OBJ: 20-5 TYPE: C

51. Adoption of the just-in-time inventory system requires
a. the elimination of raw materials wherever possible.
b. an emphasis on work in progress.
c. a reduction in the firm's finished goods.
d. close cooperation with suppliers.

ANS: D REF: p. 457 OBJ: 20-5 TYPE: C

ESSAY

1. Define total quality management and describe its importance to small firms.

ANS:
Total quality management is an all-encompassing, quality-focused approach to managing manufacturing and service operations. It is concerned with making measurable improvements to all the features or characteristics of a product so as to satisfy the needs of customers. Its goal is zero defects and complete customer satisfaction. Quality may be achieved through properly designing the product and process, using the best raw materials, and excellent performance on the part of the employees.

Small businesses must strive for quality in order to compete. TQM gives managers quantifiable methods to use and goals to reach in their quest for excellence. Emphasizing high quality and customer service while the company is small will make it easier to create the appropriate organizational culture.

REF: p. 440 OBJ: 20-1 TYPE: C

2. Explain the nature and role of quality circles.

ANS:
A Japanese innovation, quality circles are now used by many U.S. companies. Large companies have popularized them, but they are also fully applicable to small businesses. A quality circle consists of a small group of employees who meet periodically on company time to talk about quality. They analyze factors that affect quality and devise ways to improve it. Basically, quality circles constitute a worker participation plan centered on quality. Such circles need to be carefully structured to emphasize quality issues and productivity. When operated under favorable conditions (e.g., workers are trained to facilitate their participation and management provides consistent support), quality circles have the potential for making outstanding contributions to improved quality.

REF: p. 442 OBJ: 20-1 TYPE: C

3. Explain and illustrate the nature of the operations process for production of both products and services. Include references to both inputs and outputs.

ANS:
The operations process consists of the activities involved in carrying out the mission of the business, whether it be baking bread, selling real estate, cleaning clothes, or providing accounting services.

Examples may vary. For a printing plant, inputs include paper, ink, and labor. The operations, or conversion, process is the actual printing, and the outputs are the printed materials. For a car-wash business, inputs include water, detergent, and labor. The conversion process consists of the washing, and the outputs are clean cars.

REF: p. 445-447 OBJ: 20-2 TYPE: A

4. What are the major differences between manufacturing and service operations?

ANS:
Answers should include the following four items:

- Generally, productivity is more easily measured in manufacturing operations than in service operations because the former create tangible products and service operations are usually intangible.
- Quality standards are more difficult to establish and product quality is more difficult to evaluate in service operations.
- Persons who provide services generally have contact with customers, whereas persons who perform manufacturing operations seldom see the customer of the product.
- Manufacturing operations can accumulate or decrease inventory of finished goods, but a service operation typically can offer the service only when the customer is present (e.g., no service inventory).

REF: p. 445-447 OBJ: 20-2 TYPE: C

5. Explain the purpose, nature, and distinctive features of reengineering.

ANS:

Reengineering is a method designed to improve the way a business operates. Popularized by Michael Hammer and James Champy, it is distinctive in its concentration on the basic processes and purposes of a firm. It takes a cautious view of existing structures and methods, realizing that they may have become obsolete. It attempts to avoid the fine-tuning of inherently outmoded methods and processes. Proponents of reengineering expect dramatic, radical changes that improve delivery of quality products and services to customers.

REF: p. 449 OBJ: 20-3 TYPE: C

6. **You Make the Call—Situation 1**
The owner of two pizza restaurants in a city with a population of 150,000 is studying her firm's operations to be sure the firm is functioning as efficiently as possible. About 70 percent of the firm's sales represent dine-in business, and 30 percent come from deliveries. The owner has always attempted to produce a good-quality product and minimize the waiting time of customers both on- and off premises.
A recent magazine article suggested that quality is now generally abundant and that quality differences in businesses are narrowing. The writer advocated placing emphasis on saving time for customers rather than producing a high-quality product. The owner is contemplating the implications of this article for the pizza business. Realizing that her attention should be focused, she wonders whether to concentrate primary managerial emphasis on delivery time.

Question 1 Is the writer of the article correct in believing that quality levels now are generally higher and that quality differences among businesses are minimal?
Question 2 What are the benefits and drawbacks of placing the firm's primary emphasis on minimizing customer waiting time?
Question 3 If you were advising the owner, what would you recommend?

ANS:
3. As a sweeping generalization, this may well be true. In the last two or three decades, attention to quality has increased dramatically, and this has truly yielded significant results. However, the owner needs to realize that there may be vast differences from industry to industry. Also, the quality of pizza available in local markets varies widely as local pizza enthusiasts can testify. Therefore, the writer is probably right, in general, but might be wrong in this situation.

2. Benefits would include:
(a) Directing attention to an issue of real importance to most customers
(b) Possibly gaining an advantage over competitors on this feature
(c) Finding weaknesses in present delivery systems

Drawbacks would include:
(a) Overlooking quali'y problems that may exist
(b) Possibly creating quality problems by focusing on speed
(c) Giving insufficient thought to still other aspects of operations that may need improvement (that is, by trying to solve the wrong problem)

3. This question allows for individual answers that should be supported by sound reasoning. Ideally, there should be clear recognition of the great importance of quality, the present level of quality, how the owner can discern this level (e.g., through comparisons with competitors), and how this level might be measured. Getting a bad pizza fast is not a good outcome! Also, it is desirable to give some thought to the competition that typically exists between quality and speed and consider ways to minimize that conflict. We should note that speed is measured more easily than is quality.

REF: p. 440 OBJ: YMTC TYPE: C

7. **You Make the Call—Situation 2**
Derek Dilworth, owner of a small manufacturing firm, is trying to rectify the firm's thin working capital situation by carefully managing payments to major suppliers. These suppliers extend credit for 30 days, and customers are expected to pay within that time period. However, the suppliers do not automatically refuse subsequent orders when a payment is a few days late. Dilworth's strategy is to delay payment of most invoices for 10 to 15 days beyond the due date. Although he is not meeting the "letter of the law," he believes that the suppliers will go along with him rather than lose future sales. This practice enables Dilworth's firm to operate with sufficient inventory, avoid costly interruptions in production, and reduce the likelihood of an overdraft at the bank.

Question 1 What are the ethical implications of Dilworth's payment practices?
Question 2 What impact, if any, might these practices have on the firm's supplier relationships? How serious would this impact be?

ANS:
1. In failing to live up to stated credit terms to which he has agreed, Dilworth is acting unethically. Furthermore, it appears that he is doing so deliberately. In the absence of an understanding with suppliers, he is engaging in compromising behavior.
2. His practices would surely taint the firm's supplier relationships for some time to come (assuming the supplier monitors its credit accounts). He may be able to get away with it this time, but in doing so he is draining the reservoir of trust with the supplier that he may need to tap in the future.

REF: p. 454 OBJ: YMTC TYPE: C

8. **You Make the Call—Situation 3**
The owner of a small food products company was confronted with an inventory control problem involving differences of opinion among his subordinates. His accountant, with the concurrence of his general manager, had decided to "put some teeth" into the inventory control system by deducting inventory shortages from the pay of route drivers who distributed the firm's products to stores in their respective territories. Each driver was considered responsible for the inventory on his or her truck.

When the first "short" paychecks arrived, drivers were angry. Sharing their concern, their immediate supervisor, the regional manager, first went to the general manager and then, getting no satisfaction there, appealed to the owner. The regional manager argued that there was no question about the honesty of the drivers. He said that he personally had created the inventory control system the company was using, and he admitted that the system was complicated and susceptible to clerical mistakes by the driver and by the office. He pointed out that the system had never been studied by the general manager or the accountant, and he maintained that it was ethically wrong to make deductions from the small salaries of honest drivers for simple record-keeping errors.

Question 1 What is wrong, if anything, with the general manager's approach to making sure that drivers do not steal or act carelessly? Is some method of enforcement necessary to ensure careful adherence to the inventory control system?
Question 2 Is it wrong to deduct from drivers' paychecks shortages documented by inventory records?
Question 3 How should the owner resolve this dispute?

ANS:

1. The problem is that the general manager has approved the use of a faulty system (one from which all of the "bugs" have not yet been worked out.) Some control practices may be necessary, but the important lesson to be learned from this situation is that the general manager should be more careful in selecting a control system in the first place.
2. Yes, it would be wrong to deduct shortages from drivers' paychecks, unless the general manager could be certain that the system is workable and reasonably accurate (which does not appear to be the case in this situation.)
3. The only reliable and unquestionably appropriate way to resolve this dispute would be to fix the control system so that the same problem does not arise in the future.

REF: p. 442 OBJ: YMTC TYPE: C

9. **You Make the Call—Situation 4**
A college professor opened a furniture shop in Maine and has watched it grow to $5 million in annual sales volume and 85 employees. The firm produces high-quality chairs, tables, and other items for the contract furniture market. Each piece is sanded and polished, sealed with linseed oil, and finished with paste wax. No stain, color, or varnish is added, and the furniture never needs refinishing.
As the firm has grown larger, it has begun to use the equivalent of mass production. Many of the original craftspeople have moved on and have been replaced by production workers. The founder is seeking to maintain quality through employee participation at all levels. He believes that quality can be maintained indefinitely if the company doesn't get too greedy. He has expressed his philosophy as follows:
We're still not driven by profit but by meaningful relationships [among] employees and between the producer and the user. It's a way of life. We throw out a lot of good stuff. If we had to produce something just to make a buck, I'd go back to teaching school.
Source: Christopher Hyde, "The Evolution of Thomas Moser," *In Business*, Vol. 10, No. 4, pp. 34-37.

Question 1 How has this firm's growth made quality management easier or more difficult?
Question 2 The founder recognizes that people and relationships have a bearing on quality. What can he do to persuade or enable production employees to have the right attitude toward quality?
Question 3 The founder's comments suggest that profits and quality may be incompatible. When does making a profit lead to lower quality? Can or should this firm use financial incentives?

ANS:
1. Quality control becomes more difficult as the firm grows because a larger number of employees must internalize a concern for quality and reflect that concern in their work. The original craftspeople are dropping out as the firm shifts to more of a mass-production kind of production. A typical factory worker—the type apparently being recruited—does not arrive with a craftsperson mentality. New methods of quality control will be necessary—for example, relying more on inspection and less on the worker's personal commitment to high-quality work.
2. The founder must educate production employees concerning quality. This requires training sessions and/or frequent communication that demonstrates the importance of quality work. It also requires a modeling of such qualities by management—for example, refusing to ship or sell a defective product. Quality circles can develop a sense of ownership and participation in the goal of increasing the quality of the product and customer service.

3. A quest for short-run profits sometimes causes firms to sacrifice quality by becoming a little less exacting in production or service quality standards—for example, by shipping products that almost, but not quite, measure up to a high-quality standard. "Making a buck" can lead to lower quality if management loses sight of quality and its crucial importance. Most types of financial incentives emphasize quantity and thus tend to compromise quality. That type of incentive should not be used in this type of production.

REF: p. 443 OBJ: YMTC TYPE: C

Correlation Table for Chapter 21—Managing Risk

	Learning Objectives	Question Type	Definition Define new term, recall facts	Concept Understand or relate concepts	Application Apply knowledge, analyze data
1	Define risk and explain the nature of risk.	T/F	1,2,3,4		
		MC	1,2,3	18	
		ES			
2	Explain how risk management can be used in coping with business risks.	T/F	5	6,7	
		MC	4,10,11	5,6,7,8,9,12,19, 20	
		ES		1,2	
3	Describe the different types of business risk.	T/F	12,17,18	8,9,10,11,13,14, 15,16,19,20,21, 22	
		MC		13,14,15,16,17, 21,22,23,24,25, 26	
		ES		3	
4	Explain the basic principles used in evaluating an insurance program.	T/F		23,24,25,26,27	
		MC		28	
		ES		4	
5	Identify the different types of business insurance coverage.	T/F	28	29,30	
		MC	30,31,32,33,34, 38,39,44,45	27,29,37,40,41, 42,43	35,36
		ES		5	
	You Make the Call	ES		6,7,8,9	

Total Number of Test Questions: 84 (30 True/False; 45 Multiple-Choice; 9 Essay)

Chapter 21—Managing Risk

TRUE/FALSE

1. According to the textbook, risk is a condition in which there will be a known and adverse deviation from a desired outcome that is expected or hoped for.

   ANS: F
   Risk is a condition in which there is a *possibility* of adverse deviation from a desired outcome that is expected or hoped for.

   REF: p. 463 OBJ: 21-1 TYPE: D

2. Applied to a business, risk relates to the possibility of losses associated with the firm's reputation.

   ANS: T REF: p. 463 OBJ: 21-1 TYPE: D

3. Business risks can be classified into two broad categories—asset risk and pure risk.

   ANS: F
   Business risks can be classified into two broad categories—*market* risk and *pure* risk.

   REF: p. 464 OBJ: 21-1 TYPE: D

4. Pure risk refers to a situation where only loss or no loss can occur—there is no potential gain.

   ANS: T REF: p. 464 OBJ: 21-1 TYPE: D

5. Risk management and insurance management are synonymous.

   ANS: F
   Risk management has a much broader meaning, covering both insurable and noninsurable risks and including noninsurance approaches to reducing all types of pure risk.

   REF: p. 464 OBJ: 21-2 TYPE: D

6. Though common in large firms, small businesses cannot afford self-insurance.

   ANS: F
   Self-insurance is not affordable for every small firm, but this form of insurance could be advisable if a firm has a net worth of at least $250,000 and at least 25 employees to be covered.

   REF: p. 465 OBJ: 21-2 TYPE: C

7. Risk management in a small firm is essentially the same as risk management in a large firm.

   ANS: F
   Risk management in a small firm differs from that in a large firm in several ways.

REF: p. 465 OBJ: 21-2 TYPE: C

8. Fortunately for the entrepreneur, many property-oriented risks are insurable.

   ANS: T REF: p. 465 OBJ: 21-3 TYPE: C

9. Flood damage to movable property is insurable.

   ANS: T REF: p. 466 OBJ: 21-3 TYPE: C

10. Nothing can be done to prevent losses from natural disasters.

    ANS: F
    A firm can take preventive measures to reduce the risk of natural disaster—for example, locating the business in an area that is not subject to flooding.

    REF: p. 466 OBJ: 21-3 TYPE: C

11. Because of close management, small business owners are less vulnerable to business swindles than are their large firm counterparts.

    ANS: F
    Small firms are particularly susceptible to business swindles.

    REF: p. 466 OBJ: 21-3 TYPE: C

12. Real property excludes anything physically attached to land, such as buildings.

    ANS: F
    Real property consists of land and anything physically attached to land, such as buildings.

    REF: p. 466 OBJ: 21-3 TYPE: D

13. Personal property includes any property other than real property, including buildings, machinery, equipment, furniture, fixtures, stock, and vehicles.

    ANS: F REF: p. 455 OBJ: 21-3 TYPE: C

14. The three primary types of personnel-oriented risks are dishonesty of current employees, competition from current employees that take on "side jobs," and the loss of key executives.

    ANS: F
    The three primary types of personnel-oriented risks are dishonesty of current employees, competition from *former* employees, and the loss of key executives.

    REF: p. 466 OBJ: 21-3 TYPE: C

15. Most employee-oriented risks are not insurable.

    ANS: F

Most employee-oriented risks *are* insurable.

REF: p. 465 OBJ: 21-3 TYPE: C

16. Small businesses are particularly vulnerable to employee fraud because their control systems are characteristically ineffective.

ANS: T REF: p. 465 OBJ: 21-3 TYPE: C

17. A fidelity bond protects against loss from employee fraud.

ANS: T REF: p. 465 OBJ: 21-2 TYPE: D

18. Self-insurance requires designating part of a firm's earnings as a cushion against possible future losses.

ANS: T REF: p. 465 OBJ: 21-2 TYPE: D

19. Actual cash value (ACV) refers to the purchased value of a property.

ANS: F REF: p. 466 OBJ: 21-3 TYPE: C

20. Death of a key executive can be very detrimental to a small firm because, in addition to valuable experience and skill, the key executive may have specialized knowledge that is vital to the successful operation of the firm.

ANS: T REF: p. 469 OBJ: 21-3 TYPE: C

21. Product liability could be classified as a source of tort liability.

ANS: T REF: p. 469 OBJ: 21-3 TYPE: C

22. A consulting firm that typically does not have clients visit its business location would have minimal premises liability exposure.

ANS: T REF: p. 469 OBJ: 21-3 TYPE: C

23. Studies have shown that almost all small business managers carry sufficient insurance protection.

ANS: F
Many small business managers carry *insufficient* insurance protection.

REF: p. 470 OBJ: 21-4 TYPE: C

24. Because insurance companies must collect enough premiums to pay the actual losses of insured parties, the cost of insurance is inversely proportional to the probability of occurrence of the insured event.

ANS: F
Because insurance companies must collect enough premiums to pay the actual losses of insured parties, the cost of insurance is proportional to the probability of occurrence of the insured event.

REF: p. 471 OBJ: 21-4 TYPE: C

25. Transferring risk to someone else by carrying insurance is always the best way to manage business risks.

ANS: F
Insurance provides one of the most important means for small firms to transfer business risks, but it is not *always* the best way to manage that risk. Moreover, small firms usually pay significantly higher insurance premiums than do their larger counterparts, adding further justification to evaluating all available alternatives before opting for insurance.

REF: p. 470 OBJ: 21-4 TYPE: C

26. Insurance is most applicable and practical for probable losses.

ANS: F
Insurance is most applicable and practical for *improbable* losses.

REF: p. 472 OBJ: 21-4 TYPE: C

27. The ability to pay insurance premiums is all that is needed to obtain insurance.

ANS: F
Before an insurance company would be willing to underwrite possible losses, the risk must meet certain requirements (e.g., be calculable, exist in large numbers, and involve property with commercial value) and the policyholder must have an insurable interest in the property.

REF: p. 470 OBJ: 21-4 TYPE: C

28. Business interruption insurance pays for lost income.

ANS: T REF: p. 473 OBJ: 21-5 TYPE: D

29. A small company can protect itself against the death of important personnel by carrying key person insurance.

ANS: T REF: p. 474 OBJ: 21-5 TYPE: C

30. One risk that small businesses do not normally consider is loss due to the disability of a partner or other key employee of the company.

ANS: T REF: p. 474 OBJ: 21-5 TYPE: C

MULTIPLE CHOICE

1. Risk, as stated in the textbook, is
   a. a chance all entrepreneurs take.
   b. a probability that adverse conditions will result.
   c. a condition in which there is a possibility that an adverse deviation from a desired outcome will occur.
   d. usually avoidable.

ANS: C REF: p. 463 OBJ: 21-1 TYPE: D

2. Pure risk, as stated in the textbook, is
   a. a chance all entrepreneurs take.
   b. a probability that adverse conditions will result.
   c. a condition in which there is a possibility that an adverse deviation from a desired outcome will occur.
   d. the uncertainty associated with a situation where only loss or no loss can occur.

   ANS: D REF· p. 464 OBJ: 21-1 TYPE: D

3. Harold's ownership of a moving van for use in his business represents which form of risk?
   a. Uninsurable risk
   b. Pure risk
   c. Insurable risk
   d. Market risk

   ANS: B REF: p. 464 OBJ: 21-1 TYPE: D

4. Which of the following is *not* encompassed in the broad meaning of risk management?
   a. Uninsurable risks
   b. Impermeable risks
   c. Insurable risks
   d. Noninsurance approaches to reducing all types of pure risks

   ANS: B REF: p. 464 OBJ: 21-2 TYPE: D

5. A risk management program requires all of the following *except*
   a. identification of risks.
   b. evaluation of risks.
   c. controlling risks.
   d. assessment of industry risk standards.

   ANS: D REF: p. 464 OBJ: 21-2 TYPE: C

6. Which of the following is one of the three groups into which risk can be classified?
   a. Substantive
   b. Emerging
   c. Critical
   d. Reportable

   ANS: C REF: p. 464 OBJ: 21-2 TYPE: C

7. Purchasing a fidelity bond on the company treasurer is a form of risk ________.
   a. financing
   b. provisioning
   c. retention
   d. transfer

   ANS: D REF: p. 464 OBJ: 21-2 TYPE: C

8. Driving as safely as possible is an example of
   a. loss prevention.
   b. loss avoidance.

c. loss reduction.
d. loss control

ANS: B REF: p. 0 OBJ: 21-2 TYPE: C

9. One of the most important means of sharing business risks is
   a. preventive maintenance.
   b. insurance.
   c. a system of internal checks or control.
   d. good management.

ANS: B REF: p. 470 OBJ: 21-2 TYPE: C

10. In its general form, a self-insurance program
    a. designates funds for property.
    b. designates funds for workers' compensation.
    c. is a contingency fund for potential losses, regardless of their source.
    d. is administered by an insurance company.

ANS: C REF: p. 465 OBJ: 21-2 TYPE: D

11. Self-insurance means
    a. owning an insurance company.
    b. owning stock in an insurance company.
    c. saving to have money to cover possible future losses.
    d. having coverage on the owner of the business.

ANS: C REF: p. 0465 OBJ: 21-2 TYPE: D

12. Evaluation and review is an important step in the risk management process because
    a. it is difficult to select an effective method to manage risks.
    b. conditions change.
    c. it is nearly impossible to evaluate risk effectively.
    d. entrepreneurs find it challenging to identify the major risks that they face.

ANS: B REF: p. 464-465 OBJ: 21-2 TYPE: C

13. Which of the following is not defined as personal property?
    a. Buildings
    b. Furniture
    c. Fixtures
    d. Vehicles

ANS: A REF: p. 466 OBJ: 21-3 TYPE: C

14. Damage to a building by fire is an example of
    a. a benign neglect loss.
    b. a direct loss.
    c. a tort-based liability claim.
    d. a depreciated cash value loss.

ANS: B REF: p. 466 OBJ: 21-3 TYPE: C

15. Traditionally, commercial property insurance has valued all property loss at

a. the depreciated value of the damaged or lost property
b. the undepreciated value of the damaged or lost property
c. the actual cash value of the damaged or lost property.
d. the purchase value of the damaged or lost property.

ANS: C REF: p. 466 OBJ: 21-3 TYPE: C

16. Theft due to a burglary would be classified as a
a. real property loss.
b. personal property loss.
c. consumer loss.
d. direct loss.

ANS: B REF: p. 466 OBJ: 21-3 TYPE: C

17. Damage to a building due to a tornado is a ___________ loss.
a. real property
b. personal property
c. consumer
d. uninsurable

ANS: A REF: p. 466 OBJ: 21-3 TYPE: C

18. Which of the following is *not* one of the tools for managing a high severity, high frequency loss?
a. Loss prevention
b. Loss avoidance
c. Loss reduction
d. Risk retention

ANS: D REF: p. 466 OBJ: 21-1 TYPE: C

19. Which of the following is a tool for managing low severity, low frequency risks?
a. Loss prevention
b. Self-insurance
c. Contractual agreements
d. Risk retention

ANS: D REF: p. 466 OBJ: 21-2 TYPE: C

20. Which of the following is a tool for managing high severity, low frequency risks?
a. Loss prevention
b. Risk retention
c. Loss reduction
d. Self-insurance

ANS: D REF: p. 466 OBJ: 21-2 TYPE: C

21. Mistakes that an employee makes made in assembling a product for a customer could be a source of _________.
a. premises liability
b. employee liability
c. product liability
d. personal liability

ANS: C REF: p. 469 OBJ: 21-3 TYPE: C

22. Punitive damages are intended to have a ________ effect, sending a message to society that such conduct will not be tolerated.
    a. chilling
    b. deterrent
    c. provocative
    d. statutory

ANS: B REF: p. 468 OBJ: 21-3 TYPE: C

23. Compensatory damages include ___________ damages .
    a. economic
    b. breach
    c. tort
    d. punitive

ANS: A REF: p. 468 OBJ: 21-3 TYPE: C

24. The negligent act is the ___________ of the loss in a tort liability claim.
    a. circumstantial relationship
    b. obvious injury
    c. proximate cause
    d. assumed basis

ANS: C REF: p. 469 OBJ: 21-3 TYPE: C

25. _____ percent of small businesses do not even purchase business insurance to protect their enterprises.
    a. Five
    b. Fifteen
    c. Twenty-five
    d. Thirty

ANS: B REF: p. 470 OBJ: 21-3 TYPE: C

26. Insurance is most applicable and practical for __________ losses.
    a. all
    b. few
    c. improbable
    d. contingency

ANS: C REF: p. 472 OBJ: 21-3 TYPE: C

27. A business owner's policy is unique in that
    a. it contains no insurance to value feature.
    b. the business owner cannot be the designated beneficiary.
    c. property insured by the policy must have an after-loss residual value.
    d. it cannot exclude named perils.

ANS: A REF: p. 473 OBJ: 21-5 TYPE: C

28. Under a coinsurance provision requiring the building insured for at least 80 percent of its value, the recovery on an insured loss of $100,000 on the building with a replacement value of $500,000 that was insured for only $300,000 would be limited to _______.
    a. $20,000
    b. $30,000
    c. $50,000
    d. $75,000

    ANS: D REF: p. 473 OBJ: 21-4 TYPE: C

29. Most entrepreneurs do not realize the value of which of the following types of insurance?
    a. Fire insurance
    b. Business interruption insurance
    c. Property insurance
    d. Theft insurance

    ANS: B REF: p. 473 OBJ: 21-5 TYPE: C

30. Business interruption insurance covers
    a. lost income.
    b. shoplifting.
    c. debts to suppliers.
    d. defective products.

    ANS: A REF: p. 473 OBJ: 21-5 TYPE: D

31. A unique, attractive feature of a BOP is that both real and personal property are valued on
    a. an appraised cash value basis.
    b. a market-adjusted depreciated value basis.
    c. a replacement-cost basis.
    d. a proximal-to-value basis.

    ANS: C REF: p. 473 OBJ: 21-5 TYPE: D

32. BOP medical payments coverage provides payment for injuries sustained by
    a. employees.
    b. customers.
    c. business owners.
    d. all of these answers.

    ANS: B REF: p. 474 OBJ: 21-5 TYPE: D

33. A coinsurance provision requires that a property be insured for at lease ______ percent of its value.
    a. sixty
    b. seventy
    c. eighty
    d. ninety

    ANS: C REF: p. 473 OBJ: 21-5 TYPE: D

34. Doug's BOP on his fishing guide business excludes property losses due to the wakes of other fishing boats. This is an example of the _______ approach to property insurance.

a. foreseen risk
b. reasonable-person standard
c. named-peril
d. insurance-to-value

ANS: C REF: p. 473 OBJ: 21-5 TYPE: D

35. Assume that the physical property of a business is valued at $50,000. The company's commercial property policy contains a coinsurance clause with a stated percentage of 80 percent. The company insures the property for $30,000 (75 percent of the specified minimum). The company incurs a fire loss of $20,000. How much of the loss will the insurance company pay for?
a. $20,000
b. $15,000
c. $0
d. $10,000

ANS: B REF: p. 473 OBJ: 21-5 TYPE: A

36. John Dresser, who owns a small manufacturing concern, has just signed a commercial property policy with a clause requiring Dresser to maintain insurance equal to 80 percent of the property's value at the time of an actual loss. Dresser has accepted what is known as a __________ clause.
a. coinsurance
b. realty protection
c. realty reserve
d. override protection

ANS: A REF: p. 473 OBJ: 21-5 TYPE: A

37. Which of the following is an insurance coverage that is required by law in most states?
a. Workers' compensation
b. Employee bonding
c. Product liability insurance
d. Loss of key executive coverage

ANS: A REF: p. 467 OBJ: 21-5 TYPE: C

38. A customer's slip and fall injury would be covered by
a. general liability insurance.
b. surety bonds.
c. business interruption insurance.
d. commercial property coverage.

ANS: A REF: p. 474 OBJ: 21-5 TYPE: D

39. The type of insurance that provides protection against a type of customer-oriented risk is
a. general liability insurance.
b. surety bonds.
c. business interruption insurance.
d. commercial property coverage.

ANS: A REF: p. 474 OBJ: 21-5 TYPE: D

40. General liability insurance covers

a. business interruption.
b. injury to customers caused by a firm's product.
c. injury to employees.
d. explosion.

ANS: B REF: p. 474 OBJ: 21-5 TYPE: C

41. Most small business advisors recommend __________ life insurance for key-person policies.
    a. whole
    b. universal
    c. term
    d. blanket coverage

ANS: C REF: p. 474 OBJ: 21-5 TYPE: C

42. Aloft Aircraft Company can purchase __________ life insurance on its chief aircraft designer as an inexpensive way to cover its losses should something untoward happen to that key person.
    a. whole
    b. universal
    c. term
    d. blanket coverage

ANS: C REF: p. 474 OBJ: 21-5 TYPE: C

43. Regarding partners in a small business, statistics reveal that the risk of disability is __________ the risk of death.
    a. greater than
    b. less than
    c. about the same as
    d. correlated with

ANS: A REF: p. 474 OBJ: 21-5 TYPE: C

44. Life insurance purchased by a company with the company as sole beneficiary is
    a. key-person insurance.
    b. a surety bond.
    c. business interruption insurance.
    d. credit insurance.

ANS: A REF: p. 474 OBJ: 21-5 TYPE: D

45. Key-person disability insurance
    a. is common in small firms.
    b. protects the firm from losses due to the death of a key employee.
    c. replaces revenue lost when a key employee is disabled.
    d. is rarely recommended by advisors to small businesses.

ANS: C REF: p. 474 OBJ: 21-5 TYPE: D

ESSAY

1. What are the five steps required to implement risk management and its goal of preserving a firm's assets and earning power?

ANS:
The following steps are involved:
Step 1: Identify risks
Step 2: Evaluate risks
Step 3: Select method to manage risks
Step 4: Implement the decision
Step 5: Evaluate and review

REF: p. 464-465 OBJ: 21-2 TYPE: C

2. List the two basic ways to cope with risk in a small business and identify tools associated with each of these. Which method involves an insurance program?

ANS:
Risk control (tools: risk avoidance, risk reduction)
Risk financing (tools: risk transfer, risk-retention, self-insurance)
Risk financing is the way of coping with risk that involves an insurance program.

REF: p. 464 OBJ: 21-2 TYPE: C

3. List and briefly explain the different types of property.

ANS:
There are two general types of property—real property and personal property. **Real property** consists of land and anything physically attached to land, such as buildings. **Personal property** can simply be defined as any property other than real property. Personal property includes such items as machinery, equipment, furniture, fixtures, stock, and vehicles. While the location of real property is static, personal property can be moved from place to place.

REF: p. 466 OBJ: 21-3 TYPE: C

4. List the basic principles in evaluating an insurance program.

ANS:
Basic principles in evaluating an insurance program include:

1. *Identifying business risks to be insured*: Although the most common insurable risks were pointed out earlier, other less obvious risks may be revealed only by careful investigation.
2. *Limiting coverage to major potential losses:* A small firm must determine the magnitude of loss that it could bear without serious financial difficulty.
3. *Relating premium costs to probability of loss:* Because insurance companies must collect enough premiums to pay the actual losses of insured parties, the cost of insurance is proportional to the probability of occurrence of the insured event.

REF: p. 471 OBJ: 21-4 TYPE: C

5. Explain the concept of coinsurance, as found in some commercial property policies.

ANS:

Under a coinsurance clause, the insured agrees to maintain insurance equal to some specified percentage of the value of the property at the time of actual loss. In return, the insured is given a reduced rate. If the insured fails to maintain this percentage, only part of a loss will be reimbursed.

REF: p. 473 OBJ: 21-5 TYPE: C

6. **You Make the Call—Situation 1**

The Amigo Company manufactures motorized wheelchairs in its Bridgeport, Michigan, plant, under the supervision of Alden Thieme. Alden is the brother of the firm's founder, Allen Thieme. The company has 100 employees and does $10 million in sales a year. Like many other firms, Amigo is faced with increased liability insurance costs. Although Alden is contemplating dropping all coverage, he realizes that the users of the firm's product are individuals who have already suffered physical and emotional pain. Therefore, if an accident occurred and resulted in a liability suit, a jury might be strongly tempted to favor the plaintiff. In fact, the company is currently facing litigation. A woman in an Amigo wheelchair was killed by a car on the street. Because the driver of the car had no insurance, Amigo was sued.

Question 1 Do you agree that the type of customer to whom the Amigo Company sells should influence its decision regarding insurance?

Question 2 In what way, if any, should the outcome of the current litigation affect Amigo's decision about renewing its insurance coverage?

Question 3 What options does Amigo have if it drops all insurance coverage? What is your recommendation?

ANS:

1. Yes. Alden Thieme is simply assessing the amount of risk and is certainly correct in his assumption that juries are influenced by such considerations.
2. The Amigo Company should be prepared to seek additional insurance coverage if it loses the current suit, because this may be a sign of future litigation results. Premiums may be higher for this coverage, or insurance could even be denied. If Amigo wins the suit, it should not let its joy cloud its risk-management decisions and suddenly drop its current coverage. Some form of self-insurance might be coupled with its current insurance coverage.
3. Amigo, just like any other business, has the option of "going bare." This is a very risky option for managing a small firm's liability risks. It is not recommended for Amigo unless the company simply cannot afford coverage or has unusually large cash reserves—which is unlikely.

REF: p. 476-477 OBJ: YMTC TYPE: C

7. **You Make the Call—Situation 2**

Pansy Ellen Essman is a 42-year-old grandmother who is chairperson of a company that does $5 million in sales each year. Her company, Pansy Ellen Products, Inc., based in Atlanta, Georgia, grew out of a product idea that Essman had as she was bathing her squealing, squirming granddaughter in the bathroom tub. Her idea was to produce a sponge pillow that would cradle a child in the tub, thus freeing the caretaker's hands to clean the baby. From this initial product, the company expanded its product line to include nursery lamps, baby food organizers, strollers, and hook-on baby seats. Essman has seemingly managed her product mix risk well. However, she is concerned that other sources of business risk may have been ignored or slighted.

Question 1 What types of business risk do you think Essman might have overlooked? Be specific.

Question 2 Would a risk-retention insurance program be a good possibility for this company? Why or why not?

Question 3 What kinds of insurance coverage should this type of company carry?

ANS:

1. Essman may be overlooking product liability risks. Recent product liability decisions favoring the injured parties have broadened the scope of this form of risk. Essman has definitely targeted a high-risk market! She may also be overlooking several property-centered risks such as fire and burglary. Since Essman is a key executive, she should evaluate the merits of key-person insurance.
2. Essman should investigate the merits of a risk-retention group. The decisive factor will be whether or not several other businesses with common risks can be assembled.
3. Each of the different types of insurance discussed in the chapter is a possibility. Essman's personal and business situations will ultimately dictate which coverage she should obtain.

REF: p. 477 OBJ: YMTC TYPE: C

8. **You Make the Call—Situation 3**
H. Abbe International, owned by Herb Abbe, is a travel agency and freight forwarder located in downtown Minneapolis. When the building that housed the firm's offices suffered damage as a result of arson, the firm was forced to relocate its 2 computers and 11 employees. Moving into the offices of a client, Abbe worked from this temporary location for a month before returning to his regular offices. The disruption cost him about $70,000 in lost business and moving expenses. In addition, he had to lay off four employees.

Question 1 What are the major types of risk faced by a firm such as H. Abbe International? What kind of insurance will cover these risks?

Question 2 What kind of insurance would have helped Abbe cope with the loss resulting from arson? In purchasing this kind of insurance, what questions must be answered about the amount and terms?

Question 3 Would you have recommended that Abbe purchase insurance that would have covered the losses in this case?

ANS:

1. H. Abbe primarily faces property-centered risk involving offices and equipment. To a lesser extent, it is exposed to personnel-centered risk resulting from employee dishonesty, possible competition from a former employee, and losses that could occur in the event of Abbe's death. Types of insurance that should be considered include commercial property insurance, dishonesty insurance, key-person insurance, and business-interruption insurance.
2. Business interruption insurance would have helped Abbe, as Abbe's loss resulting from arson was mainly a business interruption cost. In order to buy a suitable level of coverage and avoid unnecessary coverage charges, Abbe would have to determine how much coverage would be adequate, as well as the magnitude of the loss that it could bear without serious financial difficulty.
3. Abbe should only insure against major potential losses. The goal is to insure against what the firm cannot handle financially. Thus, we would have to compare the potential loss against the cost of the coverage to make a decision. However, based on the limited information available, it would appear that business-interruption insurance would have been good.

REF: p. 477 OBJ: YMTC TYPE: C

9. **You Make the Call—Situation 4**

Lonnie Lehrer, CEO of Leros Point to Point, a New York City limousine service, thought he was prepared for anything. Then the first plane hit the World Trade Center on September 11, 2001, and all Lehrer's plans went down with it. "Ninety percent of our business is tied to the airports," says Lehrer, "We went from being a $7 million company to a $700,000 company overnight." Business slowly returned and is now better than ever. Leros recently acquired two smaller companies and expanded operations, bringing annual revenues to nearly $9 million in 2002.

Source: Daniel Tynan, "In Case of Emergency," *Entrepreneur*, April 2003, pp. 59–60.

Question 1 What kind of insurance would have helped Lehrer cope with the loss resulting from 9/11? What must considered when determining the amount and terms of coverage when purchasing this type of insurance?

Question 2 What major type of liability is faced by a firm such as Leros Point to Point? What kind of insurance will cover these risks?

Question 3 Would you have recommended that Lehrer purchase insurance that would have covered the losses in this case?

ANS:

1. Business interruption insurance would have helped Lehrer, as Lehrer's loss resulting from the 9/11 incident was mainly a business interruption cost. To obtain a suitable level of coverage and to avoid unnecessary premium charges, Lehrer would have to determine how much coverage would be adequate, as well as the amount of the financial losses that his firm could sustain without serious financial difficulty.
2. Lonnie Lehrer primarily faces vehicular liability risk involving his limousine fleet. Other risks could arise from the result of employee dishonesty, competition from a former employee, and losses associated with Leher's death. Commercial property insurance, dishonesty insurance, key-person insurance, and business-interruption insurance can provide coverage for these risks.
3. Lehrer should only insure against major potential losses. The goal is to insure against what the firm cannot handle financially (catastrophic losses). His decision on the amount of insurance to purchase would have to balance the potential loss against the cost of the coverage. Business-interruption insurance would likely have been the best result in this case.

REF: p. 0 OBJ: YMTC TYPE: C

Correlation Table for Chapter 22—Managing Assets

	Learning Objectives	Question Type	Definition Define new term, recall facts	Concept Understand or relate concepts	Application Apply knowledge, analyze data
1	Describe the working-capital cycle of a small business.	T/F	5	1,2,3,4,6	
		MC	1	2,3,4,5	
		ES		1	
2	Identify the important issues in managing a firm's cash flows, including the preparation of a cash budget.	T/F	9	7,8,10,11,12,13	
		MC	8,9	6,7,10,11	
		ES		2,3	
3	Explain the key issues in managing accounts receivable, inventory, and accounts payable.	T/F	17	14,15,16,18,19	
		MC	16,17,	12,13,14,15,18, 21	19,20
		ES		4	5
4	Discuss the techniques commonly used in making capital budgeting decisions.	T/F	25,34,38	20,21,22,23,24 26,27,28,29,30, 31,32,33,35,36, 37,39,40,42,43,	
		MC	32,40,42,43,44	22,23,24,25,26, 27,28,29,30,31, 33,34,35,36,37, 38,39,41	
		ES		6,7	8
5	Describe the capital budgeting practices of small firms.	T/F		44,45	
		MC		45,46	
		ES		9,10	
	You Make the Call	ES		11,12,13,14	

Total Number of Test Questions: 91 (45 True/False; 46 Multiple-Choice; 13 Essay)

Chapter 22—Managing Assets

TRUE/FALSE

1. Working-capital management focuses on the attractiveness of long-run investment opportunities.

   ANS: F
   Working-capital management refers to managing short-term assets and short-term sources of financing.

   REF: p. 481 OBJ: 22-1 TYPE: C

2. Net working capital includes cash and accounts receivable, among other things.

   ANS: T REF: p. 481 OBJ: 22-1 TYPE: C

3. A firm's working-capital cycle refers to the flow of cash to purchase and sell fixed assets.

   ANS: F
   A firm's working-capital cycle refers to the flow of resources through net working capital accounts as part of the firm's day-to-day operations.

   REF: p. 481 OBJ: 22-1 TYPE: C

4. The date on which accounts receivable are collected affects the working-capital cycle.

   ANS: T REF: p. 482 OBJ: 22-1 TYPE: C

5. The cash conversion period is the time period between ordering inventory and receiving cash for its sale.

   ANS: F
   The cash conversion period represents the number of days required to complete the working-capital cycle.

   REF: p. 483 OBJ: 22-1 TYPE: D

6. During the cash conversion period, the firm no longer has the benefit of the financing provided by the supplier.

   ANS: T REF: p. 483 OBJ: 22-1 TYPE: C

7. In a healthy business, cash flow is typically even.

   ANS: F
   In a healthy business, cash flow is typically *uneven.*

   REF: p. 487 OBJ: 22-2 TYPE: C

8. Net cash flow should be equated with net profit.

   ANS: F

Net cash flow is the difference between cash inflows and outflows, whereas net profit is the difference between revenue and expenses; failing to understand this distinction can play havoc with the firm's financial health.

REF: p. 487 OBJ: 22-2 TYPE: C

9. Net profit is the difference between cash inflows and outflows.

ANS: F
Net profit is the difference between revenue and expenses.

REF: p. 487 OBJ: 22-2 TYPE: D

10. Revenue and cash receipts are always recorded at the time a sale is made.

ANS: F
Revenue is recorded at the time a sale is made, but cash receipts are recorded when money actually flows into the firm.

REF: p. 487 OBJ: 22-2 TYPE: C

11. Some cash receipts are not, and never become, revenue.

ANS: T REF: p. 487 OBJ: 22-2 TYPE: C

12. A cash budget is concerned only with transactions that directly affect cash.

ANS: T REF: p. 487 OBJ: 22-2 TYPE: C

13. Cash budgets are concerned with dollars as they are received and paid out.

ANS: T REF: p. 487 OBJ: 22-2 TYPE: C

14. Accounts receivable are sometimes called *near cash* because they can be converted to cash whenever a business needs to do so.

ANS: F
Accounts receivable are sometimes called *near cash* because they typically are collected and become cash within 30 to 60 days following a sale.

REF: p. 490 OBJ: 22-3 TYPE: C

15. Aging accounts receivable can indicate troublesome accounts.

ANS: T REF: p. 491 OBJ: 22-3 TYPE: C

16. The disadvantage of accounts receivable financing is its negative impact on cash flow.

ANS: F
The disadvantage of accounts receivable financing is its *high cost*.

REF: p. 492 OBJ: 22-3 TYPE: C

17. In a practice known as pledging, a business sells its accounts receivable to a finance company, and the finance company assumes any bad-debt risk.

ANS: F
It is with a practice known as *factoring* that a business sells its accounts receivable to a finance company, and the finance company assumes any bad-debt risk.

REF: p. 492 OBJ: 22-3 TYPE: D

18. Pledging accounts receivable may limit a firm's ability to borrow from a bank because this practice removes a prime asset from the firm's available collateral.

ANS: T REF: p. 493 OBJ: 22-3 TYPE: C

19. Improperly managed stockpiling is harmful to cash flow and should be minimized if possible.

ANS: T REF: p. 493 OBJ: 22-3 TYPE: C

20. Capital budgeting primarily involves short-term decisions on the part of management.

ANS: F
Capital budgeting primarily involves *long-term* decisions on the part of management.

REF: p. 495 OBJ: 22-4 TYPE: C

21. Although the owner of a small business does not make long-term investment decisions often, capital budgeting is nonetheless important to the successful operation of the firm.

ANS: T REF: p. 495 OBJ: 22-4 TYPE: C

22. The payback period technique shows the number of years it will take to recover the cash outlay of an investment.

ANS: T REF: p. 497 OBJ: 22-4 TYPE: C

23. The accounting return on investment technique reveals how many dollars in average profits are generated per dollar of investment.

ANS: T REF: p. 496 OBJ: 22-4 TYPE: C

24. Use of the accounting return on investment technique answers the question, "How long will it take to recover the original investment outlay?"

ANS: F
It is the *payback period* technique that answers the question, "How long will it take to recover the original investment outlay?"

REF: p. 496 OBJ: 22-4 TYPE: C

25. Accounting return on investment equals the average annual after-tax profits per year divided by the average book value of the investment.

ANS: T REF: p. 496 OBJ: 22-4 TYPE: D

26. The payback period technique measures how long it will take to recover the initial cash outlay of an investment.

ANS: T REF: p. 497 OBJ: 22-4 TYPE: C

27. The discounted cash flow technique measures the present value of future benefits from an investment as compared to the investment outlay.

ANS: T REF: p. 497 OBJ: 22-4 TYPE: C

28. A disadvantage of the accounting return on investment technique is that it ignores the time value of money.

ANS: T REF: p. 497 OBJ: 22-4 TYPE: C

29. A strength of the accounting return on investment technique is that it is based on accounting profits rather than cash flows received.

ANS: F
It is a *shortcoming* of the accounting return on investment technique that it is based on accounting profits rather than cash flows received.

REF: p. 496 OBJ: 22-4 TYPE: C

30. The payback period technique does not consider the time value of money.

ANS: T REF: p. 497 OBJ: 22-4 TYPE: C

31. Discounted cash flow techniques consider the time value of money.

ANS: T REF: p. 497 OBJ: 22-4 TYPE: C

32. In using the net present value method, one does not consider the time value of money.

ANS: F
The net present value method takes into account the time value of money.

REF: p. 497 OBJ: 22-4 TYPE: C

33. The net present value method discounts future after-tax profits back to the present day.

ANS: F
The net present value method discounts *expected future cash flows* back to the present day.

REF: p. 498 OBJ: 22-4 TYPE: C

34. The internal rate of return method estimates the rate of return that can be expected from a contemplated investment.

ANS: T REF: p. 498 OBJ: 22-4 TYPE: D

35. The net present value method takes the time value of money into account in evaluating an investment.

ANS: T REF: p. 497 OBJ: 22-4 TYPE: C

36. A project with a positive net present value is acceptable for investment.

ANS: T REF: p. 498 OBJ: 22-4 TYPE: C

37. If the internal rate of return is less than the firm's cost of capital, the project should be accepted because capital for the project can be obtained more cheaply than usual.

ANS: F
The internal rate of return of an investment must exceed the firm's cost of capital if it is to satisfy the firm's investors.

REF: p. 498 OBJ: 22-4 TYPE: C

38. A firm's cost of capital is simply the interest rate it must pay on its loans.

ANS: F
A firm's cost of capital is the rate of return that a firm must earn on its investments in order to satisfy its debt holders and its owners.

REF: p. 498 OBJ: 22-4 TYPE: D

39. The firm will have difficulty attracting investors if investments in the firm have internal rates of return below an investor's required rate of return.

ANS: T REF: p. 498 OBJ: 22-4 TYPE: C

40. The payback period technique deals with accounting profits in measuring how long it will take to recover the initial cash outlay of an investment.

ANS: F REF: p. 497 OBJ: 22-4 TYPE: C

41. Calculations of net present value ignore the time value of money.

ANS: F REF: p. 497 OBJ: 22-4 TYPE: C

42. Accounting profits are not identical to actual cash flows.

ANS: T REF: p. 497 OBJ: 22-4 TYPE: C

43. The payback period technique measures how long it will take to recover the initial cash outlay and the total amount of interest unearned over the payback period as an opportunity cost.

ANS: F REF: p. 497 OBJ: 22-4 TYPE: C

44. Liquidity has very little significance to small firms.

ANS: F
The undercapitalization and liquidity problems of a small firm can directly affect the decision-making process, and survival often becomes the top priority.

REF: p. 498 OBJ: 22-5 TYPE: C

45. The limited use of discounted cash flow tools by a small firm probably has more to do with the nature of the small firm itself than it does with the owners' willingness to learn.

ANS: T REF: p. 498 OBJ: 22-5 TYPE: C

MULTIPLE CHOICE

1. The cash conversion period is the time between
   a. placement of an order and cash payment for it.
   b. receipt of inventory and cash payment for it.
   c. cash payment for inventory and collection of accounts receivable.
   d. sale of inventory and cash collection of accounts receivable.

   ANS: C REF: p. 483 OBJ: 22-1 TYPE: D

2. Which of the following is *not* a part of managing working capital?
   a. Capital budgeting
   b. Cash flows
   c. Accounts receivable analysis
   d. Accounts payable analysis

   ANS: A REF: p. 481 OBJ: 22-1 TYPE: C

3. Which of the following is *not* directly involved in a firm's management of its working capital?
   a. Inventory
   b. Fixed assets
   c. Accounts receivable
   d. Accounts payable

   ANS: B REF: p. 483 OBJ: 22-1 TYPE: C

4. Which of the following is *not* an asset used to calculate net operating working capital?
   a. Accruals
   b. Accounts receivable
   c. Cash
   d. Inventories

   ANS: A REF: p. 481 OBJ: 22-1 TYPE: C

5. Management of working capital focuses attention on
   a. cash, accounts receivable, inventory, and accounts payable.
   b. cash, accounts receivable, and fixed assets.

c. cash, fixed assets, and inventory.
d. accounts receivable, accounts payable, and long-term investments.

ANS: A REF: p. 481 OBJ: 22-1 TYPE: C

6. Cash deposits during a month less checks written during the same period equal
   a. net cash flow.
   b. net profit.
   c. operating profit.
   d. net working capital.

   ANS: A REF: p. 487 OBJ: 22-2 TYPE: C

7. Net cash flow and net profit are
   a. opposites.
   b. different.
   c. identical.
   d. identical after adjustment for depreciation.

   ANS: B REF: p. 487 OBJ: 22-2 TYPE: C

8. Net cash flow
   a. is the difference between cash inflows and outflows.
   b. is the difference between revenues and expenses.
   c. is the same as net profit.
   d. has little impact on a firm's financial well-being.

   ANS: A REF: p. 487 OBJ: 22-2 TYPE: D

9. Cash budgets
   a. treat income and expenses the same way they are treated on an income statement.
   b. treat income and expenses differently from the way they are treated on an income statement.
   c. are relatively unimportant in the life of a small business.
   d. are tools for managing revenue.

   ANS: B REF: p. 487 OBJ: 22-2 TYPE: D

10. On occasions when a small business has idle funds, cash should be
    a. used to pay creditors in advance.
    b. left in the checking account for unforeseen needs.
    c. invested.
    d. paid to investors.

    ANS: C REF: p. 490 OBJ: 22-2 TYPE: C

11. Excess cash should be
    a. invested.
    b. used to purchase assets.
    c. used to pay dividends.
    d. kept on hand.

    ANS: A REF: p. 490 OBJ: 22-2 TYPE: C

12. Which of the following is sometimes called near cash?
    a. Accounts payable
    b. Inventory
    c. Accounts receivable
    d. Pledges

    ANS: C REF: p. 490 OBJ: 22-3 TYPE: C

13. The life cycle of receivables begins with which of the following stages?
    a. A credit sale
    b. The processing of an invoice by a customer
    c. Funds remittance
    d. Collection

    ANS: A REF: p. 491 OBJ: 22-3 TYPE: C

14. Accounts receivable financing might include
    a. pledging receivables and factoring.
    b. loaning money against receivables and aging accounts receivable.
    c. providing cash discounts and charging interest on delinquent accounts.
    d. aging accounts receivable and using the most effective methods for collecting overdue accounts.

    ANS: A REF: p. 492 OBJ: 22-3 TYPE: C

15. Accounts payable __________ cash available for the firm.
    a. increase the amount of
    b. reduce the amount of
    c. have no effect on the
    d. represent all of the

    ANS: A REF: p. 492 OBJ: 22-3 TYPE: C

16. When a business sells its accounts receivable to a finance company, this is called
    a. selling short.
    b. factoring.
    c. mortgaging the future.
    d. pledging receivables.

    ANS: B REF: p. 492 OBJ: 22-3 TYPE: D

17. Wilbur is attempting to raise some quick cash for his business by selling its accounts receivable to a finance company, this is called
    a. selling short.
    b. factoring.
    c. mortgaging the future.
    d. pledging receivables.

    ANS: B REF: p. 492 OBJ: 22-3 TYPE: D

18. Inventory is called an "evil" because it
    a. ties up funds that are not actively productive.
    b. reduces cash when it is sold.

c. is subject to deterioration.
d. is a large asset for many firms.

ANS: A REF: p. 493 OBJ: 22-3 TYPE: C

19. The terms 3/10, net 30 offer
a. a 3 percent discount on purchases paid for within 30 days.
b. a 30 percent discount on purchases paid for within 30 days.
c. a 3 percent discount on purchases paid for within 10 days.
d. a 30 percent discount on purchases paid for within 10 days.

ANS: C REF: p. 494 OBJ: 22-3 TYPE: A

20. Assuming that cash is available, payment for an account payable with terms of 3/10, net 30 should be made on day
a. 3.
b. 10.
c. 13.
d. 30.

ANS: B REF: p. 494 OBJ: 22-3 TYPE: A

21. Failure to take cash discounts from suppliers
a. typically makes little difference to a firm's financial well-being, since a business does not pay a high rate for use of a supplier's money.
b. typically makes a big difference to a firm's financial well-being, since a business pays a high rate for use of a supplier's money.
c. has no effect on cash flow.
d. will result in negative credit reports.

ANS: B REF: p. 495 OBJ: 22-3 TYPE: C

22. Which of the following questions do all types of capital budgeting techniques try to answer?
a. Is the investment too expensive?
b. Do the future benefits from the investment exceed the cost of making the investment?
c. Will the investment's time requirements fit the needs of the company?
d. Will the firm's cash flows be adequate to pay for the investment?

ANS: B REF: p. 495 OBJ: 22-4 TYPE: C

23. Long-term investments are the focus of
a. cash budgeting.
b. investment planning.
c. capital budgeting.
d. corporate planning.

ANS: C REF: p. 495 OBJ: 22-4 TYPE: C

24. The main purpose of capital budgeting is to help managers make decisions about
a. long-term investments.
b. short-term investments.
c. discounts to offer to customers.
d. nonfinancial constraints on expansion.

ANS: A REF: p. 495 OBJ: 22-4 TYPE: C

25. Capital budgeting is important to the owner of a small business because
    a. long-term investment decisions are made on a frequent basis.
    b. short-term investment decisions are made on a frequent basis.
    c. correct investment decisions add value to the firm.
    d. constraints on expansion have little effect on the small firm.

ANS: C REF: p. 495 OBJ: 22-4 TYPE: C

26. The measurement techniques mentioned in the textbook include all of the following *except*
    a. accounting return on investment.
    b. payback period.
    c. discounted cash flow technique.
    d. the current accounts approach.

ANS: D REF: p. 496 OBJ: 22-4 TYPE: C

27. Discounted cash flow techniques answer which of the following questions?
    a. How much average profit is generated per dollar of average investment?
    b. Do the cash returns of the investment exceed the cash outlays?
    c. How long will it take to recover the original investment outlay?
    d. How does the present value of future benefits from the investment compare to the investment outlay?

ANS: D REF: p. 496 OBJ: 22-4 TYPE: C

28. The question "How many dollars in average profits are generated per dollar of average investment?" is answered using
    a. accounting return on investment.
    b. investment outlay valuation.
    c. net present value.
    d. internal rate of return.

ANS: A REF: p. 496 OBJ: 22-4 TYPE: C

29. The question "How long will it take to recover the original investment outlay?" is answered using
    a. accounting ratio analysis.
    b. the payback period.
    c. net present value.
    d. discounted cash flow.

ANS: B REF: p. 496 OBJ: 22-4 TYPE: C

30. The question "How does the present value of future benefits from the investment compare to the initial investment outlay?" is answered using
    a. analysis of long-term investment.
    b. investment outlay valuation.
    c. ratio analysis.
    d. discounted cash flow analysis.

ANS: D REF: p. 496 OBJ: 22-4 TYPE: C

31. Jack should use _________ to answer the question "How does the present value of future benefits from the investment compare to the initial investment outlay?"
   a. the analysis of long-term investment method
   b. the investment outlay reduce valuation method
   c. an extended ratio analysis
   d. a discounted cash flow analysis

   ANS: D REF: p. 496 OBJ: 22-4 TYPE: C

32. Average annual after-tax profits per year divided by the average book value of the investment equals
   a. average investment capability.
   b. average investment outlay.
   c. accounting return on investment.
   d. payback period.

   ANS: C REF: p. 496 OBJ: 22-4 TYPE: D

33. The amount of time it takes to recover the original cost of an investment is computed using
   a. the payback period technique.
   b. the periodic investment recovery technique.
   c. the investment return technique.
   d. the ratio analysis technique.

   ANS: A REF: p. 497 OBJ: 22-4 TYPE: C

34. In practice, a minimum acceptable rate of return on investment is usually based on
   a. industry average.
   b. outside investors' stated requirements.
   c. auditors' stated requirements.
   d. past experience.

   ANS: D REF: p. 497 OBJ: 22-4 TYPE: C

35. Failure to recognize the time value of money is a weakness of
   a. the internal rate of return method.
   b. the accounting return on investment technique.
   c. the net present value method.
   d. discounted cash flow techniques.

   ANS: B REF: p. 496 OBJ: 22-4 TYPE: C

36. The accounting return on investment technique is characterized by the fact that
   a. it is simple to calculate.
   b. it is based on actual cash flows received.
   c. it takes into account the time value of money.
   d. it is a relatively unpopular technique.

   ANS: A REF: p. 496 OBJ: 22-4 TYPE: C

37. The payback period and accounting return on investment techniques
   a. recognize the economic life of a project.
   b. ignore the time value of money.
   c. consider only the return for the first year of the investment.

d. are more difficult to use than the net present value method.

ANS: B REF: p. 497 OBJ: 22-4 TYPE: C

38. Popularity, use of cash flows rather than accounting profits, and failure to consider the time value of money characterize
    a. the payback period technique.
    b. discounted cash flow techniques.
    c. the investment outlay valuation technique.
    d. long-term investment analysis.

ANS: A REF: p. 497 OBJ: 22-4 TYPE: C

39. An understanding of the present value of a future dollar is important when one is using
    a. the payback period method.
    b. discounted cash flow techniques.
    c. the accounting return on investment technique.
    d. the investment outlay valuation technique.

ANS: B REF: p. 497 OBJ: 22-4 TYPE: C

40. Discounted cash flow techniques of analysis include
    a. return on investment and net present value methods.
    b. net present value and investment outlay valuation methods.
    c. accounting ratio analysis and internal rate of return methods.
    d. net present value and internal rate of return methods.

ANS: D REF: p. 497 OBJ: 22-4 TYPE: D

41. If the net present value of a proposed investment is negative,
    a. the cost of the investment is less than the present value of the future cash flows.
    b. the investment earns the required rate of return.
    c. the present value of the future cash flows would be unaffected by the proposed investment.
    d. the firm should not make the investment, since the present value of the future cash flows is less than the cost of the investment.

ANS: D REF: p. 497 OBJ: 22-4 TYPE: C

42. Under the NPV method, the rate of return required to satisfy the firm's investors is
    a. the cost of capital.
    b. its opportunity cost.
    c. the internal rate of return.
    d. the accounting return on investment.

ANS: A REF: p. 498 OBJ: 22-4 TYPE: D

43. Discounted cash flow (DCF) techniques compare the present value of future cash flows with
    a. the present value of capital.
    b. the investment outlay.
    c. project costs adjusted for inflation.
    d. all of these answers.

ANS: B REF: p. 497 OBJ: 22-4 TYPE: D

44. Naomi needs to earn a twelve percent return from investing in her cousin's business. Under the NPV method of discounting cash flows, if the business can earn only a ten percent return, she will not satisfy her
   a. expected cost of capital.
   b. internal rate of return.
   c. opportunity cost.
   d. required rate of return.

   ANS: D REF: p. 498 OBJ: 22-4 TYPE: D

45. In making capital budgeting decisions, small business owners tend to rely to a significant extent on
   a. intuition.
   b. government assessment.
   c. economic analysis.
   d. informed opinion.

   ANS: A REF: p. 498 OBJ: 22-5 TYPE: C

46. A reason that a small firm would not use a discounted cash flow technique in evaluating capital investments would be that
   a. the accounting rate of return is better for a small firm.
   b. liquidity is less of an issue for a small company.
   c. small firms invest more in short-term assets than do large companies.
   d. nonfinancial issues may be more important for a small firm.

   ANS: D REF: p. 499 OBJ: 22-5 TYPE: C

ESSAY

1. Discuss the working-capital cycle of a small business.

   ANS:
   A firm's working-capital cycle refers to the flow of cash, accounts receivable, and inventories as part of a company's day-to-day operations. A working-capital cycle begins with the purchase of inventory, which increases inventory and accounts payable (if the purchase is on credit). When inventory is sold, cash or accounts receivable increase. Payment of the accounts payable decreases accounts payable and cash. Payment of operating expenses and taxes decreases cash. Collection of accounts receivable when due decreases accounts receivable and increases cash. The cycle is then repeated.

   REF: p. 482 OBJ: 22-1 TYPE: C

2. Identify the key dates in the chronological sequence of a hypothetical working-capital cycle. List these in order.

   ANS:
   Day a. Inventory is ordered in anticipation of future sales.
   Day b. Inventory is received.
   Day c. Inventory is sold on credit.
   Day d. Accounts payable come due and are paid.
   Day e. Accounts receivable are collected.

   REF: p. 483 OBJ: 22-2 TYPE: C

3. Differentiate between net cash flow and net profit.

ANS:
Net cash flow is the difference between cash inflows and outflows. Net profit, in contrast, is the difference between revenue and expenses. One reason for the difference between net cash flow and net profit is the uneven timing of cash disbursements and the expensing of those disbursements. Also, there is uneven timing of sales revenue and cash receipts if credit is extended. Some cash receipts (such as borrowed money) are not revenue and never become revenue.

REF: p. 487 OBJ: 22-2 TYPE: C

4. Identify the stages of the life cycle of receivables. Why is it so important to recognize these stages?

ANS:
- Sale is made on credit.
- Invoice is prepared and mailed to customer.
- Customer processes invoice.
- Funds are remitted by customer.

It is important to recognize these stages because delays can occur at each stage of the process. The appropriate remedial action is, of course, related to the problem stage.

REF: p. 491 OBJ: 22-3 TYPE: C

5. Calculate the annual interest rate associated with each of the following terms: (a) 2/5, net 30, (b) 2/10, net 20, and (c) 3/15, net 30.

ANS:

a. Terms of 2/5, net 30: (365 ÷ (30 - 5)) x (2 ÷ (100 - 2)) = 14.6 x 0.0204 = 29.8%
b. Terms of 2/10, net 20: (365 ÷ (20 - 10)) x (2 ÷ (100 - 2)) = 36.5 x 0.0204 = 74.5%
c. Terms of 3/15, net 30: (365 ÷ (30 - 15)) x (3 ÷ (100 - 3)) = 24.3 x 0.0309 = 75.1%

REF: p. 494 OBJ: 22-3 TYPE: A

6. List the three techniques for making capital budgeting decisions discussed in the chapter. Which incorporate the time value of money?

ANS:
Accounting return on investment technique

Payback period technique
Discounted cash flow techniques (net present value method and the internal rate of return method)

The discounted cash flow techniques incorporate the time value of money.

REF: p. 496 OBJ: 22-4 TYPE: C

7. Assume that the cost of certain equipment your business is considering purchasing is $100,000. You plan to depreciate the equipment over five years, at which point the salvage value is expected to be $8,000. Anticipated after-tax profits (losses) are as follows:

Year	After-Tax Profits/Losses
1	($10,000)
2	20,000
3	25,000
4	35,000
5	20,000

Compute the accounting return on investment. (Show the formula and your computations.)

ANS:
Accounting return on investment = Average annual after-tax profits per year ÷ Average book value of the investment

Accounting return on investment =

$$\frac{(-\$10{,}000 + \$20{,}000 + \$25{,}000 + \$35{,}000 + \$20{,}000) \div 5}{(\$100{,}000 + \$8{,}000) \div 2}$$

$$= \frac{\$90{,}000 \div 5}{\$108{,}000 \div 2} = (\$18{,}000 \div \$54{,}000)$$

= 0.3333, or 33.33%

REF: p. 496 OBJ: 22-4 TYPE: C

8. Compare the two investment proposals below, using the payback period method. The projected cost of each investment proposal is $100,000.

Year	Project A (Cash flow)	Project B (Cash flow)
1	$25,000	$25,000
2	20,000	20,000
3	10,000	40,000
4	10,000	30,000
5	-	10,000

ANS:
Capital budgeting is used to compare alternatives so that the best investment decisions can be made. The total cash flow of Project A is only $65,000 from an investment cost of $100,000. The investment is unwise because the initial outlay will never be recovered. Project B is expected to generate $125,000 over its lifetime from an investment of $100,000, and the initial investment will be recovered in less than four years. Project B is the clear winner between the two alternatives.

REF: p. 497 OBJ: 22-4 TYPE: A

9. If capital budgeting is so important, why do so few firms use the techniques the textbook discusses, especially the better methods? (Mention the textbook's premises in developing your answer.)

ANS:
Capital budgeting is difficult because of the many unknowns. The issue is probably bigger than training. However, the cause for such limited use of discounted cash flow tools probably rests more with the nature of the small firm itself. Several important reasons exist, including the following:

- For many owners of small firms, the business is an extension of their lives. What happens with their firms affects them personally, and the same is true in reverse. The firm and owner are inseparable. You cannot fully understand owners' decisions about their firms without being aware of the personal events in their lives, as nonfinancial variables play a significant part in their decisions. For instance, the desire to be viewed as a respected part of the community may be more important to an owner than the present value of a business decision.
- The frequent undercapitalization and liquidity problems of a small firm directly affect the decision-making process, and survival often becomes the top priority. Long-term planning, therefore, is not viewed as a high priority in the total scheme of things.
- The greater uncertainty of cash flows within a small firm makes long-term forecasts and planning seem unappealing and even a waste of time. The owner simply has no confidence in his or her ability to reasonably predict cash flows beyond two or three years. Thus, calculating the cash flows for the entire life of a project is viewed as an exercise in futility.
- The value of a closely held firm is less observable than that of a publicly held firm, whose securities are actively traded in the marketplace. Therefore, the owner of a small firm may consider the market-value rule of maximizing net present values irrelevant. In this environment, estimating the firm's cost of capital is also difficult. If computing the large firm's cost of capital is difficult at best, measurement for the small firm becomes nearly impossible.
- The smaller size of a small firm's projects may make net present value computations less feasible in a practical sense. The time and costs required to analyze a capital investment are similar, whether the project is large or small. Therefore, it is relatively more costly for a small firm to conduct such a study.
- Management talent within a small firm is a scarce resource. Also, the owner-managers frequently have a technical background, as opposed to a business or finance orientation. The perspective of these owners is influenced greatly by their backgrounds.

The foregoing characteristics of the small firm and, equally important, the owners have a significant effect on the decision-making process within the small firm. The result is often a short-term mindset, caused partly by necessity and partly by choice.

REF: p. 498 OBJ: 22-5 TYPE: C

10. Why would undercapitalization affect a small firm's use of discounted cash flow techniques?

ANS:

If a company is undercapitalized—that is, there is not enough equity investment—its primary focus becomes meeting debt requirements. The owner must then turn his or her thoughts to survival, as opposed to taking advantage of long-term investment opportunities. The time value of money is simply not an issue. The owner is worried about *now*, not some distant future.

REF: p. 497 OBJ: 22-5 TYPE: C

11. **You Make the Call—Situation 1**

A small firm specializing in the sale and installation of swimming pools was profitable but devoted very little attention to management of its working capital. It had, for example, never prepared or used a cash budget. To be sure that money was available for payments as needed, the firm kept a minimum of $25,000 in a checking account. At times, this account grew larger; it totaled $43,000 at one time. The owner felt that this approach to cash management worked well for a small company because it eliminated all of the paperwork associated with cash budgeting. Moreover, it had enabled the firm to pay its bills in a timely manner.

Question 1 What are the advantages and weaknesses of the minimum-cash-balance practice?
Question 2 There is a saying "If ain't broke, don't fix it." In view of the firm's present success in paying bills promptly, should it be encouraged to use a cash budget? Be prepared to support your answer.

ANS:
1. The advantages are the ability to pay bills promptly and the chance to eliminate certain paperwork. A major weakness is the lower interest income resulting from maintaining such a large balance in a checking account. A commercial demand checking account cannot pay interest.
2. The firm should be encouraged to use a cash budget in order to maximize its profits. It can then transfer excess cash into interest-bearing accounts until the money is needed to pay bills. The owner of this firm may be fearful of trying a financial tool with which he or she has no experience, but cash budgeting need not be complex or burdensome.

REF: p. 487 OBJ: YMTC TYPE: C

12. **You Make the Call—Situation 2**

Ruston Manufacturing Company is a small firm selling entirely on a credit basis. It has experienced successful operation and earned modest profits. Sales are made on the basis of net payment in 30 days. Collections from customers run approximately 70 percent in 30 days, 20 percent in 60 days, 7 percent in 90 days, and 3 percent bad debts. The owner has considered the possibility of offering a cash discount for early payment. However, the practice seems costly and possibly unnecessary. As the owner puts it, "Why should I bribe customers to pay what they legally owe?"

Question 1 Is offering a cash discount the equivalent of a bribe?
Question 2 How would a cash discount policy relate to bad debts?
Question 3 What cash discount policy, if any, would you recommend?
Question 4 What other approaches might be used to improve cash flows from receivables?

ANS:
1. A cash discount is not the equivalent of a bribe. It is a payment for use of money for a longer time period.

2. If payment that otherwise would be postponed can be encouraged to come in immediately with a cash discount, that receivable will never become a bad debt. However, most companies that have trouble paying their bills do not take advantage of cash discounts. Therefore, a cash discount policy would have minimal impact on this firm's bad-debt experience. (The company does appear to have a bad-debt problem.)

3. In answering this question, the first step should be to examine the credit policies of competitors and the credit expectations of customers. There are probably standard credit terms that are commonly used in the industry. This firm may find that it is losing business from well-run companies that patronize its competitors in order to take advantage of cash discounts. Some reduction of revenue will occur as the company grants discounts to those already paying promptly. A careful estimate must be made of the degree to which payments can be accelerated and the extent to which new business can be obtained from well-managed customers. These benefits must be compared to the additional costs involved in such a policy change.

2. Cash flow might be improved by factoring accounts receivable—funds would be obtained immediately and the factor would have to collect the receivables. Reducing bad debts through improved screening and/or collection practices would also improve cash flow.

REF: p. 492 OBJ: YMTC TYPE: C

13. **You Make the Call—Situation 3**

Adrian Fudge of the Fudge Corporation wants you to forecast its financing needs over the fourth quarter (October–December). He has made the following observations relative to planned cash receipts and disbursements:

- Interest on a $75,000 bank note (due next March) at an 8 percent annual rate is payable in December for the three-month period just ended.
- The firm follows a policy of paying no cash dividends.
- Actual historical and future predicted sales are as follows:

Historical		**Predicted**	
August	$150,000	October	$200,000
September	$175,000	November	$220,000
		December	$180,000
		January	$200,000

- The firm has a monthly rental expense of $5,000.
- Wages and salaries for the coming months are estimated at $25,000 per month.
- Of the firm's sales, 25 percent is collected in the month of the sale, 35 percent one month after the sale, and the remaining 40 percent two months after the sale.
- Merchandise is purchased one month before the sales month and is paid for in the month it is sold. Purchases equal 75 percent of sales. The firm's cost of goods sold is also 75 percent of sales.
- Tax prepayments are made quarterly, with a prepayment of $10,000 in October based on earnings for the quarter ended September 30.
- Utility costs for the firm average 3 percent of sales and are paid in the month they are incurred.
- Depreciation expense is $20,000 annually.

Question 1 Prepare a monthly cash budget for the three-month period ending in December.

Question 2 If the firm's beginning cash balance for the budget period is $7,000, and this is its minimum desired balance, determine when and how much the firm will need to borrow during the budget period. The firm has a $50,000 line of credit with its bank, with interest (10 percent annual rate) paid monthly. For example, interest on a loan taken out at the end of September would be paid at the end of October and every month thereafter so long as the loan was outstanding.

ANS:

1. Monthly cash budget for the three-month period ending in December.

ASSUMPTIONS:

Collection Experience	
Cash Sales %	25%
1 Month	35%
2 months	40%
Purchases	75% of sales
Utilities	3% of sales
Short-term interest rate	10%
Minimum cash balance	7,000
Cost of goods sold	75%

		Aug	Sept	Oct	Nov	Dec	Jan
Monthly sales		$150,000	$175,000	$200,000	$220,000	$180,000	$200,000
Cash receipts							
Cash sales	25%			$50,000	$55,000	$45,000	
1 month	35%			61,250	70,000	77,000	
2 months	40%			60,000	70,000	80,000	
Total collections				$171,250	$195,000	$202,000	
Purchases	75%		$150,000	$165,000	$135,000	$150,000	
Cash disbursements							
Payments on purchases				$150,000	$165,000	$135,000	
Rent				5,000	5,000	5,000	
Wages and salaries				25,000	25,000	25,000	
Tax prepayment				10,000			
Utilities	3%			6,000	6,600	5,400	
Interest long-term note						1,500	
Total cash disbursements				$196,000	$201,600	$171,900	
Net change in cash				($24,750	($6,600)	$30,100	

2. When and how much the firm will need to borrow during the budget period.

Beginning cash balance			$7,000	$7,000	$7,000
Short-term interest		0.833%		-206	-263
Cash balance before borrowing			-17,750	194	36,837
Short-term borrowing (payments)			24,750	6,806	-29,837
Ending cash balance	$7,000		$7,000	$7,000	$7,000
Cumulative short-term borrowing		0	$24,750	$31,556	$1,719

REF: p. 489 OBJ: YMTC TYPE: C

14. **You Make the Call—Situation 4**

Gwen Malaski has called you for advice about what to she can do to increase the cash flow in her business. Later that day, you drop by her office and begin a review of her accounts. You find accounts receivable that have gone uncollected for several months. When you ask Gwen about the accounts, she responds that she tries to maintain a positive customer relationship so that she will not lose her larger customers.

Question 1 What credit management practices would you recommend that Gwen institute immediately to get her business out of its cash crunch?

ANS:

1. Credit management practices that can have a positive effect on a firm's cash flows:
    - Minimize the time between shipping, invoicing, and sending notices on billings.
    - Review previous credit experiences to determine impediments to cash flows, such as continued extension of credit to slow-paying or delinquent customers.
    - Provide incentives for prompt payment by granting cash discounts or charging interest on delinquent accounts.
    - Age accounts receivable on a monthly or even a weekly basis to identify quickly any delinquent accounts.
    - Use the most effective methods for collecting overdue accounts. For example, prompt phone calls to overdue accounts can improve collections considerably.
    - Use a **lock box**—a post office box for receiving remittances. If the firm's bank maintains the lock box to which customers send their payments, it can empty the box frequently and immediately deposit any checks received into the firm's account.

REF: p. 491-492 OBJ: YMTC TYPE: C

Correlation Table for Chapter 23—Evaluating Financial Performance

	Learning Objectives	Question Type	**Definition** Define new term, recall facts	**Concept** Understand or relate concepts	**Application** Apply knowledge, analyze data
1	Identify the basic requirements for an accounting system.	T/F		1,2,3,4,5,6,7,8,9	
		MC	15	1,2,3,4,5,6,7,8.9, 10,11,12,13,14	
		ES		1	
2	Explain two alternative accounting options.	T/F	13,16	10,11,12,14,15	
		MC	19,20,21,22	16,17,18,23	
		ES		2	
3	Describe the purpose of and procedures related to internal control.	T/F	18	17,19,20,21,22	
		MC		24,25,26,27,28	
		ES		3,4	
4	Evaluate a firm's ability to pay its bills as they come due.	T/F	23,25,26	24	
		MC	29,30	31	
		ES		5	
5	Assess a firm's overall profitability on its asset base.	T/F	27,28,29	30	
		MC	32,33	34	
		ES			
6	Measure a firm's use of debt and equity financing.	T/F		31,32	
		MC	35,36	37,38,39,40	
		ES			
7	Evaluate the rate of return earned on the owners' investment.	T/F	33	34,35	
		MC	41,42	43,44,45	
		ES			
	You Make the Call	ES		6,7,8,9	

Total Number of Test Questions: 00 (35 True/False; 45 Multiple-Choice; 9 Essay)

Chapter 23—Evaluating Financial Performance

TRUE/FALSE

1. One of the goals of an accounting system is to provide an accurate, thorough picture of operating results.

   ANS: T REF: p. 506 OBJ: 23-1 TYPE: C

2. An effective accounting system can help a small business find employee fraud, theft, waste, and record-keeping errors.

   ANS: T REF: p. 506 OBJ: 23-1 TYPE: C

3. The accounting system of a small business need not have the capacity to provide financial statements for use by banks and prospective creditors.

   ANS: F
   The accounting system of a small business should offer financial statements that can be used by management, banks, and prospective creditors.

   REF: p. 506 OBJ: 23-1 TYPE: C

4. An accounting system's effectiveness rests on a well-designed and well-managed system of record keeping.

   ANS: T REF: p. 506 OBJ: 23-1 TYPE: C

5. Though software packages can be helpful in generating required accounting records, only a limited number of these are appropriate for use in a small firm.

   ANS: F
   The accounting software options for small firms is *almost unlimited*, though some of these are more widely used than others.

   REF: p. 507 OBJ: 23-1 TYPE: C

6. Computer software packages can help a small business manager with some aspects of an accounting system but are generally not available to help prepare income statements or balance sheets.

   ANS: F
   Computer software packages are available to help a small business manager prepare income statements or balance sheets.

   REF: p. 507 OBJ: 23-1 TYPE: C

7. Small firms should never need the services of an outside accountant.

   ANS: F

Instead of having an employee or a member of the owner's family keep financial records, a firm may have these records kept by certified public accountants, bookkeeping firms, or service bureaus that cater to small firms.

REF: p. 507 OBJ: 23-1 TYPE: C

8. In choosing accounting firms, bigger is better.

ANS: F
In reality, the services of larger accounting firms are usually more expensive, and therefore are not always to be preferred.

REF: p. 507 OBJ: 23-1 TYPE: C

9. Mobile bookkeepers may provide small firms with a faster, cheaper, and more convenient approach to filling certain accounting needs.

ANS: T REF: p. 507 OBJ: 23-1 TYPE: C

10. Accounting records can be kept in just about any form as long as they provide users with the data needed and are legally proper.

ANS: T REF: p. 507 OBJ: 23-2 TYPE: C

11. Very small firms lack options in selecting accounting systems and accounting methods.

ANS: F
Very small firms do have options when selecting accounting systems and accounting methods-two such options are cash versus accrual accounting and single-entry versus double-entry systems.

REF: p. 507-508 OBJ: 23-2 TYPE: C

12. The cash method of accounting is generally selected by the very small firm that wants to help its cash flow by avoiding the payment of taxes on income not yet received.

ANS: T REF: p. 508 OBJ: 23-2 TYPE: C

13. A double-entry system of accounting is basically a checkbook system of receipts and disbursements.

ANS: F
It is a *single-entry* system of accounting that is basically a checkbook system of receipts and disbursements.

REF: p. 508 OBJ: 23-2 TYPE: D

14. The major difference between the cash method and the accrual method of accounting is the point at which the firm reports revenue and expenses.

ANS: T REF: p. 507 OBJ: 23-2 TYPE: C

15. A single-entry system does not generate a balance sheet but does generate an income statement.

ANS: F
Single-entry systems generate neither a balance sheet nor an income statement.

REF: p. 508 OBJ: 23-2 TYPE: C

16. The accrual method of accounting is synonymous with double-entry accounting.

ANS: F
The accrual method of accounting determines the timing of the reporting of revenue and expenses, whereas double-entry accounting requires the firm to include counterbalancing entries for each transaction recorded; thus, these are not synonymous with one another.

REF: p. 508 OBJ: 23-2 TYPE: D

17. Effective internal controls help to reveal employee theft, fraud, and bad decisions based on inaccurate and untimely accounting information.

ANS: T REF: p. 508 OBJ: 23-3 TYPE: C

18. Internal control is a system of checks and balances that safeguards a firm's assets and enhances the accuracy and reliability of financial statements.

ANS: T REF: p. 508 OBJ: 23-3 TYPE: D

19. Having effective internal controls is not of any concern to auditors.

ANS: F
Auditors will be unwilling to express an opinion about a firm's financial statements if the firm lacks adequate internal controls.

REF: p. 508 OBJ: 23-3 TYPE: C

20. In order to safeguard business assets and prevent errors, accounting records should be accurately maintained, transaction by transaction, by one individual.

ANS: F
To ensure appropriate internal control, the employee who collects cash should *not* be allowed to reconcile the bank statement as well.

REF: p. 0508 OBJ: 23-3 TYPE: C

21. A policy of regular vacations can be an important part of an internal control system.

ANS: T REF: p. 508 OBJ: 23-3 TYPE: C

22. It is easier to implement internal controls in a small firm.

ANS: F

It may require extra effort to implement internal controls in a small company, in which business procedures may be informal and some individuals perform multiple job duties (because of the small number of employees).

REF: p. 509 OBJ: 23-3 TYPE: C

23. A firm's liquidity is defined as its ability to meet maturing debt obligations.

ANS: T REF: p. 511 OBJ: 23-4 TYPE: D

24. To evaluate a firm's liquidity, an investor can either compare the firm's assets that are relatively liquid in nature with the debt coming due in the near term or examine the timeliness with which liquid assets are being converted into cash.

ANS: T REF: p. 511 OBJ: 23-4 TYPE: C

25. The current ratio is computed by dividing current assets by current liabilities.

ANS: T REF: p. 512 OBJ: 23-4 TYPE: D

26. The inventory turnover ratio indicates whether a company is holding excessive stocks of inventory.

ANS: T REF: p. 513 OBJ: 23-4 TYPE: D

27. The total amount of capital from various investors becomes the firm's total assets.

ANS: T REF: p. 513 OBJ: 23-5 TYPE: D

28. The ratio of operating income to total assets reveals the rate of return that is being earned on the total invested capital.

ANS: T REF: p. 513 OBJ: 23-5 TYPE: D

29. Total asset turnover is a measure of the effectiveness of a firm's credit policies.

ANS: F
Total asset turnover is a measure of how efficiently management is using the firm's assets to generate sales.

REF: p. 516 OBJ: 23-5 TYPE: D

30. The factors that determine operating profit margin are the cost of goods sold and sales revenue generated.

ANS: F
There are five factors that determine operating profit margin: volume, sales price, cost of goods sold, general and administrative expenses, and marketing and distribution expenses.

REF: p. 515-516 OBJ: 23-5 TYPE: C

31. Both the debt ratio and the debt-to-equity ratio can be used to evaluate a firm's financial leverage.

ANS: T REF: p. 517 OBJ: 23-6 TYPE: C

32. The times interest earned ratio is often used to determine one dimension of a firm's profitability.

ANS: F
The times interest earned ratio is used when assessing the firm's debt position.

REF: p. 518 OBJ: 23-6 TYPE: C

33. Return on equity is computed by dividing net income by common equity.

ANS: T REF: p. 518 OBJ: 23-7 TYPE: D

34. The turnover ratios for accounts receivable and inventories are used for one purpose—assessing the firm's liquidity.

ANS: F
These ratios have implications for both the firm's liquidity and its profitability.

REF: p. 516 OBJ: 23-7 TYPE: C

35. Typically, a thorough financial analysis will report both the average collection period and accounts receivable turnover.

ANS: F
Typically, only one of these ratios is used in analysis, since they represent different ways of measuring the same thing.

REF: p. 516 OBJ: 23-7 TYPE: C

MULTIPLE CHOICE

1. Financial statements are *not* likely to be used by
   a. a firm's management.
   b. prospective creditors.
   c. bankers.
   d. trade intermediaries.

ANS: D REF: p. 506 OBJ: 23-1 TYPE: C

2. Most small firms need to have financial statements generated at least
   a. weekly.
   b. monthly.
   c. quarterly.
   d. annually.

ANS: B REF: p. 506 OBJ: 23-1 TYPE: C

3. Most small firms generate a balance sheet at least
   a. weekly.
   b. monthly.

c. quarterly.
d. annually.

ANS: B REF: p. 506 OBJ: 23-1 TYPE: C

4. Any accounting system should accomplish all but which one of the following objectives?
a. Yield an accurate picture of operating results
b. Provide financial statements
c. Facilitate filing of tax returns
d. Reveal employer compliance with OSHA

ANS: D REF: p. 506 OBJ: 23-1 TYPE: C

5. Regardless of their level of sophistication, available accounting systems
a. rarely provide an accurate picture of operating results.
b. often do not reveal employee fraud, theft, waste, and record-keeping errors.
c. provide financial statements for internal use but not for external use.
d. should allow the firm to compare operating results from the current year with prior years.

ANS: D REF: p. 506 OBJ: 23-1 TYPE: C

6. An analysis of which of the following records reveals the degree of effectiveness of a firm's credit and collection policies?
a. Accounts payable records
b. Accounts receivable records
c. Cash records
d. Inventory records

ANS: B REF: p. 506 OBJ: 23-1 TYPE: C

7. A change in a firm's credit and collection policies will likely affect which of the following records?
a. Accounts payable records
b. Accounts receivable records
c. Cash records
d. Inventory records

ANS: B REF: p. 506 OBJ: 23-1 TYPE: C

8. Which of the following records shows what the firm owes, facilitates the taking of cash discounts, and allows payments to be made when due?
a. Accounts payable records
b. Accounts receivable records
c. Cash records
d. Inventory records

ANS: A REF: p. 506 OBJ: 23-1 TYPE: C

9. An analysis of which of the following records is important in maintaining good customer relations?
a. Cash records
b. Fixed asset records
c. Accounts receivable records
d. Accounts payable records

ANS: C REF: p. 506 OBJ: 23-1 TYPE: C

10. Carlo is concerned with his firm maintaining adequate levels of its product stocks. Which records should he to analyze to help ensure sufficient stock is on hand to meet customer demands?
    a. Accounts payable records
    b. Accounts receivable records
    c. Cash records
    d. Inventory records

ANS: D REF: p. 506 OBJ: 23-1 TYPE: C

11. An analysis of which of the following records facilitates maintenance of adequate stock levels?
    a. Accounts payable records
    b. Accounts receivable records
    c. Cash records
    d. Inventory records

ANS: D REF: p. 506 OBJ: 23-1 TYPE: C

12. Which of the following shows all receipts and disbursements and are necessary to safeguard cash?
    a. Accounts payable records
    b. Accounts receivable records
    c. Cash records
    d. Inventory records

ANS: C REF: p. 506 OBJ: 23-1 TYPE: C

13. Which of the following shows the original cost of each asset and depreciation taken to date, along with other information such as the condition of the asset?
    a. Accounts payable records
    b. Accounts receivable records
    c. Cash records
    d. Fixed asset records

ANS: D REF: p. 0506 OBJ: 23-1 TYPE: C

14. Accounting software is available for the computers of most businesses. Most software packages provide
    a. a computerized checkbook, accounts receivable managers, and financial-statement preparers.
    b. a computerized checkbook, budgeting programs, and accounts receivable managers.
    c. a computerized checkbook, preparation of a cash budget that compares actual and budgeted expenditures, and preparation of income statements and balance sheets.
    d. budgeting programs, accounts receivable managers, and financial-statement preparers.

ANS: C REF: p. 507 OBJ: 23-1 TYPE: C

15. _____ can provide firms with a fast, inexpensive, and convenient way to meet certain accounting needs.
    a. Tax accounting
    b. Cost accounting
    c. Mobile bookkeeping
    d. Public accounting

ANS: C REF: p. 507 OBJ: 23-1 TYPE: D

16. The accounting option a business chooses for financial reporting must
    a. be the same as the option chosen for tax accounting.
    b. meet legal requirements.
    c. be double entry in order to create the necessary financial statements.
    d. be computerized rather than manual.

    ANS: B REF: p. 507 OBJ: 23-2 TYPE: C

17. The major distinction between the cash method and the accrual method of accounting is that the
    a. cash method is easier to use.
    b. cash method matches revenue and expenses better.
    c. point at which a firm reports revenue and expenses is different.
    d. cash method involves less record keeping.

    ANS: C REF: p. 507-508 OBJ: 23-2 TYPE: C

18. Compared to the single-entry system, an advantage of the double-entry bookkeeping system is that
    a. no math errors go undetected.
    b. it is better suited to firms that want to grow.
    c. it doesn't have to be self-balancing.
    d. it is easier to use.

    ANS: B REF: p. 508 OBJ: 23-2 TYPE: C

19. As Benito's business grows larger, which of the following accounting methods/systems is he likely to adopt for use in his business?
    a. Single-entry system
    b. Double-entry system
    c. Accrual method
    d. Cash method

    ANS: B REF: p. 508 OBJ: 23-2 TYPE: D

20. Which of the following accounting methods/systems recognizes revenue and expenses only when cash is received or payment is made?
    a. Single-entry system
    b. Double-entry system
    c. Accrual method
    d. Cash method

    ANS: D REF: p. 508 OBJ: 23-2 TYPE: D

21. Under which method/system of accounting are revenue and expenses reported when they are incurred, regardless of when cash is received or payment is made?
    a. Single-entry system
    b. Double-entry system
    c. Accrual method
    d. Cash method

    ANS: C REF: p. 0508 OBJ: 23-2 TYPE: D

22. _____ is basically a checkbook system of receipts and disbursements.
    a. A single-entry system

b. A double-entry system
c. The accrual method
d. The cash method

ANS: A REF: p. 508 OBJ: 23-2 TYPE: D

23. _____ provides a self-balancing mechanism.
a. A single-entry system
b. A double-entry system
c. The accrual method
d. The cash method

ANS: B REF: p. 508 OBJ: 23-2 TYPE: C

24. An effective internal control system allows a small business to
a. stabilize its financial statements.
b. eliminate fraud and theft.
c. reduce the chances of bad decisions based on inaccurate accounting information.
d. maintain flexible accounting procedures.

ANS: C REF: p. 508 OBJ: 23-3 TYPE: C

25. Regardless of the method used to interpret financial statements, this should be able to answer the following question:
a. Does the firm have the capacity to meet its long-term financial commitments?
b. Is the firm producing adequate operating profits on its short-term investment?
c. How is the firm financing its assets?
d. Is the firm generating sufficient returns on sales to cover its liabilities?

ANS: C REF: p. 507-508 OBJ: 23-3 TYPE: C

26. The problem caused by Allan Lichter's graphics firm's lack of internal financial controls could have been avoided if the accounting clerk in charge of accounts receivable had not also been in charge of
a. accounts payable.
b. the company's lock box.
c. company's payroll account.
d. petty cash.

ANS: A REF: p. 509 OBJ: 23-3 TYPE: C

27. Financial ratio analysis is likely to be used to compare a company's performance to
a. that of larger firms.
b. that of smaller firms.
c. that of firms that have been particularly successful.
d. industry norms.

ANS: D REF: p. 510 OBJ: 23-3 TYPE: C

28. Jill's best use of a financial ratio analysis of her company's performance is to compare it to
a. that of larger firms.
b. that of smaller firms.
c. that of firms that have been particularly successful.
d. industry norms.

ANS: D REF: p. 510 OBJ: 23-3 TYPE: C

29. A firm's liquidity can be measured by its
    a. liquidity ratio.
    b. current ratio.
    c. turnover ratio.
    d. total asset turnover.

ANS: B REF: p. 511 OBJ: 23-4 TYPE: D

30. A current ratio is calculated by dividing
    a. current assets by current liabilities.
    b. accounts receivable by daily credit sales.
    c. current assets plus accounts receivable by current liabilities.
    d. credit sales by accounts receivable.

ANS: A REF: p. 512 OBJ: 23-4 TYPE: D

31. To determine a firm's ability to convert accounts receivable into cash on a timely basis, you divide
    a. accounts receivable by daily credit sales.
    b. cost of goods sold by accounts receivable.
    c. accounts receivable by average daily cash balance.
    d. accounts receivable by daily cash sales.

ANS: A REF: p. 513 OBJ: 23-4 TYPE: C

32. The firm's operating profit margin is computed as a ratio of operating profits to
    a. sales.
    b. inventory.
    c. assets.
    d. total debt.

ANS: A REF: p. 514 OBJ: 23-5 TYPE: D

33. The _____ is a function of how efficiently management is using the firm's assets to generate sales.
    a. total asset turnover
    b. acid-test radio
    c. fixed asset turnover
    d. current ratio

ANS: A REF: p. 516 OBJ: 23-5 TYPE: D

34. The _____ indicates the extent to which plant and equipment are being utilized.
    a. acid-test ratio
    b. fixed asset turnover ratio
    c. current ratio
    d. average collection period

ANS: B REF: p. 516 OBJ: 23-5 TYPE: C

35. The _____ is used to evaluate a firm's financial leverage.
    a. debt ratio
    b. acid-test ratio

c. current ratio
d. investment ratio

ANS: A REF: p. 518 OBJ: 23-6 TYPE: D

36. _______ ratios are concerned with how much financing risk is associated with a firm.
a. current
b. assets to liabilities
c. net cash present
d. debt

ANS: D REF: p. 511 OBJ: 23-6 TYPE: D

37. The use of debt can
a. increase a firm's return on equity.
b. reduce a firm's risk.
c. improve a firm's inventory turnover ratio.
d. enhance market response to a firm's performance.

ANS: A REF: p. 518 OBJ: 23-6 TYPE: C

38. Peter Hansom believes in using other people's money (OPM) because his firm's use of debt can
a. increase a firm's return on equity.
b. reduce a firm's risk.
c. improve a firm's inventory turnover ratio.
d. enhance market response to a firm's performance.

ANS: A REF: p. 518 OBJ: 23-6 TYPE: C

39. The debt ratio relationship can also be stated as the
a. current ratio.
b. acid-test ratio.
c. debt-equity ratio.
d. current-debt ratio.

ANS: C REF: p. 518 OBJ: 23-6 TYPE: C

40. When a firm borrows money, it is required, at a minimum, to pay
a. part of the principle (the sum borrowed).
b. the interest on the debt.
c. part of the principle and the interest owed on the debt.
d. the taxes that accrue as a result of the money borrowed.

ANS: B REF: p. 518 OBJ: 23-6 TYPE: C

41. The _____ measures the rate of return on stockholders' investments in the business.
a. return on total assets
b. profit margin on sales
c. return on equity
d. fixed asset turnover

ANS: C REF: p. 518 OBJ: 23-7 TYPE: D

42. Jackie's stockholders are primarily concerned that she constantly improve the firm's _____ ratio as it relates to their investments in the firm..
    a. return on total assets
    b. profit margin on sales
    c. return on equity
    d. fixed asset turnover

ANS: C REF: p. 518 OBJ: 23-7 TYPE: D

43. The turnover ratios for accounts receivable and inventories have implications for
    a. employee retention.
    b. asset specificity.
    c. debt position.
    d. firm liquidity and profitability.

ANS: D REF: p. 519 OBJ: 23-7 TYPE: C

44. Higher turnover ratios for accounts receivable and inventories have implications for
    a. overall employee retention.
    b. long-term asset specificity.
    c. reduced debt position.
    d. increased firm liquidity and profitability.

ANS: D REF: p. 519 OBJ: 23-7 TYPE: C

45. The turnover ratios for accounts receivable and inventories
    a. should both be included in the financial analysis of a firm.
    b. are measures of very different things.
    c. often lead to very different conclusions about the firm.
    d. represent different ways to measure the same thing.

ANS: D REF: p. 519 OBJ: 23-7 TYPE: C

ESSAY

1. List several of the objectives of an accounting system used in a small business, as discussed in the text.

ANS:
- The system should yield an accurate, thorough picture of operating results.
- The records should allow comparison of operating results across years and with budgetary goals.
- The records should provide financial statements.
- The system should facilitate prompt filing of government reports and tax returns.
- The system should reveal employee fraud, theft, waste, and record-keeping errors.

REF: p. 506 OBJ: 23-1 TYPE: C

2. What are the advantages and disadvantages of the cash method of accounting compared to the accrual method of accounting?

ANS:

The cash method is easier to use. It reports revenue only when cash payment is received, which can help cash flow in some circumstances. However, the cash method does not provide as accurate a matching of revenue and expenses as does the accrual method.

REF: p. 507-508 OBJ: 23-2 TYPE: C

3. Explain the concept of internal control and why it is important to a firm. Give some examples of internal control procedures.

ANS:
Internal control is a system of checks and balances that plays a key role in safeguarding a firm's assets and enhancing the accuracy and reliability of the financial statements. The absence of internal control significantly increases the chances of fraud and theft and also increases the chances of making bad decisions based on inaccurate and untimely accounting information. Effective internal control is required if the firm's owners ever need an audit by independent accountants. Examples of internal control procedures might include separating employees' duties so that different individuals are responsible for control over an asset and recording transactions in accounting ledgers, identifying the types of transactions that require the authorization of the business owners, establishing a procedure to ensure that checks presented for signature are accompanied by complete supporting documentation, limiting access to accounting records, having bank statements sent to the owner's attention, safeguarding blank checks, establishing a policy of regular vacations, and controlling access to the computer facilities.

REF: p. 508 OBJ: 23-3 TYPE: C

4. What are the four questions financial ratio analysis should answer?

ANS:
- How liquid is the firm—that is, does it have the capacity to meet its short-term commitments?
- Is the firm generating adequate operating profits on its assets?
- How is the firm financing its assets?
- Are the owners (stockholders) receiving an adequate return on their equity investment?

REF: p. 510 OBJ: 23-3 TYPE: C

5. Define liquidity and describe the two general methods that can be used to measure liquidity.

ANS:
The liquidity of a business is defined as the firm's ability to meet maturing debt obligations. The relevant question here is, "Does the firm now have or will it have in the future the resources necessary to pay creditors when debts come due?" This question can be answered using the following two general methods:
- Comparing the firm's relatively liquid assets with the debt coming due in the near term
- Examining the timeliness with which liquid assets are being converted to cash

REF: p. 511 OBJ: 23-4 TYPE: C

6. **You Make the Call—Situation 1**

In 2005, Carter Dalton purchased the Baugh Company. Although the firm has consistently earned profits, little cash has been available for other than business needs. Before purchasing Baugh, Dalton thought that cash flows were generally equal to profits plus depreciation. However, this does not seem to be the case. The industry norms for the financial ratios and the financial statements (in thousands) for the Baugh Company, 2004–2005, follow.

Balance Sheet

	2004	2005
ASSETS		
Current assets:		
Cash	$ 8,000	$ 10,000
Accounts receivable	15,000	20,000
Inventory	22,000	25,000
Total current assets	$ 45,000	$ 55,000
Fixed assets:		
Gross plant and equipment	$ 50,000	$ 55,000
Accumulated depreciation	15,000	20,000
Net fixed assets	$ 35,000	$ 35,000
Other assets	12,000	10,000
TOTAL ASSETS	$ 92,000	$100,000
DEBT (LIABILITIES) AND EQUITY		
Current liabilities:		
Accounts payable	$ 10,000	$ 12,000
Accruals	7,000	8,000
Short-term notes	5,000	5,000
Total current liabilities	$ 22,000	$ 25,000
Long-term liabilities	15,000	15,000
Total liabilities	$ 37,000	$ 40,000
Total ownership equity	55,000	60,000
TOTAL DEBT AND EQUITY	$ 92,000	$100,000

Income Statement, 2005

Sales revenue		$175,000
Cost of goods sold		105,000
Gross profit on sales		$ 70,000
Operating expenses:		
Marketing expenses	$26,000	
General and administrative expenses	20,000	
Depreciation expense	5,000	
Total operating expenses		$ 51,000
Operating income		$ 19,000
Interest expense		3,000
Earnings before taxes		$ 16,000
Income tax		8,000
Net income		$ 8,000

Financial Ratios	Industry Norms
Current ratio	2.50
Average collection period	30.00
Inventory turnover	6.00
Debt ratio	50.0%
Return on assets	16.0%
Operating profit margin	8.0%
Total asset turnover	2.00
Fixed asset turnover	7.00
Times interest earned ratio	5.00
Return on equity	14.0%

Question 1 Why doesn't Dalton have cash for personal needs? (As part of your analysis, measure cash flows, as discussed in Chapter 10.)

Question 2 Evaluate the Baugh Company's financial performance, given the financial ratios for the industry.

ANS:

1. Dalton's equation to determine cash flows (profits plus depreciation), although correct once in a while, can be very misleading. The company's cash flow can be more accurately determined as follows:

Firm's Cash Flows:	
Operating income	$19,000
Depreciation	5,000
Earnings before interest, taxes and depreciation	$24,000
Cash taxes	8,000
After-tax cash flows from operations	$16,000
Change in net working	
Change in current assets	$10,000
Change in non-interest bearing short-term debt	3,000
Change in net working capital	$7,000
Investment in fixed assets	($5,000)
Decrease in other assets	2,000
Firm's cash flows	$6,000
Financing Cash Flows:	
Interest	$3,000
Dividends	3,000
Financing cash flows	$6,000

2. Baugh Company's financial performance, given the financial ratios for the industry.

   When using ratios, we must remember what makes up each number we derive and that differences between ratios only suggest areas for us to study; they are not answers in themselves.

   The Baugh Company's liquidity is poor according to all the measures. Its current ratio and acid-test ratio are below the norm, and accounts receivable and inventories are both slow in converting to cash.

The firm's ability to generate operating income on its assets is above average (18.8%, versus the industry norm of 16%). This advantage is due to a superior operating profit margin, which means that the company is better at managing its income statement (refer to the five "drivers" of operating profit margin). However, the firm could do better if it could improve its management of its assets—see the asset turnover ratios. The company uses less debt financing than the industry average, which means that its financial risk is less than that of other firms. Baugh's return on equity is below average because it uses less debt than other firms, in spite of its higher operating income return on investment. However, that means the firm is less risky.

REF: p. 522 OBJ: YMTC TYPE: C

7. **You Make the Call—Situation 2**

The following financial statements are for the Cherokee Communications Corporation. The company provides pay phone service at many of the small convenience stores in the southwestern United States, primarily in Texas and New Mexico. The business was "meeting plan" until 2005, when a problem developed.

Balance Sheet

	2004	2005
ASSETS		
Current assets:		
Cash and cash equivalents	$ 668,778	$ 592,491
Accounts receivable	4,453,192	3,888,621
Inventories	137,036	112,699
Prepaid expenses and other current assets	411,990	407,274
Total current assets	$ 5,670,996	$ 5,001,085
Fixed assets:		
Property, plant and equipment (net)	$12,935,453	$16,466,001
Site licenses	1,941,467	3,771,571
Investments in affiliates	164,549	251,672
Total fixed assets	$15,041,469	$20,489,244
Other assets	681,754	455,488
TOTAL ASSETS	$21,394,219	$25,945,817
DEBT (LIABILITIES) AND EQUITY		
Current liabilities:		
Notes payable	$ 659,604	
Current portion of other notes payable	1,491,767	$ 3,320,197
Current portion of capital lease obligations	1,094,381	668,826
Accounts payable	310,358	835,384
Accrued telecommunications and other expenses	2,971,935	3,036,633
Income taxes payable	256,140	475,945
Total current liabilities	$ 6,784,185	$ 8,336,985
Long-term liabilities:		
Notes payable, less current portion	$ 6,605,835	$10,030,963
Capital lease obligations	780,593	56,219
Deferred income tax liability	342,359	306,021
Total long-term liabilities	$ 7,728,787	$10,393,203
Preferred stock	$ 2,400,000	$ 2,400,000
Common stockholders' equity:		
Common stock	$ 1,438,903	$ 1,438,903
Additional paid-in capital	10,630	10,630
Retained earnings	3,031,714	3,366,096
Total ownership equity	$ 4,481,247	$ 4,815,629
TOTAL DEBT AND EQUITY	$21,394,219	$25,945,817

Income Statements for Cherokee Communications, Inc.

	2004	2005
Sales revenue:		
Pay phone coin calls	$14,036,665	$17,615,059
Automated operator, routed calls	17,049,394	15,932,154
Other	505,581	1,363,738
Total revenues	$31,591,640	$34,910,951
Operating expenses:		
Telephone charges	$ 7,851,842	$ 9,078,851
Commissions	4,909,445	5,627,288
Telecommunications fees	1,821,930	1,519,095
Depreciation and amortization	4,298,090	5,353,797
Field operations personnel	2,016,935	2,988,456
Chargebacks and doubtful accounts	1,104,896	1,111,857
General and administrative expenses	5,520,405	6,435,919
Total operating expenses	$27,523,543	$ 32,115,263
Operating income	$ 4,068,097	$ 2,795,688
Other income (expenses):		
Interest expense	($ 1,631,416)	($ 1,816,222)
Interest income	57,278	5,069
Losses on affiliates	(34,608)	(108,556)
Unusual gains	1,160,238	27,234
Total other income (expenses)	($ 448,508)	($ 1,892,475)
Income before taxes	$ 3,619,589	$ 903,213
Provision for income taxes	1,399,140	424,831
Net income	$ 2,220,449	$ 478,382

Question 1 Using financial ratios, compare the firm's financial performance for 2004 and 2005.
Question 2 What do you think might have happened from 2004 to 2005?

ANS:

1. The ratios for the respective years are as follows:

Ratios	2001	2002
Current ratio	0.84	0.60
Quick ratio	0.82	0.59
Accounts receivable turnover	7.09	8.98
Inventory turnover	230.54	309.77
Operating income return on investment	19.0%	10.8%
Operating profit margin	12.9%	8.0%
Total assets turnover	1.48	1.35
Fixed assets turnover	2.44	2.12
Debt ratio	0.68	0.72
Times interest earned	2.49	1.54
Return on equity	49.5%	9.9%

Based on the above ratios, we see that Cherokee's liquidity declined modestly, but the real news is the firm's sharp fall in profitability. The operating income return on investment fell from 19 percent to less than 11 percent, which was mostly due to a decline in the operating profit margin. This change, along with a much smaller unusual gain in 2002 than in 2001, resulted in the large decrease in the return on equity.

2. When we look at the income statement, we see that operating expenses increased more between the two years than did sales. Almost every expense item increased significantly. However, the increase in depreciation was caused by a decision to use a shorter life in depreciating off fixed assets. The big problem that occurred was the large telephone companies going after Cherokee by instigating "call around." For example, AT&T started "1-800-CALL ATT," which allowed the caller to go around Cherokee and charge the call to AT&T. In essence, callers were using Cherokee's phones but AT&T was getting the revenue from the call.

REF: p. 523 OBJ: YMTC TYPE: C

8. **You Make the Call—Situation 3**

Alibek Iskakov has opened a small cafe, Oasis, in Kokshetau, a city in Kazakhstan. A new business in operation for only a short period on a part-time basis in a less-developed country, it has small revenues. Nevertheless, ratio analysis can be used for a quick check on its status. The following amounts are given in tenge (1 dollar = 120 tenge), the Kazakhstan currency.

Balance Sheet

ASSETS	
Current assets:	
Cash	22,000
Accounts receivable	2,500
Inventories	7,300
Prepaid expenses	6,500
Total current assets	38,300
Fixed assets:	
Plant and equipment	400,000
Accumulated depreciation	-400
Net plant and equipment	399,600
TOTAL ASSETS	437,900
DEBT (LIABILITIES) AND EQUITY	
Current liabilities:	
Accounts payable	7,000
Income tax payable	5,500
Accrued wages and salaries	7,000
Total current liabilities	19,500
Equity	418,400
TOTAL DEBT AND EQUITY	437,900

Income Statement

Sales	150,000
Cost of goods sold	80,000
Total revenues	70,000

Operating expenses:	
Selling expenses	5,000
General and administrative expenses	12,000
Other expenses	3,500
Total operating expenses	20,500
Earnings before taxes	49,500
Income tax (30%)	14,850
Net income	34,650

Source: This case was prepared by Dr. Aigul N. Toxanova and Yuliya L. Tkacheva, Kokshetau Institute of Economics and Management, Kokshetau, Kazakhstan.

Question 1 Compute the firm's accounts receivable turnover. Do you think that this ratio is relevant for this business? Why or why not?

Question 2 What is the firm's return on assets? Without the benefit of an industry norm for comparison, do you think that this is a good return on the owner's investment?

Question 3 What is the firm's return on equity? How does debt financing affect this return?

ANS:

1. Since we do not know how much of the sales are credit sales, we cannot calculate an accounts receivable turnover that is accurate. Some businesses extend credit for most of their sales, but in the restaurant business, little is sold on credit, thus an accounts receivable turnover is essentially meaningless.

2. The firm's operating income return on investment (operating income, total assets) is 11.3 percent (49,500 tenge, 437,900 tenge = 11.3%). While we do not have an industry norm, an 11 percent return on the assets is not particularly high, especially for a business that would be relatively risky.

3. The firm's return on equity, net income, common equity, is 8.3 percent (34,650 tenge, 481,400 tenge = 8.3%). This is relatively low by most standards. The firm has little debt; thus, the return on equity is not being magnified through financial leverage. Then, when you account for income taxes, not much is left for the owner.

REF: p. 524 OBJ: YMTC TYPE: C

9. **You Make the Call—Situation 4**

The following letter was written by a parent about her son:

My son was caught with his hand in the cookie jar. He has been working with me in our car dealership for the past two years, and I have been very proud of some of the ideas he has come up with to save us money and increase efficiency. Most of the other men we work with seem to respect him, not only because he's my son but because he is a talented salesman with true leadership qualities. It's because he's such a good salesman that I have allowed him to pad his expense reports. Well, I didn't exactly allow it; I simply let it go, since it didn't amount to much at first, and [I] hoped that he would eventually stop doing it. Now his expenses have gotten so inflated, our bookkeeper asked me what to do about the charges. I'm not sure how to handle this. I don't want to embarrass my son, but now that others know about it, I can't let it continue.

Source: "Confronting a Son Who Pads His Expenses," *Family Business*, Vol. 5, No. 3 (Summer 1994), p. 9.

Question 1 Given that the parent owns the business and knew what the son was doing, should the son's actions still be considered wrong?

Question 2 Do you agree with the parent's handling of this situation up to this point?

Question 3 What should the parent do now?

Question 4 What internal controls should be established to prevent padding—either by the son or by others in the firm—from recurring?

ANS:

1. Yes. The principle is unchanged and it is unethical to misrepresent the truth. Also, the son's actions set a bad example for other employees.
2. No. If what the son is doing is wrong, then it needs to be corrected immediately—not ignored until others find out about it.
3. Talk plainly to the son, indicating that his integrity is worth more than the personal financial benefit.
4. Develop better internal controls that require all employees, including the son, to submit receipts with all expense reports.

REF: p. 0 OBJ: YMTC TYPE: C